TRUE
BLUE

MATT DOHERTY
RETURNS TO CAROLINA BASKETBALL

David DeWitt

Diamond Communications
An Imprint of
ROWMAN & LITTLEFIELD PUBLISHING GROUP
Lanham • South Bend • New York • Oxford

Published by Diamond Communications
An Imprint of the Rowman & Littlefield Publishing Group
4720 Boston Way
Lanham, Maryland 20706

Distributed by National Book Network

Library of Congress Cataloging-in-Publication Data Available.

ISBN 1-888698-42-X (cloth : alk. paper)

♾™ The paper used in this publication meets the minimum requirements of
American National Standard for Information Sciences—Permanence of
Paper for Printed Library Materials, ANSI/NISO Z39.48–1992.
Manufactured in the United States of America.

Contents

Acknowledgments

W hen I began the process of writing this book I was in a position much like the new coaching staff at North Carolina: I had an *idea* of what I was taking on, but I really didn't *know*. Now that I do—or at least have a better understanding—I realize just how important so many people were to its completion.

At the top of the list of people to thank is Matt Doherty. His initial reaction to this project was predictable and imminently understandable; he was skeptical that someone would want access to him and his program during his very first season at Carolina. As time progressed (and he began to get used to me being around) he was as open and accessible as I could have hoped. His wife, Kelly, and parents, Mary and Walter, gave freely of their time. For that I will be eternally grateful. In addition, Roy and Scott Williams were gracious and accessible and incredibly honest; this project would not have been possible without them.

Doug Wojcik, Fred Quartlebaum, Bob MacKinnon, and David Cason are outstanding coaches it was my pleasure to get to know. The North Carolina basketball program is in exceptional hands, and the university is fortunate to have them as its representatives. The players were incredibly open with their time, and I am grateful for the opportunity to get to know each one: Brian Bersticker, Adam Boone, Michael Brooker, Jason Capel, Ronald Curry, Neil Fingleton, Joseph Forte, Jim Everett, Jonathan Holmes, Will Johnson, Kris Lang, Orlando Melendez, Brian Morrison, Max Owens, and Julius Peppers. I would also like to thank the many family members of the coaches and players who spoke to me at length. Managers Chad Webb and Kade Ross as well as strength coach Ben Cook are as good as it gets at what they do and were more than willing to talk about their crucial roles in the program's success.

Equally as important to this project were the tireless efforts of Jill Langford and Shari Hill at Diamond Communications. Their belief in this book from the beginning made it a reality; their calming influence and steady editorial hand made it a pleasure.

Steve Kirschner was of great assistance, as was Matt Bowers, who tirelessly tracked down players and provided all manner of help. Thanks also to David Tinson, Kevin Best, and everyone else in the UNC Athletic Media Relations Office.

My colleagues at the Tar Heel Sports Network were there whenever I had an odd request or needed a helping hand. Sincere thanks go out to Woody Durham, Gary Sobba, Missy Dike, Chris Gerhard, Art Chansky, John Rose, Bob Ellis, Jones Angell, Stephen Gates, Jake Fehling, and Ben Hayes. In addition, thanks to Dan Satter for much-needed and appreciated research assistance.

This project would not have been possible without the guidance of Mick Mixon. His humility would never allow him to say it himself, so it's left to me: He's the best broadcaster in the business and an even better friend. In addition to being one of the finest writers I know, Barry Jacobs proved to be a great source of advice and the best public servant any community could ask for. Along the way, I swapped opinions and learned a great deal from some of the best sports journalists in the country, and although the list is too numerous to include everyone, I'd like to specifically thank Tim Crothers, Barry Svrluga, Caulton Tudor, Rob Daniels, Tim Peeler, Neal Amato, Bill Cole, Lenox Rawlings, Gregg Doyel, and Eddy Landreth.

I would also like to thank all of my former coaches and coaching colleagues, whose knowledge and insights have supplied me with everything I know about the game and much of what I understand about those who play and coach it. A partial list includes: Steve Kent, Jim Kirk, John Harris, Gregg Collins, Mike Ehrenfried, Don Christian, Gary Brown, Sam Dixon, Mike Sheridan, Keith Dambrot, Jim Dipple, Steve Moore, Mike Worrell, Bruce Martin, Chris Adams, and the best coach and older brother I know, Mike DeWitt.

My parents, Dick and Bunny DeWitt, as well as my sister Lisa, sister-in-law Brenda, and niece Regan were a source of great strength, as was Barbara Burn. I can't imagine anyone is as blessed as I am to have parents-in-law like Rob and Annette Coffman, to say nothing of Rob Coffman and Brian and Stephanie Esek. I am much better for their having come into my life.

And finally, I simply cannot find the words to express my gratitude to Jennifer. She is my best editor, my best friend, and the reason I first sat down to write. It is my incredible and inexplicable good fortune that she is also my wife.

Introduction

It was an hour and a half before the start of the national semifinal game, and I was searching for my seat. This, I told myself, is why I went into college coaching; to have a chance to be here among my peers and to revel in college basketball's premiere event.

It was the 1991 NCAA Final Four.

I had spent my first year in college coaching as a volunteer assistant at a Division II school and was fortunate—since I hadn't been able to spare the membership fee into the National Association of Basketball Coaches and the right to purchase a Final Four ticket that went with it—that our team had made the NCAA Division II Tournament's Elite Eight. It meant that I would get a ticket, just one, several hundred feet above the Hoosier Dome court, for the two semifinal games between the big boys. North Carolina played Kansas in the first game, and Duke would try to upset heavily favored UNLV in the second.

This was my first Final Four, and the only reason I had been able to make it was because it was within driving distance of my north-central Ohio home. Of course, if my first year as a coach was any indication, driving distance was a relative term. As the just-happy-to-be-there low man on the totem pole, I had drawn scouting and recruiting assignments as far away from our campus as Florida and Chicago, Louisville and Massachusetts—and a Division II budget did not have a line item for first-class travel or a private jet.

Instead, I often climbed into the program's compact Mercury Topaz and drove the six or eight or more hours, scouted/recruited the game, and returned the same day to write up the report and have it on the head coach's desk by 6:00 A.M. All-night video breakdowns were part of the norm, as were tutoring players (no academic services budget), placing voluminous numbers of recruiting phone calls, and sending ungodly amounts of mail—and making the occasional run to the dry cleaners to pick up the head coach's cleaning.

All for the salary of exactly $0, before taxes (hence the title "volunteer"). It was all in a day's work as a young coach, and I loved every minute of it. I learned how to run a practice, how to coach players of all backgrounds and skill levels, and how to manage a game. I couldn't imagine doing anything else.

This Final Four trip to Indianapolis was my reward for all the hard work done during the previous year. Upon arriving, I had mingled in the lobby with all the other young coaches trying desperately to shake the requisite number of important, career-building hands, studied the one-hour practices conducted by each team, and tried not to gawk at all the big-time coaches who wandered about.

As a former small-college player and a lifetime college basketball fan, it was not easy to remain cool.

From the upper, upper, upper deck I gazed down on the Tar Heels and the Jayhawks as they warmed up for their semifinal matchup and critiqued the shooting strokes of players like Hubert Davis and Rick Fox and Adonis Jordan and Terry Brown. "No elbow lift," I muttered to myself, catching a flaw in a player's shot that Dean Smith or Roy Williams must have missed.

I imagined myself coaching players like these in a setting like this. I assumed that, at this level, everything must be different. The players, of course, were better. But the coaches must be smarter, too. They must say things that are always brilliant, never make an error in preparation for a game, and always know exactly what they're doing in managing every aspect of their program.

Could I ever be *this* good?

Warm-ups were just concluding prior to the first game when a rather tall, dark-haired gentleman sat in the seat next to mine, along the aisle. I turned and nodded and did what all coaches do when at the Final Four or at a recruiting camp with others in the profession: I stared at the school insignia on his shirt to determine where he coached.

Davidson College.

Good, I thought. Division I (no one wants to get stuck next to another Division II volunteer coach), great academic school, similar to where I went and played (Denison University, a lowly Division III institution), and rather young, just a little older than me.

When I looked up, I recognized the face immediately: It was Matt Doherty, or, as he was known nationally, "that other guy" who started with Michael Jordan, Sam Perkins, James Worthy, and Jimmy Black on the 1982 NCAA champion North Carolina team.

I don't remember if I said hello or if I was still playing it cool, but as the game progressed we exchanged a few insights and thoughts on the game. Of course, his insights were somewhat more firsthand, having played for *both* coaches on the floor, but, as I recall, I was hanging right there with the coachspeak. "Should have reversed it." "Bad rotation." "Three fouls, coach. Gotta take him out."

Doherty, as I remember it, smiled politely and engaged in conversation, mostly during time-outs. It's only now that I'm fairly certain he had me pegged as a nut.

Of course, the game would eventually go to the Jayhawks, but not before an amazing turn of events that saw Dean Smith get thrown out late in the game by official Pete Pavia. Doherty's face, I recall, turned various shades of gray during and after that ordeal, and

I was socially savvy enough, even at that young age, not to ask his opinion on it.

After that night, I went on to coach four more years at The College of Wooster, one of the most successful Division III programs in the nation, maturing as a coach and learning more each year about what was really important in the profession: the small but crucial role in educating young men, the lifelong relationships built with players and other coaches, and the powerful nature of what it means to be a part of a team. No longer was I obsessed with making that jump to Division I, pressing the flesh and working the angles that was often necessary for someone like me to make the climb to the big time.

I was in the big time, I learned, if I loved what I was doing and I was having a broader effect on others.

At some point during my coaching days I began to notice a different motivation. On long drives to see recruits or to scout opponents (some things never changed) my mind began to wander, conjuring up storylines and characters. When the season was over, I began to write them down. Several hundred pages later, I realized I had written (using a loose definition of the word) a novel.

The one thing I learned about coaching—above all else—was this: To be successful, a coach must be incredibly and completely single-minded. Coaches, for the most part, are not renaissance men. They do not paint landscapes or write (even bad) novels. Given my wanderings, I realized I no longer possessed pit bull–like determination to recruit, scout, and coach. I was doing a disservice to my players and fellow coaches, so I left the sideline, leaving my brother, Mike, to carry on the DeWitt coaching legacy alone, which he does extremely well as the head coach at Ohio Wesleyan University.

But I did not leave the game. I continued to write and do some broadcasting of basketball, and when I made the commitment to my wife to support her while she pursued an advanced degree, it led us to the cradle of college basketball: central North Carolina. Suddenly, if I turned right out of my driveway I was at Duke; left, and I was on the campus at North Carolina. And if that wasn't good enough, I could drive a little farther and be at NC State or Wake Forest.

As I tried to scrape together a living as a freelance writer—putting to good use my experience living off a $0 salary—I began to cover the Atlantic Coast Conference (ACC) for various publications as well as appear on the Tar Heel Sports Radio Network. Once I was taken into the bosom of Big Time College Basketball, my first order of business was to begin enumerating the differences between Division III (where all of the players are students and play for the love of the game) and major college (where I was certain that neither of those was true).

My heretofore sense of wonderment and longing that I held for the Big Time when I was a young coach had been replaced with a heaping supply of skepticism. I did not expect to encounter real student-athletes, and I had seen too many poor coaches make it to the Big Time to believe it was based solely on merit.

I was convinced the Big Time was all about money and fame with these so-called college basketball players and coaches. I was fairly certain that, at a place like North Carolina, no one cared about one another, the fans only wanted wins and couldn't care less about the coaches and players as people, and that administrators, media, and other ancillary people were jaded and angry individuals, jealous of the coaches' money and fame.

What I found shocked me.

The players actually *acted* like normal 18–22 year olds, showing incredible talent but also emotional vulnerability. The coaches *were* pretty smart and they *did* care about the players, and vice versa. Inside the cocoon of their locker rooms, their training rooms, their offices, their hotel rooms, their buses, and anywhere else they weren't being constantly scrutinized, the players and coaches at the country's most heralded basketball program were *real people*. On top of that, with the retirement of Bill Guthridge and the hiring of Matt Doherty (my old Final Four bleacher bum), North Carolina was about to undergo one of the most compelling years in its glorious basketball history.

I knew, from experience and late-night conversations with friends in the business, that any head coach's first year at a new school contained ten years' worth of growth, frustration, triumph, pain, wonderment, and anguish. At UNC, an alumnus was coming home to coach a program that, in Roy Williams' words, had been under "the same umbrella" for more than thirty years.

I just had to tell this story.

When I approached Coach Doherty about this project, he was understandably concerned. He had been on the job about two months and already someone was approaching him about access to his inner-most thoughts and struggles during what he and everyone else knew would be an eventful season. Worrying about a book was the last thing he wanted to be doing. But at his core—as I discovered from his players and recruits—Doherty is honest and forthright. As the season progressed—and he saw me wherever he went—he warmed to the idea. He was as free and open with his time as he could possibly be expected to be, and what he didn't allow me to witness firsthand he more than happily reconstructed. His staff was particularly enjoyable to be around and brought back memories of the camaraderie that develops between men who work so long and so close together for a common goal. The players were incredibly open about their thoughts and emotions in addition to putting away some serious breakfast food.

I am not a lifelong Carolina fan—although, as a college basketball person it was impossible not to admire what the program had accomplished and the loyalty it had fostered among its family members. Truth be told, I am not, except for a few programs where friends or relatives coach, a "fan" of any team.

I do, however, root for people. After spending a season with the players and coaches in the Carolina program, it's safe to say I'll be pulling for them in whatever pursuits their lives take them.

They are all truly Big Time.

"I'm Staying"

The sun rose slowly over the moors and pierced the morning fog, releasing the dark green, undulating hills from their gray cloak. The tees and greens of the Old Course at St. Andrews glistened under the dew as Roy Williams stepped out of the clubhouse. It was a scene and a setting that should have put Williams—an avid golfer—in as calm and pleasant a state of mind as a big-time college basketball coach could possibly be.

He was anything but relaxed.

The source of his angst was a phone call that had come several days earlier; June 7, 2000, to be exact—the day before his wife Wanda's birthday. That was the day before they had embarked on this golfing trip to Scotland with other members of the athletic department at the University of Kansas. It was a call Roy Williams, the most successful college basketball coach during the decade of the 1990s, knew would be coming.

Every day for two and a half years he had imagined what the caller would say and how he would react, so much so that he felt the constant distraction was interrupting his ability to do his job. So he had stopped wondering and focused on forgetting, but the thought never left his mind for more than a few days, when it would spring up again, triggered by a friend's polite inquiry or a conversation with a former player.

Then, just when he had succeeded in purging the curiosity, the call had come. "I think he's going to do it," said Dean Smith on the other end of the line.

"He" was Bill Guthridge, Smith's loyal assistant coach for 30 years at North Carolina. Three years earlier, Guthridge had succeeded Smith as the head coach in Chapel Hill. That tenure was going to end soon. "It" was retire.

The next day, Williams flew across the Atlantic for the 10-day golf trip in which he would play the oldest and most famous golf courses in the world. Williams, a golf fanatic, had been looking forward to it for a long time. But as he played the courses at St. Andrews, Royal Lytham, and Carnoustie, Williams could not get the call out of his mind. Soon, he would have to choose between Kansas and North Carolina. To outsiders, it seemed like a dream come true for any coach to have two of college basketball's best coaching jobs at your feet. But for Williams it was like being forced to choose which child (or parent) you liked most.

And, more important and acute in Williams's mind, which one you would inevitably hurt by *not* selecting.

Williams had told anyone who would listen, including Smith and Guthridge, that he hoped Guthridge would coach 10 more years, and then both he and Williams could retire at the same time. But it wasn't to be. When he returned from Scotland, Williams tried to resume his normal life without letting on what was about to happen. The Kansas basketball camp started, and Williams got a call from Guthridge. Yes, Guthridge confirmed, he was retiring, with the announcement to come later this week.

Williams's life changed. He couldn't sleep. He tried to think of something, anything, else. But it was impossible. His initial thoughts were that he would leave Lawrence and take the job at Chapel Hill— there was little doubt it would be offered.

Either choice meant he would be disloyal to many people to whom he owed so much.

Dean Smith had given Williams his breakthrough opportunity in college coaching. After playing junior varsity basketball and serving as a student assistant at North Carolina—from where he graduated in 1972—Williams took a job coaching basketball at Swannanoa High School near his hometown of Asheville, in the western part of the state. He never left the thoughts of his mentor, however, and after five years Smith called him home to become the third assistant at UNC at a salary of $2,700 per year. Williams jumped at the opportunity, even if it meant supplementing his salary by selling calendars in the summer and driving tapes of the coaches' television show to stations around the state.

Over the course of the next decade, Williams became an invaluable member of the staff, which included Guthridge and Eddie Fogler. Together, they brought in players like Michael Jordan, James Worthy, Sam Perkins, Kenny Smith, Brad Daugherty, Hubert Davis, Jeff Lebo, and many, many others. In 1982, the Tar Heels won the NCAA title, defeating Georgetown in one of the most memorable college basketball games ever.

But what Williams learned from Smith, Guthridge, Fogler, and all the players meant so much more. The foundations of the Carolina pro-gram were loyalty (first and foremost) and a sense of family that extended beyond merely winning basketball games and conference championships—although there were plenty of each. From the outside, the program was the Baby Blue Mafia, a core of too-perfect people that never seemed to fail on or off the court. On the inside, the team was about sacrificing for the common good, paying one's dues no matter one's talent level, and learning and growing into well-rounded people as well as basketball players.

But it was loyalty, most of all, that Williams learned from Smith. Former Carolina players never made important life decisions without consulting Dean Smith. From Larry Brown to Jerry Stackhouse, men of incomparable talent and confidence confided in Smith on issues regarding their careers, their personal lives, and their families. It was a family, and Smith was the patriarch.

By the end of the 1980s, Williams was ready to become his own patriarch. Fogler had moved on to Wichita State, and Williams himself had been courted for jobs for several years, but he was content to wait for just the right one. In 1988, Kansas, behind UNC grad and head coach Larry Brown, won the NCAA title. But Brown abruptly left the program to return to professional basketball. Kansas, a school that had, through the years, offered its head coaching job—not once, but twice— to one of its most prominent alumni, Dean Smith, went searching for a coach. The athletic director, Bob Frederick, took a major gamble hiring Roy Williams, a man with no head coaching experience from the school that had produced the coach that had just jilted the Jayhawks.

Williams got the job only to learn after a few months that Kansas would be put on NCAA probation for acts committed when Brown was in charge. Nevertheless, Williams led the Jayhawks to 19 wins in his first season and 30 the next. After that, Kansas was rarely out of the top 20, reaching Final Fours in 1991 (in which it would defeat North Carolina in the national semifinals) and 1993 (in which Carolina got its revenge, again in the semifinals). By 2000, Williams had won more games in his first twelve seasons (329) than any coach in college basketball history and had become everyone's choice to succeed his mentor, Dean Smith, as coach at North Carolina when Guthridge, who had taken the job for three seasons when Smith retired a few weeks before the 1997–98 season, decided to call it quits.

With that day fast approaching, Williams dreaded the decision facing him. Whom would he let down: Kansas, where Frederick had taken the chance to hire him and where he had felt such a strong connection that he had worked under the same contract since 1990; or North Carolina, where he was born, grew up, and learned the game, profession, and so much more from Smith? It was impossible for Williams to focus on the incredible opportunity he was being presented; instead, all the emotional Williams could think of was who he would hurt with his choice.

But the ball was already rolling, and he could no longer hold it back.

On Thursday, his wife—who thought Guthridge might be having second thoughts—called Williams at camp. "Why don't you come home and call Coach Guthridge?" Wanda said. "You may be able to talk him out of this." Williams went home immediately and called Guthridge. "He wasn't really having second thoughts," Williams recalled. "It was just going to be an emotional time for him to tell the players and staff what he was doing."

Guthridge finally summoned the strength and announced there would be a press conference the next day in Chapel Hill. Immediately, speculation ran rampant. After all, there could only be one reason for a June press conference regarding basketball: Guthridge was retiring. Reports began circulating that Williams—who was long rumored to be the coach-in-waiting—would be announced as the new Carolina coach at that Friday press conference. But it was Guthridge's night, as Smith sat next to his friend and colleague while he ended his three-year stewardship of college basketball's most prestigious program.

Williams, meanwhile, held his own press conference in Lawrence immediately after the one in Chapel Hill where he and Frederick asked for patience and time to make a decision. A reporter asked him why he needed time, given that he obviously knew Kansas and North Carolina as well as anybody could. Williams said he needed to think about a lot of things. "There was a new athletic director at North Carolina, there was a new chancellor coming in at North Carolina," recalled Williams. "I had gone seven straight years without ever seeing them play. The only reason I'd started going back was because my son was playing."

Scott Williams had heard the news about Guthridge from his father the weekend before during a family reunion in Asheville. His father, who had just returned from Scotland, sat down next to him in an old, rustic church and whispered the news. "I have a bad feeling that Coach Guthridge is going to step down," Williams had told his son.

"My first reaction was that I hated it had to be the way it was because I felt that people were unfair to Coach Guthridge that year," said Scott. "I hated that I knew he was just tired of messing with it. Secondly, I started thinking that my Pops was going to be the new head coach at North Carolina."

Scott—who had been a walk-on player for Smith and then Guthridge at Carolina—could hardly contain his rising anticipation. After graduation, he had taken a job with First Union Bank in Charlotte, and as such, he did not get to see his family as much as he would like. But now he would. He was also thrilled that Pops, always known as a tireless recruiter and worker, would now have an easier time of luring the best college players in the country. Scott remembered the time he talked to the mother of teammate Vince Carter, and how she told him that they loved Coach Roy while Vince was being recruited by Kansas, but Lawrence was just too far away. Lawrence, Scott knew from living there as a teenager, was far away from *everything*. Now, Scott knew, with the combination of his father's work ethic and North Carolina's built-in advantages, the Tar Heels could get any player they wanted.

Scott was also looking forward to the end of all the speculation about a clandestine agreement that his father would be the next coach at North Carolina. "My Pops has got to be the most honest individual I've ever been around in my life. People asked him, 'Are you coming back?' He'd say that he wanted Coach Guthridge to stay there as long as he could and he had a great situation in Kansas and he hoped that day never came. For his honesty and integrity to be challenged by people saying that he and Coach Smith had this back-door agreement that this was going to happen . . . Coach Smith would tell you the same thing: there was no agreement. . . .

"But Coach Smith, like me, would tell you he hoped he would come."

About an hour after his Friday night press conference, Roy Williams received the official offer from North Carolina athletic director Dick Baddour via a phone call.

After pleasantries were exchanged, Baddour got to the point.

"Roy, I want you to be the coach at North Carolina," said Baddour.

Williams reacted by saying he needed to talk to the people at Kansas, and then he reiterated what he had said at the press conference that he wanted to come to Chapel Hill and sit down with Baddour. Arrangements were made for Williams to travel to Chapel Hill during the family's scheduled Fourth of July vacation at their beach house outside of Charleston, South Carolina.

"It's going to be a very hard decision for me," Williams told Baddour before hanging up.

After a sleepless night, Williams arose before the sun for a scheduled tee time at Alvamar Country Club. There, he would play golf with two of his very best friends in Lawrence: Randy Towner, the golf professional at Alvamar, and Scott Buxton. All three spoke at length about Williams's options, and when the final putts were tapped in and they had made their way back to the parking lot, Williams told both men, "I've probably played my last round of golf with you that I will ever play as the head coach at Kansas." All three grown men had tears in their eyes as they embraced.

Three hours later, Williams was on a plane to South Carolina, and, three days later, he flew to Chapel Hill. He and Wanda arrived during the evening of Monday, July 3, and spent the night having dinner at the Aurora restaurant with Dick and Linda Baddour and Dean and Linnea Smith. The gathering was, for the most part, social in nature, but "we knew why we were there," said Williams. In the few days he had spent in South Carolina, he had walked the beaches seeking some sort of divine intervention.

"Going up there, the whole idea was that something would jump out and grab me and tell me it was OK to [go to North Carolina]," recalled Williams. "The problem I was having was that for 12 years I'd gone into every home and recruited the players and said if you come to Kansas I'm going to be concerned about you the rest of your life, you're going to be a part of my family for the rest of your life. I was really bothered during this time wondering if those players would feel I was disloyal or if I had been misleading them."

To try to come to grips with his feelings of disloyalty, Williams had called his Kansas staff together the Friday of Guthridge's retirement press conference and discussed with them—two of whom, Jerod Haase and C.B. McGrath, had played for Willliams—if they felt he would be deserting them should he leave.

But it was an event that took place the day before—when Williams knew of Guthridge's decision to retire but no one else at Kansas did—that left an indelible impression on Williams.

Following a camp game between current and former Kansas players, former Jayhawk player Greg Gurley—holding his three-month-old daughter—asked Williams: "Coach, how does it feel to have four of your grandchildren here?" Nearby, Rex Walters' two kids and Scott Pollard's daughter were playing. Between them, Williams and Gurley determined that Williams had 16 "grandchildren" within 40 miles of Lawrence.

It was a moment that would stick in Williams's mind throughout the week.

The dinner over, Williams and his wife went back to the Morehead residence on campus and talked until the wee hours. Roy and Wanda woke up early and walked around the deserted campus—it was July 4 and all of the students, even those on campus for the summer, were gone—and visited all the landmarks. The Davie Poplar. The Old Well. "And that's what I wanted to have in Chapel Hill is something to grab me and tell me that it would be OK to do that, that I wouldn't be disloyal to my players," recalled Williams. "That I wouldn't be phony.

"Nothing ever grabbed me."

Williams and Smith played nine holes of golf at UNC's Finley Golf Course while Linda Baddour and Wanda Williams toured Chapel Hill. The two old friends had several frank conversations about coaching at North Carolina. Smith, always the competitor, put a benevolent full court press on his old assistant. When they were finished, Smith and Williams met Baddour in the Smith Center for a several-hour talk. When it came time for lunch, Williams wanted something quick and easy, where the three of them would not have to go out. He suggested Carolina barbecue.

Assistant Athletic Director for Media Relations Steve Kirschner and Assistant Athletic Director Larry Gallo volunteered to make a quick run for the food. But a quick run turned into a two-hour ordeal, as the nearest barbecue joint that was open was in Goldsboro, 80 miles away. "I felt terrible," said Williams. "I just wanted something easy."

Smith left Williams and Baddour to talk after lunch. Williams reiterated that he did not want to haggle over any of the specifics of the contract. Baddour presented the offer. Williams did not accept it, but he did not turn it down. He asked again if he could have until Friday to decide; he had promised Frederick and Kansas chancellor Robert Hemenway that he would talk to them one last time before he decided. The two agreed that Williams would call Baddour by 5:00 P.M. on Friday and shook hands; Williams headed back to the Morehead residence to meet Scott, who had driven up from Charlotte to see him.

For the first time, Scott Williams saw what the decision was doing to his father. When the two met up in the Morehead residence, the son could see the strain on his dad's face.

They talked about what had transpired over the course of the day. Scott listened while his father told him about the round of golf, about Smith's recruitment of him, about how well he had been treated by Baddour and everyone else at Carolina. Scott recalled that "twice his eyes welled up with tears because the people on campus have been so good to him and he feels like he was going to let Coach Smith down."

It was then that Scott realized his father might choose to remain at Kansas. Williams relayed the story of Greg Gurley and Williams's 16 "grandchildren." Having spent the last decade of his own life in Lawrence—and being best friends with Brad Frederick, Bob Frederick's son—Scott knew of the pull Lawrence and KU had on his father. It was justified, he knew, as the program, the school, and the community were special.

Scott also listened to his father talk about having asked Smith and Guthridge for advice. "He asked Coach Smith and Coach Guthridge, 'What do I tell my kids?'"

It was a short reunion, as Scott knew his mom and dad wanted to get back to South Carolina to watch the fireworks with his sister, Kimberly.

The son and father hugged, and Williams's eyes welled up one more time.

 Williams spent the next day, July 5, "absolutely crazy." But his concerns had gradually changed. Before going to Chapel Hill, Williams had been concerned with how he would tell his former and current players—as well as Bob Frederick and Chancellor Hemenway—that he was leaving, when all along he had preached the importance of loyalty.

But after Chapel Hill—where he had not seen the sign he had hoped to see—his concerns were now centered on how he would tell North Carolina that he *wasn't* coming. It was July 5 in Charleston that this realization began to hit him; more specifically when Wanda drove him to the airport to return to Lawrence.

"Well, I think I'm going to go to North Carolina," Williams told his wife as they pulled up to the Charleston Airport.

"I think you ought to stay at Kansas," Wanda replied. It was the first time she had made her thoughts on the subject known.

"Why do you say that?" Williams asked.

"Because I think that's deep-down what you want to do."

When Williams got off the plane in Kansas City, he was immediately surrounded by cameras and reporters. A story was going to break in the Durham *Herald-Sun* the next morning that stated Williams had agreed to a seven-year contract to coach at North Carolina. Reporters swarmed Williams and asked him if the story was true. "I told them that no, it was not true," recalled Williams. "I had promised the chancellor and athletic director that I would talk to them before I made a decision, and that was what I was doing. I had meetings set with them that next day, the 6th. I'd promised them that. They had given me a chance here and so I wasn't going to mislead them and I wasn't going to lie to them."

About an hour later he arrived at his home in Lawrence.

 Scott Williams had spoken to his father on the phone the day he left Charleston and could hear the anguish in his voice. But it was the cause of the anguish that surprised him. His mom let him in on the source during a conversation the two of them had the night Roy flew back to Lawrence.

"Your father's not home right now, but I want you to know he feels as though he's going to let you and I down if he doesn't go to Carolina," said Wanda.

"Are you serious?" replied Scott.

"Yes, because he knows that you want him to go to Carolina and he had a feeling I wouldn't mind going to Carolina, either," said Wanda. "I've got to tell you, I don't care. But, he knows that our families are there and you're there, and he knows you want him to go, and I think that's killing him."

The next day, while Scott was still at work, the phone rang. It was his Pops and he was obviously conflicted.

As the conversation progressed, it was obvious to Scott that his mom had been right. "I don't want to let you down no matter what my decision is," Roy finally admitted.

"Listen," Scott replied, "it is obvious I think you ought to go to North Carolina. But, at the same time, you've done an incredible job at Kansas. You'd be amazing at Carolina, and there is no doubt in my mind that you would end up retiring one of the greatest coaches ever. At the same time, it doesn't bother me a bit either way, because I'll respect the hell out of your decision. I think that you have to respect the fact that you care so much about both sides." Scott then smiled into the phone: "One thing I'm going to lose is that maybe I don't get season tickets next year to Carolina games. I'd be proud of you if you decide to stay at Kansas, I'd be pumped if you decide to go to Carolina. If you stay at Kansas, you've stuck to your guns and done what you said all along. You're showing a lot of integrity by sticking with your program and with your players."

"Are you sure?" Williams asked.

"I'm serious. It doesn't bother me either way. I'll love you just as much."

Then Scott added with a grin: "But don't tell me what you decide until after it's announced. That way, when all the guys back at the office ask me what's going on, I can tell them I don't know and I won't be lying."

About the same time Roy and Scott were speaking on the phone, Dean Smith was having lunch with the North Carolina assistant coaches in Chapel Hill. Understandably, all three men—Phil Ford, Dave Hanners, and Pat Sullivan—were wondering if they would still have jobs after a new coach was hired.

But this was the Carolina Family, so maybe Williams would keep them.

Smith quickly and confidently laid out the plan. When, he said, Williams took the job it was likely he would retain at least one, maybe two, of the current coaches. Only Ford, whose DUI arrest the previous fall had been a well-publicized black mark on the program, would not come back to the staff. Instead, Ford would be reassigned to the Educational Foundation, the athletic fund-raising department.

All three assistants, even Ford, appeared relieved. Hanners was the most reserved, concerned that he would be the next most likely, after Ford, to be out. Williams was friendly with and respected all of the coaches on the current UNC staff, but with loyalties to his own staff in Kansas, they all knew their jobs were tenuous. Sullivan, because he was younger and could survive on less money and responsibility, was the most likely to be retained. When the lunch broke up, Hanners asked Smith a simple question: "What if Roy doesn't take the job?"

Smith responded as if shocked by the possibility. He quickly brushed it aside, assuring the three coaches that Williams would arrive in Chapel Hill within 24 hours to formally accept the job. All three assistants dropped the matter, knowing that if Dean Smith said it was so, it was so.

When Roy Williams had gone to Chapel Hill, he was searching for a sign to tell him it was OK to leave Kansas. On his return to Lawrence, he was now looking for one that said it was OK to say *no* to North Carolina.

The Kansas fans had thought the same thing. In a unique, genuine outpouring of emotion, fans had taped letters of support to every window and door of Allen Field House and the adjacent Parrot Athletic Center and Wagnon Student-Athlete Center, where the basketball offices are located. Messages were scribbled in chalk on the sidewalks, fans were walking around or sitting in lawn chairs on the grass outside the buildings, doing anything to be close to the situation. Nobody was there for a specific reason (other than the various television trucks, who hoped to catch a glimpse of something newsworthy), but all felt compelled to be there.

"The Williams Watch" put the eyes of the nation on Lawrence.

At around 11:00 that night, Williams drove to the campus to see for himself the letters and messages. "I went and walked around a little bit, and they asked me if I'd be on the news and I told them no, and then basically I had to get out. It was getting too emotional for me so I went on home. I was there by myself."

But the sign he sought came early the next morning.

Prior to meeting with Frederick and Chancellor Hemenway, Williams received a call at home from an old North Carolina friend. "Thirty minutes before I was leaving to meet with Dr. Frederick that morning, the phone rings and it's a former high school player of mine I coached 24 years before," recalled Williams. "I probably hadn't talked to him in several years."

"I just wanted you to know I was watching the news last night and I saw the deal when you got off the airplane in Kansas City and the look on your face," said the former player. "In high school you always told us that the players were the most important thing in the world to you. I was talking to another former player last night and we agreed that everybody would feel the same way: that *you* were the most important thing to us, not where you coached. Of course, we want you to come to North Carolina, but if you decide to stay at Kansas it's not going to change our feelings toward you whatsoever because we want what's best for you."

"I think that was the final straw," Williams said later. "I hadn't spoken to that young man in several years. That sort of told me it was all right to not go to North Carolina."

After the call, Williams drove to the office early Friday morning and asked the coaching staff to meet him downstairs in the coaches' locker room, a place he had always used as a sanctuary when the phones were ringing too much upstairs. That was most definitely the case today. When the staff arrived, Williams asked each and every one of them to write down on paper what would be best for them: Williams staying at Kansas or going to North Carolina. He also asked them to write down what they wanted Williams to do. When the staff left to complete their assignment, Williams went upstairs to meet with Bob Frederick.

Williams did not give Frederick a definitive answer. The two spoke about Williams's trip to Chapel Hill and how tough a decision it was going to be. Then it was time to go speak to Dr. Hemenway. When Williams and Frederick walked outside to Frederick's car, they were besieged by hundreds of media. "I had asked the media to give me a week, yet they couldn't allow that to happen because I guess they were afraid somebody was going to get a scoop they wouldn't have. So every time we'd walk out it would just be a sprint with people with cameras. I remember as were walking to Bob Frederick's car to go up to the chancellor's office and I looked at one guy and said, 'You're going to have a heart attack.' He was lugging around this huge camera and it's 95 degrees."

The conversation with the chancellor went much the same as the one with Frederick. Never was a new contract brought up. "If I decide to come back, I want to come back for the same contract I have now," Williams told the chancellor and Dr. Frederick. "I don't want it to be any different."

When the meeting was over—and knowing reporters were camped outside—Frederick went out the front door while Hemenway escorted Williams out the back. He walked through campus alone, but when he got to Allen Field House, he was again besieged by media. "I haven't decided yet," Williams told the throng. And it was true.

Once inside, he called upstairs to ask Haase to bring the staff's notes down. He read them alone in the locker room, believing that maybe in the prior, agonizing, week he had failed to consider some aspect of this situation. But nothing in his staff's words struck him as something he had not already thought about from every angle.

When Haase returned with lunch, Roy Williams had come to a decision.

Scott Williams tried to concentrate on work at First Union, but it was difficult. It wasn't the fact it was a Friday afternoon before a summer weekend; it was that his thoughts were with his father a thousand miles away. About 2:30 in the afternoon, his phone rang.

"I know you didn't want me to call you and tell you, but I want to tell you . . ." said Williams.

"No!" interrupted Scott. "I really don't want to know."

The two talked some more, but in adhering to his son's wishes, Williams did not let on as to what his decision would be. He didn't have to. Scott, at this point, already knew.

During the call, Scott looked up. In the doorway were several co-workers, all anxiously awaiting word so they could sprint to their own phones and e-mail and release the news to their friends.

"Don't tell me," continued Scott. "I don't want to know. Like I said I'll be proud if you stay at Kansas, I'll be pumped if you go to Carolina."

"Are you sure?"

"I'm positive," replied Scott. "You're going to make the right decision. No matter what you do, you can't lose. You're going to feel as though you let people down, but there's not a bad choice here."

"All right," Williams said, fighting back tears again. "I appreciate it."

Scott hung up the phone. "My boss, Jim, was absolutely irate," said Scott. "To his credit, Jim was great through the whole process; he didn't really bother me that much. He actually came up to me that afternoon and said, 'Scott, I got a bad feeling, he's not coming is he? I think we're going to lose Roy.'"

To which Scott honestly replied: "Jim, I don't know. I swear."

Bob Frederick was elated. His coach was staying.

Roy Williams had asked Frederick to come downstairs to the coaches' locker room in midafternoon and told him the news. "He was emotional," recalled Williams. "I think it was a relief and I think it was that he really did want me to stay. . . . I think it was a feeling of satisfaction that I would turn down North Carolina to stay here at Kansas. It was an emotional time for both of us."

Williams and Frederick then discussed how to release the news. Williams wanted to simply release a statement that he was staying.

"Roy, we have over 40 out-of-town media here," explained Frederick. "We can't do that to them. That's just not fair."

Williams agreed. If they were going to have a press conference, Williams wanted to bring his wife and daughter back from South Carolina to be there. That pushed it back to 9:00 P.M. central time. After more back-and-forth communication with the sports information staff, it was determined that the only place that was large enough to hold the press conference was in the football media room. Even with that, so many requests came into the SID's office that another release was issued saying that anyone who wanted could watch the press conference on the football stadium's jumbotron.

Williams then told his coaching staff, all of whom were relieved and thrilled at the news. But Williams was far from joyful. In fact, he was as unhappy as he had been at any time during the week-long affair. After he told his inner circle, he departed the building and went home, dreading what came next.

Later, he would have to make two of the hardest phone calls of his life.

The news of a press conference in Lawrence momentarily confused the sports world. It was obvious to most that the location of the event signified Williams was staying at Kansas. But the shock of the decision defied analysis by the many who had assumed it was a done deal. Some held out belief that maybe, due to Williams's deep sense of loyalty, he was having a last press conference in Kansas to say good-bye and would then fly to Chapel Hill for another event announcing his hiring at UNC. Many in the world of college basketball, particulary those who lived in the state of North Carolina, simply couldn't fathom that

Roy Williams would *not* come back home to coach the university he loved so deeply.

Leaving the press conference organization to the sports information staff, Williams went home and quickly felt the walls closing in on him. To get some air and clear his head, he walked out of his house and across the street to Alvamar Country Club to hit a bucket of range balls.

Two television trucks were stationed outside his house, waiting for him to emerge. The two reporters approached him as he walked down his driveway and asked for interviews. "This is hard," said Williams. "I just want some peace and to go over and hit some balls."

Both left him alone.

Dick Baddour left his office about 5:00 P.M. eastern time and headed home, setting up in his den with his cell phone next to his home phone, waiting for the call. It came a few minutes before 6:00, the deadline (5:00 central time) Williams had set for his final decision.

"Dick," Williams said immediately, "I can't come."

"Oh, Roy . . ." said Baddour.

Williams then stammered a bit in explaining his reasoning, but it came down to one simple thing: He couldn't tell his players he was leaving. Loyalty, the one quality that was so important to the Carolina Family, was exactly the reason he couldn't leave Kansas. In many ways, it was that simple.

Williams went on to tell Baddour that he, as the athletic director, had done everything right. Williams began thanking Baddour for everything when Baddour's cell phone rang.

It was Dean Smith, asking if there was any news. "Coach, I have him on the other line."

"Well, what's the answer?" asked Smith.

"Coach," explained Baddour, "he's not coming. He's going to call you right now."

Returning to Williams, Baddour asked if there was anything he could do. He asked Williams if he needed more time. "Dick," said

Williams, "I've taken too much time. The decision has been made, and I wish I made it the first day, but I didn't know it was going to go in this direction." The call ended with Baddour telling Williams he would always remain a member of the Carolina Family and with Williams, again, thanking Baddour for his time and patience.

Then Williams made the call that would haunt him. Smith was "shocked," according to Williams, and disappointed. As hurt as Smith felt, however, it paled in comparison to how Williams felt. "I felt like I was dirty," said Williams. "I felt like I was being disloyal to him."

Williams was truly traumatized by the conversation—and he still had to address the media later that night.

Sixteen thousand people showed up at Memorial Stadium and cheered wildly when Williams uttered the two words that would grace the front page of all four major newspapers in the state of Kansas the next day:

"I'm staying."

It was just after 10:00 P.M. in the east, and Scott Williams was growing tired. He had been in the office all night, not wanting to go home to the messages and calls he knew awaited him there. Since 8:00 P.M. he had checked the news every few minutes—switching between spreadsheets and an Internet browser on his office computer—to see if the official word had come. A few minutes after 10:00, he saw it: no more than a few paragraphs. Pops was staying at Kansas.

Scott smiled as he read the story. His father had stayed true to himself and, once again, taught the son an important lesson.

In the process of staying loyal to those players he had made a promise to in their living rooms through the last twelve years, Williams gave up more than almost anyone would. As one of his good friends told him later, when some of the Carolina faithful cursed his name: "How can anybody be disappointed in you? You gave up more than anybody."

Williams gave up the chance to coach at his alma mater, to take over the reigns of college basketball's premier program, a program no one loved more than he did. But he did it for great reasons: the love of people close to him and the respect for the concepts of loyalty and keeping a promise. In this day and age of college basketball coaches and players choosing a me-first attitude and taking the money and running again and again, Roy Williams stuck to what he learned first from his high school coach, Buddy Baldwin, and then from Dean Smith.

Loyalty.

But even more important, he taught his son what it meant to stay true to yourself. As the most lasting lessons always seem to be, it was difficult to teach.

"As a father, you don't want to disappoint your kids," Williams said almost a year after he made the decision to stay at Kansas. "Scott loves North Carolina basketball just like I do. [Telling] Coach Smith, that was hard. Coach Guthridge . . . Eddie [Fogler] . . . But nothing's ever been as hard as worrying and being concerned about hurting Scott. Not doing what he wanted me to do. And my wife. She wanted to go back. She wanted to be closer to her children. That was my dream. We would have been able to go back closer to our children.

"Nobody gave up what I did."

2

The Right Man for the Job

On the same early July evening that Roy Williams was holding his press conference in Lawrence, Doug Wojcik, an assistant coach at Notre Dame, was outside of the house he and his wife, Lael, had built in South Bend, mowing the lawn. It was a pleasant diversion for Wojcik, an intense recruiter/coach and former point guard at the Naval Academy during the David Robinson era. Lael, due to give birth to their first child in a few weeks, called out to her husband and asked if he wanted to watch the Williams announcement on television. No, Wojcik said, he already knew what would happen. Williams was going to Carolina, he was sure. His boss, Matt Doherty, and he had talked about it on several occasions during the week, and Wojcik was fairly certain the move would not tumble the dominoes in a way that would affect them. Doherty had spent seven seasons working under Williams at Kansas (and had played for Williams for four years at North Carolina), but it was unlikely that Doherty would want to return to Lawrence when Williams went to Chapel Hill.

So, with nothing to worry about, Wojcik returned to cutting his lawn. Another 10 minutes passed and Lael called out to her husband again, telling him that he may want to change his mind and come in and watch. Williams was not going to Chapel Hill.

The phone rang almost immediately. It was Doherty asking him to come down to his house, which was just down the block. The two had lived in the same neighborhood since soon after arriving in South Bend less than a year ago. Wojcik was there in a few minutes and the two men sat in the family room and talked about what might happen next. Doherty, like so many others, never dreamed Williams would not take the job in Chapel Hill.

Both wondered if and when the call would come.

Baddour held his own press conference shortly after the Williams announcement; he said little, other than assure the assembled media—many of whom had sources who had told them less than 12 hours earlier Williams had accepted the job—that the job search would continue in an expedient manner.

The list of candidates that Baddour, a former admissions officer and longtime athletic administrator to John Swofford (the former athletic director and current commissioner of the Atlantic Coast Conference) had compiled—the one he thought he'd never need—suddenly became crucial. When the call from Williams came to turn the job down, Baddour had begun calling around to various athletic directors and NBA general managers to obtain permission to talk to additional candidates, all of whom were members of the Carolina Family. Conversations had occurred to consider others outside the family, but the decision had been reached that so many strong candidates had Carolina ties that the list of alumni should be completely exhausted before going outside.

Dean Smith's loyalties were split, but he obviously favored three coaches: Eddie Fogler, a longtime UNC assistant who had success as a head coach at Wichita State, Vanderbilt, and early on at South Carolina, but who had hit tough times with his most recent Gamecocks squad; Larry Brown, the current head coach of the Philadelphia 76ers who had led Kansas to a national title in 1988, but had left that program on probation and had never remained with one team or program for more than five years; and George Karl, the current coach of the Milwaukee Bucks who had led the Seattle SuperSonics to the NBA Finals several years earlier, but had never coached in college.

All three men had played for Smith, and two, Fogler and Brown, had been on his staff. All three were outstanding coaches, but all had downsides as well, many of which would be outlined extensively by the media over the course of the next few days. Other alumni names would emerge, such as Randy Wiel (Middle Tennessee State), Jeff Lebo (Tennessee Tech), and Buzz Peterson (recently left Appalachian State for Tulsa), but all were considered long shots.

Baddour's list included those names, but it also included one other he immediately preferred to the others: Matt Doherty, the young and emotional head coach at Notre Dame. Baddour liked Doherty's youth, his polished appearance, and his emotion. Doherty, Baddour thought, possessed everything needed to give the program an emotional charge. He was everything Williams was, except with less experience.

All of the permissions were granted immediately, except Middle Tennessee State (Athletic Director Lee Fowler couldn't be reached) and the Bucks, who first stonewalled and eventually denied UNC the right to talk to Karl. After his press conference, Baddour was free to call as many of the candidates as he could reach.

He called only one that Thursday night: Matt Doherty.

Doherty's cell phone rang while he was in the toy aisle at the South Bend Wal-Mart, trying to fend off his son Tucker, who was filling the cart with toys when he wasn't looking. The two talked hastily as Doherty scurried to the quieter paper and napkins aisle and set it up for him and his wife, Kelly, to fly down to Chapel Hill the next afternoon. "I don't know what will happen [in the search], but I have a great deal of interest in you," Baddour told Doherty. The Dohertys left Wal-Mart with none of the items they had come to buy.

Matt and Kelly spent several hours that night discussing the possibilities of a job seemingly so out of reach Doherty had never dared dream about it.

The next day was a whirlwind from the start. Doherty called a team meeting in the Notre Dame locker room and explained in as much detail as he knew what was going on.

"Guys," Doherty said in front of the assembled players, "I got a phone call from North Carolina. They want to talk to me about the head coaching job. I don't know what I'm going to do. I don't know what they're going to do, but I'm going to explore it."

The Notre Dame players had, of course, heard about Williams saying no, and many assumed Doherty would be a candidate at UNC. Doherty could sense right away that some of the players were OK with it, while others were beginning to feel betrayed. It was only natural to feel that way, Doherty thought. He owed it to his players to be as honest as possible with them throughout the process, whatever happened.

He appointed team captain and All-American Troy Murphy to be the point man through the next few days. "I'm going to communicate with Troy pretty much every day to let him know what's going on, and he can talk with you guys." He would do exactly that, speaking with Murphy on three of the next four days and even asking Murphy's advice as the decision loomed, asking what Murphy thought of UNC and if he ever considered going to Chapel Hill out of high school.

The plane sent by UNC arrived in South Bend later that afternoon, and Doherty and his wife arrived at Raleigh-Durham airport Friday night, where they were picked up by Baddour. The three of them chatted about the flight and made other polite conversation as they drove to the Siena Hotel in Chapel Hill. A reporter greeted them in the lobby, assuring that the interview would not remain a private affair.

Later, in his room, Doherty received a call from Kevin White, the athletic director at Notre Dame. White had been working tirelessly since

receiving the call from Baddour asking for permission for UNC to talk
to Doherty. White had called his superiors and put together a very competitive contract offer in an effort to keep Doherty, the most important
component of which was its length: 10 years. Doherty was impressed
and touched by the offer, but decided to press on with the interview the
next day.

The morning of Saturday, July 8, in Chapel Hill was hot and humid,
with a haze clinging to the tops of the Carolina pines. Doherty met with
Baddour for an hour and a half in Baddour's Smith Center office, while
Linda Baddour showed Kelly Doherty around Chapel Hill. After the
initial meeting, Doherty spoke with Smith in Baddour's office and, later,
in a conference room. Then Doherty met with Bill Guthridge for an
hour. All of the meetings were much different from the conversations
with Williams a few days earlier. Instead of trying to recruit a new coach,
Baddour, Smith, and Guthridge asked more probing questions. It was
an exhausting day, but one Doherty sensed went very well. By the time
Baddour drove the Dohertys back to RDU, Doherty felt fairly certain
he had sufficiently answered all the questions he had been asked.

It had all gone so fast, Doherty barely had time to process his
thoughts.

On the plane ride back to Indiana, Matt and Kelly talked nonstop
about the opportunity that may very likely be presented to them soon.
"I could be the head coach at Notre Dame or I could be the head coach
at North Carolina," Doherty said, shaking his head and smiling. When
the plane landed in Indianapolis—where Matt was being dropped off to
attend the Nike Camp, the single most important recruiting event of the
year—both of their heads were spinning from having talked about all the
possibilities. It would be the first of many long talks the two would have
in the next few days.

Dick Baddour's next meeting did not go so well. On Sunday he
and Jack Evans, UNC's longtime faculty representative to the
NCAA, flew to California to speak with Larry Brown. Baddour had

misgivings about Brown. Although Brown was undoubtedly one of the best minds in basketball, the 61-year-old coach also had a reputation as basketball's vagabond man, having coached at Kansas and UCLA on the collegiate level and Philadelphia, Indianapolis, Los Angeles, and numerous other stops on the professional circuit. Baddour did not believe that he could hire Brown (who had led the Jayhawks to a national title in 1988 but had also left that program on probation) due to a lack of support from the UNC administration and key alumni.

But Brown was a favorite of Dean Smith. Brown had been a guard on Smith's first teams in Chapel Hill and had gone on to coach on Smith's staff. Of course, Baddour—who had once said about Smith: "I'll go to my grave remembering what that man did for me," after Smith used his influence to put Baddour in the AD's chair—knew it. Baddour owed Brown an in-person explanation.

It did not go well. Brown, a proud man who loved North Carolina and Smith, felt he should have been pursued for the job even before Roy Williams. He also did not appreciate Baddour's trying to talk him out of the job. He admitted as much later in the year to *ESPN The Magazine*'s Tom Friend: "My interview was humiliating," Brown told Friend. "The guy [Baddour] just talked about how other people were perfect for the job, and I was too old. . . . I think for me to get the job, Coach Smith would've had to go to war." Brown felt that if Smith wanted him, that was enough. But Smith, by his own admission, would be taking a few steps away from the program in the near future. His influence was not what it once was.

It was Baddour's show to run. And he had already chosen his coach.

By Monday, Fogler and Brown had released statements that they had removed their names from consideration for the job. Karl was being prohibited from even talking to UNC. Wiel had been summoned to Chapel Hill from Spain—where he was conducting a clinic—to interview, but few considered him a viable candidate. He had never led a major college program and had only mediocre success at Middle Tennessee State.

Doherty was the lone man standing.

By that evening, Doherty was growing restless at the Nike Camp. "It was getting crazy," recalled Doherty. "The media was all over the place and every time I'd turn around, someone would ask me, 'Hey, what's going on?' So I was getting a little antsy and felt like we either needed to do this or I would take my name out. I didn't want to go through it any longer. I didn't want to put Notre Dame through it any longer. I didn't want to put my players through it any longer."

Doherty spoke to his old boss, Roy Williams, at the Nike Camp as he began to realize the magnitude of the North Carolina job. In between evaluating players, Williams and Doherty backed up into a doorway and discussed the situation. "You can do that job," said Williams. Williams went on to explain to Doherty that he had the requisite toughness to handle the inevitable backlash that would come from change within a program unused to turnover. "Not that you need my blessing by any means, but I want you to take that job."

"He knows me as well as anybody, and he knows that job as well as anybody," recalled Doherty. "His saying that gave me a lot of confidence."

Doherty and Baddour talked via cell phone as Doherty drove from Indianapolis to South Bend that afternoon. Doherty asked that something be done soon or he would stay in South Bend, a place he truly enjoyed coaching and living. When he arrived at home, he told Kelly what was going on. "I think there's going to be a call tomorrow morning. I think they're going to offer me the job." Doherty called his assistants and told them the same, and then he called an old teammate, Michael Jordan, and left a message. "Hey, Michael, I need some advice here. . . ."

Then he and Kelly stayed up well past midnight, trying to reach a conclusion on what he should do when that call came.

The phone rang at 7:30 the next morning. It was Jordan. The two talked about the job and the effect being the coach at Carolina would have on Doherty's family. "He didn't really say anything that cleared my mind up," said Doherty, "except at the end when he said: 'If you don't take it, then they might have to go outside the family.' That's when it hit that I wanted to take the job."

Most observers assumed it was a slam-dunk decision. On the surface, the two jobs don't appear even close. Notre Dame was a football school in northern Indiana. Its basketball tradition was centered around the mid-1970s when, under Digger Phelps, the Fighting Irish ended UCLA's 88-game winning streak in 1974 and reached the Final Four in 1978. It was a job that ruined many a coaching career, including most recently John MacLeod, the man Doherty had replaced. With challenging academics and always in the shadow of football, Notre Dame was not viewed on the same plane as Carolina, a perennial national power in college basketball.

The fit had showed itself during the year. Doherty had taken a group of solid, if unspectacular, players and won the Irish's first game at Ohio State, which was coming off a Final Four appearance and opening a brand-new arena. Other big wins against UConn (twice), and St. John's put Notre Dame on the NCAA bubble. When it burst, the Irish rebounded and made it to the final of the NIT, where they lost to Wake Forest to finish the season at 22–15, the most wins for the program in more than a decade. With a season of recruiting under its belt, Notre Dame was projected as a top-25 team for 2000–2001.

Now, the one job in all the world that would make Doherty even *consider* leaving Notre Dame was about to be offered to him. The same questions ran through his mind over and over: Is there ever a good time to leave? Is it a good time to leave after 10 years, like Coach Williams? He had shown that was nearly impossible. Maybe the timing was bad now, but it could get worse.

When Wiel's brief interview ended in the Smith Center on Tuesday morning, Baddour placed the call to Doherty at around 1:00 in the afternoon and made the offer. "OK, Matt, now I'm going to make a formal offer to you," said Baddour. "But before we talk about numbers, I want to talk about the excitement we have for your

energy and enthusiasm, which we think is going to light up this place."
Doherty thanked Baddour and reciprocated by saying he was also
excited and thanked Baddour for the way he had been treated throughout the process. Then, Baddour got to the nuts and bolts of the offer. On
the other end of the line, Doherty, in a position he never dreamed of,
enthusiastically took the job but wanted a few provisions worked out.

"People probably don't believe this, but I wasn't thrilled with the
terms," said Doherty. "Notre Dame offered me a heckuva contract. They
offered me a ten-year contract, and I wanted something a little more than
what was being offered [by North Carolina]. And I wanted the money
for my assistants that they would have gotten had we stayed at Notre
Dame. We had to get those things worked out. People thought that as
soon as the job was offered I was running, and that was not the case."

Three issues had to be resolved: first, Doherty wanted a longer contract than UNC initially offered; second, he wanted his assistant
coaches—Doug Wojcik, Fred Quartlebaum, Bob MacKinnon, and
David Cason—to come with him from Notre Dame; and third, he
wanted those assistants to be paid more money.

Doherty and Baddour hung up, with Baddour promising to work on
the issues. Over the course of the next hour, Baddour (who had already
sent the contract to the UNC Board of Trustees for approval) adjusted the
provisions to Doherty's specifications. Baddour called back an hour later.

"OK, I can do that," said Baddour. And the deal was done. Doherty
received a six-year contract worth $145,000 annually, with radio and
television adding another $180,000 and a Nike contract that pushed it
close to $750,000. More important, he was bringing his coaches with
him, and they would get paid at the level that Notre Dame had offered.

One step remained.

Baddour wanted to have the press conference the next day.
Doherty, however, had a different idea. "I said, 'Uh, uh. Let's have a
press conference today. We need to move on this not only for me personally but for Notre Dame and North Carolina's recruiting,'" said
Doherty. "We were right in the middle of the recruiting period. We
agreed we'd have a press conference that night. They sent a plane for us.

It was crazy. I met the [Notre Dame] team at 2:00 [central time], the plane picked us up at 3:00."

The meeting with the Notre Dame players was an emotional event. "That was the hardest thing I've ever done professionally," Doherty recalled. "It happened so quickly. You can't have the proper goodbye." The meeting was too quick. There was too much to say. Doherty explained that he had accepted the job, and the emotional coach began to tear up. Some of the players did as well. Some didn't.

"I went around and hugged each guy," said Doherty. "Some gave me good hugs; some gave me not so good hugs. And that was hard. We did a lot of good things over the course of that year." Doherty understood the players' mixed reaction.

As he left the building to catch a ride to another plane—the one that would carry him to Chapel Hill to introduce him as the head coach at North Carolina—Troy Murphy caught up to him in the parking lot.

"Coach," said Murphy, "you did the right thing."

"Thanks, Troy," said Doherty, getting emotional all over again as he hugged his (former) star player. "I'll be rooting for you this season."

The plane trip from South Bend to Chapel Hill was almost surreal for Doherty, his assistants, and their families. "We just kept smiling and laughing," said David Cason, the director of basketball operations who had spent his playing and coaching careers in off-the-beaten-path places like Southern Idaho, Illinois State, and Eastern Illinois before landing the job at Notre Dame a year earlier. "It was hard for any of us to believe that we were going to be coaching at North Carolina."

The next meeting Doherty had was almost as difficult as speaking to the Notre Dame players. Not long after arriving in Chapel Hill, Doherty met with Dave Hanners, Phil Ford, and Pat Sullivan and thanked them for everything they had done for the program. Despite a record of success and through no fault of their own, they would now have to find other jobs. Their removal was particularly difficult for Smith and Guthridge, who would work tirelessly to find them jobs in the coming weeks. While the former assistants would be paid throughout the year, it was a difficult situation for a program steeped in loyalty.

Doherty then addressed about half of the players in person in the locker room (those who were on campus for the second session of summer school) while the others listened in on a conference call. His top goal was to get the players to feel comfortable with him. So he took off his jacket, rolled up his sleeves, and sat down. "I understand what you're going through," he told players who had just lost the only college coaching staff they had known. "I just went through it with my team at Notre Dame. This is a tough time. We're going to get through it, but you've got to give me a chance."

The team he inherited was not a great team by Carolina standards, but it was far from a down team, either, with four of five starters returning from a team that advanced to the Final Four the year before. Brendan Haywood, a 7'0" center still developing as an offensive presence, and Kris Lang, a 6'11" power forward with a quick, deadly jump-hook, formed a solid front line. Jason Capel was a do-everything junior forward who could handle the ball and shoot open three-pointers. Joseph Forte was a Player of the Year candidate at shooting guard who had shown a well-developed midrange game and improving ball skills during his freshman year. Two point guards, Jonathan Holmes and Ronald Curry, returned and would compete for the starting spot along with freshmen Adam Boone and Brian Morrison. Coming off the bench, Doherty had senior Max Owens, a deadly outside shooter whose defensive liabilities had cut into his playing time the past three seasons; Michael Brooker, another senior shooter who struggled to guard athletic ACC-caliber guards; Brian Bersticker, a 6'11" junior finesse player who was coming off a variety of injuries; Will Johnson, a 6'8" sophomore Morehead scholar trying to find a niche in which he could contribute on the floor; Orlando Melendez, an incredible 6'8" athlete from Puerto Rico who had yet to embrace the competitive nature of college basketball; Neil Fingleton, an enormous 7'6" freshman from England still learning the game; Julius Peppers, a 6'6", 270-pound football defensive end with surprising agility and basketball instincts; and Jim Everett, a

6'8" walk-on who worked as hard as any player in the program and would get into a game only if it was well in hand.

As the meeting progressed—interrupted only when Curry, sitting in the locker room, suffered a painful muscle cramp that radiated throughout his entire body—Doherty laid down some expectations. He spoke about how honored he was to be their new coach. He introduced the new coaching staff. He also introduced himself. "I've been in your shoes," said Doherty. "I know what it's like. I played here. I can relate to it." Before the meeting broke up, he set up times with each player to meet individually the next day.

The whirlwind continued as Doherty spent a few minutes in Baddour's office to relax before meeting the media. The press conference was set to begin at 7:30 P.M., but Doherty was running behind due to his 1982 National Championship watch having stopped about a half hour earlier. A few minutes after 7:30, Doherty, Baddour, Smith, Guthridge, Chancellor James Moeser, and SID Steve Kirschner walked downstairs and through the adjacent Koury Natatorium. A youth swim league was going on as the group walked past. The kids stopped swimming and climbed onto the deck to stare at the entourage before breaking out in applause as the men ducked through a side door.

The Bowles Room is a large open lounge that had been originally designed as a practice basketball court but had long ago been converted into a space where large, important gatherings took place. On October 9, 1997, it had been the site of Dean Smith's retirement press conference. Three and a half years later, Doherty was introduced as the new head coach at North Carolina, the first alumnus to lead the program since 1925.

He walked into the overcrowded room as lightbulbs popped, onlookers, many of them hanging from a balcony, clapped, and the horde of media personnel readied their questions. Doherty had flown his parents, Walter and Mary, in from Long Island, and they sat in a back corner, grinning from ear to ear. Along the wall sat Smith, Guthridge, and four players: Jason Capel, Brendan Haywood, Julius Peppers, and Kris Lang. His wife, Kelly, and his two kids, two-year-old Tucker and six-month-old Hattie, stood off in the wings, next to his four assistants.

Doherty, in many ways, already had a hole to dig out of.

Doherty appeared somewhat overwhelmed as he walked into the room, ducking his head slightly and gazing toward the well-wishers hanging over a balcony in the back of the room. After Moeser and Baddour made opening comments, Doherty spoke. He was reverent toward the program he had inherited and toward those who had made it what it was. The former starter on the 1982 NCAA title team gave an indication as to what he was all about as a coach when he promised that the team would work extremely hard to attain five goals: get better every day; win the next game; win the ACC regular-season title; win the ACC Tournament title; win the national championship. What he didn't say was that Carolina fans would expect those five goals to be reached, along with two (or four) that overshadowed all the rest: Beat Duke at Duke; beat Duke at home; and beat Duke in the ACC and NCAA Tournaments, if necessary.

And Carolina fans expected all of these goals to be achieved *every year*.

The Weight of History

N orth Carolina basketball, with all of its remarkable history and legendary figures and memorable games, could be described by three incredible streaks as it headed into the Matt Doherty era:

30 consecutive seasons of 20 or more wins

26 straight NCAA Tournament appearances, the longest streak in NCAA history

36 years in a row of finishing no worse than third in the Atlantic Coast Conference (college basketball's best league) regular-season race

It is a legacy that would hang over any coach, like a guillotine waiting to chop the head off of the unfortunate soul who fails to meet this incredibly high standard.

North Carolina basketball was successful prior to the arrival of Dean Edwards Smith as head coach in 1961. The first recorded game took place January 27, 1911, against Virginia Christian and was, of course, a Tar Heel victory. In 1923–24 UNC, led by Cartwright Carmichael, won the then-mythical national championship after posting a 26–0 record. Success continued nearly nonstop until Coach Tom Scott suffered back-to-back 12–15 records in the early 1950s, prompting school officials to hire a self-assured and well-dressed New Yorker, Frank McGuire, to take over the program.

Using his considerable network of underground New York talent scouts, McGuire quickly populated the Tar Heels team with his kind of players; tough, hard-nosed kids from the city or surrounding areas. Players like Tommy Kearns, Joe Quigg, and Lennie Rosenbluth. After some early struggles—particularly against NC State and legendary coach Everett Case—Carolina began to come together. During the 1955–56 season the Tar Heels posted an 18–5 record, won the ACC regular season, and appeared to have turned a corner.

The McGuire era peaked with the undefeated national championship season of 1956–57 in which Rosenbluth and his supporting cast won three consecutive overtime games in the Final Four—overcoming Kansas and Wilt Chamberlain in the final—to capture the national championship. McGuire coached four more seasons, but his recruiting victories became less frequent, and he soon wore out his welcome in Chapel Hill. With an impending NCAA investigation, McGuire left town and Chancellor Bill Aycock gave the job to a little-known assistant coach, Dean Smith, a former Kansas University reserve guard.

The Smith era began inauspiciously, with an 8–9 season in 1961–62. It was a year that Carolina spent on probation, put there by the NCAA for recruiting violations under McGuire. Things improved the next season, as Smith coaxed the team to a 15–6 record, but a 12–12 season followed. Smith was finding that following a charismatic, powerful coach was extremely difficult. After a 22-point loss to Wake Forest in January 1965—the Heels' fourth loss in a row—the North Carolina team bus pulled up outside of Woollen Gym. Hanging from a tree across the street was a likeness of Smith. It was on fire. Billy Cunningham led other players off the bus and pulled down the effigy. It was the low moment of Smith's tenure at UNC.

Carolina defeated Duke at Duke the next game and went on to win 9 of its next 12 games. Despite the strong finish, many alumni and fans called for Smith to be fired, but the furor was not the same then as it would be now, and Smith survived to coach another year.

Actually, another thirty-one years.

Over that period, North Carolina basketball became an institution, transcending the game of college basketball like few other sports franchises were able. On par with the New York Yankees, the Boston Celtics, the Montreal Canadiens, Notre Dame football, and a very small handful of other teams, Carolina basketball stood above even these in terms of consistency. Not once after 1966 has Carolina had a subpar (i.e., losing) season or one even close to it—a remarkable string of solid recruiting decisions, strong coaching, and fortunate breaks.

From the start, Smith was careful about the players he brought into the program. He wanted talented players, of course, but he also sought those who were solid people. In many ways, through developing a balanced, even program where star players and reserves were treated the same, he had constructed a program that would self-propagate, only drawing players who were willing to sacrifice for the team. Some came from single-parent homes, some from strong families, many from all over the country, but all were willing to buy into the idea of playing on a team that would not cater to their talents, but instead fold those talents into a larger concept. Because those players were treated the same and because they had all bought into the same concept, it was natural that, over time, Carolina basketball became a family that transcended generations. From Doug Moe, Larry Brown, and Billy Cunningham to Larry Miller and Charlie Scott to Phil Ford and Bobby Jones to James Worthy, Sam Perkins, and Michael Jordan to Eric Montross and George Lynch to Vince Carter and Antawn Jamison, Carolina players shared a bond of understanding of what it meant to be a part of something larger than themselves.

Of course, the bonding agent—the glue—was and is Dean Smith. Without Smith, those who played at UNC would share nothing but a diploma and memories of the same buildings and campus grounds. Along with instilling loyalty, Smith was always thinking about the game and how to teach it. His encyclopedic knowledge of the game and his pedigree (he had played for Phog Allen at Kansas, who had played for James Naismith, who had *invented* the game) allowed him to be innovative. His four-corners offense, utilized primarily at the end of games to stretch the defense and force either fouls or allow layups, brought about the shot clock. His motion offense and variations on defense were well ahead of the times, yet steeped in the game's fundamentals. He was said to inhibit the individual offensive talents of some of his players, but in fact, without the base of knowledge he taught to his players, it is unlikely their basketball careers beyond Chapel Hill would have been as successful. Dean Smith may have been able to hold Michael Jordan under 20 points per game while he was at North Carolina, but it is unlikely that Jordan would have been the player he was later without the understanding of team basketball he received under Smith.

Even with so many great players and teams, it took a couple instances of good fortune for North Carolina basketball, under Smith, to attain the game's ultimate goal: a national championship. In 1982, it was an errant pass by Georgetown's Fred Brown; in 1993, it was a time-out called by Michigan's Chris Webber—when the Wolverines had no more time-outs remaining. Both gaffes came at the ends of national championship games and obscured, in some minds, the heights achieved by those and other Carolina teams. In the television age, people remember moments, not extended periods of excellence.

Beyond basketball accomplishments and beyond the off-the-court loyalty and excellence Smith had built, Carolina basketball rose to cultural phenomenon status with the rise of Michael Jordan during the 1990s to the status of most recognized man on the planet.

Jordan was a great player at Carolina from 1981 to 1984, but he was not the greatest player in school history. That title goes to Phil Ford, who scored more points and held a more secure place in the hearts of

Carolina fans when he left UNC. But Jordan's legend grew after he arrived in the NBA, thanks to the convergence of clever marketing and an incredible drive to succeed that led to championships. Soon, Jordan was the cultural icon in a world wearing Nikes and drinking Gatorade and watching movies. When asked, he recalled his days in Chapel Hill as all other graduates of the Carolina Basketball School did: with reverence to what he learned and to the man who taught him. And wearing the Carolina shorts under his Bulls uniform didn't hurt, either.

Thanks to Jordan, Carolina basketball became cool to an entire generation, influencing everything from recruiting to road attendance to NCAA Tournament seeding to merchandising. Carolina blue became a cool color to wear, and jerseys and shirts appeared in every sports apparel store in the country, regardless of geographical location.

When Smith retired in October 1997, his longtime assistant coach, Bill Guthridge, took over. It was partially out of his own pride—nobody was a tougher competitor than Guthridge—and also out of a sense of loyalty that Guthridge took on the immense challenge of following a legend. Perhaps no one else could have handled the mantle with such grace; after all, Smith was still right down the hall, the building was named after him, and a new coach would have undoubtedly chafed under the weight of the legend and the pressure.

Not to mention those pesky streaks.

The Guthridge Era began in direct contrast to that of his predecessor; instead of struggling in the first season under a new coach, Carolina won 34 games, lost only four, and advanced to the Final Four. Along the way, the Tar Heels—led by the high-flying act of Antawn Jamison and Vince Carter—won the ACC regular-season and tournament crowns. Guthridge won many coach-of-the-year honors (despite a disappointing loss to Utah in the NCAA semifinals and an embarrassing incident involving UNC player Makhtar Ndaiye, who accused a Utah player of a racial slur that never occurred) and handled the task of immediately following a legend as well as any coach ever had.

The general consensus, however, was that Smith handed Guthridge an immensely talented team with which any coach could have won. After Jamison and Carter both left school early for the NBA, Year Two under Guthridge was expected to be a struggle.

Instead, the Tar Heels, led by junior point guard Ed Cota and senior Ademola Okulaja, won their first eight games of the 1998–99 season, rising to the No. 3 ranking in the nation. The remainder of the season was somewhat up and down (by Carolina standards), and the Heels finished second in the ACC regular season behind Duke. More important than the solid season, however, were two major disappointments: losing three times to the Blue Devils (who would go on to lose the NCAA title game to Connecticut) including the ACC Tournament Championship game by 23 points, and losing to Big Sky Conference Champion Weber State—a 14-seed—in the first round of the NCAA Tournament.

It was the loss to Weber State that began to turn sentiment against Guthridge. Because his starting center, Brendan Haywood, had played very poorly in the game (1 point, 0 rebounds, despite being five inches taller than any other player on the court), Guthridge, who was even-tempered in public, was seen as a poor motivator. The prevailing thought was that his age and gentlemanly manner had served him well with a team that was more mature, such as the 1997–98 Jamison and Carter group, but was not effective with a younger, less talented group, such as in 1998–99.

The rumblings would become a full-fledged earthquake in 1999–2000.

By the end of the century, college basketball had become a whirlwind of money, agents, players skipping college altogether to enter the NBA draft, and coaches earning millions, signing contracts with apparel companies and being paid to wear certain kind of ties and suits on the sidelines. Recruiting camps and the summer basketball circuit were completely out of control, with questionable individuals (sometimes outright criminals) masquerading as AAU "coaches" and shepherding teenagers to this event and that one all over the country. It was a scene that seemed at odds with the team-oriented, unselfish attitudes that Carolina basketball represented.

The most stark manifestation of that disconnect was Guthridge himself. An honest man and a great coach, Guthridge nonetheless appeared to lack charisma and drawing power when compared to hot young coaches like Billy Donovan at Florida, Steve Lavin at UCLA, or Tommy Amaker at Seton Hall, all of whom owned one suit that was more expensive than Guthridge's entire wardrobe. A high-level member of Carolina's athletic booster club was overheard saying about Guthridge: "A successful CEO does not wear Rockports."

Guthridge's first contract had been for five years—and he had vowed all along to coach until it concluded. It was the smart thing to do. In the cutthroat world of recruiting, one whiff of a short-timer could spell doom. So when he entered his third season, there was no sign that Guthridge would not fulfill his contract, other than the constant swirl of rumors that Roy Williams was already signed, sealed, and delivered to take over when Guthridge decided to step down.

Going into his third season, a drunk-driving incident involving Assistant Coach Phil Ford forced Guthridge to shuffle his staff, moving Pat Sullivan to a recruiting role, along with Dave Hanners. For 30 years, Smith was able to leave organizational duties to Guthridge, a highly detailed and meticulous individual, and concentrate on the basketball and public relations (which Smith disliked) aspects of the job. When he became head coach, Guthridge had no such right-hand man to take some of the pressure off.

The 1999–2000 season began like 1998–99, a torrid start followed by a lukewarm stretch. After winning the Maui Classic, the Heels hosted Michigan State, the NCAA runner-up the year before. Even without point guard and leader Mateen Cleaves, the Spartans, behind a swarming man-to-man defense, defeated Carolina handily. In the process, several UNC weaknesses were revealed: a motion offense that broke down under a physical, intimidating defense, and an inside game—led by Haywood—that had a maddening habit of disappearing, as it had several months earlier in the NCAA loss to Weber State.

And then came the injuries. Already out by the time the ACC regular season commenced were reserves Brian Bersticker and Ronald Curry, both

of whom were expected to contribute. In addition, Ed Cota missed a portion of the preseason due to a suspension stemming from a Halloween
night fight; recruit Jason Parker failed to qualify and attended Fork Union
Military Academy for the year; Jason Capel continued to battle back pain;
and Kris Lang fought through shin splints and an unknown virus.

After Michigan State, UNC lost high-profile games to Indiana and
top-ranked Cincinnati, as well as lightly regarded Louisville. The ACC
season started out well, with wins over Clemson and NC State, but then
four straight losses caused the Carolina faithful to turn their full venom
on Guthridge.

Just when the buzzards began circling overhead—and the streaks
seemed in very real jeopardy—something unexpected happened: UNC
began to show some life. The resurgence happened as unexpectedly as
a winter storm in North Carolina. A few days prior to UNC's game
against Maryland in Chapel Hill, over 20 inches of snow blanketed the
state, causing massive cancellations in an area completely unaccustomed
to dealing with such a volume of snow.

The game was postponed for a day. The crowd in the Smith Center
that Thursday night was electric, as students—the only fans who could
reach the Smith Center—were allowed in for free and permitted to sit
anywhere there was not a ticketed customer. A crowd of 15,455 attended
the 75–63 Carolina win, leaving the arena almost one-third empty but as
loud as any game in memory as the students lifted the Heels to an emotional performance. Guthridge, in his typical monotone postgame comments, called the crowd "great" and added: "Maybe the crowd helped
our team. It certainly didn't hurt us. I hope this is a springboard for us."
And then, so as not to upset the alumni who could not make the game,
he added, "I think our fans have been great all year."

The game was indeed a springboard for Carolina, as the Heels went
4–1 over their next five games, the lone loss coming in overtime to
Duke. The Blue Devils had developed into a powerhouse—despite losing an unprecedented four players in the first round of the NBA draft
the year before—further precipitating the negative feelings toward the
Guthridge regime.

Three losses in their final five regular-season games, and a quick exit in the ACC Tournament after a loss to Wake Forest, saw the calls for Guthridge's retirement resume. Still, UNC had finished in the top three of the ACC standings again and also earned a bid to the NCAA Tournament, albeit as the No. 8 seed. But it would take two wins in the NCAA Tournament to keep the third streak—20 wins—alive.

Then came the most improbable tournament run ever made by a North Carolina team. A decisive 84–70 win over Missouri was followed by a surprising upset of top-seeded Stanford. The Tar Heels had their 20 wins and, more important, advanced to the Sweet Sixteen. Hard-fought wins over Tennessee and Tulsa propelled Carolina into its second Final Four in three seasons under Guthridge, quieting his critics.

After a loss to Florida in the NCAA semifinals, Guthridge's record was now 80–28 in three seasons. He was one of only two coaches to advance to two Final Fours in his first three seasons. He had won awards for National Coach of the Year and ACC Coach of the Year.

He was also ridiculed, was second-guessed, had his loyalty questioned, and was treated like a pariah—at times—by some Tar Heel alumni and fans. He followed a legend, but even Dean Smith couldn't keep up with Bill Guthridge: Smith won 56 percent of his games during his first three seasons; Guthridge won 74 percent.

Most important, however, he had kept alive The Streaks:

30 consecutive seasons of 20 or more wins
26 straight NCAA Tournament appearances, the longest streak
    in NCAA history
36 years in a row of finishing no worse than third in the ACC
    regular-season race

Bill Guthridge announced his retirement on June 30, 2000—just a few months after telling the Associated Press that he might coach several years beyond his original contract. But he changed his mind for the same reason Smith had retired; he could not regain the enthusiasm after being worn out by the nonbasketball portions of the job.

"The spring is a real grind for college coaches," said Guthridge. "I had 12 nights in a row after we got back from the Final Four that I had to be out speaking. I had two clinics, one in Milwaukee, one in Orlando. We had the ACC meetings. Plus the normal things; the spring workouts, spring recruiting. None of it was real bad but the accumulation of it, there was no time to take a deep breath. I still think Coach Smith would be coaching if he didn't need to do all that other stuff.

"And I probably would be, too."

Eleven days after Guthridge's retirement, Matt Doherty agreed to take over the reigns of college basketball's most celebrated program. When he did, he also inherited a yoke of success—and nearly unachievable expectations—that could very well choke a man who dared to take on history and believe he could extend it.

It was now Doherty's mandate to keep The Streaks alive, to say nothing of reaching Final Fours, and, above all else: Beating Duke.

4

Pound

Looking fresh and dapper in a tweed jacket, pressed tan pants, white shirt, blue tie, and matching breast handkerchief, Matt Doherty stepped briskly and enthusiastically into the Carlisle Room at Grandover Resort in Greensboro, North Carolina.

He had no idea what awaited him.

It was mid-October, and Doherty was making his first public media appearance at Operation Basketball, the ACC's basketball media day.

In the three months since his hiring at North Carolina, Doherty had little time to unpack, let alone get acclimated to the job. His first task after the July 11 press conference had been to get back on the recruiting trail. That night. He and his staff made calls to recruits—telling them how much they were looking forward to recruiting them for UNC—until well past midnight. With July being perhaps the single most important month in the college basketball calendar (other than March), Doug Wojcik,

Fred Quartlebaum, and Doherty were on the road almost constantly. Meanwhile, their families, growing seemingly by the day thanks to births, struggled to sell houses in South Bend and move to Chapel Hill.

The day after the press conference, Doherty met with every individual player who was in town. "I wanted to find out, with them, what they liked about the last season, what they didn't like. What we needed to work on," explained Doherty. "I talked a little about my philosophy, about my staff. I wanted to explain more about the changes that were occurring. I wanted to tell them: 'I've been in your shoes. I know what it's like. I played here. I can relate to that.'"

The meetings went well. Doherty gave another indication—as he had the night before at the team meeting—that he would work the players very hard. While preseason conditioning hadn't been a walk in the park in previous years, it would have a much different feel now.

"He's intense," said Jason Capel of Doherty. "No doubt about that." But Doherty also showed an interest in being less a father figure and more of a favorite uncle, at least off the court. He made an effort to get to know the players as well as he could personally in a short period of time. Because Joseph Forte—who had set a Carolina freshman scoring record the season before—was not in town when Doherty was hired, the new coach made a special trip to meet Forte and his mother at the latter's home in Rockville, Maryland, outside of Washington, D.C. "I couldn't do it with everybody. I was up in that area, recruiting. It made sense to do that with Joe," said Doherty. "You've got to start and get that trust going."

When he greeted Forte, he did not do it with a firm handshake; he did it with a "pound" (a soft knuckle-to-knuckle punch in vogue among athletes and other young men). He also didn't just say hello, he said: "What's up, dog?" It made an instant impression. "I kind of laughed at first," said Forte. "I thought it was kind of cool. He seemed young."

Joseph Xavier Forte was big for his age when he was growing up in Smyrna, Georgia. So big, in fact, that he dreamed of being a fullback in the NFL. "I liked running over other kids," he recalled. In time, Forte lost his baby fat but not his athleticism. When he began to blossom on the basketball court ("I dribbled around my back when I was in the sixth grade," Forte said. "That's when I knew I was pretty good."), his mother, Wanda Hightower, began to notice something less constructive.

While at Griffin Middle School, Forte was gaining the attention of grown men who, as the young child became a standout player, began calling and coming around the house. None of the men ever came out and made an illicit offer, but all wanted the same thing: for Forte to go to this high school or that one. Hightower, a statuesque woman and former Spellman College student who worked in the computer sales department at Hewlett-Packard, grew skeptical. "There were a lot of people in that environment who you just couldn't trust," said Hightower. "Why would a bunch of adults want to befriend a 14-year-old boy? There is something basically wrong with that. I didn't know how a 14-year-old was going to react. It didn't seem right or healthy."

Hightower, who divorced Joseph's father when her oldest son was five years old, was not one to sit back and watch her son start down a dangerous path. She immediately began looking around for a way out. Her search yielded DeMatha High School in Hyattsville, Maryland, a suburb of Washington, D.C. After sending legendary coach Morgan Wootten a tape of her son and receiving a favorable reaction, Hightower announced that the family—which also included Jason, two years younger than Joseph—was moving.

Joseph, who had begun to enjoy the attention, was not happy. "I thought it would blow over," explained Forte. "I didn't understand why I had to change my life so dramatically."

Much of Forte's personality—a cool, often detached, exterior that covered a less sure, more easily wounded young man—can be traced to the strength and conviction of his mother and to his DeMatha experience. He recalls vividly the first time he met fellow freshman Keith Bogans, a strong and extremely gifted player for his age. "I walked up and Coach Wootten put his arm around Keith and said, 'If you can be half as good as Keith, you'll be a pretty good player.'" His demotion from star to supporting player did not sit well, nor did the strict DeMatha code of conduct, which included a dress code.

Throughout his freshman year, Forte broke the dress code and committed other small acts of rebellion as a way to try to get kicked out of school. He wore hiking boots instead of black shoes. He ripped his pants. If he committed enough violations and was expelled, he figured, his mother would have to take them back to Georgia. He hated DeMatha, and being put on junior varsity as a freshman did not help.

But things slowly got better. As a sophomore, Forte played on the varsity. By the end of that year, he began to think he could make it. That's when he began to develop confidence; not just of the "I think I can" variety, but the kind of almost regal self-assurance that comes from achieving heights no one thought he could—except Forte himself. Slowly, his vulnerability dissolved as his achievements (and the notoriety that came with them) grew. By the time he was a junior, he was on an even par with Bogans—the player who was always his litmus test and with whom Forte always had a somewhat strained friendship. As a senior, after he signed with North Carolina and Bogans with Kentucky, many recruiting publications placed him ahead of Bogans. Later that year, Bogans would be suspended from the team.

North Carolina was a perfect fit for Forte; it was the best, and Coach Guthridge's personality was most decidedly reserved and hands-off, which Forte liked. When he arrived at North Carolina, Forte felt the same doubting stares he had felt four years earlier. But he was stronger now. As the oldest male in the household with a personal mountain already climbed, Joseph took on challenges with a wink and an engaging grin. He had developed both a deep and personal desire to achieve and be recognized for his achievements, and the inner strength and confidence to believe he could do it. On the court, he had developed a unique (in the current age of dunks and three-pointers) midrange game that, combined with his explosiveness to the basket and improving three-point shooting, made him a considerable offensive force. He quickly rose above competition from teammates in practice to earn a starting position. He starred on a Carolina team that, late in the season, went to the Final

Four. During the NCAA run, in fact, Forte had become the obvious choice—the go-to guy—to get the ball when a basket was needed.

It was a role he relished—and wanted to expand upon. "I want to be remembered as one of the best players ever at North Carolina," he said. "I want my jersey to hang in the rafters."

But basketball was not Forte's only pursuit. He loved to play chess: "There are parallels in strategy, different pieces—and different players—have different strengths" but admitted it was "hard to find anyone my age who can play." He also just enjoyed "being young and having fun." During his freshman year, Forte was in the dining hall at Granville Towers when a fellow student, Chase Briggs, came up to him and began razzing him about his shorts. It wasn't rare for students to stop Forte (or any of the other players) on their way to classes or out on Franklin Street to chat. Unlike some of the players, Forte truly enjoyed it. Many of the friends he had made since coming to Carolina were not athletes, but just fellow freshmen he met on his hall or in class. This may be a common occurrence for the average college student, but for athletes—who tend to live in a cocoon that includes only teammates and other athletes—it is less so. Forte began razzing the kid back, and after a while, they began hanging out. The next year, Forte would become suitemates with him in Granville.

His sophomore season, Forte hoped, would continue his rise as a player. Unlike other teammates who would do anything to avoid having to be interviewed (Kris Lang sometimes sprinted in the other direction when he spotted reporters lurking outside the Smith Center), Forte viewed it as an honor that *Sports Illustrated* (or the *Chapel Hill News*, for that matter) would want to speak with him. He was at a place that he still enjoyed seeing his picture in the papers and hearing his name on television. His off-the-court manner mirrored his on-the-court play; he was engaging and laid-back, young and cool.

Suddenly, something out of his control had occurred; he would begin the season with a new coach. He was somewhat concerned about how it would all work out. "I'm not a rah-rah kind of guy," Forte said, well aware that his new coach most definitely was. "But I'll pound the floor if I have to."

As he learned to do during his DeMatha days, Forte was going to keep one eye on the future at all times. "Playing in the NBA," he said prior to his sophomore season, "is the first thing I think about every morning when I wake up."

During the first several months, Doherty was trading barbs with all of the players about clothing, cars, music, and all the other things young men talk about. He made a sincere effort to get to know the players—none of whom he had recruited and all of whom had signed up to play for Guthridge or, in the case of the seniors, Smith, coaches who were much different in their temperament than Doherty. Because Doherty was sincere, the players immediately began to feel comfortable with their new coach and he with them.

But that did not erase all of the pain caused by the retirement of Guthridge and the dismissal of Ford, Hanners, and Sullivan. In a program steeped in loyalty, three men—three alumni—were now out of jobs. The situation pained Smith and Guthridge most of all. Both men had moved out of the spacious, wood-paneled offices upstairs and into alarmingly small, spartan, cinder-block rooms downstairs. Both still spent considerable time in the building trying to find jobs for the three men, all of whom would continue to draw a paycheck from the university until the next spring. (After several months, Ford took a job with the Educational Foundation, UNC's athletic fund-raising department; Hanners would scout for the 76ers; while Sullivan would do the same for several NBA teams, including the Utah Jazz.)

The new staff, meanwhile, jumped feet-first into their new jobs, unable to take even a moment to marvel at their good fortune. Doug Wojcik, two years removed from the top assistant's job at the Naval Academy and a little more than a decade removed from being the first operational lieutenant on the *USS W. S. Sims*, a Knox-class frigate, was on the road almost constantly in July. The same was true for Fred Quartlebaum, who was at his fifth coaching job in five years, having first met Wojcik while the two were assistants together at Navy and coaching at Towson State, Holy Cross, and Fairfield since. Holding down the fort in the office was Bob MacKinnon, a longtime coach at virtually all levels of the game who first met Doherty when the latter was a UNC player and the former was working the Carolina basketball camp. David Cason, who had played for Kevin Stallings—a former assistant with Doherty at Kansas—at Illinois State, filled a new position in the Carolina basketball office: that of director of basketball operations. In that role, he did everything from organize film exchange to run out and get lunch for the staff.

Doherty saw to it that in August the staff took some time to vacation with their families. Knowing the season ahead would require long hours and little time at home, the coaches, their wives, and their children spent a day at the Piedmont Carolinas Train Museum near Charlotte. Throughout the late summer and early fall the bonding continued, as the staff and their families leaned on each other while living in the same apartment complex in north Chapel Hill. "We have a close group," explained Doherty. "Our wives care about each other. We watch each other's kids. We joke about moving into 82 Magnolia (an apartment complex in Chapel Hill). It was kind of our neighborhood; sort of like some old Brooklyn neighborhood or something. Doug was literally above us. Bob and Fred were literally 25 yards away from us. We'd go out to the pool and there's a grill there, and we'd cook out and hang out by the pool in August or something like that. It was fun."

On the first day of conditioning, the players walked out onto the court and saw garbage cans lined up on the baseline—just in case someone felt the need to vomit. Immediately, the players knew this would be serious. Four-player preseason workouts allowed the players to get to know their new coaches ("intense" was the word all used) and the coaches the chance to know the players. Most impressive to the coaches was Brendan Haywood, who had a reputation for being out of shape and somewhat lazy, but had shown throughout conditioning and workouts that he was anything but. He arrived in very good shape and worked as hard as any player throughout the workouts.

Inside play, Doherty knew immediately, would be a strength. He also knew exactly where the question marks lay.

So did the media.

Over the course of the first 90 minutes at ACC Media Day, Doherty answered dozens of questions thrown out by more than 100 reporters, but about 40 of those questions were variations of one topic: Carolina's point guard situation. Everyone, it seemed, wanted to know who would emerge as the leading candidate to replace Ed Cota. The only problem was, Doherty himself didn't know.

Cota's backup the previous year had been Jonathan Holmes, whose entire persona fit the stereotype of an Indiana kid. His father was his coach at Bloomington South High School, he led his team to the state finals as a senior, and he was a smart, hard-nosed player. Unfortunately, he was a step slow and his shot was a little flat. Ronald Curry was the most heralded two-sport (football and basketball) recruit in the history of Virginia's tidewater area. As a senior at Hampton High School, Curry was named the national football player of the year as well as the MVP at the McDonald's High School All-America basketball game. But he was coming off a torn Achilles tendon suffered nine months earlier when a Georgia Tech defensive lineman pulled the starting QB down awkwardly. Other options at the point were two freshmen: Brian Morrison, a great athlete with a tendency to play out of control, and Adam Boone, a solid ball handler but questionable shooter from Minneapolis.

"I'm not trying to hide anything," Doherty explained at more than one table. "I just really don't know." Again and again he fielded the same questions, and again and again he gave the same answers: "I really don't know . . . things have changed and do almost daily . . . it seems to be the topic people are most interested in . . . it's a day-to-day evaluation . . . confidence is key . . . Ronald [Curry] deserves a shot . . . when I was playing, we used to have myself or Michael bring the ball up against Wake so Kenny Smith wouldn't have to bring it up against Muggsy—it

was Coach Smith's decision . . . the two most important factors are playing defense and taking care of the ball . . . we don't want to juggle things
too much as the season plays out."

The print media—of which there were over 90 in attendance from
the *Washington Post* to the Anderson (SC) *Independent Mail* and everywhere in between—had spread out at the nine tables, with each ACC
head coach speaking at each table for 12 minutes before rotating to the
next. About an hour into the event the coaches were mentally drained
but pushed on. Steve Kirschner, Carolina's assistant athletic director for
media relations, kept a fresh glass of water in front of Doherty, who
barely had time to catch his breath between answers. This being his first
experience with the grueling format, Doherty tried valiantly to keep his
energy up and answer each question honestly and without repeating
himself. It was a futile attempt.

He pressed on, though, even making several jokes and continuing
to make eye contact with each and every inquisitor. When asked about
his relationship with Mike Krzyzewski, Doherty joked: "We got in a
fist fight on the way in." When asked who won, he added with a grin:
"You don't see any marks on me, do you?" Later, when asked about
the differences between Coach Smith/Guthridge's program and his
(another favorite question), he said, "well, the coach is taller now." The
reporters, searching for a nugget for the preseason tabs all would have
to compile over the course of the next few weeks, laughed and scribbled frantically.

When the 90 minutes of almost constant talking was over, Doherty
stood and, along with his new ACC coaching brethren, headed for the
door. Doherty glanced at Kirschner, shook his head, and smiled the
kind of smile one does when the dentist tells the patient he can get out
of the chair now. But the grueling day was far from over, as he faced 90
more minutes in front of the television and radio contingent that
awaited upstairs.

It was all a part of his new job, Doherty knew. And a long way from
Prospect Park.

From Prospect Park to Chapel Hill

It was the early 1950s, and Walter Doherty—the son of a Brooklyn cop and an elementary schoolteacher—had a decision to make. Since graduating from high school Walter had bounced around minor league baseball systems of the Phillies and the Indians as a pitcher struggling to find the control to go with the pop in his fastball. When he was twenty-three years old he had met Mary, the daughter of Irish immigrants who had come to America seeking a new life. Mary and her parents settled in New York City, working as domestics in the Connecticut mansions or in a cousin's grocery store in the Bronx, whatever paid the bills during the Depression. Walter and Mary went on their first date on Mary's 20th birthday.

Three years later and very much in love, Walter was faced with a decision as straightforward as his fastball was not: give up baseball, settle down, get married and begin a family or accept a AAA contract with the Indians, move to Canada, and continue the vagabond lifestyle of living in a boarding house and getting paid $25 for each win.

He decided it was time to settle down.

Walter got a job as a district sales manager with Pepsi Cola and then purchased a route into Greenwich Village, delivering Pepsi to restaurants and stores. With a steady income, Walter and Mary left Brooklyn and bought a comfortable two-story house on Freeman Avenue in East Meadow, a predominately Catholic area of Long Island. It's the house where they live to this day, 45 years later.

The family quickly grew by three daughters—Meg, Nan, and Maureen—who were born between 1954 and 1958. Four years after Maureen, Mary had the family's first boy, Matt, who was followed six years later by a second son, John. When they were old enough, Walter would take the two boys into the city with him on his route. "They'd love to ride into town on the truck on Catholic school holidays, supposedly to help on deliveries," recalled Walter. "But instead they'd get free ice cream and candy from all the storekeepers."

By all accounts, the three older sisters babied their brother Matt something fierce. "They took care of him pretty well," remembered Mary. "It was like having four mothers." It was probably a good thing, because it was quickly evident that Matt had other things on his mind than doing dishes and taking out the garbage.

When he was in the fourth grade, Walter signed Matt up for Catholic Youth Organization (CYO) basketball at St. Raphael's, which had a very good gym for a local parish and was run by a retired cop named John Pirkl. It was also the year that Walter signed Matt up for Gus Alfieri's All-American basketball camp. By that time, Matt had grown into the biggest kid in his grade and possessed surprising agility. He had tried baseball, but he had inherited his dad's wildness— "I thought he would hit one of the kids and kill him, so we moved him to first base," said Walter—so he had settled into basketball as his sport.

The game matched his mentality. "Matt was quiet, he worked hard in school, and did his paper route," said Mary. "He was also very neat

and organized, even as a child." Matt's solitary nature fit well into practicing the game for hours, alone.

"I really got excited about it because it was a game that captured my
attention," recalled Matt. "It was a game that, unlike baseball—which
every kid in my neighborhood started off playing—you didn't have to
have anyone else to play. You could just take your ball to a basket and
work on your game. You could imagine being every player on the
Knicks. I'd go to Prospect Park near my house and I'd be by myself and
I'd play out games by myself. I'd be Frazier or Barnett or Bradley or
Willis Reed or DeBusschere. I'd play all five spots. That was OK with
me. I wasn't as concerned about running around with a bunch of kids.
I enjoyed playing basketball."

It also helped that Prospect Park was a breeding ground for Long
Island basketball. Players such as Kevin Joyce, Brian Winters, Ernie
Grunfeld, John Roche, and even Julius Erving could be found playing
at Prospect Park, sometimes from sunup to sundown. It was a basketball version of Darwinism; lose and you sit, win and you play.

Even though he was young, Doherty was able to get into the games
and quickly develop as a player. "I was always tall for my grade," recalled
Doherty. "It was important to me to be coordinated. When you're tall
everyone thinks you're gawky or uncoordinated. I was fortunate that I
was fairly coordinated, and I worked at that, too. When I was a fourth
grader, I played with sixth graders. I always played with guys who were
two to three years older than me, or even more than that. When I was in
sixth grade I'd always try to get into games with the college guys. I may
be the last guy chosen, but I was always there snapping at their heels trying to get into those games." Early on, Doherty became very self-aware
of his abilities and how he could mold them into team success. When he
was young, he learned how to find open men, play defense, and
rebound. As he got older, his role became more of a scorer, and he'd
spend hours upon hours on his shooting.

The game had become his passion.

"I first saw him as a seventh grader," recalled Bob McKillop, then
the JV coach at Holy Trinity High School, the Catholic school in nearby

Hicksville where the Dohertys had sent both Maureen and Nan. "He came to our basketball camp. I had seen him previously at the park, playing with a lot of the older players. But it really stuck in my mind when he was at camp because he had a notebook; he was taking notes on what the coaches were saying and telling him."

Thanks to his natural abilities, physical and mental maturity, and an intense desire to reach self-determined goals, Doherty was able to become a serious contributor to the Holy Trinity varsity team as a freshman, a rare feat in a program known for consistent success. "I wanted to play varsity as a freshman," said Doherty. "I wanted to be the first person to do that. I don't think anyone else had ever done it." McKillop had moved up to varsity head coach by that time and relied on his young player heavily, at times starting him and at other times bringing him off the bench as the sixth man, to the consternation of some members of the school community. McKillop didn't care; he only wanted to put his best team on the floor. During a game against rival Long Island Lutheran, McKillop assigned his 6'5", 150-pound, freckled freshman to guard Wayne McKoy, a rugged power forward who would go on to play at St. John's. It wasn't the only time McKillop counted on Doherty.

"That year we played for the Long Island Championship against a team called St. Agnes," recalled McKillop. "St. Agnes [the school that would later produce current Florida coach Billy Donovan] had one of the great coaches named Frank Morris. Late in the game, we got a slight lead and we ran a delay game—there was no clock back then. The guy we had running the delay game, in front of 6,000 people for the Long Island Championship, was Matt. It showed great poise that he could do that on center stage as a 14-year-old freshman."

"Matt always was his own man," recalled Father Bud Ribaudo, the chaplain at Holy Trinity and the Dohertys' priest. "He set clear goals for himself, and he's been an overachiever."

The Holy Trinity varsity was even better when Doherty was a sophomore as he grew into more of a scoring role. Under McKillop's tutelage and with his parents unwavering if hands-off support, Doherty helped the team to another Long Island Championship.

On a summer day in between his sophomore and junior years in high school, McKillop visited the Doherty house, sat in the kitchen, and delivered some crushing news: He was leaving to take a job as an assistant coach at Davidson College. "It was a very difficult scene," recalled McKillop. "He was rising into his junior year, and I was leaving to go someplace in North Carolina. He had meant so much to me and my family and our program that it was a very difficult moment for me to tell him that I would be leaving."

Dick Zeitler, a good friend and old athletic rival of McKillop's, took over the varsity program at Holy Trinity. Despite scoring 27 points per game, Doherty's junior season was difficult. After losing their coach and many key players, Holy Trinity fell to 14–11.

But that didn't stop the college recruiters from their pursuit of Doherty, who had already gained a reputation on Long Island as a prep star. The first letter he had received had come from Tennessee when he was a freshman. Going into his junior season, Zeitler, Father Bud, and Jack Curran, the high school coach at Archbishop Molloy (where Zeitler had played), sat down and organized Doherty's recruitment process. All recruiting calls went to Zeitler, who would then pass them on to Matt and his parents. Before recruiters visited him, Doherty outlined his questions on paper. "Everything went pretty smoothly, because Matt knew what he wanted," said Zeitler. "For the most part, we just left Matt alone. We had a lot of faith in his ability to make decisions."

Doherty approached his recruitment in as analytical a fashion as he took notes at camp as a seventh grader. He knew he wanted a strong academic school as well as a team-oriented, successful program. Notre Dame, Virginia, Princeton, Holy Cross, Duke, and North Carolina made the initial list. Doherty kept detailed notes on each school.

"The first time I saw him was the summer before his senior year," remembered Bill Guthridge, then the top assistant at North Carolina. "It was on Long Island; I don't remember the gym it was in, but it was at night and there were several games going on. I remember how impressed I was with him. You could tell he was a savvy player and a smart player. He knew a lot about the game. I liked his size and his ballhandling abilities; his ability to play outside. He seemed to be very well respected by his teammates and by his coaches. Those are the type of things you look for. I thought he'd be a good fit for North Carolina."

Doherty entered the fall of his senior year with his head as together as could be expected. Even so, he wanted to make his college choice early so he could get on with his senior season. (The recruiting calendar was much later then, without an early signing period.) Holy Trinity was expected to rebound and have a much better season.

College coaches from his list of schools began parading into the Doherty living room: Bill Foster from Duke, Terry Holland from Virginia, Digger Phelps from Notre Dame, Pete Carril from Princeton. All made favorable impressions. But when Dean Smith came, it was an event.

"I remember the night he was supposed to come to my house and I had gone to the store to get some things for the visit," remembered Doherty. "I saw him go into a restaurant. Later, when he came by the house I thought, 'that's the guy I see on TV all the time.' I had to shake my head a couple times." Smith spoke to the family about what North Carolina could offer Matt: a great education at one of the finest universities in the country. What he did not offer was a guarantee of playing time.

"If you come to North Carolina and work very hard, you'll have a chance to play as a junior," said Smith.

The statement may have turned off other recruits who possessed a more fragile ego or less determination. For Doherty, the statement served as a challenge.

"I wanted to prove him wrong," said Doherty.

On consecutive weekends in the fall of his high school senior year, Doherty was scheduled to take official visits to Duke, Virginia, North Carolina, and Notre Dame. He was pleased with, but not blown away by, his first two visits. Then he went to Chapel Hill.

"When I got on the visit, it was fall break, so there weren't many students there," recalled Doherty. "But I felt very comfortable with the guys. I really liked everything about it. When I got off the plane at LaGuardia, I remember my mom greeting me, and the first thing she said was: 'You're going to North Carolina, aren't you?' I don't think I even said a word. She could just read my face. I called the other coaches that Wednesday and told them I was going to North Carolina."

Doherty became the first high school player to verbally commit to a college that year and the earliest commitment ever given to North Carolina at that time. "He called me up four days after [the visit] and said he wasn't going to visit Notre Dame," said Smith. "I was surprised."

"I remember the nuns at Holy Trinity were very disappointed that he didn't choose Notre Dame," remembered Mary Doherty.

Doherty's two overriding factors in choosing North Carolina were the style of play of the Tar Heels and the consistent success of the program. "I knew I wasn't going to overpower anyone with my athletic ability. My strengths were in playing a team game; passing, hitting open shots, and playing defense. North Carolina fit my style. I felt everyone else was wishing they were like North Carolina. I felt I was appreciated for what I had to offer there and that Carolina had a chance to win a national championship every year."

With his college choice behind him, Doherty was able to concentrate on his senior season at Holy Trinity, which would turn out to be a triumphant one. "He was the focus of our team," said Zeitler. "We used him wherever we thought it was best; outside, inside, low post, bringing the ball up against the press. Our point guard got hurt and he played the point for three games. He averaged about 22 points per game as a senior, and he was our leading rebounder." With Doherty playing everywhere, Holy Trinity went 27–3 and won both the Long Island Championship—on a last-second, game-winning shot by Doherty—and the New York State Championship. The only disappointment in the triumphant season was a loss to rival Long Island Lutheran, a team that was coached by a familiar face.

After one year at Davidson, McKillop had returned to rival Lutheran as its head coach. The prospect of playing one another was a painful situation for both he and Doherty, but one where a higher power intervened.

"It was difficult," said McKillop of coaching against his former team and player. "Fortunately, it was Matt's senior year, and Matt didn't play in the game. Something in the will of God would not allow us to compete against each other. He came down with the flu, was sick for about a week, and during that period, he didn't play."

At the completion of his high school career, Doherty was named a McDonald's All-American along with the likes of Vern Fleming, Derek Harper, and a rangy, long-armed kid from upstate New York named Sam Perkins, who was also going to North Carolina.

"The McDonald's game was exciting," recalled Doherty. "I didn't play in any national camps. There was no Nike camp. I didn't go to Five Star. So it was exciting to have all the best players—supposedly the best players—in one place. I joke with some of our players now. I tell them, 'I was in the McDonald's All-American game, but Clyde Drexler wasn't.' It goes to show you that [success in high school] doesn't guarantee you a right to further success. You still have to have talent, work hard, and set goals."

All of which were strengths of the fourth child and first son of Walter and Mary Doherty as he headed off to college.

6

Past Meets Present

I t was several hours until the 2000–2001 North Carolina basketball team would make its first public appearance when Charlie Scott stepped to the podium, letting his thin-as-a-rail body settle comfortably in front of those who were there to hear him speak. Light sparkled off of the glass cases in the Smith Center Memorabilia Room, which enclosed bronze basketballs, old nets, and golden trophies from long-ago triumphs. The audience included the current members of the North Carolina basketball team and assorted staff and managers. The intent of the small banquet prior to the beginning of practice was clear: Doherty would later refer to it as "past meets present."

To Scott's right sat the brand-new Carolina coaching staff, only one of whom had spent more than a few months of his life in Chapel Hill. Doherty, of course, had been a member of the 1982 national championship team that included Sam Perkins, James Worthy, and Michael

Jordan. His three assistants, however, were brand new to the mystique and mystery that is Carolina basketball. They were about to learn a lesson about what it all meant.

"It's an honor to be here," said Scott in his slow, rumbling voice. He spoke about his own experiences as a player, sharing several nods and knowing grins with Al Wood, another Tar Heel legend asked to speak at the event by Doherty. The current players, typical 18–22 year olds in so many ways, were prone to zoning out, slouching, and generally being inattentive during these types of events. Not now. Each sat ramrod straight, eyes locked on Scott, the man who, 33 years earlier, had become the first African American varsity basketball player to suit up at North Carolina.

"When you're a freshman or sophomore, it's easy to look up at the clock, late in the game when you might be behind by 4 or 5 points, and think, 'I've got another two or three years. This game isn't the end for me.'" Scott paused and looked around the room. Sophomore Joseph Forte would later swear Scott was looking right at him. So would freshman Adam Boone. "But you can't let yourself do that, for two reasons. First, you'd be letting the seniors, your teammates, down. Second, because it goes by so quickly, that when you become a senior or later when you're done playing at Carolina, you'll wish you could be back in that position, just one more time, trailing by a few points with not much time left on the clock.

"So cherish being a part of Carolina basketball now, while you can. And never, ever, think you've got enough time. Because you don't."

Doherty rose and thanked both Scott and Wood. He then covered some general team business and talked about expectations before he paused and looked at Jim Everett, a walk-on who had been on the team a year ago but had to try out again to retain his position as the 16th man on a 16-man team.

"Finally, I'd like to thank Jim for all his hard work. He's never complained a minute, he's always willing to work," said Doherty, pausing for dramatic effect, "and I'd like to congratulate him on making the team."

All of the Carolina players, coaches, managers, and everyone else in the room applauded. Some whooped, hollered, and patted Everett, the least likely Tar Heel, on the back.

Jim Everett making the Carolina varsity wasn't a long shot—it was so unlikely it wasn't even on the board. His story was at the exact opposite end of the spectrum from someone like Forte, who had been flown all over the country and received the star treatment while playing AAU ball and high school basketball for Morgan Wootten. Everett never even started a *game* at Providence High School in Charlotte, where he played three years of junior varsity before earning the right, as a senior, to come off the bench for the varsity.

Now, prior to his senior year in college, he was being told that he would be on the varsity at North Carolina for the second season in a row. He could barely dunk, but he could bang his 6'8", 240-pound body into Kris Lang and Brendan Haywood enough to provide resistance in practice. And he could show up on time every day (no one bends the rules for walk-ons), and he would be happy to put on the uniform. Make that ecstatic.

"Every time we run out of the tunnel at the Smith Center, I get goose bumps," said Everett. "The crowd's going, the band, the cheerleaders, everything. I love it every time."

Everett had held onto his dream of being on the Carolina varsity by the skin of his teeth. During summer orientation prior to his freshman year, he went in to see Phil Ford and asked about tryouts for the junior varsity. North Carolina is the only major college to have a junior varsity; the tradition goes back to the days when freshmen were not allowed to play varsity and has been continued as a way to offer regular students the opportunity to wear the North Carolina uniform. Almost one hundred players showed up the first night in October, and Everett's prospects of making the team seemed slim. But Ford liked his size, his willingness to dive on the floor, and his natural leadership qualities, so he kept him around. As a sophomore, Everett again played junior varsity, leading the team in scoring and rebounding.

Rarely does a junior varsity player make the varsity, but prior to Everett's junior year he received a call from JV teammate Matt Lezkowski telling him that UNC recruit Jason Parker was unlikely to qualify and Vasco Evtimov would be turning pro in Europe. Suddenly, two spots were open on the varsity for two nonscholarship post players. Everett, who was interning in Washington, D.C., began to work out frantically.

Everett, Lezkowski, and three others vied for the two spots. Bill Guthridge quickly cut two of the players, leaving three. The final choice lingered for what seemed like months until Guthridge informed Lezkowski and Everett that they would both be making the trip to Hawaii for the Maui Classic and, therefore, would be on the team for the entire season.

As ecstatic as he was, Everett was also prudent. Still somewhat intimidated, he remained fairly quiet as the season progressed. "I didn't want to rock the boat," he said. "Then, when we went to the Final Four, I started getting loud, more like I usually am. Brendan thought I was losing it."

For the season, Everett would score 10 points and grab 11 rebounds in 15 games, including an appearance in the national semifinal against Florida. It was a dream come true. A dream he didn't want to end.

The next summer, with an opportunity to make the team as a senior again up in the air (Parker was slated to come in after a year in prep school), Everett took an internship with Lehman Brothers in New York City. While there, he met a trader named John, who shared an interest in North Carolina basketball. When Guthridge announced his retirement, John speculated, like the rest of the country, that Roy Williams would be the next coach. A week later, both Everett and John were still in shock when Matt Doherty—who just happened to be John's brother—was announced as the new coach in Chapel Hill.

Without knowing what his chances were to make the team, Everett again worked out hard in preparation for his chance. When he returned to campus, he lifted weights and worked out with strength coach Ben Cook. He came in third place in Carolina's annual 12-minute run. But again he didn't know his fate until that night in the memorabilia room.

His teammates pulled for him and lobbied for him with the coaches, but he was in the dark until Coach Doherty announced it. Three weeks later he saw his face on the schedule card, and it hit him.

"I'm trying to slow things down and enjoy this year," he said. "Last year flew by so fast. Sometimes, I still can't believe how lucky I am."

"Midnight With Matt And The Heels" was Doherty's idea from the beginning. It had been six years since a UNC team had begun the practice season with a late-night, fan-oriented scrimmage. By all accounts, that one, set in the 21,750-seat Smith Center, had been well received, but largely uneventful.

"Midnight Mattness" quickly grew beyond a simple scrimmage. First, it was held in Carmichael Auditorium, situated just a few hundred feet from the UNC Student Union and near the heart of campus (unlike the Smith Center, which is on the southernmost edge of campus and accessible to the majority of students only by bus or car). The auditorium had also been the building Michael Jordan—and Matt Doherty—had played in.

By 10:00 that night, 6,000 fans—mostly students—had crammed into the old gym. By 11:30, the doors were closed with 10,000 inside and more than 1,000 left out. It was hot, sweaty, and tight in the House Where Michael Played, which had last seen a regular-season game on January 4, 1986—a win over NC State. Even the squirrels were jacked up—one of Carmichael's furry residents darted across center court during the student hot-shot contest.

Activities included a rousing three-on-three game between Doherty and his staff, and the all-campus intramural champs. After 14 minutes of extremely physical half-court action (the official walked over to the scorer's table at one break in the action and described his role as a "Globetrotter Official"), Doherty and his staff found themselves ahead by 1 point and in possession of the ball with one minute remaining. David Cason tossed the ball to Doherty on a wing, who promptly walked the ball to midcourt and, in a PR move any White House staffer or Hollywood executive would have been proud of, called for the Four Corners, the famous spread offense Dean Smith invented and perfected before the shot clock's introduction made it obsolete.

Ten thousand fans went berserk as Doherty, Cason, and Wojcik all but dribbled out the clock. A late turnover and missed dunk later, the coaches had won. The UNC players rushed onto the court and slapped five and chest-bumped their new staff.

The past had indeed met the present.

Hattie Doherty couldn't care less that October 14, 2000 was the most important day of her daddy's professional life. Just a few hours after "Midnight With Matt" ended, Doherty was awakened by his six-month-old daughter's crying. His first official practice was less than five hours away.

It was time to get to work.

Wojcik, Quartlebaum, Cason, and several team managers arrived around 7:00 A.M. that morning and began preparing for practice, or the beginning of "Phase Two" as Doherty had labeled it. He had referred to the preseason conditioning as "Phase One." Players referred to it by other, more colorful, names. "He likes to run you till you puke," said the always-theatrical Kris Lang. "He's good at that." Joseph Forte called it "grueling." Jason Capel was just glad it was over.

Brendan Haywood had continued to impress the coaches throughout the preseason workouts. The senior center had endured a highly criticized, sometimes bitter, season in 1999–2000. The seven-footer was the primary target of fans, talk show hosts, Internet message boards, and newspaper columnists who pinned the at-times lackadaisical team performances squarely on Haywood's shoulders. His past failings included the oft-repeated 1 point and 0 rebound effort in the NCAA first-round loss to Weber State two years ago. Continued subpar play into the first one-third of 1999–2000 caused a furor over his apparent lack of desire and intensity. The barrage resulted in Haywood becoming exceedingly distrustful and sometimes outright disdainful of reporters.

More so than any Carolina player—maybe more than any college athlete—the public perception of Haywood was directly opposite from his actual personality. Thought to be a morose, angry young man with a chip on his shoulder, Haywood was, in fact, a very thoughtful, highly sensitive person who cared deeply for his mother, his aunt, and for those he trusted.

"He's a great person," said Guthridge. "But he's guarded. Once you get to know him, he's got a great sense of humor. And he's a very kind and considerate person." During Haywood's sophomore season, Assistant Coach Dave Hanners fell ill and was forced to miss a couple days of practice. The only player to call and check on him was Haywood. "Just little things like that he would do are very considerate," said Guthridge.

Haywood was also the team's funniest guy. His dead-on impersonations of Smith and, in time, Doherty, left players and coaches alike in stitches. If no reporters were around, he'd tell stories and have the other players rolling on the floor in laughter. One of his favorites occurred when he was being recruited as a high school senior and received a call from Dean Smith.

"Brendan, you know if you come to North Carolina and work hard you can end up like [former UNC and NBA star] Brad Daugherty," Haywood would say imitating Smith's voice (renowned for its nasal quality). "Or, if you come here and don't work hard, you can end up like Geff Crompton."

"Coach," Haywood would retell himself asking, "who's Geff Crompton?"

"Exactly," Haywood would deadpan in Smith's voice.

Haywood was the most universally well-liked player on the team and could interact and hang out with everyone, from the religious Jon Holmes to the more cynical Jason Capel. In many ways, Haywood was a big kid; he entered UNC when he was just 17 years old. By far his favorite activity was playing video games, either in the players' lounge or in his apartment. Haywood did not like to go out much and had earned a reputation as someone who was somewhat frugal: Every time he went to a movie (always the matinee) at the theater down the street from his apartment, he'd stop in at the grocery store in the same shopping center for a packet of Twizzlers to sneak into the movie with him to avoid paying too much for candy.

Growing up, Haywood was always big for his age, but lacked coordination. Due to a difference in what school-age was in New York (where he was born) and North Carolina, Haywood was always a year younger than others in his grade. Despite some early setbacks in the game, he continued to work hard on developing his abilities and skills, thanks to his mother Barbara, who somehow found the money to send him to basketball camps. But it was also his mother who, when Brendan began to slack off on his schoolwork during his early years in high school at Greensboro's Dudley High, took basketball away. The lesson was learned quickly, and as his coordination caught up with his size—and thanks to the coaching of David Price—Haywood went from struggling to make the varsity to a star, leading the Panthers to the state title as a senior.

His late development continued into his years at North Carolina. As a 16-year-old freshman, he was the seventh player in a six-man rotation that featured Antawn Jamison and Vince Carter. When Jamison and Carter left, Haywood became a starter as a sophomore and quickly earned a reputation as a shot-blocker and occasional scorer. He shot rarely and led the league in field goal percentage but did not have the requisite number of attempts to qualify for inclusion in the official league stats. He showed flashes of brilliance, scoring 24 points and grabbing 12 rebounds against California, but sometimes disappeared in other games—the most glaring example being the game against Weber State in the first round of the NCAA Tournament that would be synonymous with his up-and-down Carolina career. In that game, Haywood scored just 1 point and did not grab a rebound. It was a game for which he would be resoundingly criticized and would sour him on both the game and UNC fans and media.

Many believed Haywood's junior season would be his breakout year. Again, it was a case of playing well one game and struggling in others. He led the league in blocked shots, but at times did not work as hard to get the ball in the post as his coaches and teammates would like. The results were some games in which Haywood would be a nonfactor on offense. Retribution came, ironically enough, during the NCAA Tournament as Carolina advanced to the Final Four behind Haywood's inside dominance.

But even the late run and Haywood's solid play did not impress many college basketball observers. Prior to the 2000–2001 season, one preseason basketball publication listed Haywood as the eighth best post player in the country, behind those he had clearly bested previously such as Alvin Jones of Georgia Tech and Kaspars Kambala of UNLV. Publicly, Haywood brushed it off. Privately, it didn't hurt so much as motivate. It was his senior year, and Haywood would not let the criticism get to him. He would work hard, do the best he could, and let the chips fall where they may. If fans loved him or if they hated him, he didn't care. He only wanted to win.

Thanks to the improved confidence generated by a successful fall, it was a different Brendan Haywood that met the media and the fans a few days prior to the team's first practice. He admitted to having lost 10 pounds and appeared markedly thinner in his waist and leaner in his chest and neck. He ran the mile (a Carolina tradition) in just over six minutes—impressive for a man his size.

The effect of his weight loss was not readily apparent until the team scrimmage during "Midnight With Matt." During the 20-minute scrimmage, Haywood ran the floor with more speed and desire than he had ever shone. On several occasions he beat guards and forwards up and down the floor, grabbing fast-break offensive rebounds and dunking with his usual ferocity.

About 15 minutes into the scrimmage, with Lang obviously tiring, Haywood only looked stronger when he received a pass on the left block. Haywood's primary move in that position—one he used almost exclusively unless double-teamed—was an energy-conserving baseline turnaround jumper that he could get off simply because he was taller than anyone he played against.

But on this occasion, he stayed on balance and moved across the lane, finishing with a right-hand lunge-hook on the other side of the hoop. It was a simple move that required quickness, balance, and patience: three traits Haywood had rarely before displayed.

The other star of the short scrimmage was Forte. Forte, unlike Haywood, was revered by fans. He had captured their hearts with a wildly successful freshman season that put his picture on the cover of magazines and invited the inevitable comparisons to Michael Jordan. Jordan may have been the most famous freshman shooting guard in school history—memories of his 18-foot jumper that won the 1982 NCAA title still bring mist to the eyes of Tar Heel fans—but Forte averaged more points, 16.7 per game, in his first season than any player ever to wear a UNC uniform.

With Haywood and Forte impressive in their first showing—and Doherty getting the crowd excited with his Four Corners routine—Carolina fans began to believe that maybe, just maybe, this could be a better team than many predicted.

7

Living in the Now, Building for the Future

Matt Doherty was a spectator during his team's first public appearance on the court of the Smith Center. As his assistants readied the 14 players for the 40-minute running-clock scrimmage known as the Blue–White game, Doherty sat behind the scorer's table in the first row of the stands. Several thousand hard-core fans were in attendance, as was one very special guest.

Sitting in between Doherty and his wife, Kelly, was the last remaining and unsigned top recruit for the Tar Heels, DeSagana Diop, a well-proportioned, 6'11" center from Senegal, now playing at Oak Hill Academy in Virginia. A day earlier, Doherty, Fred Quartlebaum, and David Cason had picked Diop up at the airport and driven him to campus. The visit, thus far, had gone well. "Let's just say he had a good time," said Jason Capel, whose record as a host for recruits was stellar. "For the record, anyone I've ever hosted has come to Carolina."

Diop had made it known to the UNC staff, as well as to the coaches at Virginia (his other top choice), that he would not make his final selection until the spring. This decision put the Carolina coaches in a bind: Did they wait for Diop and their second choice at center, David Harrison (who also publicly claimed he would wait until the spring but was considering at least four schools), or should they move farther down the list and take a center that may be less talented but more willing to accept a scholarship for the fall signing period, which started November 8?

This decision had crucial repercussions throughout the program. Carolina needed to bring in a quality center this season. Haywood was graduating, and Kris Lang and Brian Bersticker would be seniors next year. If Diop or Harrison would not commit in the fall and the UNC coaches chose to wait, then they would have to continue recruiting at least four players—all centers—throughout the winter. That took time away from focusing on the current team's development, preparing for opponents, and recruiting the current class of juniors, and it would generally add stress—and increased speculation in the press about recruiting—to the program.

One of the stark contrasts between Doherty's Carolina program and those of his predecessors came in the creativity with which the current staff went about recruiting. The top prep players—and even some of the average ones—received thousands of pieces of mail, talked to hundreds of college coaches, and sometimes made dozens of official and unofficial visits to college campuses. Even North Carolina could have difficulty setting itself apart in that climate of overkill.

Doherty's recruiting system is one that is highly personalized and uses methods that impact typical 18 year olds. It also helped that the general student population—which was knowledgeable when it came to recruiting matters—would welcome their prospective fellow students when the recruits visited campus. Two weeks earlier, when escorting Jackie Manuel, a guard recruit from Florida who had committed to Carolina in July, and Jawad Williams, a forward from Cleveland still

uncommitted, through the football stadium, Doherty walked both players through the student section. The savvy students picked up on the
cue and began cheering and chanting for the players.

Williams would verbally commit that weekend.

In Diop's case, a student contingent had gathered in the stands during the Blue–White game and hoisted signs, such as "Dunk in our place,"
and chanted Diop's name prior to the game. Doherty gave a thumbs-up
to the students for their efforts. In a further attempt to make a point cre-
atively, Doherty had Cason ask the producer of Doherty's television
show to produce a highlights video of Haywood to show to Diop. The
video, complete with the hard cuts and booming music set underneath
Haywood's most vicious dunks and adept post moves, was designed to
show Diop that Carolina valued and developed its big men—and got
them the ball. Similar videos were shown to other high-profile recruits
Jawad Williams (showing Vince Carter) and Manuel (Joe Forte).
Williams had been so excited by the video, in fact, that he had offered
his verbal commitment almost as soon as the screen went dark.

 Doherty's recruiting strategy was one part Dean Smith, one part
Roy Williams, and one part Matt Doherty.

From Smith, he learned to be brutally honest. Just as Smith had
done while sitting in his parents' living room 20 years ago, Doherty liked
to challenge the high school players he recruited. Never did he make a
promise about playing time, and if anything, he'd make the mountain
seem higher to climb than easier.

"I've lost kids by being honest," said Doherty. "But again, I go back
to my experiences with Coach Smith. I was a McDonald's All-American,
and he sat in my living room and told me I would be lucky to play by the
time I was a junior. I took that as a challenge, to be honest with you. But
it was kind of refreshing, because everyone else told me I would start my
freshman year. Michael Jordan was not told he would start as a freshman. The thing I want is to be honest with kids. I don't want them to
come here and then I can't look them in the eye because I told them a

story. The trust starts in recruiting. If you start telling them stories that won't come true, then the trust has broken down and you won't have the relationship you want to have with them.

"I'd rather undersell it a little bit and have them pleasantly surprised than oversell it and have them disappointed."

One of the recruiting rules observed by Smith was to not over-recruit. It was a simple strategy; instead of stockpiling players and thus having the potential for talented players wiling away on the bench (and negatively affecting team morale), Smith chose to recruit a handful of exemplary players each season and fill in with role players (thus allowing other talented players to pursue options at other schools). It was a strategy that worked exceedingly well for decades.

But the recent trend toward players leaving early for the pros had damaged Carolina in recent years—more so than any other college program—and had rendered this strategy obsolete. With barely decent players leaving college after just two seasons for the professional ranks, Carolina had to readjust and recruit more and more talented players to increase depth for the very real possibility that many of those players would not stick around Chapel Hill for all four seasons.

From Roy Williams, Doherty learned resiliency and toughness. The nature of recruiting is losing more than winning. The whims of 18 year olds change with the wind. Never giving up—and handling losses with class—are trademarks of Williams. And both can prove fruitful.

A perfect example came when Doherty, then the coach at Notre Dame, began recruiting Jawad Williams, a rising senior from Lakewood St. Edwards High School, just west of Cleveland. A 6'8", athletic wing player who showed great potential to be a scoring small forward, Williams was exactly the kind of player Doherty coveted. "Speed kills," Doherty explained it simply.

As one of the top players in the class, Williams—the son of a former professional boxer who traveled an hour each way to get to school across town—was being recruited by a great many of the top basketball programs in the nation. Notre Dame, despite a solid first year under Doherty, was not one of the schools that enticed Williams.

"The last time we talked on the phone, I told him that I had narrowed my choices to five schools, and Notre Dame wasn't on the list," recalled Williams, who was nonetheless fond of Doherty. "He asked me which schools I was thinking about and I mentioned North Carolina. He said, 'Well, if you aren't going to come to Notre Dame, I think you should go to North Carolina,' and he went on to explain why. He wished me well."

A few months later, of course, Doherty was the head coach at the school he had recommended to Williams. Williams was excited when he heard the news; he had liked Doherty immensely, but wanted a bigger program. Now, he had the best of both worlds. Williams was scheduled to take an unofficial visit to Maryland when he got the call from the new North Carolina coach.

Williams never made it to College Park.

"He was honest," said Williams. "He told me how it would be if I went to North Carolina. He didn't pull any punches."

Doherty, of course, must be himself when he recruits. With a background as a Wall Street trader and a coach, Doherty has the salesman's ability to sense what is important to a recruit and highlight that aspect of North Carolina. "It's a lot like cold-calling," said Doherty of making the initial contact. Effusive and comfortable talking to most anyone, Doherty also works harder at finding and attracting the best players than his two predecessors at North Carolina. It was rare that a top recruit, such as Williams, was contacted by anyone from Carolina other than Doherty.

"He works harder at recruiting than I did," said Dean Smith. "It's not all bad being 38."

But working hard doesn't always assure that everything will go smoothly.

Earlier in the fall, when Doherty was making home visits to recruits, he took a private plane (furnished by a Carolina alumnus) to Montgomery, Alabama, to meet with Ousmanne Cisse. At least he thought it was Montgomery.

"I got to the airport, just rolled up 50 feet from the plane, feeling big-time, the head coach at North Carolina," recalled Doherty. "So I jump in the plane, probably take a little nap, land, get a rent-a-car, and the directions were to get on I-65 North. So I find it and I'm on I-65 North for 20 minutes. I'm looking for the exit. And I don't see the exit. As I'm driving around, I'm saying to myself, 'Boy, this town looks familiar.' But I've never been to Montgomery before; but we had been to Birmingham when I was at Kansas and we lost to Arizona in Birmingham in the NCAA Tournament. So I pull out the map, and the map is of Birmingham, not of Montgomery. I'm in the wrong town."

Despite that slight miscalculation, Doherty and his staff were able to obtain verbal commitments from Williams, Manuel, and Melvin Scott of Baltimore Southern High School—the same high school Cason had attended—after a few months. But he still needed a big man, a center to replace Haywood.

It would be the toughest sell Doherty ever had.

The Blue–White intrasquad scrimmage served many purposes, but none more important than putting the three starting point guard prospects—sophomore Jon Holmes and freshmen Adam Boone and Brian Morrison—up against one another in a gamelike situation.

Prior to the scrimmage, the assistant coaches (MacKinnon and Cason versus Wojcik and Quartlebaum) drafted the players onto the respective teams. With the first pick Wojcik selected Haywood, who had been unstoppable in the Midnight With Matt scrimmage and in the first week of practice. MacKinnon then got the next two choices, and he took Forte and Lang. The two sides then chose one at a time until the teams were full.

Holmes and Boone were both drafted on to the White Team, while Morrison would man the point for the Blue. Holmes got the starting nod and played very well throughout the first half. His defense, particularly off the ball, was fundamentally sound and he even hit 3-of-4 from the field. Boone was also solid, hitting an open jump shot and running the offense adequately.

Morrison, however, struggled. Unquestionably the best athlete of the three, Morrison was also the most erratic and the quickest to get down on himself. Even with Forte—with whom he had formed a personal friendship already—on his team, Morrison's concentration wavered on both ends of the floor. He would end up with five turnovers, but even worse showed a lack of consistency on the defensive end.

Haywood dominated the first half, scoring 10 points and taking his White Team to a 17-point lead. Bersticker also impressed, although he was matching up against the undersized Will Johnson—solidifying the three-deep rotation Carolina would have up front until Peppers came out from football.

Forte picked up the ballhandling slack on the Blue Team and led them to a bit of a second-half comeback. He would finish with 28 points and eight assists and send the attending press scurrying back to their laptops to file stories on his candidacy as the new point guard. Unfortunately, most of the reporters failed to realize that the majority of Forte's scoring plays and assists came when either Morrison or the defensive rebounder pushed the ball ahead to Forte—pushing the ball up the court had been a point of emphasis for the coaches during the first week of practice—and he had been able to get into an uncongested lane. If he was the point guard, he would be the one pushing it ahead, not receiving the long sideline pass, thus reducing his scoring chances in the open floor.

Forte could, however, play the point guard position in the half court. In fact, it was obvious that, when the shot clock was running down, the number one option was for Forte—the best player on the roster at creating his own shot—to be isolated on a wing or the top. "The thing that he is, above everything, is a basketball player," said Doherty after the scrimmage. "He comes off a pick, he hesitates, he reads it, he sees what the defense does, then he makes his decision. They're overplaying him on the wing—we haven't put in any back-door plays—but they're overplaying him and so he cuts back-door. He just makes eye contact with the passer and makes the play. He knows how to play basketball. I would have enjoyed playing with Joe in college. He knows how to cut, where to deliver the basketball. And he's a scorer. He can put the ball in the hole." Forte could also guard an opponent's point guard, which would eventually be the number one criteria for whomever would become the starter at the position. The test, in Doherty's mind, was Duke's Jason Williams, a big (6'2"), strong point guard whose strength and quickness in getting into the lane had demoralized Carolina in the Blue Devils' three wins the previous season.

Forte, at 6'4", could guard Williams. But what effect would that have on his own offense? Morrison had the physical tools to guard Williams, but not the fundamentals or mental resolve. Boone was not quite as strong or athletic, but might stand a chance. Holmes, at 5'10" and a step slow, would struggle. Ronald Curry was still throwing footballs and was at least a month away from even joining the team.

Two important pieces to the puzzle going in to the weekend had been the great point guard debate and DeSagana Diop, who would leave Chapel Hill without offering a verbal commitment. While neither had been answered, the coaches were far from defeated.

Nobody said it was going to be easy, even at North Carolina.

8

"Let's Get Better Today!"

The most energetic and useful practices—particularly in the pre-season when, with no specific games to prepare for, practices can become monotonous—tend to occur immediately prior to or immediately following a day off. Such was the case on this Wednesday as the Tar Heels were happy, smiling, and getting ready for a two-and-a-half-hour workout before a rare weekday off the next day. Thursday's break had been on the schedule since Doherty first laid out the calendar in early October, but the day off the team enjoyed two days earlier on Monday was unscheduled.

"We're all tired. I know you guys are tired and, to be honest, the staff's tired, too," said Doherty at Sunday night's practice, the sixth consecutive without a day off. "If you work hard tonight, we'll take a day off tomorrow." The players looked around at each other until one finally asked if Monday's day off took the place of Thursday's. No, Doherty assured them, if the practice—which was mostly a scrimmage in front of selected Educational Foundation (alumni club) members—was spirited and they worked hard, they would get both Monday and Thursday off. Energized by the possibility of free time, the scrimmage was intense, if a little rough, and Doherty kept his promise.

Doherty's admission that the staff was tired was putting it mildly. October is always hectic for any college basketball staff, with the effort of putting the final touches on the high school seniors it still coveted—big men DeSagana Diop, David Harrison, and Ousmanne Cisse (who was a long shot, at best)—prior to the November 8 signing date as well as sending out creative letters and cards to the juniors they could finally contact. Add in practices, staff meetings, and individual player meetings, and any staff in the country is exhausted before the first exhibition game. The Carolina staff had the additional stress and strain of uprooted personal lives: Quartlebaum's son Trey was less than three months old, Wojcik's son Paxson was a newborn, and Doherty himself was rotating bottle duty with his wife Kelly for their daughter Hattie.

After Tuesday's day off, the team and staff went back to work on Wednesday with an increased level of enthusiasm and a renewed sense of purpose. As the players walked the short distance from their locker room under the Smith Center seats to the floor, MacKinnon, always among the most vocal coaches on the staff, stood in the tunnel yelling, "Let's go Heels!" The admonition to hurry to the floor was delivered with a smile, but the message was clear: It was time to go to work.

Once on the floor for prepractice, the players shot on their own (with a manager rebounding) or worked out with strength and conditioning coach Ben Cook. In one of the drills, Cook had Brian Bersticker and Kris Lang do what he called a "crab," in which the player is parallel to the ground with his back facing up and, on all fours, moves laterally along the floor, sideline to sideline. Both Lang and Bersticker found the exercise difficult, moaning and grunting, but both pushed on as Cook yelled to keep their backside down and their back straight.

Doherty, meanwhile, took a moment to talk to Forte and Holmes about a play the staff had put in the day before. Both players had run the play correctly, but Doherty wanted to point out a subtle timing issue that would allow Forte to get open just at the time the point guard would be ready to deliver him the ball. Forte asked Doherty a few questions for clarity, which Doherty obviously saw as a good sign. A well-thought-out question is the best sign that a player understands.

All of the coaches gained great enjoyment from prepractice. Quartlebaum stood under one of the main baskets (in addition to the two main hoops, six other baskets are brought out for practice) and rebounded for Max Owens, who drained 15-of-20 three-pointers from various points behind the arc. Quartlebaum smiled, offered challenges with a grin, and whistled at Owens when he missed.

Wojcik, meanwhile, played a game of one-on-one with junior Orlando Melendez at another basket. There was a lot of friendly woofing between the two, particularly when Wojcik hit a shot. Melendez, one of the best athletes on the team and an incredible leaper, let Wojcik have any shot outside the arc. When he missed, other team members who were shooting nearby let their coach know about it.

After all the players were on the court, MacKinnon also took on a few players at one of the side baskets. He defended Forte and forced him to miss four straight shots—and razzed him mercilessly when he did. Brian Morrison was equally unlucky against MacKinnon's defense—which included more than a few jabs with his forearm—and MacKinnon walked away in triumph, telling the two players over his shoulder that he was going elsewhere to "find someone who will challenge me."

The buzzer went off and head manager Chad Webb (he has six assistants at each practice helping him run the clock, collect the balls, lay out water and towels, and attend to all manner of needs of the players and coaches) put five minutes back on it. The team circled around Cook and stretched at midcourt while the coaches briefly discussed some of the finer teaching points of that day's drills. MacKinnon continued shouting enthusiastically: "Nine more days!" "Let's get better today!" When the five minutes were up and the buzzer went off, the team jumped to its feet and surrounded Doherty at midcourt.

Doherty's voice was calm, almost reticent, as he addressed the players. All were fidgeting from nervous energy, but attentive. Doherty talked about some of the things he saw on the tape from yesterday's practice. (All practices were taped by a manager from one of the radio booths under the upper deck.) He talked about general improvements the team had made, but also pointed out the work of several players, including Owens. He lauded the senior for his defensive work, an area of his game for which Owens had been publicly criticized in the past.

At the end of his comments, Doherty raised his voice markedly. "Let's go!" he yelled, and the team broke up and ran to preassigned baskets for shooting drills. The entire team shot one-handed shots up against the glass. After a dozen or so "air shots," they shot short jumpers, concentrating on good form. Only after many shots in close did the guards move out to the free throw line and the elbow (the juncture of the free throw line and the lane line) to shoot off the pass from a coach or a manager. Post players also moved out to fifteen feet or so, but didn't venture out farther when the guards shot a few three-pointers from the top of the key.

The horn sounded, and the players sprinted to one of the baselines for a full-court, three-man weave drill for five minutes. Another horn, and the players split up into a perimeter and post groups, with the guards working on doubling down on the post and the post players working on one-on-one post defense. During the drill, Bersticker and Lang got tangled up and fell, with Lang's leg rolling awkwardly underneath. A manager, Kade Ross, immediately sprinted to find trainer Marc Davis. Lang was OK and was back in the drill a few moments later. (But the incident only added to the constant needling from his teammates about the amount of time the rugged post player spent in the training room.)

After what he called the "individual work" portion of the practice was complete, Doherty called everyone back to the center circle. He again gave out platitudes for play in the first few drills, singling out

Morrison and Lang's effort. He added: "The shooting stats look great, too. We're really shooting the crap out of the ball. Great job." Another horn and another shout, and the players again sprinted to preassigned baskets while the coaches called out drill names and shouted for players to assume positions on the court. "Joe, you're on the wing . . . Wood, you're defending in the post . . . Cape, you got Joe . . ."

Coaches constantly referred to certain players by nicknames, if they had them. It was a small but telling point in the relationship between the players and the coaching staff that had developed in the few short months. It was a close relationship, almost like big brothers, in which the assistant coaches, in particular, had fun with those whom they coached. The tone, however, also relayed to the players that it was time to get to business. And the coaches were never afraid to admonish, in no uncertain terms, when they felt a player was being lazy or not concentrating. A few times each practice Doherty would remind his players sternly, "When I'm talking, look me in the eyes and stop talking!" But when the players did something worthy of praise, the coaches were quick to give it, even going so far as to rush in with players to help a teammate off the floor after taking a charge or fighting for a loose ball. At other, more informal times, the coaches would offer the player a pound. Doherty, in fact, greeted almost every player who came onto the floor prior to practice with a pound.

Defensive stations included work on guarding the on-the-ball screen and the back-screen. In all of the drills, the coaches were animated and intense, unafraid to jump into a drill themselves to show how a fundamental should be executed. When the defensive stations were completed, the players again rushed to the center circle, where Doherty gave more instant feedback on how the drills looked and which players stood out. The players were already feeling a burn in their legs and lungs. Practice was less than one-third completed.

At the halfway point, they changed into clean jerseys and toweled down, leaving their drenched mesh tops on the floor. Chad Webb picked them up and handed them to an assistant manager, who jogged into the locker room with them as the players moved on to a controlled scrimmage. Every move the players made was critiqued and either corrected or lauded. It was a draining workout—mentally and physically—that the coaches agreed was adequate, but could have been better.

The players counted the days until they could play against someone else.

In case they forgot how long until that happened, MacKinnon was there to let them know as they left the court after nearly three hours: "Nine more days, gentlemen!! Nine more days!!"

9

"Can You Believe We're Here?"

Jon Holmes walked into the Smith Center locker room well before the required game time deadline for sophomores. One of the team rules that had survived the change in coaches was that freshmen were required to report an hour and a half prior to tip-off, sophomores one hour and 15 minutes, and juniors and seniors one hour. It was rare that anyone on the team came close to missing those deadlines. Tonight being the first game against Winthrop in the NABC Classic on their home floor, all of the players were in and dressed at least two hours prior.

Holmes went about the business of preparing for the game as he always did. He dressed quickly—putting a wrist band on his left forearm last—before going out to the court for some informal shooting and stretching. Hanging heavy on his mind were the minutes he would get tonight. Publicly, Coach Doherty had yet to announce his starting point guard. But Holmes knew it would be freshman Adam Boone, who had earned the majority of work with the White (first) team in practice all week. Freshman Brian Morrison had also worked in with the Whites, while Holmes had run the Blue (second) team.

One of Doherty's more private pronouncements was that, if the game went according to plan, he would rotate point guards every five minutes. It was a loose plan, however, as he also stated and believed that he would stay with someone if that player and the team were playing well.

While he was shooting, Holmes found his mom, dad, aunt, and uncle in the stands behind the scorer's table. He glanced their way but did not acknowledge them—his dad, being a longtime high school coach, would not look kindly on such a distraction so close to game time. Keep your mind focused on what you're going to do, he'd tell Jon.

At this early point in the season, Holmes was keeping his head up and biding his time, waiting for his chance. He knew Coach Doherty would keep his word and he'd get a chance tonight. He hoped it would come early, but whenever it came, he would do what he always did: play as hard as he could, get the ball where it needed to be, and hit an open shot if it came his way. It was the only way he knew how to play.

Jon Holmes was a true-to-life stereotype: an Indiana kid who lived and breathed basketball, whose life had been the game since before he could remember. His dad, J.R., was the coach of South High School in Bloomington; his mom was also a teacher. He had always been the point guard on every team he had played on, from the time he was just a little taller than the ball.

His teenage years were consumed with the game, from falls, winters, and springs spent practicing with whatever team he was on to summers spent on the AAU circuit. Every day of his life he played basketball somewhere, working on some aspect of the game. At six-feet tall by the time he was a junior and not possessing of blinding speed, he had little choice if he was to realize his dream of playing college basketball.

It was a dream that nearly caused Holmes to lose his faith.

Jon's religion was a large part of who he was. He drew particular strength from his mother, Martha. During his senior year in high school, he would need it. After drawing a great deal of attention from major college programs during his junior year in high school, Holmes had a somewhat disappointing summer. And in this day and age, players are made (or unmade) during the month of July. Holmes received calls and serious interest from Duke, Michigan State, and some other Big Ten schools as well as Kentucky, Kansas, and Clemson. After several unofficial visits, several schools, including Clemson, made him a scholarship offer.

On August 6 prior to his senior year, Holmes had made a decision; he wanted to go to Clemson. He had family in South Carolina and decided to end the speculation. He called Coach Larry Shyatt to tell him he wanted to come, but Shyatt was on vacation and wouldn't be back until the next week. Instead of calling back, Holmes decided to wait and look to even bigger programs. Duke was waiting on a decision from Jason Williams, a point guard from New Jersey, but wanted Holmes if Williams said no. Williams said yes, as did other point guard prospects at Stanford, Michigan State, and Northwestern. By the time he finally grasped what was happening, Holmes's suitors were all gone.

Salvation came from an unlikely source. Holmes's aunt lived in Columbia, South Carolina, down the street from Eddie Fogler, the coach at South Carolina and a former player and assistant coach at North Carolina. Due to his aunt's persistence, Fogler continued to recruit Holmes, but with his point guard situation covered, he never offered a scholarship. Fogler eventually called Bill Guthridge, who was in the market to sign a point guard after Ed Cota began to make some noise about leaving to go to the NBA after his junior season. Guthridge needed a solid backup for a year, at the least.

Guthridge went to see Holmes in December of his senior year. By that time, Holmes was a nervous wreck, believing his chance to play college basketball at the highest level may have passed him by. After Guthridge watched Bloomington South practice, he called back on December 14, a Monday night. Holmes remembered it well.

"He called and asked me if I wanted to come to North Carolina and play," said Holmes. "He offered me a scholarship. I almost dropped the phone. I committed on the spot."

Holmes had achieved a goal, but he was not about to rest on the fact that he was on the team. He truly believed that if he worked hard enough and did everything possible to improve, he could be the starting point guard for the Tar Heels for three years, after serving as an apprentice to Cota (who decided to remain in Chapel Hill his senior year, after all).

His freshman season, Holmes made one start—when Cota was hurt at Georgia Tech—and played 22 minutes against Florida State at home when Cota was out with the flu. But the latter game was a loss and, more important for Holmes, showed that he struggled against ultraquick point guards.

During the preseason four-player workouts Holmes had spent considerable time with Bob MacKinnon on a variety of exhausting drills designed to improve quickness, including lane slides, where the player stays in a defensive stance—a low crouch—and slides across the lane, touching each line with his foot, for anywhere from 30 seconds to 2 minutes. When classes interrupted the normal workout times, Holmes would call MacKinnon and ask to work out individually. MacKinnon was glad to oblige.

With no one else in the arena, MacKinnon would work Holmes out to the point of complete exhaustion. Holmes, of course, loved it. When the workout was over, Holmes would spend hours shooting—with MacKinnon rebounding. The two had formed a close bond in the few short months they had known each other. But that made MacKinnon only push the sophomore harder the next time, and it made Holmes only that much more determined.

He knew that this year was his chance to fulfill his dreams—or watch them slip away, maybe forever.

Matt Doherty's first game day as the head coach at North Carolina began with him staying at home throughout most of the morning, watching videotape of Winthrop. It was a routine he would fall into for home games: stay at home (where the phone wouldn't ring) and polish up the scouting report and game plan until the scheduled walk-through, usually some time about midmorning.

At Notre Dame, Doherty liked to have a walk-through an hour and a half prior to the tip-off, but without an alternate gym (other than the Smith Center) he had decided that was impossible. Walk-throughs almost always consisted of the same routine: free throws, some light shooting, maybe a full-court drill or two to loosen up the legs, some time spent working on offensive plays, and then a 15-minute (or so) scouting report on the other team.

Pregame meals for the upcoming season would be held primarily at Michael Jordan's 23, a new restaurant in town that had a convenient back room. Following a meal of steak or chicken and corn, potatoes, pasta, and salad, Doherty would begin quizzing players on the opponents' players and sets.

"Joe, what does Winthrop want to do when they call out Play 'X'?" or "Brendan, which way does Effiong turn when he shoots his jump-hook?" The exchange was serious, broken only momentarily by a giggle or a smile if a player was stumped. Doherty was stern, delivering admonishments in a way that did not embarrass a player but got his point across: don't make a mistake next time.

After pregame, which usually took place four hours before tip-off, Doherty headed to the office. The hours before a game, Doherty has found, are typically quiet and a good time to get some office work done. This being his first game at North Carolina, Doherty had to spend an inordinate amount of time on ticket requests, requests for parking, and other nonbasketball-related issues. All of those are taken care of in the days leading up to the game, so Doherty spent a few hours writing correspondence to recruits as the hours wound down until game time.

The North Carolina basketball offices underwent a gradual but not drastic change when Doherty and his staff took over. One of the most difficult transitions came back in the late summer, when Guthridge and Smith were removing pictures and mementos from their office walls—

and asking Doherty if he wanted any of the stuff. The only trophies he kept were the national championship trophies—prominently displayed in the outer office—and the national player-of-the-year trophies won by Antawn Jamison, Michael Jordan, and Phil Ford, which sat in Doherty's wood-paneled office.

It had taken Doherty some time to get accustomed to working in Smith and Guthridge's old office. The electronic gadgetry alone—which controlled the track lighting, the blinds, and a video screen that descended from the ceiling—was enough to overwhelm him. In time, Doherty had made himself more comfortable by hanging some of his own North Carolina photos. A stickler for organization and detail (he often referred to himself as "anal," a judgment shared by many close to him), Doherty had a system of piles on his desk that only he and his assistant, Jennifer Holbrook, knew the key to. He had eschewed the large video screen across the room for a small television monitor and VCR that sat immediately to the right of his desk. In an office that was 40 feet long, Doherty had pushed his work space into an area less than one-quarter that size, leaving the rest to two lounge chairs and a coffee table.

Still hanging on the walls of the office lounge were photos of every Carolina basketball alumnus. Doug Wojcik and Fred Quartlebaum occupied adjoining offices that, like Doherty's, looked out onto the walkway between the Smith Center and the adjacent natatorium. During the late summer, it was common for the staff to host cookouts on a small patio outside Doherty's office for all the players and managers who were in town. David Cason's "office" was the video room. Two monitors and the latest digital recording equipment dominated one wall, with Cason crammed into a dark corner. Bob MacKinnon's small, windowless office was down the hall.

Throughout the remainder of the office, little had changed, but what had changed had been done for a specific purpose. In the outer office, across from the glittering national championship trophies and against a gently curving wall, a blown-up photo of the 1982 NCAA title game had been installed. It showed a young, skinny Michael

Jordan in midjump, his elbow tucked perfectly under the ball moments before The Shot that would win Dean Smith his first national championship. Only one other Carolina player was in the frame; a gangly, dark-haired forward named Matt Doherty, who was standing in the lane, his legs slightly bent and his hands up, just in case Michael might want to pass.

On the wall in the main hallway outside the office is the most striking change: a large interlocking NC on top of the words "Carolina Basketball." Underneath it are all the national championship years—off-center—and all of the ACC championship seasons—also with plenty of room at the right end.

The message was clear: There are more championships to add.

About an hour before the Winthrop game, Doherty walked out of his office and downstairs to the coaches' locker room, adjacent to the players' locker room and down a back stairway from the office suite. The coaches' locker room is surprisingly small, with lockers for each staff member (with a chair in front of each) and a small lounge area with a television and VCR. It is a room that is Doherty's sanctuary. When the office upstairs is hectic and he is finding the intrusions and distractions too much, he retreats to the coaches' locker room. It is a trick he learned from Roy Williams.

On this day, like many game days to come, the staff was already there. All the coaches shared some thoughts on the upcoming game and exchanged friendly banter. Doherty checked over a blue index card that he would keep with him in his shirt pocket during the game. On it, he had notes on what plays he believed would be best suited against the different defenses Winthrop would employ, as well as a few general thoughts on the game. It was a habit he had started while at Notre Dame, and being a fairly (although not overly) superstitious coach, Doherty had gotten into the habit of using a blue index card for each game.

After a while, the room grew silent as the weight of the moment seemed to come over them. Sitting in front of his locker, Cason looked to his right at Quartlebaum, who glanced over at Wojcik and to MacKinnon and Doherty. All of their eyes locked, and everyone broke out into a huge, knowing smile.

Cason said what they were all thinking: "Can you believe we're here?"

When the scoreboard clock showed 32 minutes until tip-off against Winthrop, Holmes called to his teammates to head into the locker room. A few took last-second shots and sprinted down the tunnel to a smattering of cheers from the notoriously late-arriving Smith Center crowd.

Once inside the locker room, Holmes was surprised at the anxious feeling that permeated the room. The players milled about, getting gum or a drink, going to the bathroom, and taking care of last-minute alterations to their shooting shirts and warm ups, before Coach Doherty began his first pregame speech before an official game.

Doherty again went over what MacKinnon and he had prepared for Winthrop (the assistant coaches rotated scouting assignments). The champions of the Big South conference—and thus the recipients of the automatic NCAA bid—the previous two seasons, the Eagles were expected to be a solid test. The players—particularly those who remembered the embarrassing loss to Weber State in the first round of the NCAA Tournament two seasons ago—were not going to take Winthrop lightly.

"They're athletic," said Doherty, in his pregame talk. "They'll play hard and get after you on defense." Holmes again thought about what he had to do when he got into the game. To his left sat Forte, who, as always, was quiet and staring down at the floor. Most of the other players fidgeted, bouncing their legs up and down, ready to go. Although this season started earlier than most—the team had had just 21 practices—the players were anxious to go against someone other than themselves.

When the scouting report was over, Doherty took a small piece of paper from his inside jacket pocket and paused.

"I received a note from Coach Smith today, and I wanted to read it to you guys." The players immediately looked up from whatever they were doing. Only two of the players—Brendan Haywood and Max

Owens—had played for Dean Smith, but several others were recruited by the legendary coach. All felt Smith's presence in almost every aspect of the program. In many ways, the players felt Smith was a powerful, unseen force that was always watching them and making his will felt in a number of ways. When he was referred to in any situation, they always stopped and listened.

Doherty, noticeably emotional, read the note, which wished the new coach well in his first game and displayed confidence in his abilities to prepare the team. The note did not speak to the team directly, other than to wish them good luck, but all of the players had the same general thought: Smith still cared deeply about the players on the team and the program, and showed confidence in Doherty as the new coach. It was an important message to deliver before the first game.

After a brief huddle, the players made their way to the court.

The Matt Doherty era was about to begin.

One of the activities that fans and reporters alike were partaking in during the first few public appearances of the Carolina team was to count how many longstanding game traditions the program was keeping— or breaking. Most of the changes were simply a reflection of the personality of the coach. For instance, Doherty preferred to be on the court and active while his team warmed up. "Coach Williams used to do that," explained Doherty. "What am I gonna do, sit in the locker room? I'd rather come out. I like greeting people. I like making sure our kids are going through warm-ups hard. I like to kind of eye the other team a little bit and see if that kid is really 6'8". At home games, I enjoy the give-and-take of students. Most of the time you just sit there and take it in. It's an exciting time."

The watch continued, as longtime Carolina observers made mental notes on where Doherty sat on the bench (between the players and MacKinnon), where the team sat during time-outs (in five chairs pulled out from the bench), whether the players still pointed to the passer (a Smith invention), and so on. Most observers were pleased that many of the traditions were intact.

But one of the changes most would approve of—one that was every bit as obvious to those same observers—was the intensity with which Doherty's Carolina team played. Despite the amazing success under Guthridge that included two Final Four appearances in three seasons and more wins than any coach ever in his first three seasons, a knock on the Heels was that they weren't as tough, mentally or physically, as they might have been.

Comparisons are seen as a birthright to Carolina fans, and no comparison is complete without a reference to the school up the road. Referred to as anything but the actual school name by real Tar Heel fans (some of the favorite derogatory names are "Dook"—emphasis on the "ooh" and "The State University of New Jersey at Durham"), Duke had enjoyed tremendous success against Carolina during the Guthridge era, including five straight wins. The Blue Devils' three-year run included just two regular-season ACC losses total (including an undefeated conference season in 1999—the first since Carolina's in 1987) and two ACC Tournament titles. Although UNC did defeat top-seeded Duke in 1998, the Devils returned the favor the next year.

Doherty and his Duke counterpart Mike Krzyzewski had spoken on a couple of occasions during the summer (Krzyzewski had sent Doherty a note of congratulations after getting the job) and had run into each other at an AAU event in Las Vegas, but the first extended conversation since Doherty's ascension to UNC head coach was in the parking lot at ACC Media Day a few weeks earlier—after which Doherty joked with reporters that the two had gotten in a fistfight. ACC coaches are amazingly cordial and supportive of one another, perhaps more so than in any other conference in the country. Although they compete intensely, the nine coaches who make up the league—led by veterans Krzyzewski and Dave Odom of Wake Forest—have a great deal of pride in the conference and pull for each other in nonleague games. "I was amazed at how nice everyone was," remarked new Georgia Tech coach Paul Hewitt.

But the rivalry would heat up soon. Duke was picked by the media to win the ACC and was ranked anywhere from first to third in the nation in the preseason polls. All-American Shane Battier was back, as were three other starters: point guard Jason Williams, off-guard Nate James, and center Carlos Boozer. Mike Dunleavy, son of the Portland Trailblazers' coach who had chosen Duke over UNC two years earlier, would come off the bench and was maybe the best all-around player on the team. Defeating SUNJ–Durham this season would not be easy, Doherty knew.

He also knew that Winthrop was not Duke. And while the Tar Heels wouldn't have to face the Blue Devils until February 1, that didn't stop fans from wondering how this team would fare against their biggest rivals.

Exactly six minutes into the 2000–2001 season, the Carolina faithful knew this was a new era. Doherty—irate on the sidelines following what he thought was a poor call awarding the ball out-of-bounds to Winthrop—began gesturing and yelling at official Tim Clougherty. The crowd responded with a furor, jumping to its feet in a show of support of Doherty's animated sideline demeanor. Doherty then attempted to get the attention of Brian Morrison, who was milling about in the lane waiting for a defense call, by shouting his name toward the court. "I can't whistle," he'd say after the game. "The crowd was too loud to yell, so I stomped my feet. I've got size 14s and the official must have thought I was stomping at him."

The result was a technical foul, which brought what remaining fans were still sitting to their feet. A thirty-second ovation ensued as fans applauded their new coach, whose fire and intensity were obvious as he complained vehemently to Clougherty: "I was talking to my team!" Doherty repeated over and over. At Midnight With Matt in Carmichael six weeks earlier, Doherty had half-jokingly worked the "Globetrotters" official to a similar ovation. This time, it was for real—and the UNC fans, starved for emotion on the sideline and from their team, responded. This was a different coach on the sideline, one who threw T-shirts to the crowd on his entrance into the arena and now showed the raw emotion so many of the fans felt during a game. Guthridge, who was watching the game with his wife, Leesie, in the second row of the upper deck behind the bench, remained stoic, a slight grin on his face.

The technical inspired the Heels, who were trailing undersized Winthrop at the time, 12–4. As Holmes had thought, Boone had started the game, and while he had not played poorly, the offense struggled. The reason was simple: missed shots. Forte, whose midrange, pull-up jumper off the dribble was one of the best in the country, misfired repeatedly. Boone was able to get the ball to Forte and Capel on the wing and also made some nice entries into the post to Haywood and Lang, but none of them led to scores.

Morrison entered the game after five minutes had elapsed and the tempo changed immediately. The freshman from Redmond, Washington, sprint-dribbled the ball up the floor, found Capel for a breakaway dunk, and hit two quick three-pointers. His play, and Doherty's technical, energized the crowd as the Heels tied the game at 13–13 with 11:40 remaining in the first half.

Holmes finally got his chance with 9:40 remaining in the first half when Doherty called his name to go in. In his first possession on offense, he did what he always did: snapped chest passes quickly around the Winthrop defense. His ability to move the ball quickly around the perimeter—called "reversing" the ball—was one of the reasons Doherty and the staff believed that when it came to running the team, Holmes was as good as anyone. It was also true that Holmes, at 6'0", needed to improve his quickness and shooting consistency.

Holmes' effect on the game was limited, and after five minutes Morrison was inserted back into the lineup. The game continued to go back and forth until Forte, driving the left side, wrapped the ball around his waist as he went in for the layup to put Carolina ahead, 28–25. A late mini-surge, led by another three from Morrison, pushed the advantage to 39–33 at the half, but the team—and the coaches—were not pleased.

In the locker room at halftime, Doherty urged his team to continue playing with the kind of fire and determination they had shown on defense over the last 10 minutes of the first half. Overall, the coaches were pleased with the effort, but not with the offensive execution. They had failed to take advantage of their substantial height advantage: Haywood was four inches taller than anyone Winthrop had on its roster, but two fouls in the first 20 minutes had limited his minutes. Lang had picked up the slack with 10 points and five rebounds, but the Eagles were outrebounding Carolina as a team, 18–16.

Doherty tried to keep a positive frame of mind about the first half. His team had simply missed shots while Winthrop had made some tough looks. Sometimes, despite everything you practice, all the preparation, and with all the desire you display on defense, the other team still shoots the ball in. Certainly, Doherty thought, Forte wouldn't continue his poor shooting (1-for-7 from the floor for two points) and Haywood would be able to play more than six minutes. He kept his team's spirits up and encouraged them to keep playing hard.

Winthrop, coached by Gregg Marshall, continued to play right with the taller Heels well into the second half. Boone again started— "I don't want to jerk guys in and out of the starting lineup," Doherty had proclaimed prior to the game—and the defense continued to play well. Doherty stuck with man-to-man defense, except when Winthrop had the ball out-of-bounds under its hoop, to keep pressure on the outside shooters. Forte continued to misfire, however, and Carolina's offense struggled.

Underlying everything, Winthrop continued to get to the offensive boards. All week in practice, Doherty had stressed rebounding. After an exhibition game win over the CBA's Yakima Sun Kings four days earlier, Doherty had become incensed while watching the film at the lack of Carolina's rebounding effort. When the players came to the Smith Center for practice the next day, they were greeted by dozens of flyers posted to the walls of the hallways, the inside of their lockers, and even in the toilet stall, all of which screamed for them to "BOX OUT." Doherty had reiterated the message during the pregame meal, the morning walk-through, and his pregame talk.

It wasn't working.

Despite the rebounding woes, Carolina slowly pulled away late to win, 66–61, thanks to a nine-point advantage from the free throw line.

"We out-field-goaled them and out-rebounded them by nine," Marshall lamented after the game. "It came down to free throws. I just wish we had gone to the line more."

After the game, Doherty thanked his team for getting him his first win as the Carolina coach. It was a sincere moment, but the players did not feel euphoric in the victory. Forte had shot 2-for-11 from the field. Haywood had hardly dominated the paint as he had all fall. An oversized, outmatched team had hung with them through all 40 minutes. Doherty told the players not to stick around to watch the second game of the tournament, between Arizona State and Tulsa, but to get back to their rooms and get some rest.

Sitting in his locker and staring at his shoes, Holmes tried not to get down. It was the first game, he told himself. But he had played just six minutes, only one in the second half. Hardly enough time to do anything to impress the coaches. He knew his dad, mom, and other members of his family were waiting outside, but he didn't want to face them. To his left, reporters crowded around Boone, who had played 19 minutes, and Morrison, who had scored 14 points. Freshmen were not allowed to talk to the media at all until after their first game. With the curtain of silence removed, the print and television media surrounded the two first-year guards.

Holmes showered and left without saying much to anyone. After picking up a few things in his dorm room, he ate a quick dinner with his parents and tried to get some sleep at the Hampton Suites (players who lived on campus were sequestered in a hotel the night before games because their dorm, Granville East, could "get a little rowdy on the weekends," according to Doherty, who had lived there himself not so long ago).

As the players bedded down in the hotel, the coaches scouted Tulsa and Arizona State. When that game was over a little after midnight, the staff broke down and graded the film from their own game. The screening out situation was worse than even Doherty thought; on over 50 occasions the Tar Heels had graded out as "no box out," meaning the opportunity arose when a player should have screened out and did not make the effort or executed the fundamental incorrectly.

At around 2:30 A.M., the film had been dissected and the scouting report on Tulsa, a 69–67 winner over the Sun Devils, was ready. Instead of heading home, the staff, knowing it would have to return in four hours or so, searched for a place to sleep in the Smith Center. Doherty bedded down on the couch in his office, while Quartlebaum commandeered the one in the coaches' locker room. Wojcik wound up in the players' lounge and MacKinnon in the training room.

Matt Doherty was not the only Carolina alumnus in the coaching ranks who had moved over the summer. His good friend and former teammate, Robert "Buzz" Peterson (perhaps best known as Michael Jordan's roommate at UNC), had left Appalachian State to take the job at Tulsa to replace Bill Self, who had moved on to Illinois.

The Golden Hurricane had enjoyed a remarkable season under Self in 1999–2000, going 32–5 and reaching the NCAA South Regional final. As fate would have it, Tulsa lost that game to North Carolina in what was, although no one knew it at the time, Bill Guthridge's final win. Fate further intervened as Peterson was introduced as the Tulsa head coach on June 20, nine days before Guthridge announced his retirement. If not for the timing, Peterson may very well have been in the mix for the job in Chapel Hill.

As it was, however, Peterson was faced with rebuilding a Tulsa front line that was decimated by graduation. His backcourt was solid with two starters, Dante Swanson and Greg Harrington, returning. His biggest problem in the championship game of the NABC Classic—although he wouldn't know it until game time—was that Forte and Haywood had played so poorly the night before.

That would not be the case against Tulsa. Unlike the night before, Forte felt the touch early, hitting his first three shots. During the day, Doherty had said little to Forte other than to continue taking his shots. Never one to suffer from a confidence problem, Forte took and made a tough fallaway on the baseline with 0:50 gone in the game. On the bench, MacKinnon grinned, knowing Forte's offensive game developed slow and then built, like a tidal wave.

Similarly, Haywood felt good about how he played early against Tulsa. Unlike Forte, Haywood had to rely on others to get him the ball, a fact that had been in evidence far too many times the season before. With no foul trouble to worry about, Haywood banged inside for a monstrous dunk then followed it up with two free throws, a short jumper off the glass, and two more free throws. By the time he came out for his first rest, Haywood had 8 of his team's 18 points.

Despite a much better offensive flow early, Carolina could not pull away from Tulsa. When Holmes entered the game—for Morrison, who earlier replaced Boone, the starter—at the 9:15 mark of the first half, Carolina owned just a five-point lead, 21–16. Haywood returned at the same time, and Holmes had the fleeting thought that his one advantage over the other two point guards was that he knew how best to get the ball to Haywood (the center preferred high lobs to his right hand as opposed to bounce passes low). Holmes knew he only had a few minutes to try to make a mark in the game or he might not get another chance, like last night.

And if he didn't make an impression now, he might not get another chance the rest of the season.

On the first offensive possession, Holmes hit Haywood on the left block and the big man was fouled going up for a jump-hook. He made both, pushing the lead to 23–16. Swanson scored a layup in the lane to cut the Carolina advantage back to five. Holmes immediately pushed the ball up the floor, got it back, and quickly reversed it. Forte then entered it inside to Haywood for a layup and a foul. During Haywood's free throw, Holmes jogged to the bench. "Good reversal, Jon!" yelled two of the assistants. He felt good, but refocused quickly. Doherty called for a zone. Holmes relayed the call.

Tulsa had not worked much on its zone offense—"I didn't expect that Carolina would play much zone," admitted Peterson after the game—and it showed. After each miss, Holmes pushed the ball up-court, reversed it, and found open players. The Carolina offense, for the first time in three halves, began to find a rhythm. Forte scored on a baseline fadeaway; Lang dunked and was fouled; Forte knocked down a three. With 3:15 remaining before halftime, Carolina had taken a commanding 17-point lead.

Holmes was juiced. He dove on the floor twice for loose balls, which elicited an immediate reaction from the bench and the crowd. Tulsa, however, found its shooting touch and hit 3 three-point bombs; 2 of which, from Marcus Hill, could have brought rain.

With just over a minute on the clock before halftime, Holmes set up to take a charge on David Shelton, Tulsa's 6'6", 230-pound senior forward. As this game was part of an exempted preseason tournament game, the NCAA Rules Committee was experimenting with a dotted circle on the floor around the basket. A defensive player set up outside the circle could take a charge; if he was set up inside, it was either incidental contact or a block.

Holmes' back heel was on the perforated circle as Shelton slammed into him, the full force of the Tulsa player landing on top of Holmes as his head hit the floor. No call. Johnson tipped the miss in to pull the Golden Hurricane to within six points. Holmes missed the tip-in completely, as he was momentarily woozy from the blow and couldn't get up.

Longtime Carolina trainer Marc Davis—known as "Skate" to the players, a nickname given to him (even before Doherty's playing days) because of the way Davis shuffled his feet when he walked—was on the floor in seconds, asking Holmes a series of memory questions. Holmes was OK—Doherty came out to check on him, and Holmes told him quickly that he was fine—and jumped up to tell Boone, his replacement, what defense they were in and who he was guarding.

At the half, Doherty was pleased, despite seeing the 17-point lead whittled down to 6. Forte and Haywood combined for 33 of Carolina's 42 points. Doherty told the team to do more of the same on offense and to continue to locate Tulsa's shooters on defense. The staff urged Doherty to continue using the zone.

Haywood and Lang continued to dominate in the second half. After Haywood was fouled and hit a turnaround jumper, Peterson turned to no one in particular and said, "He's just too big." Quickly, Carolina's lead was back up to 18 points after Forte hit another three. Holmes was again the third point guard into the game, but he played the majority of minutes as the offense again clicked when he ran it. He hit his first jumper of the season when Shelton left him to double Forte: As he received the pass in front of the Carolina bench, Holmes could hear Doherty yelling behind him, "Shoot it!" He did. The three-pointer at the 3:38 mark effectively ended the game. When Holmes was taken out with 23 seconds left he had scored nine points, two more than he had all of last season.

"You played a helluva game, Jon. You ran the team," Doherty told him as the team exited the floor after the 91–81 victory. He'd smile at that later when his dad and he relived the game at his parents' hotel room late into the night.

After the game, Doherty hugged his old pal Peterson, shook everyone's hand, and watched the short trophy presentation. He was drained but energized as he jogged off with his players.

He was 2–0 as the coach at North Carolina.

Once everyone was in the locker room, the coaches shut the door so just the players, managers, and coaches were present. The players noticed immediately that their coach was emotional, but they weren't surprised. They knew him well enough by now to know that they were playing for an intense, wear-his-heart-on-his-sleeve coach. The enthusiasm was becoming infectious.

"We played well tonight, guys," said Doherty. "We won a tournament on our home floor, and that's always a positive. We've got three more of these tournaments to win, one in Charlotte (the Hardee's Tournament of Champions), the ACC Tournament, and the NCAAs."

Doherty paused and looked around the silent room.

"But Coach MacKinnon," Doherty continued, "do these guys look like they know how to celebrate a tournament victory?"

"No coach, they sure don't!" MacKinnon said in an overly loud voice inside the tiny space.

With that, Doherty animatedly instructed the players to get up and back their chairs up against the wall, clearing the middle of the locker room. All of the coaches walked into the center of the room as the play-ers and managers looked on with quizzical looks.

The chant—more of a barking sound, really—began first. Then Doherty put his long arms in the air and began jumping up and down, whooping and hollering. Wojcik, Quartlebaum, MacKinnon, and Cason all joined in the spontaneous mosh pit, chest-bumping tie-against-tie amid the cacophony of shouts and cheers. The players and managers fell over themselves laughing, stunned at watching their coaches "teaching" them how to celebrate. Soon the players joined in, and the room erupted in sound and large, gyrating bodies.

The season had begun.

10

Role Player

With a Long Island basketball pedigree, a New York state championship, and an appearance in the McDonald's High School All-American game under his belt, Matt Doherty arrived in Chapel Hill the summer before his freshman season for a three-week stretch to work and play with the North Carolina players—both past and present. It was a period Doherty both looked forward to and feared.

When he walked into Carmichael Auditorium in June 1980 he looked around and saw Dudley Bradley, Tommy LaGarde, John Kuester, Mitch Kupchak, Walter Davis, and Mike O'Koren—all of whom were or would be professional players—as well as James Worthy, Al Wood, and others with whom he would play that season. The first pick-up game started, and it was incredibly competitive and fast-paced, unlike anything he had experienced before, even at Prospect Park. Just a few plays in, he found the ball in his hand and an open shot from the free throw line. Instinctively, he rose up and shot, anxious to show that he could play.

The shot missed everything.

"I started to think 'Oh my gosh, can I play at this level?'" remembers Doherty. "I didn't realize, well, these guys are the pros. These are the best players in the world. Guys like Kuester, O'Koren, Kupchak, they really made me feel comfortable and gave me confidence. I felt like I got better in that week." But that didn't help his homesickness. Missing his family and feeling overwhelmed by his surroundings, Doherty cut the three-week trip to Chapel Hill short and headed back home after only seven days.

A few months later, he was back in Chapel Hill with a better idea of what he was up against, but nonetheless anxious to take on the challenge of playing at North Carolina. With Mike O'Koren—a player Doherty looked up to a great deal—leading the way the previous season, the 1979–80 Tar Heels had tied for second place in the ACC with NC State (behind Maryland). But the season ended in disappointment as the Tar Heels lost their last two games; to Duke in the ACC Tournament semifinals and to Texas A&M in its first NCAA Tournament game.

O'Koren was gone, but Smith had brought in Doherty, Cecil Exum, and Sam Perkins—at the time a shy, soft-spoken kid who had been mentored by his high school coach in upstate New York. With incredibly long arms, a sleepy-eyed expression, and large feet, Perkins was thought to be a project. But he also had great hands and a deceptive shooting touch. "From the first few pick-up games, it was pretty obvious that Sam was a special player," said Doherty.

Walter and Mary Doherty made the trip with their son—in a station wagon borrowed from Matt's sister—to drop him off in what would be his home for the next four years. An emotional family to begin with, the Dohertys were all in tears as they dropped their son and Perkins off for a Spanish placement exam, after which they were leaving to head back to Long Island.

"They were going to leave right from there to go back to New York with my brother," remembered Doherty. "We were saying good-bye and getting emotional, as we do. And as I walked away from the car, I turned to Sam and said, 'I'm glad that's over.' I was wiping tears from my eyes.

"So, we take the test and go to the gym to play some ball, and I'm running back on defense and I see my family walk in the gym. After a moment there was a break in the play and I walk over. 'What are you doing here?' I asked. 'The car broke down,' they said. So they had to stay an extra day.

"And we had to go through that whole good-bye ordeal again."

Doherty's emotion would soon have to exist in a program that took a strictly businesslike approach to winning.

Adjusting to college life, Doherty began to learn about living with others (Jim Braddock was his first roommate) and life in the south. "He [Braddock] was the first guy I had ever known who dipped Skoal." Doherty continued to get homesick, but less and less as the days went by. "[Former UNC assistant coach and then assistant athletic director] John Lotz was a major influence on Matt," said Mary. "He went over to Mr. Lotz's house when he was homesick to watch TV, eat dinner, and just talk." Knowing that time home would be scarce after basketball practice started, Doherty took a long weekend trip to Long Island in early October. When he got back to Chapel Hill and practices kicked into high gear, he rarely had time to think about anything other than basketball and school.

Smith, as Guthridge had been before, was impressed by Doherty's ability to handle the ball on the perimeter. More specifically, Doherty could pass and play defense, although the latter was improving. Smith's practices were incredibly organized and intense, with no wasted time between drills.

The orderliness suited Doherty well.

While he was being recruited, Doherty had analyzed Carolina's roster, looking to see who would be his competition for playing time. When he looked at the Carolina roster, he saw that Mike Pepper would be a senior. "My thought was that, hopefully, I could play behind them for a year and then step up when they graduate," he said.

It happened exactly as he had hoped. When the season began in Alaska, Doherty was the first player off the bench for either Pepper or small forward Al Wood. In winning the Great Alaska Shootout, a home game versus Mercer, and splitting two games in the Big Four Tournament, Doherty averaged 25 minutes per game. In just his first six weeks Doherty had gained the confidence of his coach—not an easy task—and had even contributed the deciding free throws in the first game of the Big Four, a win over Duke. "He was not a starter, but yet, was extremely important to us," recalled Roy Williams, then a Carolina assistant coach. "He was a young man going through a process of deciding how he was going to be important. He was trying to find his niche. He was trying to find a way he could get on that court and help our team win."

Doherty had found a way to contribute—by finding the open man on offense and playing solid position defense—and his confidence began to grow. The team was winning, and he was playing an important part. It was exactly what he had imagined while working on his game, alone, in the early mornings and late evenings at Prospect Park.

Exams were just getting over in mid-December when Doherty decided to take a break and go to the Varsity Theater, where the new hit *Stir Crazy* was playing. He was there with friends when, about halfway through the movie, he got up to get some popcorn. As he scrambled over legs and feet as he headed for the aisle, Doherty tripped over teammate Pete Budko's leg and began to fall. As he did, he instinctively put his left hand out, trying to catch himself on the back of a theater seat. But his hand landed awkwardly on the seat back, and Doherty heard a sickening pop as he fell.

He had broken his left thumb.

"We were playing Indiana in two days," Doherty recalled. "It was on national TV, I remember, and the NBC trucks were outside, and I was upset because I couldn't play. I missed five weeks."

Dr. Tim Taft (who was then and still is the team surgeon) put a metal pin in Doherty's thumb to fit across the joint and fused a wire into the joint to hold the fragments together. Taft took the cast off of Doherty's thumb on January 16, and Doherty played eight days later against Wake Forest. But his timing was off, and his play was sporadic for the remainder of the regular season. The Tar Heels would eventually finish in second place in the ACC, losing an overtime game at Duke in the regular-season finale.

Doherty's struggles continued in the ACC Tournament ("I played like crap," he told reporters then), but Carolina won the crown, defeating Maryland by a single point in the final. Entering his first NCAA Tournament, Doherty was personally discouraged, but his spirit was buoyed by the team's play. During the tough stretch, he went back to his roots, consulting Bob McKillop and Father Bud. "Don't sit back and watch. Go ahead and do what you can do," McKillop urged.

On the trip to El Paso for a first-round NCAA matchup with Pittsburgh, Doherty did not know how much he would play. When he entered the game for Pepper, he hit his first shot and, suddenly, his tentative play disappeared. He took shots—and made them. In 16 minutes he scored seven points and grabbed four rebounds. It wasn't much, but it was an important confidence booster. Carolina won the game 74–57 and advanced to the West Regional Finals in Salt Lake City.

There, Doherty shined. In two decisive wins Doherty scored 28 points and played almost 50 minutes. It was a decisive weekend in his playing career, but more important, Carolina was heading back to the Final Four.

Prior to the national semifinal game with Virginia, Smith bumped into Mary and Walter Doherty, who had made the trip from Long Island. "We don't get to these every year, so don't get too used to it," said Smith. A 13-point win over the Cavaliers put the Tar Heels into the national championship game. The run ended when Indiana, led by Isiah Thomas, defeated North Carolina in the championship game. The loss was tough for Doherty to take, but the talk that followed about Smith's inability to win "the big one" strengthened the players' resolve to get back to the final game.

And win it.

With every player who played a significant role on the team returning except Al Wood and Mike Pepper (the two players, coincidentally, who played ahead of Doherty), North Carolina was everyone's pick to win the NCAA title in 1981–82. With one superstar (Worthy), a great rebounder (Perkins), a solid point guard (Black), and a savvy role player (Doherty) already in the mix, Smith needed only to add one piece to the puzzle to push Carolina over the threshold that would make a good team great. He needed an athletic shooting guard; someone who could rebound, make open shots, and play defense.

What he got was Michael Jordan.

Matt Doherty recalls seeing the then-skinny kid from Wilmington while Michael was on his official recruiting visit the year before: "I remember seeing him take a basketball and go up and dunk with two hands with no problem—in his jeans and a polo shirt."

"He was very gregarious, very confident," Doherty remembered. "As a freshman, Michael was a very serious kid. Very neat. His clothes looked nice. They were always neatly pressed. He was very aware of his presence. He always had a clean haircut and things like that. He really listened—he was a good listener. And he played hard."

Doherty was hoping to start at his normal position—the 3-spot, or small forward position—which meant Jordan would be the 2-guard, if he could make the leap from Laney High School star to member of the Tar Heels. After just a few practices, it was apparent to the upperclassmen and even to Smith that Jordan could and would be able to handle the pressure.

A special team was born that fall. Despite the hype and obvious talent level of this squad, Smith continued business-as-usual, running his program with a strict set of rules and pecking order. When *Sports Illustrated* wanted to put the Carolina starting five on its college basketball preseason issue, Smith said OK, but only the four returning players. Freshmen—who were relegated to chasing down errant basketballs in practice and carrying the dreaded "green bag" on road trips—were not going to be on any magazine cover.

When the season began, Doherty's confidence grew and his play blossomed. He had found the niche in which he could contribute and, unlike most high school all-Americans, was more than content with the inevitable "role player" label. It was an angle played up in the local and national media ad nauseam. (Later, when Doherty was hired as the head coach at North Carolina, Sports Information Director Steve Kirschner would go back through the files of articles about Doherty and be amazed that nearly every single one contained the term *role player*.)

"We got along very well," Doherty said about that 1981–82 team. "We respected each other. On a team, you don't always have to be best friends with everybody; you don't always have to hang out with everybody. But I think we got along well. We had good leadership with Jimmy Black and James [Worthy]. We were all pretty serious about it—and unselfish. James could have averaged 30 points per game if he wanted to. But his personality was great. He's a very welcoming guy. James would make everybody feel comfortable. We just wanted to win. We had great balance on our team. We didn't have that much depth, but we had great balance."

It was evident early that this team could handle the expectations of being ranked No. 1 in the preseason as it won its first 13 games. Doherty played well during the stretch, scoring 61 points in the team's first five games. When Wake Forest came to town in mid-January, however, Doherty had cooled down and was beginning to question his shooting. Local beat reporters began to write that Doherty was the master of the shot fake, often passing up wide open shots to try to force the ball to Worthy or Perkins, the first two options in the Carolina offense.

It all came to a head at home against Wake Forest when the Tar Heels, playing without an injured Sam Perkins, scored just 48 points (it was another year before the ACC would bring in a shot clock). Even with their record, the Tar Heels, and Doherty, came under fire. "Maybe a few times I didn't shoot when I should have." Doherty said then. "Coach Smith said not to worry about the armchair coaches and to keep doing what I had been doing." After three straight ACC wins, Carolina was thumped by a Ralph Sampson–led Virginia squad in Charlottesville, 75–58.

It was the last game Carolina would lose that season.

Clemson would employ the same strategy as Wake had, letting Doherty and Black alone while blanketing Worthy, Perkins, and

Jordan. Eventually, Doherty began to feel more confident with his shooting, and with all pistons firing, Carolina breezed all the way to the ACC Tournament Final, where it won, 47–45, over Virginia in a game that saw Smith go into a six-minute stall in the second half before coach Terry Holland finally came out of his zone and began to chase. Doherty hit 3-of-4 free throws down the stretch to secure the win.

But it was in the NCAA Tournament that this team would either become the one that finally won Dean Smith his first NCAA title or be yet another disappointing chapter in a painful story.

"It was definitely a conscious thought between me and my team-mates; we wanted to win a championship for Coach Smith," recalled Doherty. "He had won so many things, and everyone was talking about how he had never won a championship, so it was important to us to do that for him. And it was important to do it for us. Our goal all year was to win a national championship. We had come up a hair short the year before. We were preseason No. 1 in the country, and we wanted to fin-ish it off."

It would not be easy. After a serious scare against James Madison in the opening round, Carolina rolled over Alabama and Villanova in Raleigh to reach the Final Four in New Orleans. A slug-fest semifinal win over Houston—which featured Clyde Drexler and a young, raw Hakeem Olajuwon—put UNC in the final against Georgetown, a team coached by Smith's good friend John Thompson.

It was a classic game, one that would earn distinction as one of the greatest NCAA final games ever played. Moments from that game are burned not only in the minds of Tar Heel fans but in the memories of all sports aficionados: Patrick Ewing goaltending Carolina's first five shots. . . Worthy's incredible scoring duel with fellow Gastonia native Sleepy Floyd . . . Jordan hitting The Shot . . . Fred Brown's ill-advised pass.

But for Doherty the memory that sticks with him all these years is one that was not so sweet and underlined a vivid fear of failure that extended throughout his playing and coaching career.

With a little over a minute to go and Carolina ahead by one point, Doherty was fouled by Eric Smith. Having dreamed about this moment,

Doherty strode confidently to the line. He was the team's second-best free throw shooter, behind Jimmy Braddock. If he made the two free throws he knew his team would be in the driver's seat, forcing Georgetown to have to score on two consecutive possessions to tie. (The three-point line was not yet in effect.)

Twenty feet from the man for whom he desperately wanted to win, Doherty cradled the ball, bounced it three times, and shot the front end of a one-and-one. No good.

"I was really . . . that shook me up," said Doherty, still bothered to this day. "You dream about being in that situation, making foul shots at a key moment in the game, and I missed one."

Floyd immediately scored on a 12-foot jumper, putting the Hoyas up by one point. Dean Smith called time-out and gathered the team around him, speaking as calmly as if it were the first day of practice back in Carmichael. "I had to look up at the clock to make sure we were the team behind," said Roy Williams. When the huddle broke after he had drawn up a play to go to Worthy, Smith—knowing that Georgetown would do everything it could to deny Worthy the ball—told Jordan and Doherty in separate comments to be ready to knock in the shot if it came to them. Of course, the shot came to Michael, and one legend—Smith's—was cemented, while another one was born.

In the end, Doherty's missed free throw was a side note. He had not lost the game—he had, in fact, with his solid floor game, gone a long way toward winning it. He still remembers that victory (just as he views winning today) as a relief, rather than as a celebration. "I remember sitting in the locker room after the game, just the satisfaction of looking around the locker room and looking into your teammates' eyes and saying, 'We did it.' "

Doherty's junior season, 1982–83, was punctuated by the loss of Worthy to the NBA, Michael Jordan coming into his own ("he improved more between his freshman and sophomore seasons than during any other period," said Smith), and a need for Doherty to score more. He did, averaging in double digits (10.5 points per game), the only season in his career when he would do so. But it was a disappointing season in many ways, as Doherty was required to move to the 4-spot frequently until freshman Brad Daugherty could overcome injuries and develop into the player he would later become.

The team achieved mixed results, by Carolina standards. It started out disastrous as the Tar Heels lost their first two games to St. John's and Missouri. (North Carolina had not lost its opening two games of the season since 1928–29 and has not lost its first two games since.) A three-overtime victory over Tulane in their third game did not build a great deal of momentum, as a loss to Tulsa three games later attested.

But then the Heels went on a 17-game winning streak and built a 9–0 record in the ACC. The 17th straight win was perhaps the most exciting, as Carolina roared back from a 10-point deficit against Virginia with just over four minutes remaining to trail by just three with 1:20 on the clock. After Braddock missed a three, Jordan rebounded and scored to pull the Heels to within 63–62. Jordan then stole the ball from Rick Carlisle at midcourt and dunked for a one-point Carolina lead and— after Virginia failed to score on its final possession—the win.

But the thrilling victory had its cost, as Carolina lost the next three games it played. Four regular-season wins followed and gave the Heels a share of the regular-season ACC title, but the team was not playing well as tournament time neared. Daugherty was hampered by a stress fracture in his foot, forcing Perkins to play center and moving Doherty to power forward. The result was a semifinal loss to NC State in the ACC Tournament. After two wins in the NCAAs, Carolina was upset by Georgia, and its season was over.

Despite the best scoring output of his college career, Doherty was bitterly disappointed after his junior season. The team had not performed up to what he saw as its ability, and what was worse, his shooting had been suspect yet again. In back-to-back wins over Wake Forest and Georgia Tech in the middle of Carolina's 17-game win streak, Doherty had missed 14-of-15 shots. He rebounded to play well in the ACC Tournament, earning second-team honors, but the lingering doubts were beginning to trouble him more and more as he entered his senior season.

Ever the perfectionist, Doherty was greatly disturbed after the team came back from a preseason trip to Greece prior to the 1983–84 season. He had not played well on the trip, and he was at his wit's end trying to solve his shooting woes. He had begun to question his technique as he shot, reminding himself about putting backspin on the ball or shooting with enough arc. With his senior season—a season prognosticators said could be the best UNC team ever—in jeopardy of unraveling before it started, Doherty went searching for help.

"He really had a tremendous battle trying to make himself into a great jump-shooter," recalled McKillop. "He thought that Brian Winters, who had played at Molloy High School and at South Carolina before going on to the NBA, had the most picture-perfect technique and form. Matt, in a very conscientious way, would always say that 'I'm not good enough as a shooter. I have to get better as a shooter.' It was something he consistently worked on throughout his college career."

Doherty found Dr. Richard Coop, a sports psychologist on campus, and had several sessions with him. Coop subscribed to the theory of right brain versus left brain, which stated that the areas of the brain that controlled instinct (the right brain) and analytical thought (left brain) often fought over control. "I need to be more right-brained," Doherty joked then. "I'm very analytical. With me, it's always been that the harder I work, the better I do. But with the jump shot, that's not necessarily so." Throughout the season, Doherty would remind himself to be more "right-brained" by whispering words to himself when he felt himself overanalyzing. "Flow," he'd say to himself, or "smooth."

While Doherty struggled with his shooting, the team was coming together as Brad Daugherty became healthy and Kenny Smith, a freshman from New York City, grew into the role of point guard. Of course, Jordan and Perkins were the most potent one-two punch in college basketball, both coming into their own as well-rounded players. Doherty again filled a role, finding open men, playing solid defense, providing leadership, and doing his best to hit open shots when they came to him. "I don't think he was as vocal or demonstrative, but he was every bit the leader," said Dave Odom, then a Virginia assistant and later the longtime head coach at Wake Forest. "Outward emotion wasn't part of the modus operandi. They took a more businesslike approach."

The result was a 21-game win streak that stretched from the opening game win over Missouri through a February 9 victory at Virginia. Even a one-point loss at Arkansas the next game did not dampen the expectations that this Carolina team was the best ever, as the Tar Heels won the ACC regular season by an astounding *five games*.

Doherty's entire family made the trip from New York to see him play in his final home game in Carmichael. The opponent was Duke. In his fourth season, Blue Devils' coach Mike Krzyzewski had finally broken through (and likely saved his job) by putting together a team that would finish 24–10 and included the nucleus of Johnny Dawkins, Tommy Amaker, Jay Bilas, David Henderson, and Mark Alarie. Still relatively young when they came into Carmichael to take on the No. 1 team in the nation, the Blue Devils were nonetheless hungry for an upset.

They almost got it.

Ahead most of the game, Duke entered the final 20 seconds with a 73–71 lead, thanks to a three-point play by Alarie. With 10 seconds remaining and Carolina on offense, Steve Hale missed a shot from the corner, and Duke's Danny Meagher collected the rebound. Daugherty immediately fouled Meagher, who went to the line with a chance to put Carolina away. But he missed the front end of the one-and-one, and Perkins rebounded, immediately calling time-out.

Carolina was down by two points and had to go the length of the floor in seven seconds.

Krzyzewski instructed Dawkins and Amaker that under no circumstances was Jordan to get the ball. "They were all over me," Jordan said. The two Duke guards were successful in denying Jordan, so Joe Wolf was forced to inbound the ball to Doherty. Without hesitation, Doherty began sprint-dribbling up-court. "I'm looking for Michael and I can't find him," he recalled then. "I *had* to put it up."

Doherty did, jump-stopping and launching a jumper from about 12 feet over Meagher. He did not think about it; he just shot.

Flow.

The shot went in, and Carmichael nearly lost its roof. On the second row of stands behind the Carolina bench, Walter and Mary cried tears of joy. The game went into two overtimes before Carolina finally got control and won, but history would remember Doherty's shot and what it meant; North Carolina had become the first team to go undefeated in ACC regular-season play since 1974.

"You look back on several games as a player, and that game was probably one of the most memorable for me as well as the 1982 championship game," said Doherty. "That game, your last home game, to hit a shot at the buzzer to put it into overtime . . ."

In the ultimate cruelty of college basketball, the euphoria would last exactly 19 days, when it would be replaced by the thing he feared most: losing.

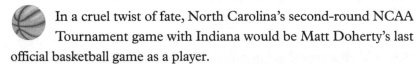 In a cruel twist of fate, North Carolina's second-round NCAA Tournament game with Indiana would be Matt Doherty's last official basketball game as a player.

The pain from that loss was the type that transcended the years. One reason was that the Hoosiers that season were not a great basketball team. Bobby Knight, their coach, was known for his ability to prepare his team exceedingly well for an opponent, particularly when given time. But North Carolina had its own legendary coach in Smith, and being outclassed in preparation for a game just didn't happen.

The Tar Heels were also not playing particularly well in the weeks leading up to the NCAA Tournament, having lost to Duke in the ACC Tournament semifinals just one week after Doherty bailed them out with his late-game heroics. But that was to be expected after losing just one regular-season game *all year*. A slight letdown before a march to a second championship seemed natural and might even serve as motivation, the Tar Heel backers believed.

Nothing occurred in the days leading up to the game or during warm-ups that even hinted at the disaster to follow. The baskets in the

Omni in Atlanta were 10 feet, there was no poor shooting background or breeze coming through the arena. It was just the basketball gods reminding Carolina that it was not always a just world—and that in the one-and-done world of the NCAA Tournament, anything could happen.

The causes, in hindsight, were easy to determine. Foul trouble plagued the Tar Heels almost from the beginning, as junior Player of the Year Michael Jordan picked up two early fouls and played little in the first half, as Smith elected to save his best player from getting his third foul in the first half. (Ironically, Doherty, in his first season as coach at Carolina, would consider the same strategy and be counseled by Smith to *leave a player in* with two fouls in the first half.) Over the years, the story of Indiana's Dan Dakich (now head coach at Bowling Green State University) having shut down Jordan has grown into legendary status, but the truth was, it was the Hoosiers' offensive execution, continually splitting UNC traps for easy baskets and utilizing their passing proficiency for back-door layups and easy jumpers, that won the game.

North Carolina never led after the middle of the first half, despite a manic second half in which the Tar Heels and Dean Smith tried everything. Carolina would get to within two points late, but as time wound down, it became evident to seniors Sam Perkins, Cecil Exum, and Doherty (and later Jordan, who would skip his senior season and declare for the NBA draft) that their college basketball careers were over.

For Doherty, it came like a punch in the gut.

Late in the game, Doherty fouled IU's Mike Giomi on a breakaway layup in a last-ditch effort to stop the clock. It was his fifth foul. The intense disappointment washed over him after the referee's whistle. It was all over. He walked in a fog toward the Indiana bench and shook Knight's hand (beginning a habit of never forgetting to publicly congratulate an opponent after a bitter loss) and then walked with his head down to the end of the Carolina bench, sat down, and buried his head in a towel.

It was the only college basketball game in which Matt Doherty had ever fouled out.

After the final buzzer sounded on the 72–68 defeat, Smith spoke to his team briefly in the locker room, unable to hold back tears of his own.

He reminded them that the best team didn't always win. He thanked them for their effort. He could speak for only a few moments. "I knew it was over then," recalled Doherty. "I remember in the locker room after the game; Woody Durham was trying to interview me. I was so upset, I couldn't talk."

After speaking to the players, Smith tried to make sense of it in front of the media.

"The reason it is disappointing," Smith said, "is because this is the third time I thought we had the best team in the country. I thought we were the best team in 1977 . . . and again in 1982, when we did win."

The finality of his college career coming to a screeching halt is a situation no college athlete can fully come to grips with, often for several years. For Doherty, to have it end so harshly and so publicly, it was all that much worse. His acute fear of losing now had a benchmark.

Seventeen years later the pain is so real and so fresh he can almost touch it.

"I'm still not over it. I'm really not. There will be moments when it will pop into my head, maybe when I'm getting ready to close my eyes at night or driving down the highway or on a plane, something, for whatever reason, the thought will pop into my head. I don't know if I'll ever get over it. That loss hurts more than any loss I've ever had because we had the best team in the country. We had the best coach in the country. And that's the cruelty of the NCAA Tournament: If it was a best of seven series, we'd have won the national championship, no problem."

Although he didn't know it at the time, Doherty was heading into a six-month period where failure, for the first time in his life, would have its way with him. Following the Indiana loss, Doherty went on a barnstorming tour across the state with other college seniors whose eligibility was used up, playing basketball in the evenings and golf in the afternoons. The rigorous schedule added to back pain Doherty first felt during his senior season, but he kept pushing himself, hoping to stay in shape and improve his chances at playing professional basketball.

Doherty attended predraft camps in Portsmouth, Virginia, and Chicago that showcased players to professional scouts. Scouting in the mid-1980s was not nearly as comprehensive as it is today, despite the draft containing nine rounds and over 200 selections (as opposed to the two rounds it is today). Doherty's game—unselfish, strong passing skills, based more on a good head than a quick pair of feet—did not exactly fit into the me-first style exhibited in the meat market setting of such an event.

"I went to those camps and my game wasn't suited to what they were looking for," Doherty recalled. "They wanted guys who could beat you off the dribble. I wasn't a great shooter. You're hoping you're going to knock down shots. So I understood a little bit, but I was hoping I'd be drafted in the third round."

The day of the draft, he was speaking to several hundred campers at the Campbell College Basketball Camp. Prior to giving his talk, Doherty called Linda Woods, the longtime secretary in the UNC basketball office, to ask if there was any word. The draft had begun several hours prior.

"Not yet," she said.

Doherty started to grow concerned. He began speaking to the kids, who were attentive and lively, but his mind was elsewhere. About halfway through, the camp director interrupted, stepped up beside him, and spoke in his ear. He had just been selected in the draft. In the sixth round. By the Cleveland Cavaliers.

It was not good news.

"I'm in front of 200, 300 campers and I'm starting to lose it," recalled Doherty. "That was not what I wanted to hear. I'm fighting back tears, trying to keep my composure, trying to talk to these kids, and all I can think about was: Cleveland Cavaliers? They were terrible. Sixth round? Nobody makes it in the sixth round. I thought I'd be drafted higher. The thought occurred to me that it was probably George Karl doing Coach Smith a favor." Karl, a UNC guard in the early 1970s for Smith, was the coach of the Cavaliers at the time.

"I saw this young man invest every muscle, every fiber in his body to become the greatest he could become and sacrificing in the process not only relationships and time and energy but also a role," said Bob McKillop. "He chose to be a champion instead of an individual star. Then, to be selected in the sixth round, it was very difficult for him. He may not say that, but I know it was very difficult for him. It was shocking to me. Absolutely shocking."

Doherty, ever the competitor, was intent on proving everyone wrong by making the team, but his back pain precluded him from playing in the Cavs' rookie camp. When he could finally play, he went to camp with the veterans in September. After only a few days, it was apparent that his playing career was over.

"George Karl put his hand on my shoulder and said: 'There comes a time when you've got to look for something else to do in your life,'" Doherty remembered. "Again, I'm trying to fight back the emotion of it. I did hurt my back—I ended up getting back surgery a couple years later—but that wasn't the reason I didn't make it. I just wasn't good enough."

Coming out of North Carolina as a three-year starter, Doherty had assumed that professional basketball was a viable option. "There was a little false sense of security, I think, having been a three-year starter at North Carolina and being around all these NBA players," Doherty said. "[You think] you're a good player and you'll have a chance to play in the NBA. And looking back, that wasn't good. I should have had a little more of a sense of fear, a sense of desperation."

When he was cut, Doherty immediately began to purge basketball from his life. "It was like a girl who breaks up with you. You've been loyal to her, done everything right. All of a sudden she turns her back on you. I felt like basketball did that to me. It was such a big part of my life. I didn't know what to do without it. It hurt."

Always the model student-athlete, Doherty had been preparing for life after basketball without ever really thinking he'd have to use the student internships he'd had on Wall Street.

The life of a trader appealed to him because it had nothing to do with basketball, but it had a similar feel; an excitement and a rush, where his competitive instincts could flow. A former UNC football player, Max Chapman, was the president of Kidder-Peabody at the time. That was his in. Doherty interviewed in the fall of 1984 and was working on Wall Street by January of 1985.

"I thought that would be a cool thing to do," Doherty said. "Part of the reason I went to Wall Street, it was a lot like a locker room setting. The energy you get from the trading floor. You can make money. And it was a cool thing to say to people. They'd ask, 'What are doing now?' And I could say, 'Well, I'm not playing in the NBA, but I'm working on Wall Street.'"

Doherty had found a sedative for the pain of failing to achieve his goals and dreams as a basketball player. But it would be a temporary relief.

Boone, NC

The celebration of the first two wins of the season was short-lived. Despite a 2–0 start and the arrival of the three letters of intent from recruits Jawad Williams, Jackie Manuel, and Melvin Scott over the weekend, Matt Doherty and his staff were discouraged by the rebounding problems. The good news was that Carolina had a full week of practice to work on rebounding and other fundamentals prior to a game on Friday at Appalachian State.

Typically, North Carolina would never have played an in-state school out of its own arena. For years, Dean Smith and Bill Guthridge had avoided playing schools such as UNC–Charlotte or one of the other schools in the state that was not a member of the ACC. The exceptions came when schools were coached by a UNC alumnus, which was how the Appalachian State game came to be on this year's schedule.

Buzz Peterson had been the coach at Appalachian when the game—that would open ASU's brand-new 8,325-seat Seby Jones Arena in Boone, North Carolina—was scheduled. Of course, Peterson had left Appalachian during the summer to take the job at Tulsa, the school Carolina had just defeated in the final of the NABC Classic.

Doherty was not thrilled by the game, but he had no choice but to play it. In many ways, it was a no-win situation for Carolina: win, and you were supposed to win; lose, and it's a disaster that wouldn't be forgotten about for a long, long time, particularly by alumni of both schools, many of whom worked and lived side by side. In the week prior to the game, Doherty restated a slightly altered UNC policy to not play an in-state opponent unless there was a personal or alumni connection. That left North Carolina A&T, coached by UNC alumnus Curtis Hunter, and Davidson, where Doherty got his start in coaching under his old high school coach Bob McKillop, the head coach at the 1,700-student school.

Practices that week were particularly intense as Doherty and his staff zeroed in on the fundamental errors they had seen in the tapes of the two games. Early in the week, practices were attended by faculty members who had a UNC player in their class and by select Educational Foundation members. By Wednesday, practice was again closed to all but two members of the Tar Heel Sports Network broadcast team, who got a taste of Doherty's intensity and attention to detail.

The practice began simply, with almost 45 minutes of shooting drills. The poor shooting performance against Winthrop still bothered Doherty, so he put a special emphasis on the perimeter players being ready to shoot when the pass arrived. He went over several fundamentals: "Have the left foot already pointed at the basket . . . hands up, ready to catch the pass . . . when the ball arrives, already be moving your feet into position." In addition, Doherty and his staff emphasized confidence to his young point guards. Boone, the starter, had yet to score in a game; Morrison had shown little fear in putting the ball up, but Doherty liked that about his young gunslinger; Holmes also had to be ready to shoot when his man left to double-team one of the other players, as he was against Tulsa.

As Wednesday's practice progressed, Doherty became increasingly frustrated with the lack of enthusiasm. Midweek practices—particularly during weeks where there was just one game on the weekend—could sometimes suffer from this type of malaise. With nothing immediate to focus on—practicing specifically for Appalachian State would not begin in earnest until Thursday—players often lost focus as their minds wandered. Doherty and his staff were trying to combat that, to little avail.

Wandering the most was Brendan Haywood. Haywood was usually a hard worker who, like an increasing number of players in his generation, required a good-sized amount of outward discipline. If he was given the opportunity to relax and not work as hard as he should, he—like almost any other college-aged male—would take that opportunity.

He was pushing his coaches today, and Doherty was letting him know it. One of Doherty's most oft-repeated directions was for the players to halt immediately in place when he stopped the action and to watch him closely as he instructed a specific player or the group on what he wanted accomplished. Frequently, his comments on this day were directed at Haywood.

Sensing the session was going quickly downhill, Doherty threatened significant running after practice if things did not improve. They didn't, as plays were being botched (even with no defense) and defensive intensity waned. When senior reserve Michael Brooker took a charge, the entire team followed the team rule and sprinted over to help up their fallen teammate. The entire team, that is, except Forte, who bent over to tie his shoe.

Incensed, Doherty immediately stopped the action with a shrill blow on his whistle. "Get back on the ground, Mike!" Doherty shouted. Brooker immediately resumed his position flat on his back. "Joe, when your teammate falls, go PICK HIM UP!!" When Doherty blew the whistle again, Forte sprinted over, grabbed both of Brooker's hands at the wrists, and nearly pulled his arms out of his sockets as Brooker rocketed to his feet. Creating an on-the-spot drill, Doherty then had Forte repeat picking Brooker up twice.

The final straw came a few minutes later after the players were finishing up shooting free throws when Haywood, out of the action and on the sideline, decided to sneak a drink of water from the coaches' own water cups when they weren't looking. Doherty, who gave the players several regularly scheduled drink breaks (typically after a prescribed number of free throws had been made) during a two-and-a-half-hour practice, turned and saw Haywood just as the seven-footer was tipping back one of the coaches' water cups.

Without hesitating, Doherty pointed at Haywood and then at the tunnel. "Brendan, get out!!!" Haywood sprinted for the locker room. (Following practice, Doherty told Haywood he would get no water breaks with the rest of the team during practice for the remainder of the season; he could get water only when a coach specifically told him he could.) After banishing Haywood, Doherty then turned to the two members of the radio broadcast crew and asked them to leave. "We have some work we need to do."

It turned out to be the threatened running, which was beginning early on this day.

The town of Boone, North Carolina, had never before seen anything like this. A popular tourist town nestled in a fold of the eastern slope of the Appalachian Mountains, Boone was also home to Appalachian State University. The most exciting events in Boone were App State football Saturdays and the Olde Boone Streetfest in September.

Until now.

North Carolina playing in Boone was a major event. Every sign on every hotel and restaurant welcomed the Tar Heels to town. When the Tar Heels arrived on Friday after spending the night in nearby Blowing Rock, their bus was followed by scores of screaming kids (and adults) hoping to catch a glimpse of their heroes.

The game, the first ever in Seby-Jones Arena, sold out in 12 minutes. The building itself had received its certificate of occupancy less than 24 hours prior to tip-off. Several of the bathrooms did not have soap or paper towels, and offices, classrooms, trophy cases, and even picture frames were empty.

Although they were treated like visiting dignitaries (or rock stars), the Tar Heels were hardly gracious. Sporting serious, glum scowls, the players went through warm-ups in the cold arena. The Mountaineers, meanwhile, appeared more than a little nervous—almost every player had come out to shoot around two and a half hours prior to the tip-off.

Moments before the game began, Joe Forte stamped his feet and blew warm air into his hands as he leaned toward official Mike Wood. "Man, it's cold," Forte said. Wood was still grinning when he tossed the ball into the air to officially christen the new arena, which was filled to capacity and rocking with noise.

Seven seconds later Adam Boone—fundamentally sound with his left foot pointing at the basket, as Doherty had coached earlier in the week—took a pass and calmly and confidently hit the first jump shot in the new building and scored his first points as a Tar Heel. The raucous crowd did not even flinch. This was the Tar Heels, and the students were going to take advantage of their one chance to prove they could harass and heckle just like the big-time schools.

The Mountaineers of brand-new Coach Houston Fancher hung with the Heels in the opening minutes, thanks to 6'8", 280-pound Corey Cooper, who hit a three-pointer over Haywood to match Boone's. A made jumper by Buddy Davis put ASU up by two a few seconds later, and the crowd was euphoric, raining the "overrated" chant on Carolina's bench.

Forte may have been cold before the game, but during it he was anything but. His steal and layup gave Carolina an 8–7 lead with 17:48 remaining in the half. He followed it up with an assist on a Boone three-pointer (another confident, fundamentally sound shot) and a three of his own in which he was tightly guarded by App's Noah Brown but cut the heart out of the basket off the dribble. The look on Brown's face when, after he just missed getting a piece of the ball only to watch it arc convincingly through the hoop, was telling: No matter how well we play, the look said, we can't hang with these guys.

Doherty, up and out of his chair from the start, implored his team to continue to push the ball up the floor and to get back in transition defense, sensing they had Fancher's club on the ropes. Over and over Carolina pushed the ball ahead, found either Haywood or Kris Lang inside, and kicked it back out for open jumpers. Carolina would go on to hit an incredible 10-of-13 three-pointers in the first half to push the Heels to a comfortable 54–29 lead. As if it wasn't bad enough, Lang and Haywood, both of whom were significantly bigger than anyone on the Mountaineers, roster, hit several 15-foot jumpers from the free throw circle near the end of the half. Boone, Morrison, and Holmes, spurred on by their coaches' confidence, combined to connect on 6-of-7 from behind the arc.

At halftime, Doherty tried not to let his team get complacent.

Before addressing the players, Doherty, as he always did, huddled with his coaches. Each offered an opinion on points to pass on, but Doherty knew the real challenge would be to keep the players aggressive, even with a big lead. The year before, Carolina had enjoyed precious few blowouts (only an 86–53 win over Howard exceeded 30 points). The lack of a killer instinct had been particularly evident at Buffalo, a game in which Carolina struggled against a weak team before pulling away late.

In an effort to give his team something to play for in the second half, Doherty asked the players what they wanted if they went out and won the second half. He expected the request to be a day off or the coaches to do sprints. Taking the leadership role Doherty wanted him to take, Haywood had an idea.

"How about if we win the second half, I get my water break back?" Haywood said with a straight face. The rest of the team immediately agreed. Doherty chuckled and asked Haywood if he hadn't conspired with his teammates beforehand. But he let the goal and reward stand: If Carolina could win the second half, Haywood could have his water break back.

The overmatched Mountaineers battled in the second half's opening minutes. The boyish-looking Fancher kept his team's spirits up, despite what had to be a heavy heart. At halftime, he had stayed out on the floor as part of a presentation which included the mother of Rufus Leach, a young man who would have been the Mountaineers' leading returning scorer but had drowned during the summer in a lake just across the Tennessee state line. The loss was stunning for the close-knit school and team. His jersey and degree were being awarded posthumously to Leach's family and Fancher—who, as an assistant, had recruited Leach—was there to present them to her.

The Mountaineers never got closer than 25 points, despite a valiant effort. With 13:30 remaining in the game, Michael Brooker stepped in front of Mountaineers' guard Shawn Alexander on the left baseline, drawing a charge. Forte, recalling his blunder in practice earlier in the week, sprinted to his fallen teammate, even boxing out several of them, in an effort to be the first one to lift Brooker off the ground. Doherty, at the far end of the court on the bench, didn't notice at the time. But he would later while watching the film.

Forte and Carolina were simply too much for Appalachian State as the hot-shooting continued. A Morrison 10-footer was followed by a Forte three, and the lead was 32 with just over 12 minutes on the clock. After Forte's basket, he gestured for the App State students to have a seat as he ran back down the court. They didn't, but the chants of being overrated had stopped.

The game mercifully ended with the score 99–69. Carolina had won the second half by three points. True to his word, Doherty gave Haywood his water break back.

Within an hour after the final buzzer sounded, all of the players were on the bus for the three-hour ride home. Forte and Haywood were the last to leave the locker room, and as they headed out of the tunnel to the bus, they were swarmed by autograph seekers of all ages. "It reminds me of the old days," said Woody Durham, the radio play-by-play voice of the Tar Heels, "when the Carolina players were like rock stars. Everyone wanted a piece of them."

In another minute, the Tar Heels' bus pulled away from the arena and headed out of Boone, probably forever.

A Life to Live

The holidays are always a difficult time for any college basketball player. As their fellow students prepared to head home for Thanksgiving dinner, the Tar Heels players—with no classes to worry about—were faced with two and sometimes three practices per day, even though they did not play a game for a week and a half. Late November was a grueling time.

What they did have, however, was an exhibition game. The players looked forward to playing the California All-Stars on the Tuesday prior to Thanksgiving—which many would spend at the houses of teammates who lived close by. Max Owens, Neil Fingleton, and Michael Brooker were headed to the Dohertys' for Thanksgiving dinner.

The exhibition game's presence on the schedule (after three regular-season games had already been played) seemed odd to many, but it was being played at that time, in part, because of Doherty's desire to bridge a perceived gap that existed between the basketball team and the students. More accurately, the rift existed between current Carolina students (who, in the Smith Center, were allocated seats under one basket and in the upper corner of the arena) and Carolina alumni (who had the best seats courtside and in the lower arena). At times during games the previous seasons, the current students had chanted "get up" to the alumni who occupied the best seats—and rarely stood during a game to cheer.

That rift became a story following the "Snow Game" versus Maryland the year before, when the administration decided it would allow students to sit anywhere they could find an open seat in an attempt to fill the arena. The game with the Terps was inaccessible for many fans due to more than two feet of snow dropped on the Carolinas, so the students took over the lower level. Even with the arena one-third empty, the atmosphere was electric as the Heels won a tough game. Almost immediately, the students and media clamored for better student seating—like the students at Duke enjoyed—so that the atmosphere could be as charged on a regular basis.

In response, the school had redesigned the student seating arrangements in the off-season, giving them more lower-level seating, including a paddock area along the baseline closest to the Carolina bench. The paddock gave rowdy students a place to do their best to intimidate the other team—and a place for Doherty, a student-friendly coach, to target his energies.

Doherty's student-friendly campaign would involve him bringing doughnuts to students camped out during ticket distribution, "Midnight With Matt" (and pre-event hype speech to students in "The Pit" area of the student center), as well as several other well-publicized personal efforts to make the students feel more a part of the program.

Doherty, in fact, enjoyed his interactions with students as much as any part of his job. In his first few months on the job he would often eat lunch with his wife, Kelly, in Lenoir, the main dining hall on campus. "One of our first times there," Doherty recalled, "it was pretty crowded. I saw that there was only one table in the back that was open, so I used my big body and boxed a few students out to get it. Just as I arrived, another student was putting his tray down, so I asked if we could join him." Doherty then introduced himself and they started chatting during lunch. The student mentioned that he was in ROTC, which was paying his way through school. After they discussed his major the student, in all sincerity, asked Doherty, "So, what do you do on campus?"

Another of Doherty's student public relations ideas had been to play an exhibition game in Carmichael Auditorium. Thus, the November 21 game against the EA California All-Stars that followed a women's game against North Carolina A&T was scheduled.

After the Friday night win at Appalachian State, Doherty was feeling better about how the team was progressing. They had worked steadily on shooting the ball in the practices leading up to that game, and they had shot the ball better. They had worked on boxing out, and that had been somewhat better. Most of all, they had worked on maintaining intensity, and that had been there from the opening tap through the final horn against the Mountaineers.

But the exhibition game was a step backwards. Playing a team of ex–college players who were not picked up by NBA (or even CBA) teams, the Heels came out flat and uninspired. Carmichael was about two-thirds full, with many of the students having already left for the break, and not nearly as energized as it had been for Midnight With Matt. The result was an inexplicable 8–0 run to start the game for the "All-Stars," thanks to three-pointers from Drew Barry and Kenyon Weeks.

The lack of Carolina's focus was obvious from the beginning. In the game's first minute, Brendan Haywood took a post entry on the right block and turned meekly, with the ball around his waist. After it was stripped and knocked out-of-bounds, Doherty wasted no time. He took Haywood out and inserted Brian Bersticker. On the bench, Doherty reiterated to Haywood—in no uncertain terms—the importance of him being aggressive. Haywood listened and understood. His point made, Doherty immediately reinserted his big man.

But that did not change the course of action. Lang hit a 15-foot jumper with two minutes gone to make the score 8–2. As he ran back down the court Lang shook his head, knowing this was not his team's best effort. At the first official time-out, the Heels had cut the margin to 12–8, but former Oklahoma State point guard Doug Gottlieb scored on a driving layup, and Barry (a former standout at Georgia Tech) hit another deep three to push the score back up to 17–8. The All-Stars continued to bomb from deep, and Carolina continued to make unforced errors on offense. With 5:48 remaining in the first half, Carolina trailed by 10 points to a team with just eight players on its roster—three of whom had been recruited to play a day earlier.

Just before the half, the Heels woke up. Forte hit a three and a floater in the lane to cut the deficit to five. More important, Carolina began to play more aggressively on defense, denying into the passing lanes and extending its zone out farther to take away Barry's set-shot threes. The result was the first involvement all night of the crowd. Gottlieb was able to get into the lane for another layup, but the last five minutes belonged to Carolina as it took a 39–37 lead when Haywood blocked a shot, recovered it, and was fouled with 1.4 seconds remaining. He sank both free throws.

At halftime, Doherty was not appeased by the late surge. The pre-holiday crowd, the eight days before they would play again, the poor shooting, nothing was an acceptable excuse. After discussing the matter with his assistants, he walked into a quiet locker room and threw down the gauntlet. "Who in here wants to win a national championship?" he asked. Everyone's arm shot up. "Well, we took a step backwards out there in the first half." He went on to talk about the mental errors—not boxing out, not taking care of the ball—that would undoubtedly get them beat against any team in the conference, not to mention the NCAA Tournament. Against the California All-Stars, for crying out loud, it had gotten them in a hole.

The Tar Heels responded with a 17–4 run to start the second half. Eventually, with the EA All-Stars tiring and Carolina forcing the action, the Heels would pull away to win by 23 points. The crowd would get back into it only when it was time for Doherty to insert the two newest members of the squad, Ronald Curry and Julius Peppers, both of whom were dressed just days after they had trounced Duke in their final game of the *football* season. But only Curry would get into this game, however, as he had practiced the previous day while Peppers had not. "It's always good for Ronald to touch a basketball," Doherty said, although the fourth point guard he would have to find minutes for would air ball a three-pointer in his only shot attempt.

As setbacks go, anything that could possibly go wrong for Ronald Curry on the basketball court would never approach the tragedies he had already suffered.

 Ronald Curry was in the eighth grade when everyone around him began dying.

By the time he was entering his teens in Hampton, Virginia, Curry had already become something of an athletic legend in the Tidewater area. The stories about his pre–high school exploits were almost mythic: he could throw a football 70 yards; he could dunk a basketball; he was the fastest eighth grader anyone had ever seen.

The summer before he would begin ninth grade his grandmother, Mattie Curry, had a stroke. His mother, who had given birth to Ronald when she was just 14 years old, had already moved to Rocky Mount, North Carolina, when he was 12. All along it had been Mattie who had raised him. Ronald's father was just 16 when he was born and had been in prison since Ronald was six. Unable to stay with his grandmother after the stroke, Ronald went to live with his aunt, Lillian Crawford— known to everyone in town as Big Momma—and his cousin Joemel Dennis. Joemel, four years older than Ronald, was the younger boy's hero and everything Ronald wanted to become: a big strong football and basketball star with a presence that his peers and adults alike admired. Going into high school, Ronald wanted to be just like Joemel. More accurately, Ronald wanted to *be* Joemel.

And then Joemel was killed—shot while he was a bystander during an armed robbery. Ronald was devastated. He sat in the bathtub for days on end, unable to summon the strength to get up and go outside or go to school until Big Momma finally got through to the only son she had left.

"Boy," she said one day, "you'd better get yourself outside and play. You got a life to live." So Ronald got out of the bathtub and lived his life, one day at a time. He had gone into the tub a boy; he came out a man.

As a freshman, Ronald started at quarterback, the first freshman to do that at Hampton High. He was big for his age—for any age, really—and strong. And what an arm. But it was his manner, his gracious, quiet, humble manner, that made an impression. "He was the best kid that we ever had," Lanier Sanders, a Hampton High teacher, told writer Eddy Landreth. "You will not find anybody in this building that did not like Ronald. He was very respectful. I had him as a student. He was almost too perfect. He could score 10 touchdowns, come to school the next day, get a book and sit by himself. He didn't want it any other way."

At 6'2" and almost 200 pounds, Curry could do anything he wanted on the football field and the basketball court. Above everything else, he was a winner, leading Hampton to three consecutive state titles in football and two as the point guard on the basketball team. Playing both sports—even in high school—was tough for most kids. Not Ronald.

"His junior year, three days after the [football] state championship game and with only three days of practice, he played in the first game and scored 44 points," said his high school basketball coach, Walter Brower. "I'll never forget that."

The beginning of Curry's junior year was also the first chance for college coaches—both football and basketball—to begin contacting him. It was a wild time, one that Curry wanted to get over with as soon as possible. So he verbally committed to Virginia, which touched off a war of opinions and advice and guidance between Brower (who wanted Curry to consider other schools), Mike Smith (the Hampton football coach who pushed for Virginia), and AAU basketball guru Boo Williams (whom Curry played AAU basketball for in the summer). Curry found himself in the middle of it all.

By the time it was all over, never-proven allegations of involvement by Nike, some confusion in Charlottesville, and diligence on the part of North Carolina's Phil Ford resulted in Curry backing out on his original (though never official) commitment to Virginia and signing instead with North Carolina to play both football and basketball. Along the way, he earned awards as the top high school football *and* basketball player in the country.

Built up as the savior of Carolina football and the next great point guard for Carolina basketball, the legend of Ronald Curry arrived in Chapel Hill long before Curry did. Just five snaps into his first college football game, Curry found himself under center due to an injury to starting QB Oscar Davenport. By the end of his junior season in football, he had played for two different offensive coordinators and his head coach had been fired. He had also suffered a torn Achilles tendon on October 9 of his sophomore season, ending that year on both the field and the basketball court.

In his only season of basketball, Curry had displayed great quickness and strength on the defensive end, but an erratic jump shot on the offensive end. He played in 26 games and made some big shots—none bigger than a three-pointer from the corner at NC State that put Carolina ahead to stay—but he had hardly dominated as he had in high school.

Every day during Curry's collegiate athletic career, the expectations threatened to overwhelm him. In high school, he had won every football award in the Tidewater area—ahead of even a rival high school QB named Michael Vick, who would go on to win a Heisman Trophy two years later at Virginia Tech. At Carolina, Curry was only the second most effective football-turned-basketball player, behind teammate Julius Peppers, whose incredible combination of strength and agility had earned him national publicity. But through all of the setbacks and all of the incredible pressure to perform, Curry had remained centered and stoic, unrattled by events in the athletic arena.

"He's not going to let anything bother him, and if he does, the world will never know," said Jason Capel, who had played AAU basketball with Curry since the seventh grade before the two became Carolina teammates. "You rarely see him show any kind of expression—happy, sad, anything at all—and he's just always been that way. He's been through a lot and he's had to grow up fast. He's had a hard time and luckily he's used athletics as a vehicle to get where he is. He'll be successful, he's overcome so much this past year, getting hurt, it's probably the first time he's ever had to overcome anything athletically."

In time, Curry had become a beloved figure on the North Carolina campus, particularly by his fellow students who cheered emphatically when he entered a basketball game. It was that quiet presence—the same trait that his cousin Joemel had possessed, the one whose initials Ronald had tattooed on his arm—that made Curry a leader.

It was a trait that would make Curry a key member of Matt Doherty's first North Carolina team.

13

See Where We Are

I t was with a new sense of purpose that the Tar Heels entered the week after Thanksgiving. The Appalachian State blowout and the comeback against the EA All-Stars had raised the team's collective confidence, but it was preparation for a national television matchup with defending national champion Michigan State that led to a week of focused, intense practices.

It was rare when Carolina entered a game as an underdog, but it would do so against the Spartans in East Lansing.

While Doherty may not have been overly thrilled with the level of play from his team in its first three games, he felt confident that he knew what needed improvement. And he knew that Michigan State—a well-coached, sound team with great athletes—would be a solid early-season test.

The ACC Big Ten Challenge is the best kind of made-for-TV event. In an attempt to build fan interest in college basketball in

November and December, ESPN had put together the two-day event in 1999 as a way to bolster its schedule following the end of the college football regular season. The challenge quickly (thanks to clever and ceaseless on-air promotion) grew in stature. A trophy was even presented to the winning conference commissioner at the conclusion of the second night of games.

A year earlier the marquee matchup had been North Carolina and Michigan State. The Spartans, two-time Big Ten champions, were expected to make a run at the Final Four, while Carolina—in its second season under Bill Guthridge—had won the Maui Classic and was seemingly better than advertised. The bloom was taken off the game somewhat when Mateen Cleaves' ankle injury precluded the star point guard from suiting up for MSU, but the early-season matchup was expected to be a great test for both teams and a thrilling early-season, intraconference showdown.

It wasn't. Michigan State dominated the Tar Heels in Chapel Hill, utilizing a stifling, swarming man-to-man defense to dismantle Carolina's offense. The defeat was decisive and blew apart the Heels' confidence. It would take almost five months to get it back.

The 2000 game between Michigan State and Carolina was also a showcase in the challenge, along with the Illinois–Duke matchup the night before, which the Blue Devils had won. With the win, Duke cemented its early-season No. 1 national ranking, a position it had taken over from Arizona, which had fallen to Purdue a week earlier.

For three key members of the Carolina program—Matt Doherty, Joseph Forte, and Brendan Haywood—this would be their first appearance on the national stage in 2000–2001. All had high expectations.

After watching film on Michigan State for a week, Doherty had little doubt how good Tom Izzo's team was. The defending national champions were without Cleaves and Morris Peterson, seniors who had graduated and were now playing in the NBA, but the talent and the mentality were still there to form a very, very good basketball team. Charlie Bell had already risen to the leadership position vacated by Cleaves, while Andre Hutson and Jason Richardson formed a talented nucleus. Added to the mix were heralded freshmen Zach Randolph and Marcus Taylor, players who would have easily started in any other program in the nation, but who came off the bench for the deep Spartans.

Tom Izzo was someone Doherty admired greatly. Izzo's team was an extension of himself—blue collar, hardworking, and relentless. All of these qualities could also be said of Doherty—but not yet of the Tar Heel team he had inherited.

If nothing else, playing the Spartans in East Lansing would tell Doherty exactly how tough his team was. He had no illusions about going into East Lansing and blowing out Michigan State, but he wanted to be able to walk off the Breslin Center court (noted as one of the loudest college arenas in the country) with his head held high, knowing the Heels had competed hard and matched Michigan State's intensity. "My goal is to have other teams have to raise their level of intensity to match ours," he said during the week. "But we're not there yet."

Forte wanted a win as much as any player on the team, but he also wanted to continue his hot shooting and solid all-around play against a good team—and to play well on national television. Perhaps no other player on the team paid as close attention to what the media said and wrote as did Forte. Not only did he watch ESPN *SportsCenter* (as did almost every college athlete—or nonathlete, for that matter), but he also read local papers and occasionally would venture onto Internet message boards and see what was being said. With the Michigan State game on ESPN—and Dick Vitale announcing—it gave him another reason to be ready.

For Haywood—who paid much less attention to the media but still felt the sting when he was disrespected—the game was more personal. In its preseason college basketball magazine, the *Sporting News* had ranked the top centers in the country. Haywood was 13th on that list, a fact that did not go unnoticed by the seven-footer. It was a slap in the face that Haywood could address in the Michigan State game. Randolph, a freshman who had never started a college basketball game, was rated No. 3 on the same list.

With a chance to show the world the "new" emotional and reenergized North Carolina basketball program, the final practice before the team flew to Michigan was spirited, competitive, and energetic.

A light snow greeted the team in East Lansing when it arrived on Tuesday evening, but it paled in comparison to the blizzard of defense that hit the next night inside the Breslin Center.

Forte turned the ball over on the first possession of the game—an unforced turnover at that—as he penetrated into the lane and tried to kick a pass out to Boone, who was moving right as the ball flew out of bounds to his left. Normally not one to show any emotion on the court, Forte jogged back down to the defensive end shaking his head, knowing that Michigan State would force their share of turnovers and he had just helped their cause.

On his second pass, Forte tried to get it inside to Haywood. But Andre Hutson was able to get a hand on the pass to knock it loose and force a held ball. Two offensive possessions, two turnovers.

At the first media time-out, Carolina trailed 10–7. Doherty had opened the game in a man-to-man defense, but it was obvious to him that he'd have to switch things up a bit due to the difference in quickness. He'd have to play some zone and maybe even try to trap some to get Michigan State out of any offensive rhythm. Since it was the Spartans' ball after the first break—and Izzo had just inserted his two freshmen into the lineup—Doherty decided to come out of the time-out and play a possession of trapping zone and maybe catch the Spartans unaware.

After the ball was inbounded, Marcus Taylor dribbled exactly where Doherty wanted him to, into the teeth of a Boone–Capel trap. But Bersticker and Lang miscommunicated on who had next-pass coverage (and both were late in getting there, anyway), which resulted in Jason Richardson receiving the pass on the sideline (directly in front of where Doherty was standing, arms wide as if in the trap himself) with a clear, unabated lane to the basket. One of the most spectacular athletes in college basketball, Richardson dribbled twice and threw down a monstrous two-handed dunk that caused the Breslin Center to explode.

Although Carolina would continue to battle, it was obvious from that point it would be uphill.

The Spartans' obvious offensive game plan was to pull Carolina's bigger interior players out of the middle. Brendan Haywood began the game matched up with Hutson, a lithe, 6'8" slasher type, who immediately began to float out to the corners, enticing Haywood to chase him. Like a guard dog not sure whether or not to leave the house unattended, Haywood snuck out, only to watch Hutson drive by him and score.

The Tar Heels hung tough and put together an 8–0 run, punctuated by a Kris Lang alley-oop dunk off a pass from Brian Morrison, that gave UNC a one-point lead with 11:42 remaining in the half. But a minute later Haywood picked up his second foul when he got too aggressive with Zach Randolph trying to rebound a Capel miss. Haywood turned to argue the call, but instead just threw up his arms in disgust. Haywood was still trying to adjust to the way officials were calling post play—in the off-season the NCAA had mandated a closer scrutiny of interior defense by officials—with little luck. During the summer the NCAA had produced a video that it sent to all college coaches showing illegal post play and how calls would be made when certain tactics were employed. The two stars of the video were Haywood and Lang, whose "illegal" play constituted at least 70 percent of the footage.

The Tar Heels were down by one, 16–15, when their center went to the bench.

On the perimeter, Forte couldn't get free. Thomas, Bell, and Richardson switched on every Carolina perimeter screen, bringing the UNC offense to a standstill. Doherty had preached ball reversals all fall, but now Carolina couldn't swing the ball from one side to the other due to Michigan State's switches and quickness. When Forte did get the ball on the wing, he was molested into forced jumpers or off-balance leaners over Hutson, Randolph, and Aloysius Anagonye, who quickly shut down the middle. "I'd get around a guy and there'd be another guy sitting there waiting for me," said Forte after the game. "There were no easy shots out there. I'd never really seen that before."

Adam Boone, who had been so steady at the point in the first three games, made a mental error with just over five minutes remaining in the first half. Down by five points, he mistakenly thought the shot clock was about to expire (it had been reset after a kicked ball), and he dribbled frantically into the lane and hoisted an off-balance shot. Even though he was bailed out by a foul call, Doherty admonished his freshman to know the situation.

Doherty knew this game was going to be a mental and emotional war, as the Spartans fed off the sellout and raucous crowd. With Haywood sitting next to him, Doherty watched his team fall behind by five, then seven, and finally ten after Bell hit a three from the left wing when Boone and Owens miscommunicated in the zone. Watching the game slip away, Doherty put Haywood back in, and he immediately scored on a put-back off a missed three by Brian Bersticker to cut the lead to 35–27.

But Richardson again displayed his incredible athletic ability when he caught a pass in midair and seemingly changed direction for a spectacular layin. The crowd, sensing that one more punch might send Carolina reeling, exploded. A Maurice Taylor jumper in the lane with six seconds remaining before the half sent the Heels to the locker room, down 42–29.

At halftime, Doherty challenged his team to not back down or give up. Coming back would be difficult, he told them, but not impossible. "Match their intensity," he said. "Don't let up."

Normally, teams come out for second half warm-ups with no more than two or three minutes on the clock before the start of the second half. With few changes to their strategy or game plan, the Heels were back on the floor with almost five minutes on the clock. The message was clear: it was not about strategy, it was about effort and desire. "Whoever wants this game more will win," Doherty told his team simply in the huddle before the start of the second half.

A fast start to the half didn't happen. Starting in a zone, the Heels were quickly down by 15 points after Anagonye hit two free throws. But

Carolina again battled back, culminating with Lang scoring inside in transition while being fouled by Mike Chappell (a transfer from Duke) with 15:38 remaining. A free throw would cut the lead to six, but Lang's shot clanked off the back rim. Capel rebounded and kicked it out to Boone, who had a decent look at a three-pointer that would cut the lead to four points and decidedly change the complexion of the game. But at the last second his shot was blocked by Bell. Michigan State recovered the loose ball and scored on its next possession—on a six-footer by Richardson—and the threat ended.

Later, Forte, who was still struggling to find room to score, had another chance to get the deficit to below seven but missed the front end of a one-and-one. It would be the Heels' last chance.

Bell, Richardson, and Randolph all scored to push the lead back up to double digits. After a Haywood turnaround jumper cut the lead to 58–47, Doherty and the UNC bench rose up and urged the Heels to get a stop. But Forte fouled Bell on the ensuing possession, and Doherty, incensed, turned and slammed the scorer's table in disgust. Immediately, he turned and apologized to the Michigan State official sitting closest, but the frustration permeated the evening for Carolina. A late run cut the lead to eight points twice, but Michigan State was never seriously threatened.

Despite the late double-digit deficit, Doherty continued to coach as if the Heels could stage a miraculous last-minute comeback. Ordering fouls and calling late time-outs—with his team down by as many as 14 points—sent a message to the players: The game is never over until the buzzer goes off. He would never allow his team to quit, even if it meant the score might look worse in the paper the next day than it actually was.

This one would end up a 13-point loss, 77–64.

After the game, Doherty shook hands with Izzo and the rest of the Spartan team and then jogged off the floor with his head held high. Athletically, Michigan State was simply better, Doherty knew. But that did not lessen the pain of the loss. In truth, he had conflicting thoughts about the game immediately after it was over.

"I think we learned a lot," he said. "I'm excited, as excited as I've ever been about our team right now, which is crazy because we just lost. But you play these games to see where you are, and I'm excited because they are one of the best teams in the country."

But the frustration from Haywood and Forte—both of whom had hoped to use this game as a springboard—was obvious, as well.

"A lot of people say I'm not aggressive, that I don't hit the boards," said Haywood. "Well, every time I got aggressive and hit the boards, I got hit with a foul. I guess I'm going to have to get smarter, and I'm definitely going to have to get smarter about what I say to the press because I'm very upset at this point."

Forte's frustration wasn't with the officials, but with the stifling defense he had just experienced. "This is probably the best defense I've seen," he said. "If I see it again, I'll know how to deal with it better."

Armed with more knowledge about the team he had inherited, Doherty began watching the game tape on the bus ride to the airport.

In just three days, the Tar Heels played Kentucky.

Rock Bottom

One of the best aspects of college basketball, Matt Doherty would say to anyone who would listen as November rolled into December, was that you always (except in the NCAA Tournament) had another game to play, and it usually came pretty soon after the last one.

Following the emotional and difficult loss to Michigan State, Carolina had plenty of time to consider what went wrong in East Lansing, as an electrical problem in the charter plane's cockpit (the light indicating the cabin door was not closed properly stayed illuminated) caused an unscheduled landing in Toledo. A few hours later—after more time to stew about the loss to the Spartans—the plane was back in the air and touched down at Raleigh-Durham airport about 3:00 in the morning.

The mechanical difficulties of their aircraft, however, were nothing compared to the malfunctions that had occurred within the university's athletic department several months earlier.

 North Carolina wanted Jason Parker, and Jason Parker wanted North Carolina. But sometimes even that's not enough.

Parker, a burly 6'8" man-child as a high school senior in Charlotte, is the son of schoolteachers who grew up dreaming—like so many other sons of Carolina—of suiting up for the Tar Heels. Blessed with incredible agility for his size, Parker was able to run the floor faster than players much smaller than he and catch the ball no matter where it was thrown. Any casual basketball observer knew immediately that Parker, who tipped the scales at almost 260 pounds by the time he turned 18, was a special athlete.

Carolina's recruitment of Parker was a comedy of errors almost from the beginning. Bill Guthridge began the process, inquiring about Parker when he was a student at West Charlotte High School at the beginning of his junior season. Initially, Carolina was somewhat apprehensive; although Parker was obviously a great player, he had struggled in school, with a grade point average that hovered just above a C. As Parker's junior season progressed and his academics did not improve, Guthridge informed him that Carolina would no longer recruit him. Guthridge was brutally honest for a simple reason; it was in the young man's best interests that he do so, in order for Parker to focus on his other options.

Parker was extremely disappointed by the decision, but appreciated (once he got by his emotional first reaction) the upfront way Guthridge had informed him.

Over the course of the next few months, Parker's stock as a player increased and so did his efforts at raising his academic standing. Guthridge and the Carolina staff kept an eye on him, but it wasn't until a few weeks before the early signing period that their minds began to change. Parker's size and speed were impressive, but his academics were still sketchy. He had yet to achieve a qualifying test score on the SAT or ACT despite several attempts at each.

The other factor that so impressed Guthridge was that Parker truly wanted to come to North Carolina, despite the rejection a few months earlier. Knowing the risk was small but the reward could be great, Guthridge gave Parker an option: Carolina would hold a scholarship for him until he made his score, whether it be during his senior year of high school or if it required him to attend a prep school upon graduation. Parker jumped at the chance and verbally committed to Carolina on the spot. He was thrilled to be given the opportunity to fulfill his dream, even if it meant having to postpone it. (Parker could have gone virtually anywhere in the country—and maybe even turned pro—as a partial qualifier and played after sitting out a year whether he achieved the score or not. But the schools in the ACC have a gentleman's agreement that they will not accept partial qualifiers.)

Despite buckling down and studying for the standardized tests, Parker did not get the score he needed, missing by just a few points on several occasions. On the basketball court, however, he flourished, leading West Charlotte to the state title, scoring 38 points and grabbing 12 rebounds in the championship game on the Smith Center court. But without the academic qualifications—and true to the promise he made to Guthridge—Parker left for Fork Union Military Academy, where he would spend the next year getting up at dawn, going to class, playing basketball, and living the military lifestyle. He initially hated it, as most young men would, but he stuck it out. He even got a taste of his future in a game against the Carolina junior varsity in the Smith Center.

Then, in the spring, on his very last chance, he received the good news: He had made the score on both the SAT and ACT. He signed the letter of intent and was in Chapel Hill just a few days after he was done at FUMA, working out with the other Carolina players. Guthridge retired, Doherty was hired, and Parker was ready to live out his dream.

Then the bottom fell out.

In August, just days before classes began in Chapel Hill, Parker was told that his test scores were being flagged by the Educational Testing

Service, the organization that administered the SAT. His score had increased several hundred points on the SAT—enough to raise suspicion and launch an inquiry into the legitimacy of the test. On a previously scheduled family vacation in Charleston (where he was staying in Roy Williams's beach house), Doherty kept on top of the situation via telephone. By the time he returned, he and Guthridge met with Parker and his parents to tell them that North Carolina would not be admitting him due to this latest development.

The dream was officially and irrevocably over.

Parker was devastated. The entire situation had been covered like a presidential scandal, and when the news broke that Parker would never be a Tar Heel, reporters began to swarm in full force, calling the Parker house at all hours. UNC officials released a statement only after the Parkers released one of their own. Doherty would say later that it was the hardest thing he had ever had to do as a coach; Guthridge could think of only one other more distressing situation: when he and Dean Smith had to inform former UNC center Scott Williams of his parents dying in a homicide/suicide.

Parker's options were murky. He was too late to enter the NBA draft. He could go to another school, but he'd have to sit out *another* year because of his recently disqualified test score. Other factors—was he a transfer since he signed a letter of intent?—were not as clear. The CBA or Europe were also possibilities.

Despite the mess, college coaches called in droves. UNC–Charlotte's Bobby Lutz knew Parker from the recruiting process and desperately wanted him to stay close to home. Kentucky's Tubby Smith also inquired, as did Wake Forest's Dave Odom. Cincinnati was very interested, as well. Parker was simply too good not to at least inquire about.

Parker liked Odom and Smith and scheduled two visits. Prior to doing so, his family sent his high school and prep school transcripts and test scores to both places. But there was one last bizarre twist in the saga. Upon further review of his two high school transcripts, it was discovered that a clerical error had been made. A course he had taken as a freshman at North Mecklenburg High School had not been given proper weight

by the school he had transferred to, West Charlotte. His grade point average had been miscalculated; it should have been slightly higher. It was a
miscalculation that was not caught by the North Carolina basketball
office or by the Office of Admissions. The razor-thin margin was just
enough to make him eligible—on the NCAA's sliding scale of grades and
test scores—while counting one of the test scores that had *not* been disqualified. Parker was now, miraculously, instantly eligible.

Parker and his family were shocked at the news. The administrators at North Carolina were equally surprised, but would not discuss
the issue, citing student privacy regulations. Doherty, through Parker's
former high school coach, made some subtle inquiries about the possibility of Parker considering coming back to Chapel Hill. No matter
how much he had once wanted to be a Tar Heel, Parker wasn't willing
to go that far.

Within a week, Parker had chosen Kentucky and enrolled immediately, impressing his new teammates with his strength and skill during
pick-up games. Tubby Smith and the Wildcats had received the most
improbable of gifts, and Parker would begin the season as the Wildcats'
starting center and, in a postscript equal to the bizarre nature of the
entire ordeal, would line up against his almost-teammates in a regular-
season game against North Carolina in Chapel Hill just a few short
months after the ordeal.

But he wouldn't be allowed to talk about it. Never before, in Tubby
Smith's 11 years as a head coach, had he instituted a rule that did not
allow freshmen to speak to the media. Until Jason Parker came along.

Knowing the scrutiny on Parker would be intense and ceaseless, Smith
made his first-year players off-limits to the media. When asked if the rule
seemed silly by a disgruntled reporter, Smith responded, "Not to me."

As if the Parker subplot wasn't enough, the Carolina–Kentucky
matchup grew into a crucial early December game for both teams. The
Wildcats were off to a poor start, and the pressure on Smith in Lexington
was increasing with each loss. The Tar Heels were coming off a decisive
loss to Michigan State and needed a get-well game on the national stage.
Even CBS, the multibillion-dollar holders of the NCAA Tournament

rights, needed a big game in its first broadcast of the season between two of college basketball's most storied programs.

In many ways for CBS, it was a dream matchup. Carolina versus Kentucky. Parker's return. A matchup of Joe Forte and Kentucky's Keith Bogans, who had played high school basketball together at DeMatha for Morgan Wootten and had been intense competitors in high school.

As the Kentucky game loomed, no Carolina player was more anxious than Forte, whose relationship with Bogans had actually improved once the two of them went to college. "We talk quite a bit on the phone," said Forte, who never forgot Morgan Wootten's holding up Bogans as the player he hoped Forte was half as good as when the both were freshmen in high school.

"We're both looking forward to this one."

The Kentucky game also marked the first Smith Center game in which the risers, like those at Duke and Michigan State, had been installed in the end zone of the Smith Center for the students. Given the buildup for the game and the students' new vantage point, it was expected to be a raucous crowd—by Smith Center standards.

Matt Doherty knew what the environment would be, and ever aware of public relations, he launched a preemptive strike. The man who, a few months earlier, had done the hardest thing he had ever had to do as a coach in telling Parker he would never wear Carolina Blue, sent a letter to the *Daily Tar Heel*, the UNC student paper, asking that Parker be given a warm welcome when he was announced to the Smith Center crowd.

"Obviously, a lot has been written and talked about Jason Parker and his enrollment at UNC and Kentucky," the letter said. "Jason and his family are first-class people and longtime fans of our program. I want to take this unusual step of asking our fans to respectfully welcome Jason and his family to Chapel Hill. He wanted to attend Carolina and play for the Tar Heels. An unfortunate series of events made that impossible. However, I wish him and his family the best and want them to be treated with Carolina Class on Saturday. In fact, I would like to ask our fans to please give Jason a warm ovation when he is introduced."

The request was eerily similar to one Dean Smith had made back in the mid-1970s when Tom McMillan, whose recruitment was a legendary series of events that eventually saw the Pennsylvania native choose Maryland and not Carolina, made his first appearance in Carmichael.

Matt Doherty was in his pregame mood for Kentucky the moment the plane from East Lansing had landed at 3:00 A.M. three days earlier, and his mood had not changed. He was markedly different when he was like this; instead of bantering with players he would be stern and unapproachable. His focus was complete and single-minded, and practices, while still upbeat, were not social events.

A typical day during the season in the basketball office started for Doherty about 8:30 or 9:00 A.M. Sometimes, Doherty would eat breakfast alone at a downtown eatery called Breadman's, which was also favored by many of the players. There, he would sit at the far end of the counter near the television, which was tuned to a replay of *SportsCenter*. As he ate, he read *USA Today* or one of the local papers, scanning for articles or quotes he could use to motivate a particular player or maybe the entire team. He would do the same thing when he arrived in the office, getting on the Internet and scanning for articles about Carolina or one of its opponents. It was a duty of David Cason to do the same, but it was often that Cason would present the list to his head coach only to find out Doherty had already found most or all of the items on his own—and already printed them out for placement on the bulletin board in the players' locker room.

On the day before the Kentucky game, Doherty worked on the scouting report throughout most of the morning, walking down the hall-way and talking with each of the assistant coaches as he did so. It was rare that any of the staff arrived in the office after 8:00 A.M. "One thing that I learned from Coach Williams is that you have to hire people that are hard workers, that are loyal and intelligent, and you set them free," said Doherty. "I don't want to look over their shoulder. I don't want to have them punch a clock. I don't have time for that. I don't want to work that way."

Around midmorning, Doherty walked downstairs to the coaches' locker room—his sanctuary away from the ringing phone—to work on the practice plan. Typically, planning a practice takes an hour or a little more. On this day, it took a little longer and Doherty worked through lunch, which was pizza and was brought downstairs by Cason. It's an unwritten policy that none of the staff goes out to lunch during the season.

Doherty returned to his office around 1:00 in the afternoon and began making phone calls—including one to Tom Izzo, the Michigan State coach. The two shared some thoughts on the game just played—sort of a postgame scouting report. For Doherty, the conversation was enlightening. "He thought our zone was effective in slowing down their transition," Doherty said. "He also admitted to going small and trying to get our big men out on the floor."

At 1:30 Forte came in for an individual film session. "I want to sit down with everybody and show them some films of our first couple of games," Doherty explained to Forte. The Forte film, edited by one of the assistants, was specifically to show Forte what he could do better on defense, which included applying better ball pressure. The session—in which Doherty cracked his only smile of the day—lasted less than a half hour.

By the time practice rolled around, Doherty was the last one on the court. When stretching was complete, the team huddled around him, and he reiterated the Thought of the Day, which was printed at the top of each practice plan and was handed out to the players prior to practice. Sometimes the Thought is basketball-related, sometimes it isn't. Often, Doherty will ask an unsuspecting player what the Thought was for today. If the answer is incorrect, the team will run a quick five-second sprint to half-court and back.

After the two-and-a-half-hour practice, Doherty showered and headed back upstairs to his office to watch more Kentucky film and make some more recruiting calls. Near midnight, he headed home—to his home office, actually, to watch one last film before he tried to sleep for a few hours.

The difference in the atmosphere in the Smith Center for Kentucky—as opposed to Winthrop or Tulsa—was obvious, and not only because of the new student seating. The television trucks and the afternoon start translated into much more of a carnival atmosphere. It was a juiced place when the Carolina players, led by Jonathan Holmes, rushed out onto the court for warm-ups. Doherty followed the players and his assistants, tossing T-shirts into the student section.

The euphoria didn't last long.

After jumping out to a 7–0 lead to start the game—including a tip-in by Forte just 10 seconds in—Carolina controlled most of the first half. The Wildcats appeared much as they had in their previous four games (of which they had lost three) in missing open jump-shots and relying too much on one-on-one moves in the half-court. Tubby Smith searched for a lineup that played well together, substituting seven times before the second media time-out.

Another 7–0 Carolina run in the middle of the first half—punctuated by a Lang dunk on the same out-of-bounds play he had dunked on just three minutes earlier—gave Carolina a 10 point lead at 21–10 with just over 10 minutes remaining in the first half. Smith immediately yanked Tayshaun Prince, whom he believed had failed to recognize the play and knock down Lang's path to the basket. Smith would admit later that he was wrong and that Prince wasn't responsible.

But after looking so sharp on offense earlier, Carolina suddenly turned the ball over on four of its next six possessions—and missed two other shots badly—while Kentucky scored on four layups to cut the lead to one point. The surge seemed to give the floundering Wildcats confidence and shake the Tar Heels. The remainder of the half would go back and forth, with Kentucky taking the lead on two Bogans free throws, but Carolina getting it back with two of its own with 15 seconds before the break.

But a Marquis Estill free throw and a put-back following a miss on the second shot gave the Wildcats a three-point lead at the half, 38–35.

The Carolina locker room was deathly quiet before the UNC coaches came in. The players, normally animated as they made their way through the tunnel and into the locker room, were in stunned silence. A game they controlled was suddenly out of control—and very much in doubt.

Doherty's instructions were rapid-fire: fight, claw, play smarter on the offensive end, and communicate better in transition defense and in the zone. Reenergized by Doherty's enthusiasm, the Tar Heels took back the lead when Haywood corralled a rebound off a missed Lang jump-hook, muscled the ball back in, and was fouled less than two minutes into the half. He missed the subsequent free throw, however, and UNC clung to a one-point lead.

The lead seesawed until Prince, back in Smith's good graces after his first-half defensive struggles, knocked in a deep three against the Carolina zone, giving the Wildcats a 50–48 advantage. Beginning with those points, Kentucky went on a 13–2 run in which Carolina appeared anemic and tentative on offense. The Wildcats were exactly the opposite, cutting through the lane with a burst of speed and shooting as if they knew it was going in.

Suddenly the game had become a forest fire, burning in so many different places that the Tar Heels appeared paralyzed as they tried to figure out what to put out first.

On the bench, Doherty continued to urge his team to play with energy, cover shooters, and block out. Between the 9:00 and 4:00 marks, Carolina played even with Kentucky. But another 13–2 run gave Smith's team a 23-point lead with 1:18 remaining. The Smith Center crowd quickly dissipated—all but the students in the risers, who began chanting "goodbye, alumni" when much of the crowd made for the concourse. Doherty, as he had in the Michigan State game, kept coaching until the final buzzer, but when it went off, Kentucky had handed Carolina its second-worst defeat ever in the Smith Center.

After a brief conversation with Parker, who had been a nonfactor due to foul trouble, Doherty ran down the tunnel with his head down to a deathly silent locker room. He addressed the team, trying to focus on the next game, two days later against Miami. When he was done, he walked outside into the hallway and saw Vince Carter, whose jersey had been retired at halftime, and his mother.

"I'm sorry," said Doherty, shaking Carter's hand. "I'm sorry we lost on the day you got your jersey retired." Carter tried to console Doherty, but it was of little comfort.

"Coach Doherty has a lot of pride, and he puts a lot into this team emotionally and physically," said Forte, who had missed 14-of-19 shots from the floor. "For us to go out there and lose like that, it's very embarrassing to him and to the team."

Doherty would apologize to the fans for the team's performance a few minutes later in his postgame press conference. "We play again in two days," he said to the media, reiterating what he had said to the team immediately following the game.

"That's the only good news."

Rock bottom for Matt Doherty and his assistant coaches came later that Saturday night. Hours after the last fan had left the arena and the custodians had picked up the final hot dog wrapper, Doherty stood outside his office in the hallway, leaning against the wall. He had watched the game film—twice. He would watch it many more times over the course of the next few days and nights. His eyes drooped and his shoulders hunched; he looked like a beaten man. His voice was low as he explained what happened.

"It was . . . it was just a total collapse," he said. "That's my fault. A lot of it was transition defense."

It would be many more hours before he made his way home and very few before he was back, trying to find the key to turning around the season. It was December 2, 142 days after he was hired as North Carolina's head coach, and he had led the Tar Heels to a 3–2 record and one of the worst home losses in the program's history. It was the lowest moment of his coaching career.

He was the last person in the world who thought it would be over two and a half months before Carolina lost again.

A Team in His Own Image

Matt Doherty made a crucial decision—one that would have a season-saving effect—in the wake of the Kentucky debacle. In essence, it was a basketball decision, but in reality it had the effect of completing the transfer of ownership of the North Carolina men's basketball program to the hard-nosed Irishman from Long Island.

The opponent on December 4, just 48 hours after the Kentucky loss, was the Miami Hurricanes. The Hurricanes were, like UNC, a team adjusting to a new coach. Leonard Hamilton was gone, having taken Michael Jordan's offer to coach the Washington Wizards. In his place was Perry Clark, who had taken the job after several successful seasons at Tulsa. But the talent needed to be replenished; just one Hurricanes starter who had taken the floor the year before against Carolina was still in uniform.

Before they could concentrate on Miami, Doherty had the entire team in the locker room on Sunday, watching the Kentucky tape for an hour. Typically, tape sessions last no longer than 15–20 minutes. This session, which was followed by a full practice, was anything but typical.

During the pregame meal at 23 on Monday, Doherty was on edge—but the players weren't. As the meal progressed, the jocularity around the room began to wear on him. "I don't mind you being loose," Doherty told the players when the meal was over, "but we'd better come out mad. We just suffered the second-worst loss in Smith Center history."

The Smith Center was barely half full at tip-off—and significantly below that when the Tar Heels took the floor for warm-ups. Although the attendance would swell to 19,859 as the late-arriving crowd filtered in, it was hardly a raucous throng. The one exception was the new student risers at the end of the Carolina bench; students who sat there had already earned a place in Doherty's heart with their enthusiasm and pre-arranged cheers.

But it wasn't the opponent or the student crowd that made the team Doherty's and dramatically changed the course of the season. What turned the Heels' year was a simple and crucial happening: The team finally took on the personality of its coach.

A few minutes into the Michigan State game six days earlier, Doherty knew he could not hang with the Spartans by playing man-to-man defense. He had an inkling going in, but the athleticism and the intensity of Tom Izzo's team confirmed it. Carolina had stayed in the game by playing a zone, but it was obvious that this would not be Doherty's team until it played his style: hard, aggressive man-to-man with a trapping zone or matchup zone mixed in.

Due to continuing foul problems with his big men and an inability to match up at key perimeter positions, Doherty was forced to play more zone than he wanted in East Lasing and again against Kentucky. It's not that he disliked the zone or that the team played it poorly—as Izzo later confirmed, the zone was very effective. It was that the zone wasn't Doherty. A zone is not about getting after it, outhustling the other guy, wanting the game more. Doherty is about all those things, and as long as he wanted his team to be an extension of himself, he couldn't play zone as his primary defense.

"I was more committed to man defense as opposed to zone or bouncing back and forth between the two," he admitted before the Miami game. It wasn't that Miami was a prime candidate to matchup man-to-man against. The Hurricanes were athletic but not highly skilled—a perfect team against which to play zone.

But Doherty had made up his mind: If Carolina was going to be his team, it had to go after a team like Miami.

And that's what the Heels did from the opening tip. Starting the same lineup he had all year, Doherty began the game pressuring the Hurricanes' ball handlers and forcing bad shots. Unfortunately, the Carolina offense couldn't take advantage, and the first six and a half minutes of the game resembled a soccer match—a lot of guys playing hard but not a lot of scoring. Haywood, who came out energized, nonetheless missed his first four free throws. Like all the other Carolina players who were shooting less than 70 percent from the line for the season, Haywood was required to make 9-out-of-10 before he could leave practice every day. He almost always made nine on his first attempt.

Carolina could manage only a Boone layup before the first media time-out, and UNC trailed early, 4–2. The late-arriving crowd snoozed. Forte broke the drought with a three-pointer out of the time-out, and Haywood scored on a layup—but missed a fifth straight free throw—for a 7–4 lead.

Despite the slow offensive start, Doherty began to see some good things happening on the court: Forte battled for a defensive rebound . . . Owens worked hard to get around a perimeter screen . . . Haywood got off his feet quickly to challenge shots, blocking several early and changing others.

But the rustiness and mental errors returned. Brian Morrison replaced Boone and immediately threw the ball away trying to toss a lob on the break to Capel. Immediately, Doherty sent Ronald Curry to the table to check in. Curry had played well in practice the day before, but even up to the tip-off, Doherty was unsure if he would use Curry. He wanted to make sure his quarterback/point guard—who had practiced only two weeks since football ended—was mentally prepared.

"Ronald," Doherty asked Curry as the team came to the huddle after warm-ups, "if we decide to use you tonight, are you ready?"

Curry's reply was swift and to the point. "Absolutely, Coach."

With 11:31 remaining in the first half, Curry got the chance. Immediately, the crowd got back into the game, cheering Ronald's appearance at the scorer's table. On his first possession in the game, Miami went zone and trapped Ronald as soon as he touched the ball. But Curry calmly handled the trap and hit Owens in the corner with a quick pass. Not getting out of control, as was his habit as a freshman, Curry ran the offense and played harassing full-court defense. Soon, the offense began to click and the ball started going inside. Lang hit a layup on a pass from Forte, which started an avalanche of scoring inside, all by Lang. The ball moved up the court, and the half-court offense clicked, thanks to Curry's sharp passes. Before he had come in, the Tar Heels had made only 3-of-11 shots from the field. With him on the floor, they had hit 6-of-9.

Meanwhile, the Carolina defense continued to stymie Miami's offense. Again, the key was Curry. He picked up point guard Michael Simmons as soon as he crossed half-court, forcing the Hurricanes' offense to start 35 feet from the basket. On the sideline, Doherty liked what he saw.

His team was playing his style.

When Curry came out six minutes later—after holding up a fist to indicate he was tired—the Heels led 21–12. Doherty reinserted him after a minute and a half, just in time to snap a 30-foot chest pass on a rope to Will Johnson, who was fouled at the basket. Curry remained in for the remainder of the half as Carolina extended to a 33–18 lead.

As pleased as Doherty was with his team's defensive performance, the first half wasn't all positive. With 8:24 remaining in the half, Capel was on the right side on the break, took a pass from Curry, and attacked the rim as Miami's Dwayne Wimbley slid in to attempt to draw the charge. His legs taken out, Capel turned as he fell and landed hard on his lower back. Immediately, he twisted in pain and yelled out. The

Smith Center crowd went quiet, remembering that Capel had battled through his freshman season with a disc problem in his back that eventually required off-season surgery.

Marc Davis quickly made his way to Capel, followed closely by Doherty, who knelt next to Capel as Davis checked him out. Capel would eventually make it off the court under his own power, but would not return.

In the locker room, Doherty pointed at Curry, but spoke to Boone and Morrison, his two freshmen point guards. "Guys, all he's doing is hitting the open man and guarding the ball. That's it, it's simple, but that's what we need."

Then, Doherty turned to Curry. "Now Ronald, don't start having Hampton flashbacks and start going between your legs and going crazy on me." Curry grinned and shook his head.

Doherty and his staff liked what they had seen, particularly when they had their small, athletic lineup—Curry, Forte, Owens, Capel, and either Lang or Haywood—on the floor. They could get into passing lanes, get out on the break, and generally turn up the speed a notch. With Capel out, Doherty talked about going with Will Johnson.

The second half began where the first half left off as Haywood blocked a shot on the baseline, giving him seven blocks on the night so far. At that point in the game, Miami had hit only seven field goals *total*. Haywood would end the game with 18 points, 14 rebounds, and 10 blocks—the first triple-double in North Carolina basketball history. On the bench, when Haywood's triple-double was announced, Doherty turned to several players and deadpanned: "I had a triple-double once, 10 minutes [played], 10 cups of water, and I set 10 screens."

As Miami grew increasingly frustrated, Carolina's confidence soared. The result was a rout that would swell to as many as 28 points with just under four minutes remaining. When Jon Holmes made a bittersweet entrance with 1:36 to go in the game, Carolina was already well on its way to a 67–45 win.

More important than the final score—and the first win in three games—was the way in which it was attained. Doherty's way: hard-nosed defense, pushing the ball on offense, going for the jugular. "That was fun," said Doherty after the game, flashing a smile that was making its first appearance in the month of December. "I don't think they got many open looks. It was fun to get into somebody and guard them." Doherty had taken the chance, and his team, finally released from its slumber, had responded. Finally, the Tar Heels were playing the style Doherty wanted. They were getting after it. They wanted it more.

Now, all they had to do was repeat it for about 30 more games.

16

Out of the Shadows

Two hours before his Tar Heels took the floor against Buffalo, Matt Doherty sat in the coaches' locker room wondering which team was going to show up. Would it be the team that had won eight days ago at Texas A&M, 82–60, by persevering through a game Joseph Forte had called "weird, it had no flow to it"? Or would it be the Carolina team that was coming off of the worst practice of the season the day before, when the Blue Team had made the starters look like the JV squad?

It was a practice that seemed upside down from the start, as the reserves defeated the starters in virtually every drill. It came to a head during a drill called "three and out" in which the defense had to string together three stops in a row. Doherty had allotted 10 minutes for the drill, but when the White Team couldn't stop the Blue Team, he extended it until they did. "I had to talk to some people," said Doherty, whose frustration and anger with the practice had caused him to lose some sleep.

"We got killed," said Jason Capel. "The Blue Team really gave it to us. We didn't think we were going to start today until he wrote it on the board."

When Doherty did write the starters on the board, it included the name Ronald Curry.

Prior to the win at Texas A&M, Doherty had met with Jonathan Holmes to explain why he was going to bring Curry off the bench as the second point guard.

"It's nothing you did wrong, Jon," Doherty explained in a low tone. "But Ronald gives us what we need defensively. We're better when he's on the floor."

Holmes was devastated. He stared at the carpet, visions of the thousands of hours he had spent in the gym with his dad back at Bloomington South, all of the line drills he had done in individual workouts in the fall, everything, filtering through his mind. None of it had amounted to anything.

Doherty, of course, knew what Holmes was going through. But the hard truth was that the team *was* better with Curry in the lineup and that all of the players had worked exceptionally hard. But only five players could play at once, and that reality meant that there would likely be 11 players at various stages of unhappiness or unrest on the bench. He empathized with Holmes, as well as the other players whose time on the court would soon be diminished, but it was a choice that had to be made. It was just as hard on the coach as it was on the player, and Doherty hardly took the conversation lightly. He did, however, try to end it on an upbeat note.

"Jon, you are still an important part of this team," Doherty said. "We'll need you to stay ready, because I might call on you at any time. You need to be ready like you were early in the season."

Holmes looked up at his coach and nodded.

Prior to revealing to the team that Curry would start against Buffalo, Doherty had told both Holmes and Adam Boone—who would now be relegated to a reserve role—about the change. Doherty informed Curry he would be starting when Ronald arrived at the Smith Center for the game. He reacted to the news as he did to most questions or pieces of information, with a slight nod and no discernible change in expression.

Doherty was more concerned with how Boone—who graduated from high school with a 4.11 grade point average and was one of the four finalists for the Franklin Watkins Award given annually to the top African American scholar-athlete—would react. He told Boone just after telling Curry, pulling him aside in the coaches' locker room. Doherty had been pleased with Boone's reaction, which was somewhat dispirited, but not crushing, like it had been with Holmes in Houston. If he hadn't been somewhat disappointed, it would mean he didn't care. Doherty wasn't worried about that—he knew Boone cared, too much at times. What he didn't want was for Boone to see it as a final defeat. It wasn't; Doherty knew (and explained) that Boone would still play about as many minutes, but Doherty wanted Curry to set the tone defensively from the game's outset.

Against Buffalo, that's exactly what Curry did. Feeding off the crowd's reaction to his start, Ronald harassed Bulls' point guard Louis Campbell, Buffalo's best all-around player. A message had been sent: Carolina was now a team that would be aggressive instead of passive.

At the end of the Sunday afternoon game, which Carolina would go on to win easily 95–74, several trends would be eliminated (at least for a time) and others established.

First, Doherty had found himself a point guard. Curry made all three of his field goal attempts, two of them threes. During his freshman season, Curry had needed 19 attempts to make 3 three-pointers; this season, he needed only four. More important, Curry had set the tone with his defense and taken care of the ball. Boone, meanwhile, played 11 minutes and did not sulk through his time on the floor, showing impressive maturity for a freshman. Holmes did not play until mop-up time. "I just wanted to work hard and let Coach make the decisions," said Curry. "I just wanted to do everything the coaches asked me to do, and I felt I had done that. I'm just glad Coach made the decision as early as he did."

Second, Haywood and Lang were beginning to understand how to play within the new confines of the postplay mandates issued by the NCAA Rules Committee. Haywood would pick up just two fouls for the game; Lang none.

Third, Forte returned to the free throw line, going 5-for-5 from the stripe against the Bulls. In the two earlier losses to Michigan State and Kentucky, Forte had gone to the line just once—and missed the free throw. It was a point of emphasis Doherty had made to him in the eight days of practice between the Texas A&M and Buffalo games; be aggressive on offensive and don't settle for jumpers. His line against Buffalo was 23 points on 9-for-15 from the field, five assists, and seven rebounds. He forced nothing, scoring all his points within the framework of the offense.

Finally—and remarkably—a Carolina player recorded a triple-double for the second time in three games. Capel's 16 points, 11 rebounds, and 10 assists came in 35 minutes, the last 1.5 of which was a gift from Doherty.

"Cape, we've got 3:14 left," said Doherty during the final media time-out. "I'm sending in a sub for you with one minute left. You need two rebounds for a triple-double."

Capel looked up and smiled. "I'll get it."

He did, grabbing his first rebound on a missed three-pointer by Gabe Cagwin—in which Bersticker shielded his man, Clement Smith, so Capel had a clear path to the ball. The history-maker would come on an offensive rebound at the 1:25 mark—:25 before the deadline— off a missed Holmes' three. Capel missed the put-back and was tied up, forcing an alternating possession, but he didn't care. For the second time in Carolina basketball history—a span of over 2,300 games—a Tar Heel had recorded a triple-double. Remarkably, the two had come 13 days apart.

Doherty's decision to leave Capel in to pursue the triple-double was a watershed moment, not because he had achieved the record, but because it signaled a coach willing to give a player a chance to pursue an individual goal. Never, experienced Carolina watchers would say, would Dean Smith have allowed such a concerted effort for an individual goal.

Smith, after all, was so adamant in his adherence to downplaying individual achievement and creativity that he once ordered that a Michael Jordan dunk—a legendary one that occurred in the waning moments of a win over Maryland in which Jordan literally invented the windmill dunk he would later use to win the NBA Dunk Contest—be edited out of the weekly coaches' television show highlights.

"I don't want to sacrifice things for individual success," explained Doherty. "But in certain situations like that I think it's the right thing to do. And there's no one more deserving than Capel to do that because he works so hard and does all the little things."

Despite the obvious difference in philosophy, Doherty's decision to leave Capel in further built a bond between the players and their coach. Capel had been one of those who had been sitting in the Bowles Room the day Doherty was announced as the new coach. As one of the players closest to Phil Ford and the other deposed assistant coaches, Capel appeared less than happy, sitting slouched on a couch, his jaw set and eyes staring straight ahead.

On this day, Capel's mother, father, grandparents, and godson were in the stands to witness an event that would not have been possible if Doherty had strictly adhered to a policy of suppressing any and all individual achievements. "I've never seen one in all my years as a coach," said his dad, Jeff Capel Sr., the head coach at Old Dominion. "I'm thrilled we could all be here today to see this."

Ever since the eighth grade, Jason Capel has sought a place to call his own. That was the year his father moved the family from Fayetteville, North Carolina (where Jeff Sr. had been the coach at Fayetteville State), to Greensboro to become the head coach at North Carolina A&T. Left behind in Fayetteville were family and friends; ahead of Jason was a year in a private school (Greensboro Day School) that he hated, another in Virginia (after his dad became the head coach at Old Dominion), and two more at St. John's Prospect Hall, a private school in Maryland.

Despite the bloodlines of a father and an older brother, Jeff Jr., who had great success with the game, Jason did not gravitate willingly to basketball as a youngster. His brother, five years older, was a legend at Hope Mills Southview High School outside of Fayetteville. "He was like the town hero, and I didn't want to be some scrub and bring down the family name," said Capel. "So I shied away from it and tried to make my niche in something else."

That something else was baseball. But eventually Jason's talent—and size—allowed him to achieve success in the family pastime. Playing against his older brother's friends built his confidence and kept him out of trouble. "I was one of those guys who could have gone either way," he said. "Basketball helped steer me the right way. I was a little troublesome, probably because I wanted attention. I just wanted to be different than my brother."

When Jeff underwent intense recruitment, Jason watched and learned. He opened every letter his brother received and went on every official visit. When Jeff chose Duke, Jason spent many weekends in Durham. When it came time for him to choose a school, Jason—who had never spent more than a few years in any one place since elementary school—wanted stability.

"My dad, when we moved to Virginia, told me that I would play my high school at the school I was at. And I left after two years," said Capel. "When I was making my college decision I could have gone to a place where I'd have been the star of the team and maybe have a chance to leave after two or three years. But my dream had been to come to Carolina, to be a part of a family."

More so than any other player in the program, Capel had a difficult adjustment to the changes that had taken place in the program since his arrival. First, Dean Smith retired soon after he committed. Then, Bill Guthridge was gone, and so were the assistants—coaches with whom Capel had grown close. The stability he had sought had vanished before his eyes.

"Things just aren't the same around here anymore," he said. "Take it however you want, they're just not. If I would have known that going into it, I can't say that would have changed my mind, because I've experienced so many good things, but it's just not the same."

Capel's strengths on the court are eerily similar to those of a small forward who played 20 years earlier and would become his coach prior to his junior year at Carolina. "Cape plays the game the way it should be played," said Matt Doherty. "He's a leader on the court who knows what needs to get done."

Unlike Doherty 20 years earlier, Capel often bristles at the role player label, but due to his wide-ranging skills and willingness to do many of the things that don't appear on a stat sheet, Capel's contributions on the floor are not as recognized as some of his teammates.

Due to his background and maturity, Capel rose to a leadership role by the time the 2001 season rolled around. "He'll tell people anything," said Ronald Curry. "He keeps everybody in check. He doesn't show any favoritism. If Joe's in the wrong, he'll go talk to Joe. If it's Brendan, he'll talk to Brendan. It's not to say, 'This is my team.' It's just to say, 'I want to win.'"

Capel's leadership and his willingness to accept a secondary scoring role on the team would both be tested as the season progressed.

Merry Christmas

Abasketball season is a lot like life in one very important way: You can sit down and look at a schedule and *think* you can predict when and where the important events (or games) will be, but more often than not, you'd be wrong.

The key games on Carolina's preseason schedule appeared to be Michigan State, Kentucky, and UCLA. The first two had been losses, with the Kentucky game having been a particularly tough pill to swallow.

In the two days following the Kentucky game and prior to Miami, Matt Doherty (and his staff) hardly went home or slept. The misery was obvious on his face. Around the coaches, he was ashen, as if he'd lost a loved one. In practice and around the players, he was extremely tough and demanding.

"He takes it really hard," Forte said before practice on December 3. "We all hate to lose, but I've never seen anyone take it like he does."

The Kentucky game had long-ranging effects. Doherty reevaluated every aspect of what they as a team were trying to do. The last three games against Miami, Texas A&M, and Buffalo had allowed him to rededicate the team to aggressive man-to-man defense. Rarely had the Heels played a possession of zone in the three easy wins.

In many respects, it had been the Miami game that had been the critical juncture of the early season, the game during which the Tar Heels discovered they could play Doherty's style—hard-nosed with a lot of emotion—and win. After that game, the players began to buy into the new system—which was much like the old one, with some changes in terminology and an infusion of energy.

The test was going to be UCLA. "We really haven't had a big win," said Jason Capel during the week. "We have to do it now so we can set a tone for the rest of the season." The Bruins, under Steve Lavin, had already suffered through a season-long series of ups and downs, bad breaks, and criticism.

Picked anywhere from 12th to 16th in the nation in the preseason polls, the Bruins had performed admirably and displayed a lethal full-court press in a 99–98 loss to Kansas and a 97–92 overtime win against Kentucky in the Coaches vs. Cancer Classic.

But since then, UCLA had been horrible and inconsistent in a home loss to Cal-State Northridge, a close win over Santa Barbara, a loss on the road at Georgia Tech, and another slim victory over UC–Irvine. The result had been loud and frequent calls for the head of Lavin, who had never completely won over the fans in Westwood when he had replaced Jim Harrick.

In the days leading up to the UCLA game, Doherty had scheduled several "fundamental" practices, during which the team would get back to the type of work they had done in October, working on individual skills and team concepts. Exams were over on Tuesday, December 19, which meant Doherty had the team's undivided attention for three days prior to taking on the Bruins.

It was a time he relished.

"It's like the guys become professional players, in a way," said Doherty of the time over the holidays. "With no class and no other distractions, they can think about basketball all the time."

Two-a-days returned, with the morning practice consisting of a combination of light shooting, running their offense against no defense, and lifting weights. Then, before the afternoon practice, the team would return for a videotape session. In all, the players would be in the Smith Center 8 to 10 hours per day while their fellow students were home for holiday break.

On Wednesday, the team received a bit of a surprise when Julius Peppers walked into the basketball office to tell Doherty he was ready to join the team. Peppers, an incredible athlete who possessed rare speed and jumping ability for a 6'6", 268-pound defensive lineman, had played a critical role the previous year off the bench when Carolina had made its run to the Final Four.

This season, Peppers, after a slow start in football, had come on to lead the nation in sacks for the football Tar Heels. But his coach, Carl Torbush, had been fired after the season and rumors immediately began that Peppers would leave school and make himself eligible for the NFL draft. In fact, when Peppers walked into the basketball office that Wednesday (he had been in contact with Doherty and the coaches throughout November and into December and had been expected, at least initially, to join the team after the last football game on November 18), many in the program believed it was to tell the coaches he wouldn't be coming out for the team and would declare for the NFL.

Peppers had told the press that he wanted the time off after the football season to work on his class work. That was only half true. While Peppers was certainly working on his grades, he was also testing the waters and collecting information on his football draft status. What he learned may have been sufficient to lead any other athlete to the decision to leave school, but Peppers had other reasons for wanting to play basketball: It was fun, and if pressed, he'd admit that he enjoyed the spotlight playing basketball afforded him.

So there was genuine surprise and delight when Peppers walked into the office and announced to the coaches he was ready to join the team. He still had not decided on the NFL yet—he would wait until just before the January 12 deadline to make a final decision to come back to UNC the next fall—but he committed to finishing out the basketball season. Peppers' obvious strength and athletic ability fit well into Doherty's rededication to aggressive man-to-man defense.

What no one expected was how quickly Peppers would fit in both on the court and off.

The year before, Peppers, who hailed from the small, down-east North Carolina town of Bailey, had been very quiet and never fully let the other players get to know him off the court. But almost from his first day back everyone noticed how loose Peppers was in the locker room, laughing and joking like he had never allowed himself to before.

On the court, he was an instant presence.

"I initially thought there was no way he could be ready for UCLA," said Doherty on Friday. "But the closer we get, the more I thought he could help. He's been through it before. And he's a player in a position where we need some help."

And Peppers was a quick learner on the basketball floor. To help him get acclimated to the new system, the assistants would work with him in prepractice on learning the plays. Wojcik or MacKinnon would grab Everett, Holmes, and a few others and run through all the sets in dummy offense, focusing on where Peppers should be.

But most of all, Peppers just played. His speed and quick-jumping ability amazed even the players who had played with him before. The assistants, many of whom would have given their right leg for a player with Peppers' ability when they worked at Navy or Fairfield, just shook their heads and smiled. At North Carolina, one of them lamented, guys like Peppers just walk into the gym one day from the *football* team.

Peppers made his first appearance against UCLA at the 7:44 mark of the first half. Up until that point, he was hardly needed as Carolina roared out to an 11–0 lead by the first media time-out. Despite it being a nationally televised game on CBS, Pauley Pavilion was a morgue at the tip and only got quieter once the game began and Carolina jumped out to a lead. When point guard Earl Watson made a free throw with 14:02 remaining in the half, the fans sarcastically cheered the Bruins' ineptitude.

On the other bench, Doherty was all over the sideline. The CBS cameras caught him several times in a textbook defensive stance (the UNC defense was in front of the bench during the first half), knees bent, arms active, communicating the trap.

The atmosphere and the anemic play of the opponent only made Doherty ride his players harder. "In that kind of situation you have to fight human nature. It would be easy to play to the level of your opponent. But as coaches, we have to keep pushing our guys not to let down or look ahead."

Doherty implored the bench to get into the game, which was rarely a problem. Bersticker, Melendez, Holmes, and Everett formed a vocal (if nonplaying) group. After big baskets or athletic dunks, they'd literally jump off their seat and bump chests. If a run caused an opposing coach to call a time-out, all three would sprint out to greet their teammates. When Doherty called on them to keep the intensity up, they were only too happy to oblige.

Through most of the first half, enthusiasm from the bench wasn't needed. UCLA did start to score, but Carolina did as well: Forte hit a floater in the lane, Curry knocked in a short jumper on the break, and Lang slung in a left-handed jump-hook. When the steadily improving Will Johnson ("he never misses a shot in practice" said Forte) took a pass on the break and hit an 18-foot jumper on the right wing, Lavin had seen enough and called his second time-out. Carolina had taken a 22–9 lead and appeared to be well on its way to erasing the pain from the Kentucky loss.

With a somewhat comfortable lead, Doherty felt it was the right time to insert his new post player, even though Peppers knew only a handful of the plays. UCLA, in many ways, was the perfect first opponent for an instinctual player like Peppers: their defense (particularly in the half-court) was not going to take anyone out of anything; so much so that Carolina had called very few set plays and had instead been able to score out of its secondary break. Peppers, therefore, could just play.

And, as it turned out, play well. He immediately set an on-the-ball screen that completely wiped out Matt Barnes ("I felt like a limp noodle," Barnes would say after the game) and allowed Morrison to hit a 16-footer and extend the Carolina lead to 18 points. It would get as high as 19 a minute later on another basket—this time a three-pointer—from Morrison.

Peppers' first bucket came on, appropriately enough, a dunk. Capel, after diving on the floor, shuffled the ball to Peppers alone under the basket. He jumped and tomahawked it with one hand. On television Billy Packer likened him to Charles Barkley. It was the kind of national exposure Peppers had never received on the football field. He would add two free throws later in the half, and North Carolina took a 16-point lead, 46–30, into halftime.

With a rain of boos cascading on the hometown Bruins as they left the court, Doherty turned to his assistants. "We're turning the ball over too much against the press," he said. Carolina indeed had 11 turnovers; entirely too many. Six had come in the last three minutes of the first half against UCLA's press. Doherty knew what would be coming in the second half.

In the locker room, the players felt good about what they had done. The mood was loose. Until Doherty came in. He railed against the turnovers. He implored the guards to be stronger with the ball and to get the ball into the middle of the floor and attack. A few easy baskets, maybe even dunks, and the UCLA press would be demoralized and fold. Human nature, Doherty explained, would lead to a letdown.

"Don't let it happen to us."

But it did. The second half was a different game as UCLA began hitting the same shots it had missed in the first 20 minutes, allowing the Bruins to get into their full-court press. Over the course of the next 11 minutes, Carolina would turn the ball over on nine occasions (on a variety of bad passes and violations) and miss all seven of its free throws. When Barnes hit two free throws following a Capel charge, the UNC lead was just 56–54 with 8:46 remaining.

Suddenly, a sure Carolina win was turning into what would be a crushing defeat. Not only could UNC lose, but it would have imploded. Given the game away. On national television. Two days before Christmas.

The next play was one of those that every player dreads and every television highlights producer covets: With UCLA in its diamond press and the Pauley Pavilion crowd smelling blood (as much as a SoCal crowd can smell blood), Capel began moving up-court with the ball. Met at midcourt by Barnes and Watson, Capel tried to throw a high pass to Lang, who was positioned just over the midcourt line. It was a bad pass for several reasons. One, he traveled when he first tried to make the pass—but the officials didn't call it. Two, the pass was to Lang in a position that Lang was unaccustomed to handling the ball. Third, the pass sailed high, over Lang, and hit Doherty—who was standing on the sidelines—right in the numbers.

Immediately, Doherty slammed the ball to the floor in disgust with one hand. Capel wanted to hide. The crowd erupted. It was turnover number 21. CBS showed the replay four times. ESPN, CNNSI, and every other sports highlights show, national and regional, had a clip for the evening show.

UCLA did not convert on the other end, but Capel *again* gave the ball away on the next possession (on a fast break when he tried to dribble in a crowd). It was the 22nd turnover of the game for North Carolina, and this time UCLA tied the score when Barnes lofted a short jumper over Haywood on the other end. The lead was gone with over eight minutes remaining in the game.

Doherty stood on the sideline with his hands on his hips. "I thought I wouldn't be having a very happy Christmas morning opening up gifts with my family," he said later. "The highs and lows in this profession are crazy." UCLA had come back from 19 points down, and after Watson hit two free throws to push the Bruins into a 58–56 lead, the home team looked well on its way to winning a game Carolina had already put in its stocking.

In the first twelve and a half minutes of the second half Carolina had turned the ball over 11 times and made just 2-of-12 from the field.

Doherty made a last-ditch effort to stem the tide. He was tired of being timid and complacent. His team had lost its edge when they were forced to go zone due to foul trouble. If they were going to lose, they were not going to lose bouncing up and down in a zone. They would go man-to-man. The assistants all agreed. If we go down, let's go down swinging.

Forte tied the score with two free throws. Carolina gave up two offensive rebounds in its first possession of man-to-man, but something else had happened, too. UCLA, now forced to execute an offense instead of stand around and shoot jumpers, took two bad shots. Haywood dunked to again tie the score. Carolina had dug its feet in the California sand. It wasn't going anywhere.

Watson scored on a lob, but Carolina handled the press and Capel was fouled by Watson, his fourth. Capel made two free throws—making it four straight made from the line. Forte stole the ball and scored on a short jumper to take a 64–62 lead with just over five minutes remaining. Capel was fouled again after Barnes missed a jump-hook. He made two more free throws, and suddenly UCLA—and Pauley Pavilion—had lost its steam.

The Bruins' Jason Kapono, who had declared for the NBA draft after the previous season only to change his mind, missed a three-pointer badly. Another press break and Forte was fouled again going at the basket. Against Michigan State and Kentucky, Forte had gone to the line just once. Against UCLA, Forte went 10 times, making eight.

The game's last four minutes were now just as the first 32 had been: UNC in control and UCLA giving chase. The switch to man-to-man defense was the key; it forced UCLA to execute, something it could not do very well. UNC had outscored UCLA, 14–1, over a four-minute period after UCLA took the lead. Carolina had answered the bell under the most difficult of conditions. Away from home, in a hostile environment, with all its weaknesses exposed.

After the game, an 80–70 Carolina win, Doherty was even able to joke about Capel's pass. "I know I was open," he deadpanned. "But I wasn't wearing the right color jersey."

It would be a merry Christmas after all.

18

Charlotte, NC

The Carolina players had experienced Matt Doherty's anger on several occasions during their nearly six months together, and they had come to expect outbursts when they played poorly or without any emotion. So what they went through at halftime against Massachusetts—in the first game of the Tournament of Champions in Charlotte three days after Christmas—was nothing new.

Doherty never got angry without good reason. He was not a coach who yelled and carried on simply for getting mad for mad's sake, nor did he do so to play mind games or for the sake of the television cameras. He used the outbursts as a way to motivate, to inspire a sense of fear, and to push his players out of their comfort zone. "Fighting human nature," he would call it. Getting mad was just a tool; in fact, Doherty was much more likely to speak to players individually, show them films, put an arm around them, or otherwise motivate and cajole than to yell.

But when he did lose it, watch out.

Joe Forte first heard of Doherty's temper from Notre Dame All-American Troy Murphy, who gave him the rundown on his new coach while the two of them played on the college-select team against the U.S. Olympic team in Honolulu during the summer of 2000. Murphy relayed a story that had made the news in South Bend the season prior when, during a practice after a loss, Doherty had made the Irish run 309 consecutive sprints. The incident made such a deep impression that several Notre Dame players wrote the number "309" on their shoes as a constant reminder of what had transpired.

Many of Doherty's tirades quickly became sources of great humor and bonding, even to the players who had gone through the tongue lashing. They knew that Doherty, who possesses the ability to laugh at himself or make a snide comment a day or two after he gets angry, was only trying to make the team better and had their personal interests at heart.

It didn't take long for Forte and the others to feel the wrath, love, humor, and sense of closeness Doherty emanated once their new coach took over in Chapel Hill.

"Michael Brooker was supposed to say good-bye to a recruit during a visit in the fall," Forte recalled. "But he didn't make it. So he told Coach Doherty that his car broke down. And Coach Doherty just flipped on him. He said, 'If we had a game, you'd have been here.' Of course, he didn't exactly say it like that. This was early in the fall and was probably only the second time I had seen him get mad, as I had just gotten back from Hawaii. So Coach is yelling at Brooker and I'm standing behind him, trying not to laugh.

"But Coach caught me when he turned around quickly. Without hesitating and in a joking manner, he said: 'What the hell are you laughing at?!'

"And I just lost it," said Forte.

Doherty quickly learned who could take his stronger forms of criticism and who might better be handled with kid gloves. Forte, Jason Capel, Brendan Haywood, and Kris Lang, for example, reacted well to being pushed. So did Brian Morrison and Max Owens.

Doherty could motivate differently depending on the time and the setting. Forte, for example, reacted very well to being challenged, even when he was walking down the stairs to the locker room in the off-season.

"Joe," Doherty said one day as Forte was making his way to change for a preseason October workout. "I was just watching the Duke game [from last year] and Chris Carrawell was scoring on you anytime he wanted to."

Forte was somewhat taken aback, but the comment, and others like it, found their mark. "I immediately tried to come up with excuses," said Forte. "I was thinking that I was just a freshman then and stuff like that. The truth of it is, he was right, and I needed to learn how to play some defense and stop some people."

The players made the adjustment to Doherty's various motivational styles well and by late December reacted as needed when he playfully needled them in hotel lobbies or, when the situation called for more drastic measures, he rearranged the furniture in the locker room.

Which is exactly what he did at halftime against UMass in the first game of the Tournament of Champions in Charlotte. The Minutemen were in the midst of a difficult season, having lost seven of their first nine games, albeit against a difficult schedule. (A UMass beat writer referred to it as a "firing schedule," suggesting that Massachusetts athletic director Bob Marcum scheduled games at Oregon, Ohio State, and against UConn and North Carolina as a way to ensure a poor record and be able to show Coach Bruiser Flint the door at season's end.)

But UMass had come out inspired against Carolina and scrapped its way to within seven points at the half, 40–33.

As soon as he walked into the locker room, the players knew their coach was incensed. He had talked all week—the players had returned to campus early on December 26 to resume practice—about setting the tone defensively. The UCLA game, and the return of Curry and Peppers, had convinced Doherty that his Tar Heels could play defense the way he had wanted all along: aggressively. Doherty had wanted to take UMass out of what it did best, which was to run single and double screens for shooter Monty Mack.

The Tar Heels had failed, as Mack had scored 16 points in the first half.

At halftime, Doherty railed against the inadequate ball pressure. He blasted Forte—Mack's primary defender—and the rest of the perimeter players for being lazy and letting UMass dribble and pass anywhere it wanted to on the floor. On offense, Carolina had settled for jump shots and wasn't working to get the ball inside to Haywood and Lang. The tirade could be heard throughout the back corridors of the Charlotte Coliseum.

Finally, unable to contain himself, Doherty spied an unoccupied metal chair in the corner of the room. In one quick, deft maneuver, he stepped over to the chair and stomped his size 14 foot on the seat. The chair crumbled, startling the players momentarily. No one dared move or let out a sound.

Carolina came out and outscored UMass by 24 points in the second half, while allowing Mack just one more basket on eight shot attempts.

Afterward, when the reporters filed in, the chair, just like the sprints at Notre Dame and Brooker's failure to say good-bye to the recruit, became an after-the-fact punch line.

"It looks like I'll be paying for a chair," deadpanned Doherty after the game.

"At this point, I don't think we're going to be alarmed by anything Coach does," said Forte through a grin. "We've seen it all."

Back-to-back games are hard on players, but they're hell on coaches. During the first game of the tournament between Richmond and the College of Charleston, two very respectable midmajor clubs with NCAA aspirations, assistants Doug Wojcik and Fred Quartlebaum sat at one end of the court, scouting both teams. In this day and age of satellite television and tape exchanges between schools, it was rare that a coach got a firsthand look at an opponent. Just for good measure, Carolina's tape coordinator/strength coach Ben Cook had brought along more than enough tapes on each team, which were back in Doherty's presidential suite at the South Park Suites Hotel.

John Kresse's College of Charleston Cougars won the hard-fought battle against Richmond, meaning Wojcik would be preparing the scouting
report on the Cougars. It would take him until 6:00 the next morning to
get the tapes broken down and the highly detailed report completed. He
was up two hours later to go over it with Doherty and the rest of the staff.

Later, during the walk-through, Wojcik went through the Cougars'
offense with the players on the Coliseum floor. Charleston was an
exceedingly well-coached team that didn't utilize the press as much as
Kresse teams in the past, but was very solid in its half-court man-to-man
and zone and ran a number of offensive sets to get the ball to their two
stars, 6'8" center Jody Lumpkin and 6'3" guard Jeff Bolton.

Due to the first-person account, Wojcik had audible calls to go with
the various plays. With many tapes, it was a near impossible chore to get
calls for plays unless a courtside microphone picked it up or a hand signal
could be seen clearly enough. It was not uncommon for the coach with
the scouting responsibility to press his face up against the television screen
(or his ear to the speaker) while watching a tape, trying to determine if the
point guard was signaling or calling out a "1" or a "thumbs down."

At pregame meal, Doherty quizzed the players on various Cougar
players and plays. "Joe, which way does Bolton like to drive when he's
on the left wing?" "Jason, when Charleston calls play '5,' what are they
going to run?" Almost always, the players got the questions right to
Doherty's satisfaction.

Doherty came out for pregame warm-ups as he always did, about 25
minutes before tip-off, and immediately spied Dave Hanners, the former
Carolina assistant whom Doherty had displaced when he brought his own
staff with him from Notre Dame. The two greeted each other warmly.
Hanners, a central figure in the Carolina basketball family for almost three
decades, had gone through the expected range of emotions after his dismissal. He had been shocked at first, then slowly picked up and moved on
with his life. He had attended some of the early-season Carolina games,
watching from a seat in the upper deck of the Smith Center, before UNC
alumnus Larry Brown had given him a job as a scout for the Philadelphia
76ers. It was in that capacity that he had come to Charlotte.

In early November, Roy Williams had asked Hanners and Pat Sullivan to come to Lawrence to scout his team while it played in an intrasquad scrimmage. Hanners and Sullivan had gone and given Williams their opinions on the Jayhawks' strengths and weaknesses. After watching and reporting on the Kansas team, the two former UNC assistants sat down with Williams in his office for a more personal discussion on the lingering effects of Williams' decision to remain at Kansas.

The Williams affair had, as might be expected, created a fissure in the Carolina Basketball Family. South Carolina coach Eddie Fogler was incensed with Williams and had refused to return any of Williams' repeated phone calls since early July. Larry Brown harbored ill will about the way his interview with Baddour had been conducted. Other former players and Carolina coaches held strong feelings about various aspects of the coaching change, as well. Universally, none liked the way in which the loyal assistant coaches had been summarily dismissed.

Standing above the fray, Dean Smith had resumed a close relationship with Williams, and the two had talked often, further cementing Smith's reputation as an individual who possessed a remarkable ability to forgive former players and coaches. No one had been more positively affected by this Smith quality than Larry Brown himself when the latter was the coach at Kansas and hired Ed Manning (the father of then–top recruit Danny Manning of Greensboro) as an assistant coach, despite Manning's lack of experience in coaching.

Following Brown's hiring of Manning (and the inevitable decision by his son to attend Kansas) many in the UNC basketball office— including then-assistant Bill Guthridge—were incensed and refused to speak with Brown. But not Smith. He almost immediately forgave Brown and never held a grudge against his former player and assistant. Brown remained enough of a Smith favorite to become Smith's top choice to take over the program after Williams chose to remain in Lawrence.

As the year after Doherty's hiring progressed, Williams and Doherty spoke to as many members of the Carolina Basketball Family as possible in an attempt to smooth the rough waters. After many frank conversations and, more important, with Smith's inclusive manner, it was only a matter of time before old grudges were forgotten.

The Charleston matchup turned out to be more of a test than anyone in Carolina blue would have liked. Again, Carolina's defense did not stop its opponent from running what it wanted to. Against a weak UMass team, the poor defense had only hurt the Tar Heels in the first half. But Charleston was significantly better; the Cougars, in fact, had beaten Carolina in this very tournament two years earlier.

From the second Charleston possession—when Bolton blew by Capel for an uncontested layup for the Cougars' first hoop—Doherty was up off the bench. The Tar Heels looked heavy-legged versus the smaller, quicker Cougars. Lang played well inside, working hard to get position on the 6'6" Leighton Bowie, but Charleston was able to run its sets unimpeded.

Carolina was in for a battle.

By the second media time-out, Charleston had taken a 15–10 lead. Doherty subbed in four new players—Haywood, Morrison (playing in his new role as backup to Forte), Curry, and Capel. Boone and Peppers had already made an appearance. The infusion of energy worked, as Carolina quickly tied the score on a twisting, full-court layup by Curry, who was looking more and more comfortable running the offense and scoring when he had to.

But the rest of the half was a possession-by-possession war, with six lead-changes and neither team gaining more than a two-point advantage until Bowie's layup with 2:30 to go before the half gave Charleston a three-point lead, 26–23. Carolina got the lead back on a Lang jump-shot and a Forte tip-in, but Charleston again answered with a Lumpkin dunk and a Rudy Rothseiden drop step against Capel. Forte's baseline reverse layup brought the Heels to within one, 30–29, at the half.

Doherty was every bit as upset at the half as he was the night before, but he sensed his team needed something different. Again, he was angry, but instead of releasing his emotions—as might be expected of any young coach in his position—he was more constructive while addressing his team. Sounding more like a professor, he pointed out the mistakes and spoke in muted tones about what type of effort they would need to win. Better than the first half, he noted.

Inside, Doherty was twisted in knots. Not only was the defense not doing what he wanted, but an upset hung in the air. Doherty knew such a loss would be disastrous, not just because it would be to a lesser opponent, but because it might come this early in his coaching career and in a city he had once called home.

The second half began in the worst possible manner, with Lumpkin—who had made Haywood appear slow and sluggish all night—catching an errant post pass from Bowie and laying it in against Carolina's set half-court defense.

After two free throws, Haywood picked up his third foul with 17:27 remaining in the game, which allowed Doherty to insert Owens into the lineup and go small. Defensively, it was a much better matchup; offensively, it negated Charleston's strategy of double and triple teaming Haywood as soon as he touched the ball.

Thirty seconds later Capel wrestled the lead back with a baseline drive. Another Lumpkin layup put the Cougars in front, but Forte answered with a 12-foot jumper in the lane off a set play following a media time-out. The play—an on-ball screen for Forte on the left wing while a double screen was set up for Owens on the opposite side—would become a key set for the Heels the rest of the way.

Following Forte's hoop—the 16th lead change in the game—Carolina would hold a slight advantage until just before the game's final minute. But only once would that lead reach as many as five points, as Kresse masterfully switched defenses and mixed offensive sets, sometimes calling two or three plays at a time—to be run in successive possessions—during time-outs.

The only offensive constant for UNC was Forte, who would go on to score 29 points on a masterful array of midrange jumpers, three-pointers, and layups. Defensively, Forte was matched up on Bolton, who was having a magnificent game himself. Together, the two would put on a tremendous individual battle throughout the second half.

Bolton would finally tie the score with a twisting, driving, jump-hook in the lane—against Forte—with 1:12 remaining. Capel answered with a left-handed leaner—as the shot clock wound down—for a two-point lead.

Thirty-eight seconds remained. Kresse, who had no time-outs, had already called the play he wanted in the prior time-out. Carolina set up in its man-to-man. Whereas early in the game the Tar Heels' defensive stances had been lazy, with their hands down at their side, they were now poised, legs bent, eyes darting around the court. This was it; one stop for the win. Without it, Carolina would lose.

The year before, this was exactly the kind of game North Carolina would lose; one in which it played anemic but thought it would escape with a close victory over a lesser opponent. Too often, it hadn't happened. Several players would think that very thought as Charleston began its play: a clear-out for Bolton on the left wing.

Having been beaten on defense for most of the night, Forte decided to roll the dice. Starting on the baseline, Bolton flashed up the lane to receive the pass at the top of the key. Only the ball never got to him: Forte, a step behind Bolton, lunged into the passing lane as the ball left Charleston point guard Tyrone Nelson's hand. Forte just got the base of his left hand on the ball, knocking it loose and back toward Nelson. Already with a head of steam, Forte outran Nelson for the ball and streaked down-court. One dribble, two dribbles, layup. Four-point lead, 11.5 seconds remaining.

"He's that talented," Doherty said of Forte and the defensive play. "He's that competitive. He's an All-American and that's what All-Americans are supposed to do."

Bolton made it interesting with a deep three-pointer just six seconds later, but Lang, knowing the Cougars had no time-outs, quickly inbounded to Owens, who had snuck behind the Charleston press, and scored the layup and was fouled with two and a half seconds on the clock.

Carolina had survived, nearly done in by human nature, but not quite.

Back on the Inside

Matt Doherty was on the outside, looking in. It was the spring of 1986, and it had been one year since he last played college basketball. While Wall Street had brought him a lifestyle—living in an apartment on Manhattan's Upper West Side, eating in expensive restaurants, working on Wall Street—many his age would relish, it was making him less and less happy.

He missed the game.

Slowly, basketball began to creep back into his life. He began to get involved as a member of the media, taking time off of trading to work as an unpaid runner for CBS during the Final Four and doing radio color commentary on St. Francis games in Brooklyn (where Bobby Valvano, the brother of Jim, was the coach). Slowly, he began to realize it was possible to make a living out of basketball. But coaching was not yet in his system.

The firm he worked for, Kidder-Peabody, began to change as well. When it was bought by General Electric in the late 1980s, the firm became much more cutthroat. No longer were managers giving out leads; they were keeping them for themselves. Any semblance of a family atmosphere began to fade, and Doherty, realizing he was living for the weekends and had little passion for trading, began to look for a way out.

At 11:00 A.M. one morning in 1987, Doherty strolled into his bosses' office at 10 Hanover Square. "I'm leaving," he said. They thought he meant for lunch, but Doherty meant forever.

Without a job, Doherty moved to North Carolina, the site of so many of his athletic triumphs. It was the turning point in his professional life. "When he moved down south, he came back to an environment where basketball memories were very, very vivid," said Bob McKillop, his high school coach and close friend. "He could really sort out the experience of that end to his playing career." Over the course of the next two years, Doherty moved first to Greensboro and then to Charlotte, working as an executive recruiter. It was a job similar to Wall Street—"just different products," he said—and offered little more than a paycheck.

While in Charlotte, Doherty began to dabble again in radio, doing color for Davidson College basketball. With his name and reputation, Doherty was still well known throughout the state. Almost on a lark, he got involved with UNC grad and former football star Charles Waddell as a coach for a traveling AAU team called the Charlotte Sonics. The coaching bug bit, and when it did, Doherty knew he was hooked.

He planned practices. He planned road trips. He coached several talented players, including future Tar Heel point guard Jeff McInnis. When Davidson's coach, Bobby Hussy, was fired in 1989 after a 7–24 season, Doherty began lobbying for his old coach McKillop to get the job. "I was at Davidson before he was, so it was kind of like I was trying to help him in any way that I could, talking to [then–athletic director] Kit Morris, talking to prominent boosters, knowing that I'd probably end up working for him." When McKillop got the job, Doherty was his first hire.

He was finally back on the inside.

"He was never a spectator," said McKillop. "He always wanted to be a participant."

Davidson College is a unique dot on the college basketball map. The program's current standing in Division I can be traced to a period of two years in the late 1960s when Lefty Driesell led the Wildcats to two consecutive improbable seasons and two NCAA Regional Championship games (both close losses to North Carolina) that defined the program while at the same time relegating it to a position of forever trying to recapture old glories. Davidson is small, private, and one of the finest academic colleges in the south. While most other colleges with its profile compete in Division III, Davidson, thanks to a past both remarkable and damning, chooses to compete at the Division I level. And while it is highly unlikely that lightning can be trapped in a bottle more than once, that is the task put before any succeeding Davidson coach by the prominent alumni, many of whom live and work in nearby Charlotte and remember what Driesell did and wonder why, if it happened once, it can't happen again.

Davidson, with its challenging academics and small, rural campus, can be a tough sell to recruits. It requires a coaching staff that knows, appreciates, and can uncover recruits who will be attracted to an outstanding liberal arts college while not lamenting the big school, big city experience. It can be a trying experience for any coach, let alone one in his first season.

When McKillop and Doherty (joined by Don Hogan, now the head coach at West Florida who played for McKillop in high school; John Corso, a high school teammate of Doherty's; and Larry Garloch, who played at Miami of Ohio and was on the previous Davidson staff) started, the school had just completed construction on Belk Arena, a tiny jewel of a gym, but hardly a big-time facility. They also inherited a program struggling to compete amid increasing speculation that the school would deemphasize the sport and athletics in general.

The first year, 1989–90, was a disaster. Everyone knew it was coming— given the dearth of talent left over from the Hussy era—but it was hard on the staff, particularly McKillop. "I had never experienced losing like that before in my life. Basically, he [Doherty] went about doing his job, knowing he had a clear vision that we were going to bring good players in here and we were going to turn this around." With Doherty beating the bushes—and in the process, developing a straightforward, relentless, and creative recruiting style—Davidson did slowly improve, from winning four games in their first season, to 10 in 1990–91 and 11 in 1991–92.

"We'd be in the office about 8:00 A.M., we might go get a bite to eat, work until dinner, maybe work out—we'd play three-on-three, two-on-two—go get something to eat, and then we'd be back at the office until midnight," recalled Doherty. "We'd do that, it seemed like, every day for a couple months. I enjoyed it. I enjoyed calling recruits. It was like selling stocks and bonds. Cold calling. I enjoyed the camaraderie with Coach McKillop and Hogan and Corso and Garloch. I was single, so I could be very selfish with my time. And that's what I enjoyed doing."

Each year, McKillop, Doherty, and the other coaches brought in better players, and Doherty developed as a coach, relying on lessons learned from Dean Smith, Eddie Fogler, Bill Guthridge, and Roy Williams. "He'd be talking on the phone at 11:30 at night with a prospect, having talked to the guy already for an hour and having the staying power to go another half hour," recalled McKillop. "He was meticulous in his approach to analyzing opponents, analyzing strategy, and developing our strategy against it."

McKillop remembers sitting in a hotel room, watching Doherty come back from an AAU event at 1:30 in the morning and going right to the table and sending out recruiting letters. "I think it was that sense of purpose, that sense of commitment, that was a constant that gave me a clear indication that he was passionate enough to get it done."

His former coaches, who were first surprised that Doherty gave up a successful career on Wall Street for coaching, also noticed his dedication to his new profession. "He's always had a great desire to learn more about the game of basketball and the little ins and outs of it," said Bill Guthridge. "And then when he did decide to get back in coaching, he worked our camp, and in the afternoons during free time he was on the phone calling prospects."

The recruits noticed his dedication, as well. "You knew his name," said Jason Zimmerman, a Davidson guard from 1990–94 who was courted by Doherty. "He had played at Carolina, played with Michael Jordan. He came into my house and he had a national championship ring on. I wasn't getting recruited by major schools like North Carolina, so when he came into the house, it made an impression." Later in the recruitment process, Zimmerman would come on his official visit to Davidson, where he was met at the airport by Doherty, who was carrying a jersey with Zimmerman's name on the back.

Doherty also had an instant and long-lasting affect on the players he recruited and coached. "He was very neat. Very sharp," recalled Matt Matheny, a walk-on then and an assistant coach at Davidson now. "He always looked good and dressed well, like he does now. He was also very in-tune with what was going on at the time."

It was not unusual for Doherty to jump into drills or scrimmages when he felt the intensity needed a boost. "He was better than most of the guys on the team," said Matheny. "He was still pretty young and he could still play. That's one of the things I remember is that he would compete in the drills. And he was *very* competitive. To the point, in practice, it would get pretty intense."

And just as he had learned from Smith, Doherty created a family atmosphere with those he recruited and coached. It made it that much more difficult when it came time to leave.

In the spring of 1990, Doherty, taking a break after the spring recruiting grind, decided to take a night out and relax. He drove the 20 miles to Charlotte—there was not much to do in Davidson if you were not a college student—to an "Alive After Five" party put on by a local television station at the Charlotte Convention Center. While there, he met a beautiful woman about his age and, never shy, Doherty introduced himself.

Kelly Propst, who split time between her hometown of Concord, North Carolina, and Miami, Florida, was not a sports fan and most certainly had never heard of Matt Doherty. "I had never followed basketball in my life. I knew of Michael Jordan, but that was about it." Kelly was so unimpressed that she initially gave Doherty a fictitious name: her friend's. "After 30 minutes, when I realized how nice and sweet he was, I confessed."

By the end of the evening, Kelly knew she was in trouble. By November, she moved back to Charlotte full-time to be close to Matt; by May—one year after they met—they were married.

It was the spring of 1992, and Matt Doherty was more nervous than he had ever been. It had been three years since Doherty had arrived at Davidson, three years spent learning the coaching craft under McKillop. In March, Jerry Green was hired as the head coach at Oregon and had taken Mark Turgeon with him, opening one spot on Roy Williams's staff at Kansas. (The NCAA had mandated a three-assistants rule that year, meaning that instead of two vacancies on the Jayhawks staff, there would only be one.) Doherty wanted the job as badly as he had wanted anything in his professional life.

"I had talked to several people and had more than several apply but there were only a couple guys I was going to even really seriously consider and I wanted it to be someone I knew, someone I could trust and knew would be loyal," said Williams.

Williams settled on two final candidates: Doherty, who had played for him while he was an assistant at North Carolina; and Joe Holladay, the coach at Jenks (OK) High School who had gotten to know Williams when Carolina recruited (and eventually signed) a player of his, Steve Hale. Williams agreed to meet with Doherty at the 1992 Final Four in Minneapolis. Kansas was coming off three consecutive seasons of 27 or more wins and was one year removed from reaching the national title game in 1991 (after defeating UNC in the semifinals).

Doherty arrived in Williams's hotel room, and the two began to catch up with each other. In his three seasons at Davidson, Doherty had bumped into Williams at recruiting camps and other functions where coaches congregated. "As a player, he had my total respect because he was a guy who wanted to do things exactly right," said Williams. "He wanted to be perfect." As a coach, Doherty had earned a reputation as a diligent recruiter. Whenever Williams would speak to colleagues from the Southern Conference or those who had ties to Davidson, he'd inquire about Doherty. "The reports that I got were that he hadn't changed. He was still the kind of person I'd want to be with."

The meeting went on for about an hour and a half. "I was so nervous meeting with him," said Doherty. "Here's a guy I've known for a long time. I'm in his hotel room, and I'm telling him how much I want to work for him. My wife, when I left, said, 'You were so tight.'"

Williams's wife, Wanda, who was also there, had the same thought. Williams knew Doherty, however, and took that nervousness as something else.

"I took it as more of how much he wanted the job as opposed to being nervous," said Williams. "That part didn't bother me, but he was very intense. . . . I have heard him say several times about how he was so nervous. But I took it as a positive of how intense he was because of the degree to which he wanted the job."

When the interview was over, Wanda asked her husband, "Is he always like that?"

Williams responded, "No, he just really wants the job."

Doherty got the job, and before he and Kelly moved to Lawrence, Kansas, he had to tell the Davidson players his decision. Given his training in the family atmosphere of Carolina basketball and his own emotional investment in the players in the program, they were difficult conversations to have.

"It was a Friday night and he called me up in my dorm room," recalled Zimmerman. "His voice was shaking and he was pretty upset. He said that he was leaving to go to Kansas. He didn't have to call me and tell me, but he felt he had to. He wanted to make sure I knew why he had to make the decision."

Several years later, when Doherty had become the head coach at Notre Dame, he displayed rare loyalty and devotion to his former players.

"He got my mom and dad tickets to the Ohio State game, his first game as a head coach," said Zimmerman. "He didn't have to do that. My dad got there two hours early, and Coach Doherty spent 45 minutes talking to him before the game. He gave my mom a hug after the game. That relationship he continues to build is something he doesn't have to do, but it's special to my family and me."

Doherty left Davidson in much better shape than when he arrived. With many of the recruits he brought in—including Brandon Williams, who would go on to score over 1,500 points at Davidson and earn an NBA championship ring with the San Antonio Spurs—the Wildcats would go on to solid success in the mid-1990s, winning 20-plus games twice in a three-year span.

"He had stamped his name on the program by what he had accomplished," McKillop said of Doherty. "We really struggled. We had not had a 500 season yet [when Doherty left], and he had this wonderful opportunity for him to be in a program with a guy who had coached him and recruited him. It was the next step in his progression. He was ready."

Once at Kansas, Doherty was on track to attain his goals in the coaching profession. He knew it would take exceptional dedication and hard work, but neither had ever been a problem for him. If anything, Doherty needed to learn to back off a little bit, to realize that players were allowed to make mistakes, that they were human.

In St. Louis for the NCAA Regionals in 1993, Kansas was preparing to play California in the Sweet Sixteen. During a particularly heated practice a few days before the game, Doherty—serving as an official during an intrasquad scrimmage—called a foul on one of the team's best players, Richard Scott. Scott reacted with a cross look at Doherty, who responded by yelling back at Scott. Williams immediately stopped practice.

"Here I am, trying to get to the Final Four and I've got to worry about people's feelings?!" Williams yelled. "It's not a problem, Richard, for him to correct you. Coach Doherty, it's not a problem for him to be stubborn and give you a dirty look. He may not think he did something wrong. He may think your call was a bad call, but there's no problem with that, but I'm tired of worrying about people's feelings. We're trying to go to a Final Four. We're in this thing together!!"

An assistant coach in that situation, like a player, is likely to sulk or become sullen when taken to task by the head coach in such a public fashion. But not Doherty. "Immediately, instead of going over to the side and pouting, he was right back into it," Williams said of Doherty. "He walked over past Richard two minutes later and patted him on the back and said, 'Let's go.' And I think that focus is something that's been important to him."

Kansas would go on to the Final Four that season, only to lose to North Carolina in the semifinals in New Orleans. Carolina went on to win the National Championship two nights later with a win over Michigan, with Williams and Doherty in the stands, cheering on their alma mater.

Maturing and gaining confidence every day under Williams's tutelage, Doherty became one of the most recognizable—and thus sought after—assistant coaches in college basketball. In his seven seasons in Lawrence the Jayhawks reached the NCAAs every year, won five conference crowns, and advanced to the Sweet Sixteen or beyond on five occasions.

Along the way, Doherty was courted by several universities seeking a head coach, but like Williams had been at North Carolina, Doherty was patient and bided his time for the right opportunity to come along. When Doherty would be contacted by a school, he'd go to Williams. Their conversations always went the same way, with Williams careful not to offer too much advice, but Doherty actively seeking it just the same.

Some of the jobs that, for one reason or another, were not right were Long Beach State, Manhattan, and UNC–Charlotte. The latter was a job that kept him up nights while he decided whether or not to take it. He had lived in Charlotte, and his wife was from nearby Concord, but after consulting with Williams and Smith, he chose to stay at Kansas. The next season, when Charlotte went to the NCAA Tournament,

Doherty felt as if he may have missed his opportunity. All through the spring of 1999, Doherty felt as if his chance came and he had blown it.

Until Notre Dame came along.

The fit seemed perfect. Doherty was an Irish Catholic guy from Long Island, where, as McKillop put it: "Notre Dame has instant recognition, instant notoriety, instant respect. Growing up Irish Catholic in New York there's Notre Dame, the Knicks and Yankees, Giants, Mets and St. John's."

Doherty went after the job with everything he could.

Notre Dame was a unique basketball job that perplexed and enticed many coaches and college basketball insiders. It had its downsides: the facilities were average, the shadow that was created by football (which would always be king) was considerable, and the former coach, John MacLeod, had struggled. But it also had a great many positives: it had a great academic reputation, a national name, and competed in a big-time conference (the Big East).

"Ideally, you want a great job that's always going to be great, like a North Carolina, or you want a job that was beaten up," said Doherty. "It's like buying a stock. You want to buy a stock that's been beaten up but has great infrastructure for success. And Notre Dame did. It needed work and I wasn't afraid of that. It had just been beaten up for a while, for whatever reason. Some of the reasons you know, some you don't know until you get there, and that's scary, too, the unknown."

Notre Dame was in a position where it could hire a coach with considerable head coaching experience, if it so chose. Athletic Director Mike Wadsworth had many fine midmajor coaches to choose from—and as much advice as he could handle. As it turned out, the type of person he was looking for was Matt Doherty.

Williams immediately got involved in trying to get Doherty the job. "I thought it was going to be difficult for him to get it, but I thought it was the perfect job for him," recalled Williams. "I challenged the athletic director and [others involved with the search] and said, 'You guys are going to [have to be] really tough. You've got to really have enough courage to hire a guy who's never been a head coach. Everybody is going to say you're stupid to do that but [Kansas athletic director] Bob Frederick did and it worked out all right here.'"

As it turned out, Wadsworth had the same idea.

"He didn't want to take somebody else just because somebody else said so and he'd done this and this at other schools," said Williams. "He wanted to find the one guy that he thought was perfect. So he didn't shy away from that challenge. I told him that three years from now the Notre Dame job will be better off with Matt Doherty than anybody else that you can hire, so what makes the difference whether he has head coaching experience or not?"

The search was highly scrutinized by the media, but no one picked up on Doherty's involvement until very late in the process. When his name did come up, several days after he had interviewed, it was cast aside as a long shot at best. Digger Phelps, a former Notre Dame coach and current ESPN analyst, told a national television audience that Notre Dame would never hire an assistant coach. When he heard that, Williams immediately called Wadsworth and left a message: "See, I told you. It's a challenge."

Doherty was offered the job a few days later.

The night before Doherty was to travel to Notre Dame to attend the press conference announcing his hiring, he and Williams spent several hours going over what he would say. Williams had jotted down some notes earlier that day on the flight back from the 1999 Final Four in Tampa. As the two men watched Connecticut defeat Duke in the National Championship game in Doherty's living room, Williams and Doherty covered every possible scenario. Around midnight, Williams was leaving to go home when he had one more thought.

"You've got to do one more thing," Williams told Doherty on the phone.

"What's that?" Doherty asked.

"Call your mom and dad and tell them that you want them on the first possible flight from Long Island to South Bend," Williams said.

Doherty agreed and immediately consulted every major college coach's best friend: the Official Airline Guide (or OAG). Doherty called the airline, made the arrangements, and then, early the next morning, called his parents. Doherty told them to be on the plane later that day; he wanted them in South Bend when he was announced as the new head coach at Notre Dame.

"I think I was probably more proud of him for that than any other thing he'd done," said Williams. "He got his mom and dad to the press conference. I thought that was just going to be a truly touching moment for them."

A little more than a year later, one of the first tasks Doherty would attend to after accepting the North Carolina job was to consult his handy OAG, arrange another flight, and call his parents to tell them to meet him in Chapel Hill.

In becoming the head coach at Notre Dame, Matt Doherty had finally attained the job he always wanted. His personal life was also cruising along, as his wife, Kelly, had given birth to their first child, Tucker, after which Matt slept on the floor of the Lawrence Memorial Hospital.

His first assistant coach hire was the easiest. Doherty first met Doug Wojcik while the latter was on Don DeVoe's staff at Navy. Doherty and Wojcik ran into each other often on the recruiting trail while both pursued the small pool of talented players and students who were qualified for places like the Naval Academy and Davidson. Doherty admired Wojcik's dogged style and work ethic, and the two soon became friends, meeting at Final Fours for dinner.

"He's the hardest worker I'd ever seen in the summer recruiting," said Doherty, adding with a smile, "Oh, we'd [Davidson] beat him for every recruit he ever tried to get, no question. So I felt sorry for him."

Above all, Wojcik was a winner. It's a trait he learned, in part, from his father, Fred, a three-sport star at Wheeling Central Catholic High School in the 1950s (a few years prior to John Havlicek's rise to local prominence across the Ohio River in Bridgeport). Thirty years later, Fred's son Doug would follow in his footsteps, playing quarterback, point guard, and pitcher at Central Catholic.

In the economically depressed Steel Valley during Wojcik's childhood, high school football reigned supreme. In 1979, Central Catholic won the West Virginia state title in that sport, with Wojcik as a backup quarterback. Basketball was just what you played at Central Catholic after football season was over. That is, until the arrival of a new coach, Skip Prosser.

Prosser, who would later go on to become the head coach at Xavier and Wake Forest, became the basketball coach at WCC prior to Wojcik's freshman year and put an emphasis on the sport like no coach prior. His devotion to the sport and to his players was infectious: He would open the gym at any hour—even during the summer—as well as drive players to summer camps at Notre Dame or Five-Star. Wojcik took to the new emphasis, and soon basketball was his favorite sport.

Wojcik would cap his high school career with a 25–2 record and a state championship as a senior, but at 6'0" and possessing more desire than natural ability, the Division I schools stayed away.

The Naval Academy didn't so much find him as he found it. Mike Sonnefeld, an athlete (nearly every male was an athlete at Central Catholic) a year ahead of Wojcik, would return home from Annapolis with his plebe friends wearing their dress uniforms. Wojcik began casual conversations with Mike (who was the brother of a friend in his class) and began to think more seriously about the Naval Academy as his senior year progressed. The more he thought about it, the better it looked to him: a free education at a top school and the chance to play ball. His parents overwhelmingly approved. Prosser was himself a graduate of a service academy (the Merchant Marine Academy in King's Point), and Wojcik would become the first and only player he sent to Division I while at Central Catholic.

Wojcik suffered through a year at the Navy Prep School in Newport, Rhode Island, adjusting to the rigors and regimented lifestyle. After some rough times, Wojcik's own dedication to excel meshed well with the military academy's demands, and he thrived. He was chosen the captain of the prep school team and led it to an undefeated season, playing a number of the other prep school teams in New England as well as some college junior varsity teams.

But it was during his four seasons in Annapolis that the incredible happened. Paul Evans was putting together a program that would have a magical run—the kind of basketball success never before experienced before or since at a service academy. The major reason was a skinny, 6'7", 185-pound classmate of Wojcik's who possessed incredibly large feet and long arms. His name was David Robinson. Over the course of their four years together, Robinson and Wojcik (along with other great players like Vernon Butler and Kyle Whittaker) would lead the Midshipmen to the top of the college basketball world.

After a year on the junior varsity, Wojcik started the next three seasons. His sophomore year the Middies went 26–6, beat Richmond in the finals of the ECAC South Tournament, and beat LSU by 23 points in the first round of the NCAAs at Dayton, Ohio. With the confidence that comes from playing and beating the best, the Middies went on a tear during Wojcik's junior season, winning 30 games for the first time in school history. After capturing the inaugural Colonial Conference Tournament (following which Robinson gave his MVP trophy to Wojcik for his unselfish play), Navy made a run in the NCAA Tournament, defeating Tulsa, Syracuse (in the Carrier Dome), and Cleveland State to reach the Elite Eight. Duke ended the dream in the NCAA East Regional final, but no nonscholarship team had gone so far since Penn reached the Final Four in 1979.

But the Middies had lost Butler and Whittaker and were not nearly as deep or talented as the year before. Fans all over the country—so many of whom had fathers or brothers or other relatives who had been in the Navy—pulled for the Middies wherever they went. Robinson, now close to seven feet tall, faced double- and triple-teams inside. The entire team, other than the Admiral, was made up of step-slow battlers that no other Division I team wanted. All were basking in the glow of big-time college basketball. The dream run came to a close for Wojcik and Robinson in the first round of the NCAA Tournament against Michigan when the two combined for 51 points—with Robinson getting 50. Wojcik still holds Navy records for assists in a game (14), season (251), and career (714).

With his playing career over, Wojcik was uncertain about his future. A three-year commitment to the Navy loomed, which he began in May as a graduate assistant basketball coach. That appointment lasted six months before he was shipped to Surface Warfare School in Newport, Rhode Island. In April 1988, Wojcik reported to the *USS W. S. Sims*, a Knox-class frigate, as the first operational lieutenant in charge of various ship duties such as anchoring, mooring, and overall appearance.

Days on the ship passed slowly for Wojcik, who found himself with plenty of time to consider his future as the ship sailed around the Caribbean and South American seas. Thinking back to the success he'd had as a player and still influenced by Prosser, Wojcik began to think about college coaching. After two years onboard the *W. S. Sims* he was due to be rotated to shore duty. He lobbied hard for a return to the academy as a PE instructor and coach and was granted the position in April 1990.

He immediately was sent on the road recruiting by then-coach Pete Herrmann. The Naval Academy spends a lot of its resources in attracting recruits of all types, whether they can play basketball or not. Wojcik traveled all over the Midwest and West, looking for athletic, slightly undersized players who were smart enough to handle the academic rigor and disciplined enough to handle the academy.

It was about that time he ran into Matt Doherty (then an assistant at Davidson and recruiting the same kind of players) during a summer camp in Cincinnati. The two quickly struck up a friendship based on similarities in their backgrounds: both were the product of tight families and Catholic schools, both believed in hard work, and both faced the difficult challenge of recruiting top-flight student-athletes. A friendship developed, with Wojcik never failing to remind his colleague that the all-time series record between Navy and UNC was 14–6, in favor of the Cadets.

Don DeVoe replaced Herrmann, and Navy's basketball program— thanks in large part to Wojcik's efforts—rose back to midmajor prominence in the Patriot League. "I'd get a call from him in the spring and he'd be going from Kentucky to Ohio to Michigan to Minnesota to make home visits, and he'd make two or three home visits in a day sometimes," recalled Doherty. "It was incredible the organizational skills and the work ethic that took. And, the realization that you might get 1 out of 100 of those players."

But after nine seasons, Wojcik knew he needed to move on if his career goal of becoming a head coach was to become a reality.

And then an old friend called. Would he be interested in coaching at Notre Dame? Despite his history and love for Annapolis, it was an easy choice.

For several months after moving to South Bend, Doherty and Wojcik were the only two members of the staff, actively pursuing some late recruits and scoring some solid recruiting victories in Ivan Kartelo and Jere Macura, both from Croatia. Finally, in May, Doherty hired Bob MacKinnon, who was then the head coach at the Merchant Marine Academy, as the third assistant.

MacKinnon was a basketball lifer, a man completely devoted to the game and the profession since he could remember. His dad was a college and professional coach at some of basketball's more obscure outposts, but as the family traveled between Canisius and St. Bonaventure and St. Louis and New Jersey, there was always one rule: "None of the kids were allowed to go to a home basketball game until they reached the age of seven," said MacKinnon. When young Bob reached the required age, he never again left the court.

MacKinnon's basketball education at his dad's knee took him from ball boy for the Spirits of St. Louis of the ABA—where Bob Sr. coached one of the legendary collections of misfits and head cases, led by Marvin "Bad News" Barnes ("News used to pay me $20 to go out and wipe down his Rolls Royce after every game," recalled MacKinnon), and where the young radio play-by-play man was Bob Costas—to the New Jersey Nets to King's College as a player.

Being a coach was a foregone conclusion, building a career was a long road. After King's, MacKinnon became a coaching nomad, working on the staffs at Mercyhurst, George Washington, Niagara, and finally

Back Home. Doherty addresses the media for the first time as Carolina's basketball coach, just a few days after his mentor, Roy Williams, turned the job down.

Doherty and the coaches take on the campus intramural champs as part of Midnight With Matt and the Tar Heels festivities. One of the pleasures Doherty derives from his position as head coach is his interaction with students.

Doherty and Joseph Forte discuss the finer points of an offensive play prior to a Carolina practice in October.

Doherty is never afraid to jump into a drill and aggressively demonstrate how a fundamental should be executed, as he does here against Brian Bersticker and Jim Everett.

Freshman Adam Boone (background) watches sophomore Joseph Forte as he gets interviewed in October. Freshmen basketball players at Carolina are not allowed to give interviews until after they play in their first game.

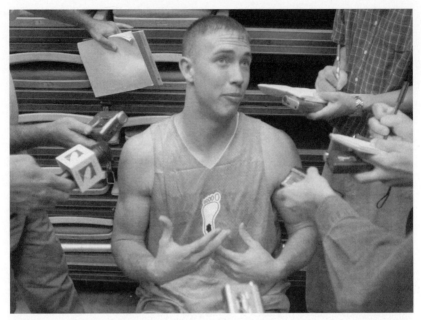

The constant media scrutiny is a burden for some of Carolina's players. Kris Lang enjoys the banter on some days, but has also been known to duck quickly into back doors when he sees reporters lurking.

Doherty chats up recruit DeSagana Diop during the annual Blue–White intrasquad scrimmage. Diop later chose the NBA over Carolina.

Success, frustration, motivation, concern. Doherty demonstrates it all on the sidelines during the course of a game.

Doherty makes a point to an official.

Doherty demonstrates a defensive stance at Duke. . . . Note the ever-present blue index card in the shirt pocket.

Doherty is often the first one on the floor when one of his players goes down, as he is here with Jason Capel.

Joseph Forte (left) and Ronald Curry (right) sandwich Brendan Haywood following his last-second, game-winning basket against Wake Forest.

Jonathan Holmes battled all season for more playing time—and to prove he was good enough to play at Carolina.

An incredible athlete at 6'6" and 285 pounds, Julius Peppers electrified crowds with his force-ful dunks, like this one at Wake Forest.

Jason Capel, shown here dunking against Maryland, hated to be known as a "role player."

After setting a Carolina single-season scoring record as a freshman, Joseph Forte became an
even more important offensive force for the Tar Heels as a sophomore.

Senior Max Owens unselfishly came off the bench and often provided an offensive spark.

Sophomore Will Johnson played a crucial role in practice and was a model student-athlete off the court.

Kris Lang is a favorite target of opposing fans, as he is here on the road against rival NC State.

Ronald Curry gave the Tar Heels much needed defensive intensity, but his shooting difficulties in the NCAA Tournament added to Carolina's offensive woes.

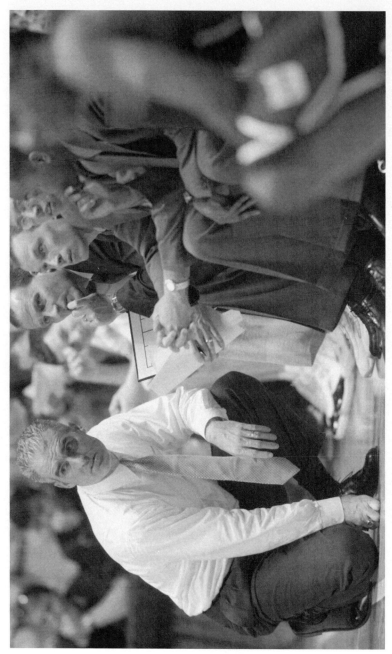

Doherty and his staff (from left: Bob MacKinnon, Doug Wojcik, Fred Quartlebaum, and David Cason) try to figure out what's going wrong during Carolina's worst loss of the season, at home against Duke on Senior Day.

working as a head coach at the Merchant Marine Academy in King's Point. During that time, he also worked the North Carolina basketball camp, where he ran into a player preparing for a potential professional career during the mid-1980s.

Matt Doherty and MacKinnon struck up an instant friendship, with MacKinnon working out with Doherty as the graduated senior tried to work through injuries and prepare for a career in the NBA.

Twenty years later, Doherty remembered his old friend.

"He loves the game of basketball and has the most enthusiasm I've ever seen," said Doherty. "And he's a true team player. He doesn't care, whatever I ask him to do, he'll do it with great enthusiasm. He has gotten beaten up in this profession and has come back for more."

His first summer at Notre Dame was fading fast, and Doherty still had two positions open on his staff. He would fill one of them with Fred Quartlebaum (after a protracted search for the last coaching/recruiting position), a former colleague of Wojcik's at Navy and coaching vagabond in his own right; Notre Dame would mark Quartlebaum's fourth straight summer of switching jobs (and coaching shirts) just before the summer recruiting period.

"Coach Williams always said: 'Hire people you know, or people that they know, know them very well,'" said Doherty. "I knew Doug, I knew Bob, I knew Q through Doug. So I called Q and it was pretty much done over the phone." Doherty liked Quartlebaum's engaging nature and skills of organization. David Cason, a former player for Kevin Stallings (a Doherty colleague at Kansas) at Illinois State, was hired to be the director of basketball operations and the staff was finally complete.

The staff was assembled and the season was soon upon them. The Irish set the tone early with a win over Ohio State, a Final Four participant the season before. Before they knew it, the season had flown by (and was much more successful than the prognosticators had predicted) and Notre Dame was the NIT runner-up.

Along the way, the Dohertys added a baby girl to their family. A story surrounding the birth was particularly telling about Doherty, who constantly felt the pull of his high-pressure job and the commitment he felt to his family.

"The hospital called and they told me they wanted to induce labor on a Monday," recalled Kelly Doherty. "So I called Matt at the office to tell him and the first thing he says is: 'Can you ask them to switch it to Tuesday? I have to go see a kid play on Monday.'"

As soon as the words left his mouth, Doherty knew he'd made a mistake. He called his wife back, apologized profusely, and Hattie was born on Monday, with her father crying tears of joy in the delivery room.

20

The ACC

I mmediately following North Carolina's win over the College of Charleston in late December, Matt Doherty expressed his displeasure with how his team had played defensively, but he also recognized an important fact: his team could play poorly against a solid opponent and still find a way to win. The Tar Heels had the toughness to overcome; not an insignificant trait to possess.

No one had displayed that more than Jason Capel, who had been so ill after the Charleston win that Bob MacKinnon had to physically carry Capel from the training room to a waiting car to take him to the hospital. Capel stayed there overnight while the team returned to Chapel Hill.

Doherty immediately immersed himself in preparations for Georgia Tech. Like Doherty, Paul Hewitt would be making his ACC debut. Hewitt, who had replaced the popular Bobby Cremins (who had resigned from Tech after 19 years), had quickly endeared himself to

Yellow Jacket fans with some impressive upsets in the pre-ACC season. Hewitt had come to Tech from Siena and discovered that while the cupboard was hardly bare, it would need some serious carpentry work. Center Alvin Jones and point guard Tony Akins were talented but often lazy and tended to brood when things didn't go well. Starting two-guard Shawn Fein was a Division II transfer. The rest of the roster was made up of undersized or underquick players no other ACC team had wanted.

But Hewitt had brought this group together into a formidable force that had already defeated UCLA *and* Kentucky—only one of which Carolina had defeated—and thus opened the eyes of many conference observers. Picked in the preseason to finish anywhere from fifth to eighth, Tech was suddenly a team to contend with and had already built up an impressive NCAA resume, despite a loss to in-state rival Georgia.

Tech was an example of how the ACC had improved from the last two seasons—in which the conference had earned just three invitations to the NCAA Tournament each season. In 2000–2001, the ACC had already had as many as five teams—Duke, Carolina, Maryland, Virginia, and Wake Forest—in the AP Top 25. NC State and Georgia Tech were considered strong contenders for NCAA play, as well.

Duke had been Duke in the early season, demolishing nonconference opponents by an average of 28 points per game. The Blue Devils had lost once—to the smirks and winks of Carolina players—to Stanford, but had been challenged by Temple and Illinois. In the Stanford game, the bigger Cardinal players had simply worn down Duke's frontline. After Carlos Boozer had fouled out late, Stanford scored at will, making up a 14-point deficit to win in Oakland. Still, Duke had a lineup of two potential National Players of the Year in Jason Williams and Shane Battier as well as Mike Dunleavy, Nate James, and Chris Duhon, who, despite coming off the bench, was probably the best freshman in the league.

Since the season started, Carolina's players and coaches had kept a close eye on Duke's every move. With the local media and the intense fan interest, it was impossible not to.

Maryland, after losing three of its first four games, had reeled off eight straight wins. Gary Williams had the most experienced group in the league, and his was the only team to defeat Duke (in Cameron, no less) the previous year. Terence Morris, Juan Dixon, and Lonny Baxter were stars, while Steve Blake and transfer Byron Mouton added depth. What was worse, the Terps loved to press (they had scored 100 points in four of five games against nonconference foes). Carolina had not shown it could handle even marginal pressure.

Wake Forest had been the major surprise of the early season. Dave Odom's team was thought to be solid, with the return of Carolina killer Robert O'Kelley and Rafael Vidauretta, probably the best post defender in the league. But the development of Josh Howard, Craig Dawson, Ervin Murray, and Broderick Hicks had vaulted the 2000 NIT Champions (the Deacs had defeated Doherty's Notre Dame squad in the final) into the top five in the country. A 30-point demolishing of Kansas in Winston-Salem in December opened eyes all over the ACC, and the nation. Wake Forest, some reporters were writing, might be the best team in the conference.

Likewise, Virginia had been impressive early and also had a lopsided win over a top-five team—Tennessee, in the Coaches vs. Cancer Classic in Madison Square Garden—to show for it. What's more, Pete Gillen's team had a chip on its shoulder: the Cave felt they were jilted when North Carolina—a team they had defeated twice last season—got the ticket to the 2000 NCAA Tournament that they believed was theirs.

NC State had struggled somewhat early, but Herb Sendek had good talent and could beat anyone if the Wolfpack had a good shooting night. Likewise, Clemson had improved under Larry Shyatt and had some depth to go with the leading scorer in the league, Will Solomon. Only Florida State was a fairly sure conference win; the Seminoles were 4–8 in nonconference play, with losses to Furman, South Florida, and Cleveland State.

The Tar Heels had two good—not great—days of practices heading into the ACC opener at Tech. With the Charleston game on December 30 and the Tech game on January 2, just two days of preparation were available, with one of those days coming after a hard-fought (and late) game, and the other day being New Year's. Doherty admitted he was a bit nervous as the ACC season approached: "I feel like I did before the first game of the season against Winthrop. I feel like my heart is going to explode."

Several players noted that the coaches, although energized, seemed to be less jocular and more serious over those two days of practices, films, and walk-throughs. "You could sense Coach was nervous," said Kris Lang. "He's trying to find every nook and cranny in our game and polish it up." In truth, Doherty had ridden Lang particularly hard after the Charleston game, almost begging Lang to be more aggressive on both ends of the floor. "Don't you want to get me off your tail?" Doherty had asked Lang during practice.

During workouts, it was becoming more obvious that Julius Peppers was working into the lineup as if he had never left to play football. "He's an incredibly smart player," said Doherty. "He remembers the plays well and he has good instincts." The other thing Peppers brought was toughness, both mental and physical. With Peppers on the floor, practices were instantly more physical. No longer were Kris Lang and Brendan Haywood beating up on Brian Bersticker and Jim Everett who—despite the latter's handiwork with the padded blocking dummy—were not big enough to keep the starters out of the lane during scrimmages. With Peppers' presence, it improved how the starters could prepare.

Curry was also improving at a rapid rate. His ballhandling was coming along, but it was his presence as a leader and defender that was having the greatest impact. "He has our instant respect because we know he's been there before," said Jason Capel. As the football quarterback, Curry had endured a great deal of pressure from opposing defenses. Personally, he had come through much more. The players not only liked Ronald, they respected him—and, most important, they would listen to what he said.

With Curry and Peppers coming on, the Heels were becoming a team in Doherty's image: tough, hard-nosed, and emotional.

 At the top of Doherty's keys for Tech—as well as New Year's resolutions—was taking care of the basketball. Hewitt had brought the press with him from Siena, and the results had been that the Yellow Jackets played harder than any Tech team in recent memory.

Utilizing a 10-man rotation, Tech had scored an average of 86 points in its eight wins and forced almost 17 turnovers per game.

Knowing all this, Doherty had boiled down the key to victory in Atlanta to one not-so-simple task: take care of the ball. If his Heels did that, Doherty knew, they would be able to get the ball inside where the height advantage would force Tech to make a choice: double-down (in which case UNC would get open outside jumpers) or let Alvin Jones and Jon Babul go one-on-one with Haywood and Lang.

At walk-through and in the locker room before the game, every point Doherty made reiterated the need to limit turnovers: take care of the ball, be strong in traps, make yourself available for the pass, and, above all else, make good decisions.

Carolina was able to do that—for about five minutes.

With just one turnover—a bad pass by Curry—in its first 11 possessions, Carolina was able to get good shots. Lang got inside for an offensive rebound and later scored on a jump-hook; after the first media time-out the Heels appeared in total control, leading 14–5.

Then the dam broke. Tech's Halston Lane hit a three-pointer, Jones scored inside, and Marvin Lewis stripped Capel at half-court and converted the layup. Suddenly the game was tied at 14 and the momentum had turned. On the next possession, Lang got free against the press for an open layup, but before he could score Babul came out of nowhere and blocked it.

It was going to be anything but easy.

The next five minutes lived out Doherty's worst nightmare. Carolina was tentative against Tech's press, and the results were predictable. Morrison came off the bench and promptly was beaten back-door. Max Owens and Adam Boone both committed ugly turnovers. Akins hit two threes. Fein scored on a layup. When Babul—overplayed by Peppers—went back-door and was fouled, his two free throws at the 9:07 mark gave Tech a 27–17 lead.

Tech's defensive scheme was exactly what Doherty thought it would be: in both the zone and man-to-man, Tech was doubling down extremely hard on Haywood and Lang. Outside shots were there, when (or if) Carolina could handle the pressure and get the ball inside.

But the Tar Heels couldn't handle the pressure. Curry threw it away trying to find Lang on the blocks. Owens was stripped trying to drive. Doherty, trying to find someone who could take care of the ball, inserted Jon Holmes into the lineup at point guard, but the sophomore promptly threw a pass into Lang's kneecap.

In all, Carolina turned the ball over 11 times in the first half. The result: Georgia Tech led 44–32 at the break.

Walking back to the locker room, Doherty, who had been irate during halftimes before, knew that wasn't the best course of action in this case. Surely, he had to feel the pressure: first ACC game, losing on the road to a team picked in the third division of the conference. A loss in this game would be devastating. (It didn't help that Billy Packer, perhaps the most influential commentator in college basketball, was saying exactly that on television.)

But instead of yelling and screaming, Doherty sensed his team needed reassurance. In his very first conference game, in just his second season as a head coach, Doherty made a decision many more experienced coaches would not have been able to make: instead of succumbing to his own emotions (frustration, anger, pressure) he handled his team in a way he sensed would be more effective and would restore the players' confidence.

"Let's relax out there, guys," he said to his team in conversational tones, just moments after he had chewed out official Les Jones while he was leaving the court. "We don't need to go so fast. We need to take our time and play our game. Don't get caught up in running up and down the floor, making passes we can't make. Play smart, be calm, and *get the ball inside.*"

It was the last point he wanted to emphasize. Even though Haywood had missed all three of his shot attempts in the first half, Doherty knew that if they could get the ball down low, good things would happen. Tech was doubling down hard. If Haywood and Lang could handle the traps, open shots would be there on the perimeter.

Curry was the key, Doherty knew. He took his point guard aside and spoke to him as the team prepared to go back onto the floor. "It's your game, Ronald. Relax."

Carolina came out of the locker room earlier than usual, beginning warm-ups with more than five minutes remaining before the start of the second half (just as they had done at Michigan State). Doherty, as he usually did, came out with the team and walked among the layup lines, offering words of encouragement and the usual "pounds."

It was only in the huddle immediately prior to the start of the half that Doherty was more energized and fiery. Never once did he give an ultimatum about winning the game or else. Instead of being emotional, he trusted his coaching instincts.

And it worked. Carolina looked like a different team. Where in the first half, the Heels were trying to speed up and get frenetic when trapped, they instead handled Tech's pressure as if they knew it was coming. The results were immediate: passes were completed, good decisions were made, and the ball got inside.

It also helped that Forte and Peppers made two of the more amazing plays of the year at the beginning of the half.

Forte's came when his team needed it most. After Lang dunked to cut the deficit to 10 points and following a Babul miss inside, Forte took the rebound and started down the right side. With no one from Tech picking him up, he was able to get all the way to the baseline, but when he rose up (taking off from just outside the lane), Jones, who led the ACC in blocked shots, was suddenly in his path. Forte, already in the air, floated all the way under the basket and—fully extended—hesitated before he threw up a hook shot just as his feet hit the ground. "I just wanted to get it up there," Forte explained later, "much less try to make it." It was a shot that had no earthly business going in.

It did.

The bench exploded. The crowd gasped. Most important, the whistle sounded. Babul had fouled Haywood while trying to ride him under the basket for what everyone expected was going to be a rebound on

Forte's miss. The basket, however, was good. Carolina got the ball back and immediately went inside. When Haywood was doubled hard, he kicked the ball back out to (fittingly) Forte, who hit a three from the top of the key to complete the five-point possession.

On the other end, Fein missed a three and Carolina came down on the attack. Forte got a seam and dribbled into the lane, hit a tough one-hander, and was fouled by Fein. Suddenly, Carolina, which had been down by 12 points, was within two.

Forte had scored eight points in two possessions.

Tech weathered the onslaught for a few more minutes—even increasing the lead to seven points on a Lane three-pointer from 22 feet—but Carolina was doing exactly what Doherty wanted: taking care of the ball and handling Tech's double-teams inside. The result was a layup by Peppers and another three by Forte. By the 13:50 mark, Carolina had tied the score on an Owens jumper from left of the lane. On the next possession, Lang would score on a jump-hook—following a pass inside from Owens—and the Tar Heels led 53–51.

Carolina gradually increased its lead over the course of the next seven minutes. Tech could not get into its press due to missed shots and fewer free throw attempts. When it did, Carolina—now more confident with the lead—handled it easily by being stronger in the traps and making long passes down the sideline. In addition, Carolina's half-court defense began to push Tech further out on the floor. Shots that were open in the first half were contested in the second.

The final shot of adrenaline came when Peppers made his own incredible athletic play. With just under seven minutes remaining and Carolina up by eight points, Tech began getting even more frenetic on defense. When Forte was doubled coming off an on-ball screen, he was able to get the ball to Lang inside, who took a short baseline jumper.

On the other side of the lane, unguarded, stood Peppers, bouncing on his toes. As soon as Lang's shot was in the air, Peppers gathered and leapt as high as he could off two feet from outside the lane. When Lang's shot hit the back rim, it appeared as if Peppers had mis-timed his jump and the ball would sail over his outstretched hands.

At the last moment, Peppers extended just an inch or two higher and clasped the ball in his fingertips. Already moving downward and fully extended, he snapped the ball through the basket for a vicious dunk. It was an incredible athletic move that was made all the more unbelievable because it was performed by someone who was nearly 270 pounds. "Earlier I had gotten on him for missing a layup," Doherty said afterward. "I told him to rip the rim down the next time he had the chance. He almost did." The Carolina bench erupted, but more importantly, the crowd gasped in deflated amazement.

Carolina led by 10 with 6:49 remaining, but the game was over. North Carolina would go on to commit just two turnovers in the second half on the way to an 84–70 victory—outscoring Georgia Tech by 26 points in the second half.

In a game where panic could easily have ensued due to poor play in the first half, no one had lost his cool, specifically Doherty. Twice in a row now, in games that could easily have been lost, Carolina had won. Call it confidence or call it a fresh perspective, this UNC team was tougher mentally than in the past.

And the players knew it.

"We'll just have to keep Coach Doherty's confidence up," said Forte with a grin on the way to the bus.

Confidence flowed elsewhere in the ACC that night, as Wake Forest—the surprise powerhouse in the ACC thus far—demoralized Virginia, 96–73.

"Wake Team To Beat In The ACC," read the headline of the AP game story the next day. By 8:00 A.M. the next day, the headline was already highlighted in yellow and hanging on the wall of the Carolina basketball locker room.

In four days, the Demon Deacons were coming to town.

21

Wake

Later that night, with their first ACC win safely tucked away, the Carolina players sprawled out in a waiting area of the Atlanta airport, legs and arms splayed across three and sometimes four airport bench seats. The mood, as might be expected following the win, was relatively light and upbeat.

Prior to the season, Doherty had outlined a specific team rule that was nonnegotiable: no cell phones on the team bus or plane. "If you want to carry them, turn them off," he had said. Several players had already circumvented the rule, turning their phones to "vibrate" instead of ring, but talking had to be done under jackets and with a barely audible voice. No one dared be seen talking into a cell phone.

But sitting in the airport lobby waiting for their charter—and in a semigiddy mood following the Tech win—Doherty pulled out his own

212

cell phone and began to make a few phone calls he had been putting off. Likewise, Assistant Coach Bob MacKinnon called his wife.

Doherty had just hung up after call number one and was about to make another when his cell phone rang.

"Hello?" Doherty answered.

"Coach," the voice said in a serious tone, "I thought you said no cell phones?"

Doherty immediately recognized the voice and turned around, staring at Joe Forte, who had his own phone pressed to his ear and a devilish smile.

The entire team began laughing uncontrollably and rolling around. Haywood nearly fell out of his chair.

So did their coach.

Upon returning to Chapel Hill, Matt Doherty could hardly take a moment to relax. He gave the team Wednesday off, while he and his staff sequestered themselves in the office and tried to figure out a way to beat their next opponent: Wake Forest.

A few weeks earlier, he had been in Michael Jordan's 23 Restaurant broadcasting his weekly call-in show the night Wake had demolished then-No.2 Kansas in Winston-Salem. During breaks he and Woody Durham had caught snippets of the game on the bar's big-screen TV. His mood dampened as he watched his old team go down by 30 points to the Deacs in the second half. A few days prior to playing Wake, Doherty called Roy Williams, and the two talked about the Deacons. "They're very athletic," Williams told Doherty. "They demoralized us."

Dave Odom's 2000–2001 squad was unique in college basketball (and the pipeline of underclassmen going to the NBA) in that it had been able to develop across several seasons into a team that was now athletic, experienced, and seasoned. Led by shooting guard Robert O'Kelley—a notorious Tar Heel killer who had single-handedly beaten Carolina the year before in Winston-Salem—and post players Rafael

Vidauretta and Darius Songaila, the Deacons had won the NIT the year before, defeating Doherty and Notre Dame in Madison Square Garden.

But the key to Wake's development had been 6'6" wing guard Josh Howard, 6'9" post player Josh Shoemaker, and supersub Craig Dawson, the nephew of former Carolina great Jerry Stackhouse. This trio—which had taken time to develop into more than just athletes—gave Odom's team the quickness and depth it had lacked in previous seasons.

Wake was also the media's team du jour. Many of the local ACC beat writers as well as the national media expected a Wake rout in the Smith Center. Their articles and commentaries quickly found their way into the Tar Heels' locker room that week.

The amount of pressure Doherty would put on himself, his staff, and his players reached a crescendo during the two days of practice preceding Saturday's Wake game. The players, who had been in more "must-win" games than their coach, were nonetheless cognizant of the importance of this game.

Doherty would not admit it, but he wanted this game more than any other that Carolina had played this season. In earlier national television games against top-flight opponents—Michigan State, Kentucky, and UCLA—he had pushed his team hard and prepared exhaustively, but had still been getting to know his players. Now, he felt they had embraced his system—particularly on defense—and were on the verge of becoming a very difficult team to beat. Wake Forest, Doherty hoped, would be a sort of coming-out party for his Carolina team; one that played as hard—and was as talented—as any in the country.

In the middle of two very long days of preparation, Doherty took time out to do something he and his coaches had discussed for several weeks. It was something he looked forward to.

Prior to Friday afternoon's practice, Doherty sent for Jim Everett to come to the coaches' locker room. Everett's primary duties that week had been to pound on Haywood and Lang with a football blocking dummy during post drills and to imitate Wake's Songaila during scrimmage preparations. The latter duty was a challenge for Everett, whose skills were not nearly those of Songaila, who had been a key member of the Lithuanian Olympic team that had nearly defeated Team USA in the Olympics earlier that summer.

When he appeared in the coaches' locker room, Everett was nervous; partially because he rarely was called to the locker room (he had been in the room only once before) but also because he had just dinged up his mom's Ford Expedition pulling out of a Kinko's in downtown Chapel Hill and was a little rattled.

"Jim, we need you to sign this paper," said Doherty, a serious look on his face.

Petrified, Everett signed it in the wrong place. When he had fixed his error, he looked up at Doherty, who was not smiling.

"Jim, do you know what you just signed?" Doherty asked. Everett just shook his head. "That paper means you're not a walk-on anymore."

Perhaps more than any other player, Everett cherished being a part of the team and wearing the Carolina uniform. Doherty had immediately taken a liking to Everett, calling him "Big-Jim-Sports-Camp." Everett's face never changed, not knowing what Doherty meant and looking around the room at the other coaches, who were all stone-faced, just like Doherty.

Doherty let the comment hang in the air, but not for too long.

"We've decided to put you on scholarship for the second semester," said Doherty, his face breaking into a wide grin. "Congratulations. You're now a scholarship player at North Carolina."

Everett's eyes went wide, and he smiled a huge smile as all of the assistants came over to shake his hand and slap him on the back. He had never even thought of being put on scholarship. It was not something Doherty needed to do, even if he had the extra scholarship with Jason Parker's nonadmission, nor was it something Everett needed—a scholarship for an in-state student for one semester came to about $4,000. Everett had just received his signing bonus for his postcollege job at Lehman Brothers, the investment firm at which he had interned the summer before, and could have paid for the semester himself. But Doherty wanted to do it, to reward Everett for his hard work.

When Doherty told the players a few moments later—when they collected around him in the center jump circle prior to practice—they all applauded for their new "scholarship" teammate.

And then they went to work.

The first truly big game of the year in the ACC began with Doherty's suit jacket already in its place in the locker room. Rarely does the Smith Center—outside of the annual battle royale with Duke—truly feel electric. Against Wake Forest, it was. The 400 students who were fortunate enough to be standing in the risers at the end of the court were nearly lost in the pregame noise. When tip-off time came, the atmosphere was truly intimidating.

And then, on the first shot, Forte threw up an air ball.

Songaila, matched up against Haywood, then drove into the lane and threw in a one-handed runner. But the place only got louder. Curry took a three-pointer from almost the same spot where Forte had shot—and barely glanced the backside of the rim.

Howard then blew right around Capel, drove baseline, and had his layup goaltended by Haywood. Right away, it was 4–0. But still, the crowd only yelled louder.

Forte found Haywood inside and, shrugging off a Shoemaker–Howard double-team, Haywood spun baseline and laid the ball over the rim. Haywood had not scored a point against Georgia Tech, but his coach had stood by him, claiming he had played unselfishly against double-teams. "His play was crucial to us winning, even if the media didn't think so," Doherty said.

Songaila scored again, but Carolina drew a foul on Shoemaker by again looking for Haywood inside. The call: pushing with the hips. It would be a harbinger of things to come. After missing two jump-hooks, Lang finally scored on an offensive rebound, put-back, and hit the free throw. The foul was called on Songaila, his second, with just 3:18 gone in the game.

On the defensive end, Carolina was surprisingly aggressive; jumping into passing lanes and challenging Howard, O'Kelley, Dawson, and

Scott when they caught the ball. Combined with the fouls being called, the first 10 minutes of the game were choppy, with Wake maintaining a two- to six-point lead throughout. On the sideline, the always-active Doherty was maniacal, jumping on rebounds and displaying a perfect defensive stance technique. When Haywood threw an outlet pass into the scorer's table, Doherty bellowed toward the court and stomped his feet, urging his team to play with intensity. On the next possession, Capel dove onto the floor and outfought two Deacons for the ball.

Message received.

When both teams substituted at the next media time-out, Wake immediately took the advantage. Against the UNC zone (one of the few possessions of zone Carolina had played in its last five games), Dawson hit a three-pointer from the baseline that careened off the side of the board and in. After Capel's inside shot was blocked, O'Kelley got a step on Morrison on the baseline, leaned in, and scored as the whistle sounded. Bucket good, and one. When he hit the free throw, Wake led by nine points with just over seven minutes remaining in the first half.

The crowd, for the first time, showed signs of quieting.

Doherty immediately reinserted Forte. On the next possession, Haywood—fighting his way through a double-team inside—kicked out to Curry on the right wing. Without hesitating, Curry shot—and missed badly. Wake had the ball and a chance to push the lead to double digits.

On the sideline, Doherty did not panic. When the ball was knocked out-of-bounds by Forte, Doherty even shared a chuckle with official John Clougherty. During the break in action, his eyes met Curry's. "Keep shooting, Ronald!" yelled Doherty. "That's your shot!" Curry nodded.

Carolina got the stop it needed when Lang slid over to help on Dawson, who had driven by Capel, and forced a tough shot. Lang rebounded and got it to Forte, who sprint-dribbled to the other end. Haywood got position inside, took a pass from Capel, and was fouled by Shoemaker—his third. With Carolina in the bonus, Haywood walked to the free throw line for two crucial shots. He hit both.

Haywood's energy on defense often was a result of his doing well on offense, and in this game, it was again the case. Haywood dogged

Vidauretta's every step on the next possession and forced an air ball. On the other end, Capel hit a three-pointer on a pass from Curry to cut the deficit to 27–23. On the sideline, Doherty leaped into the air. When he came down, he slapped the floor.

Forte cut it to one point with a three-pointer a minute later. But it was on defense that Carolina had gotten back into the game, holding Wake scoreless for four minutes since the Deacons had taken a nine-point lead.

Haywood tied the score with a put-back with 1:45 remaining before the half. He then gave Carolina a lead with two free throws 15 seconds later. Buckets by Owens and Forte pushed the lead to five points, but Scott cut it back to three, 37–34, by the break.

In the locker room, Doherty huddled with his coaches. He was pleased with the effort as well as the execution on offense. The plan coming in had been to get the ball inside and read the defense; if Wake double-teamed, Haywood and Lang were to kick it out for open shots. If not, they were to score.

In the first half, Wake had double-teamed, sometimes triple-teamed, hard on Haywood and Lang. Unfortunately for Odom's team, Wake had been called for fouls. Shoemaker had three, Songaila two (in just three minutes of play). The other result had been open shots for Curry, who had turned down most of the chances and missed the only two he took.

Doherty knew Wake would double-team even harder inside in the second half—and leave Curry open.

"Ronald," Doherty said to his point guard in the locker room. "I know you can shoot the ball. Your teammates know you can shoot the ball. If you have an open shot, don't even hesitate."

In the first minute of the second half, Wake had tied the score on a Songaila reverse layup. Worse, Curry had hesitated, turning down an open shot when Hicks cheated inside to guard Lang. "Shoot it, Ronald!" Doherty bellowed from the sideline.

Two minutes later, Haywood, triple-teamed inside, fought for position, bulled Vidauretta under the basket, and dunked for a three-point lead. It was the largest margin Carolina would have in the game.

Dawson hit a hanger in the lane to cut the Carolina lead to one. A few possessions later, Curry again turned down an open shot to feed Haywood, who was quadruple-teamed. Curry got the ball back and hesitated, but finally took an 18-footer that clanged off the front rim. Lang was called for an over-the-back foul on the rebound.

Curry had missed four shots, all of them wide-open. Still, Doherty encouraged him on the sideline. "Don't hesitate, Ronald!" Two minutes later, Curry turned down another wide-open shot against Wake's zone, forcing Forte to take a contested jumper from the top of the key. Hicks rebounded the miss and pushed the ball ahead to Howard, who hit a 15-footer along the baseline. Wake led, 45–44, with 15:38 remaining.

Owens' three-pointer from the top-of-the-key broke a two-and-a-half-minute scoring drought for both teams and gave Carolina a two-point lead with 13:04 remaining. Curry had another wide-open look from the top-of-the-key and missed his fifth consecutive shot in the midst of a 7–0 Wake run. With 10:36 remaining, Carolina trailed 52–47.

But the Tar Heels stormed back, thanks again to aggressive man-to-man defense. Doherty took Curry out—"Keep shooting, Ronald. We need you," Doherty whispered in Curry's ear as he passed by him on the bench—but immediately put him back in two minutes later. Lang scored twice inside and Peppers took a baseline pass from Haywood and dunked, bringing the crowd alive again. He missed the ensuing free throw, but not his next chance to electrify the Smith Center.

It was a play that began innocently enough. O'Kelley missed a three-pointer—largely due to Peppers running at him—from the left wing, and the ball rebounded long to Curry, who started up-court. Howard reached from behind and poked it loose, but Curry ran it down. Looking up, he saw Peppers, his arm raised and running down the left wing. Curry took another dribble to collect himself and lofted a pass near the rim. Pepper bent his knees and, at 6'7", 270 pounds, rose off the floor, caught the ball slightly behind his head and slammed the ball through the rim, hanging on it and jackknifing for added effect.

The Smith Center exploded. On national television, Vitale almost fainted. The Carolina bench began celebrating like it was Mardi Gras.

Only Curry kept his calm, running back down to the other end of the court with his fist raised, signifying Carolina's defense.

The game was tied 55–55, but the shaking arena caused Odom to call a time-out.

During the time-out, the in-house video boards—of which there are four, one in each corner of the arena—showed the replay of the dunk six straight times. Each time, the crowd responded with a collective "Whhooosh!" The noise was deafening, and even the players snuck a look over the coaches' shoulders. "How does it look, Joe!!" yelled Doherty, in the huddle, with a grin.

Carolina came out in a zone, hoping to throw Wake off. It didn't work, as Songaila drove baseline and fed Shoemaker for a layup. Haywood answered with a fade-away jumper, but missed the free throw that would have given the Tar Heels a lead.

It had turned into exactly the kind of game Doherty wanted: every possession was a war and every basket was hotly contested. The coaching staff and the players were anxious to prove this was a tough, hard-nosed group capable of beating good or very good teams in close games.

Wake took the lead on an O'Kelley runner in the lane with 6:11 remaining. Forte answered with two free throws 40 seconds later. As Forte lined up his second shot, Odom called over Murray, his point guard. "You're guarding Curry again," Odom pleaded. "Get down in the lane. He's not going to hit one from now . . . until the next millennium."

The next millennium dawned exactly one minute and nine seconds later. After missing the front end of a one-and-one in the prior possession, Curry took a pass from Haywood on the left wing but immediately turned down an open shot. Instead, he dribbled to the other side of the court—directly in front of Doherty—and fed Haywood again. Murray— as he had been instructed—dutifully played off of Curry, who floated to the open spot at the top of the key. Haywood again hit him, and this time Curry rose up and shot without thinking about it.

Swish.

Carolina led by three, 62–59, with 4:30 on the clock. With two minutes remaining, Curry fouled O'Kelley, who hit both free throws. Curry threw it away trying to get the ball inside to Haywood. Wake came down-court, and Dawson took an off-balance three that missed. But the ball bounced long to Songaila, who hit Dawson streaking to the basket for a layup.

Wake 67, Carolina 66; 1:22 remained.

Just six seconds later, Forte missed a three and Wake rebounded. Carolina desperately needed a stop. Wake called a 30-second time-out to set up a play for Dawson. But Carolina fought over every screen and pressured the ball. With just three seconds on the shot clock, Hicks drove right, trying to make something happen. Forte, guarding Dawson, made a calculated gamble—similar to the one he made against the College of Charleston a week and a half earlier. This one paid off similarly: Forte stole the ball cleanly from Hicks and sprinted down-court for a layup that gave Carolina a one-point lead.

Wake chose not to call a time-out, instead spreading the floor and getting the ball inside to Shoemaker, who hit Songaila at the free throw line. Forte got crossed up and let his man, Dawson, slip inside. Songaila spotted him immediately and whipped a pass inside for a layup and a one-point Wake Forest lead. Moments after making a crucial defensive play, Forte had made a terrible mistake.

Doherty called a time-out with 14.2 seconds remaining and calmly designed a play to get the ball to Forte up on the left side of the floor, with Capel cutting to the baseline. Forte was to look for Capel on the cut.

The play developed exactly as it was designed. Forte, showing that great players sometimes knew when to make the play and when not to force it, hit an open Capel as he cut to the corner. Capel immediately drove the baseline, but was cut off by Shoemaker and Songaila, who had helped off of Haywood. Capel jumped back into the lane and forced up an off-balance shot that was blocked from behind by Shoemaker with just five seconds on the clock.

The ball ricocheted off of Songaila's back and fell to the floor, where it bounced directly into Haywood's hands. Songaila saw him and tried to foul, but it was too late: Haywood went up and scored off the glass with 3.3 seconds remaining. Carolina led 69–68 as the bench and the players on the floor celebrated.

Doherty pumped his fist in the air once, but he knew it wasn't over and quickly tried to calm everyone down and get the players' attention. Haywood, who had just equaled his season-high with 24 points the game after he was held to zero points at Tech, held his arms out as he walked to the free throw line. Capel walked over to his coach and relayed instructions to his teammates.

Odom instructed his team to run a home run play after Haywood's free throw. But the foul shot missed, and Shoemaker could only get it to Songaila for a running 40-footer that was well wide.

Matt Doherty held his arms high up in the air, threw his head back, and momentarily stared at the far-off white ceiling of the Smith Center. Around him, bedlam ensued. His mind raced as all around him, players, students, and fans rushed the court. On autopilot, he moved to shake Odom's hand and then turned his head and found his wife, Kelly, and the dam burst as the last five and a half months of emotion poured out. Moving his young family . . . working in a fish bowl of media and fan scrutiny . . . questioning himself at the same time he reassured himself that, yes, he could do this job. This win solidified that voice that kept telling him he was equal to the challenge of running the North Carolina program. He had earned it. And more important, he could do it.

As he is apt to do, Doherty let his emotions pour out. His eyes welled with tears, his throat choked, and he wept openly in front of 21,000 people and a worldwide ESPN audience as he joined the celebration at midcourt. Fans hugged their coach and he hugged back. A few minutes later, he wept again in front of the media—his perfectly tailored white shirt streaked with blue from the painted fans who had embraced him. "The blue guy got me," Doherty said. He talked about the importance of his brother John being there, the highs of winning a big game, and the lows of where he'd been just a few weeks earlier after the Kentucky loss.

While Doherty addressed the media, the players and assistant coaches were much more subdued downstairs outside the locker room. Haywood, whose 24 points were a vindication, leaned back on the couch in the players' lounge, a short smile on his face. Reporters tried to get him to comment about his game-winning shot, but he refused to get too excited about it. "The ball just went down. Nobody knew where it was. But I saw it."

The other players were equally nonchalant about the victory. "We should win at home," said Forte. The one exception was Everett, who had not played but was still ebullient. Outside the locker room, the newest scholarship player was hugging his parents when Wojcik came up to congratulate the family.

"Maybe you can spend the money you'll save on driving lessons," Wojcik said to Everett's parents.

22

The Teacher and the Student

The morning after his team had defeated fourth-ranked Wake Forest for its eighth-straight victory, Matt Doherty called Dean Smith at home. "Coach," he said, worried that he had displeased his mentor, "I hope you don't mind that I got all emotional like that, celebrating with the fans at midcourt."

"Matt, you've got to be you," said Smith. A long pause ensued, before Smith added, "I wouldn't have done it, but that's OK."

At about the time his former players began to become head coaches in college and even professional basketball, Dean Smith began hosting an informal gathering every summer that quickly became a retreat of the highest order, an Algonquin Round Table of basketball and golf. Over the years, Larry Brown, George Karl, Eddie Fogler, Roy

Williams, Bill Guthridge, and others would meet for several days in the off-season in a publicly undisclosed location.

When he was hired at Notre Dame, Matt Doherty finally earned his first invitation to the event.

"Immediately, I felt one of the group, one of the boys in the club," said Doherty. "As an assistant you're kind of peeking in, hoping to join them for these coaches' meetings, for the golf outings." A year later, he found himself in an even better position, as Smith was walking the same hallways.

"Now, I was closer to Coach Smith and Coach Guthridge," said Doherty. "We go to lunch. We talk. There's more opportunity to share ideas and thoughts about different things because now I'm around them more. It's exciting for me."

Doherty quickly began to welcome and count on input from his two predecessors. From Guthridge, he would inquire about organizational issues regarding best utilizing the staff, academic counseling, camp issues, and the like. "I only watched one practice," said Guthridge. "Matt had me sit with a recruit for one practice. I thought the practice was very good."

From Smith, Doherty solicited any and all basketball knowledge Smith was willing to offer. In the preseason, Smith, Doherty, and the assistant coaches had participated in an all-day basketball session in the coaches' locker room. "It was like learning math from Einstein," said Doherty. The two also talked after every Carolina game, which Smith either watched on television or, during the two games all season that weren't televised, attended in person. And for every game, Smith kept notes.

One of the games he attended—to almost no one's attention—was the nontelevised exhibition game in Carmichael against the EA All-Stars.

"We talked the next day," explained Doherty, "and he said, 'you guys played well, those guys were better than you gave them credit for.' I asked him how he knew and he said, 'Well, I was at the game.'"

It turned out Smith had snuck in just before tip-off and sat in an area designated for the band.

As the year had progressed and Doherty had come to rely on the insights of both Smith and Guthridge, his respect and admiration for the two men grew.

"Those meetings were great for me," said Doherty. "To be with Coach Smith in the coaches' locker room, drawing up plays, talking about personnel. . . . Sometimes it might have been 20 minutes on the phone, other times it might have been an hour and a half on the board. I'm getting a private tutoring session from someone I think is the best coach in all of team sports.

"Both [Smith and Guthridge] were very generous with their time. They want this program to do well and will do anything to help me get that done, whether visit with a recruit or offer some advice. They're careful not to come out and offer the advice, they usually wait until I asked, but if it was important enough to either person they would offer the advice, and it was always well received because of the experience they have. I knew they were caring people, but now, being on the inside, I realize the many things that separate Carolina basketball from other programs, there's a lot of factors, but number one is the way those two people care about the people who have played and worked for them."

Several factors, on and off the court, came together that made the win over Wake Forest big, even for a program as storied as Carolina.

For one, Ronald Curry made a big shot. Odom's strategy was one that past and future teams would employ; double-down hard inside and leave Curry open on the perimeter. All he needed to do was hit every once in a while, and Curry could single-handedly make Carolina much tougher to beat. "I am *not* going to be the weak link on this team," Curry had said during the week.

What he and Julius Peppers had brought to games and practices since joining the team in late November was a mental and physical toughness that was not there consistently the year before. Peppers' sheer athletic ability also brought a buzz to the team; he had already become a *SportsCenter* staple. Prior to the Maryland game, ESPN would devote almost its entire pregame video tease to Peppers. That buzz not only put the gloss back on the program that had been surviving in the afterglow of the Michael Jordan image for over a decade.

Now, it was becoming cool again to be a Carolina fan.

On the court, Curry's ability to pressure the ball had changed the Carolina defense from one that reacted to one that attacked. Doherty had taken a major gamble in pressuring Wake. The Deacs were widely viewed as superior athletically to UNC, but the Heels' perimeter defense had bothered the Deacons. The team had believed in what Doherty had preached, and it had paid off. If it hadn't, the team could have begun to question their coach. Carolina now had confidence, but for how long remained to be seen.

"The most important game of the year is the next one," said Doherty often. He rarely knew who was ahead on the schedule, beyond the next game.

That next game was Maryland at Maryland, a place where Carolina's ability to handle the press—a problem earlier in the season against UCLA—would again be tested.

The Terrapins, more than any other program in the ACC, had a chip on their shoulder when it came to North Carolina. Gary Williams was just 10–16 against the Tar Heels in his coaching career, but it was on the recruiting circuit that Williams had already suffered at the hands of Doherty. Two top-flight prep players, Jawad Williams and Melvin Scott, had spurned the Terps and chosen Carolina since Doherty had become the coach in Chapel Hill.

The game, while important to Carolina, was critical to Maryland. After starting the season 1–3 (with losses to Illinois, Dayton, and Wisconsin), the Terps had reeled off 10 straight wins. They were 2–0 in the ACC. This showdown, on national television, was primed to vault either Maryland or North Carolina back into college basketball's elite.

But not both.

Like Wake, Maryland was one of the more experienced teams in the country. Terence Morris had turned down the NBA to return for his senior season and would be an exceedingly difficult matchup for the bigger but slower Kris Lang. Juan Dixon, a jet-quick shooting guard, was one of the most active and talented players in the league. Inside, Lonny Baxter—a quick and agile post player who caught everything thrown his way—had always given Brendan Haywood fits.

Doherty came down quickly from the high of the Wake win and refocused his team. A sloppy practice on Monday was almost welcomed. It started in the perimeter-post breakdown drills, when players struggled to get over a baseline back-screen that Maryland employed in its "flex" offense. The scrimmage session wasn't much better, and Doherty continued to get animated, employing the "don't rest on your laurels theme" liberally.

By Tuesday, practice was better, and the players appeared ready and relaxed when they boarded the flight for Washington, D.C., that night. By the time they arrived at the Watergate Hotel, the mood was appropriately tense.

For Forte, the Maryland game was a trip home. He had lived just a few miles from Cole Field House while attending DeMatha High School and his mother, Wanda Hightower, and his brother Jason lived in nearby Rockville. If he was nervous about the homecoming, it didn't show, as Forte maintained his quiet, reserved demeanor.

Forte's defense had improved dramatically since his freshman year, when he had played conservative, contain man-to-man, defending as if he was waiting for the defensive possession to end so he could get his hands back on the ball. His outstanding hands, long arms, and quick feet gave him the physical skills to be a stingy defender. All he lacked was the motivation. When Doherty arrived, so did the will.

Doherty took a great deal of pride in Forte's development as a defensive player. In his first-ever face-to-face meeting at Forte's house in Rockville a few days after he had been hired, Doherty outlined a plan to make his star guard a better defender. Forte had reacted well to the shock of suddenly being yelled at in practice and immediately improved. Now, he had become the team's perimeter stopper. His high school coach, the legendary Morgan Wootten, had even called Joe during the early part of his sophomore season to tell him he had noticed his improvement on defense and encouraged him to keep working. For good measure, Wootten would be in Cole Field House to watch his former player.

Carolina began the game—in a rollicking Cole Field House—as if it was reliving Wake Forest, with Curry missing a wide-open three-pointer. Due to four turnovers and missed shots, the Tar Heels didn't score a basket until Jason Capel hit a 15-footer over Byron Mouton with 16:36 on the clock. But the play wasn't all bad, as Haywood sprinted the floor with Baxter and the Heels' defense again forced the action, proving it could pressure Maryland effectively in the half-court.

As the first half progressed, Carolina continued to look more comfortable against Maryland's press. Curry also settled down, hitting a three at the 13:23 mark to draw Carolina to within one at 11–10. A minute later, Curry poked the ball free from Maryland point guard Steve Blake, outraced Blake to the ball, and scored on a layup to give Carolina its first lead.

Maryland came back with a rush as Baxter and Morris both scored inside. The Terps' lead would swell to six, 29–23, following a Dixon three with 6:33 remaining in the first half. On the sideline, Doherty was calm. With the defense in front of him during the first half, the majority of his attention had been focused on alerting his players to getting through Maryland's screens and cutting off dribblers.

On offense, Forte and Capel, normally reliable scorers, were having off-nights. Curry, however, was gaining confidence. His three-pointer with 3:31 remaining—he was left wide-open on the left wing when Blake left him to double Haywood—cut the Terps' lead to three, 31–28.

At the half, Carolina trailed 36–32.

In the locker room, Doherty was calm, much the same as he had been at Georgia Tech. "Joe and Cape aren't shooting very well, other than that, we're in pretty good shape," he said to his assistants. Carolina had committed eight turnovers, but had hit 4-of-6 three-pointers, including Curry's 2-of-4. Only when the subject of Maryland's field goal percentage came up did he raise his voice to the team. "Guys, they're shooting 42 percent on us. That's not good enough."

At the beginning of the second half, Forte broke out of his mini-slump with a three-pointer to open what would be Carolina's best 12 minutes of basketball to that point in the season. On offense, Carolina passed the ball through Maryland's press with daggerlike effectiveness in the full court and seemed to adjust to Maryland's double-down strat-egy in the half-court. Capel's three from the right wing 38 seconds after Forte's put Carolina on top, 38–36.

The Tar Heels would not trail again.

A beautiful full-length pass from Morris to Dixon got the Terps to within one at 41–40, but Curry drilled his third three-pointer of the game when Blake *again* left him wide-open to double-team Lang inside. From there, the rout was on as Carolina went on a 17–4 run over the next four and a half minutes.

The advantage would balloon to 19 points at the 8:14 mark when Lang hit 1-of-2 free throws. Cole was suddenly cold and quiet as Carolina was loose and confident on offense and tenacious on defense. At the next media time-out, Doherty told his players not to look at the clock or the scoreboard and just play. "Continue to be aggressive against the press. Don't settle for jump-shots. Take it inside." Doherty did not want a repeat of UCLA, when Carolina's guards were tentative in the second half and began turning the ball over.

Immediately after the time-out, Forte had a layup blocked by Baxter. Then Haywood missed an easy one inside. Carolina suddenly went cold, making just three free throws in over five minutes of play. But the Tar Heels' defense continued to slug it out in the half court. Forte fought through screens set for Dixon; Lang did everything he could to stay with Morris; Haywood battled Baxter for position all over the floor. Elsewhere, Carolina's other players completely shut down Mouton (who would finish 1-for-6 from the field), Blake (2-for-9), and Mike Mardesich and Danny Miller (a combined 2-for-9).

Maryland chipped away at the lead, cutting it to single digits on a deep three by Morris with exactly 4:00 on the clock. An important minute passed with neither team scoring until Forte—running a play Doherty called during the time-out—answered with a fall-away three at the 2:49 mark. But the tentativeness continued for Carolina, and, like a shark smelling blood in the water, Maryland kept attacking. On the sideline, Doherty couldn't yell and scream; that would only make his players tighter. Instead, he kept yelling encouragement and trying to settle everyone down.

It didn't work.

Lang fouled out battling for a rebound with Maryland's Drew Nicholas. Owens turned the ball over when his pass to Curry hit the sideline. Curry then broke the press, but missed a contested layup. A Haywood block and a Forte layup put the Tar Heels up 78–68 and seemed to put the game out of Maryland's reach with 1:43 to play.

Following two Morris free throws that cut the lead to eight with 1:27 remaining, Blake stole the ball from Peppers at midcourt and drove to the basket. He missed the floater, but Morris tipped it in and then immediately fouled Forte. Playing in front of his mother, brother, and high school coach—not to mention 14,500 red-clad lunatics—Forte calmly hit both free throws.

Carolina led 80–72 with just over a minute remaining.

But Carolina's defense was now as tentative as its offense. Twenty seconds later, Chris Wilcox stole the ball from Owens near midcourt, and Dixon outraced Curry to the ball near Maryland's basket. Curry was unable to stop his momentum as he slid under Dixon while he shot the layup. The bucket was good, and Dixon was going to the line with a chance to cut the lead to five points with 44 seconds remaining.

Owens, who had already been lazy with the ball twice in the past two minutes, was hammered on the head on the inbounds pass. Woozy, he staggered to the line with Doherty trying to get his attention to ask if he was all right to shoot the crucial free throws. Owens did not respond, but he was obviously not all right. Owens, who was shooting 81 percent from the line, missed both badly. Playing for the three-pointer, Carolina allowed Mouton to score inside with 0:27 on the clock.

Carolina led by just three points when Maryland fouled Forte on the inbounds play.

Forte dropped the ball and immediately swaggered the 75 feet to the free throw line. The importance of having a player like Forte—who not only wanted the ball, but the intense pressure that came with it at the end of games—flashed through Doherty's mind. "It's unfair to compare anyone to Michael Jordan," Doherty would say later. "But Joe has the same confidence in his abilities and same desire to win." On the bench, Haywood and Lang held hands in solidarity and silent prayer as Forte stepped coolly to the line.

Nothing but net. Twice. Carolina led 81–77 with 25 seconds remaining.

Carolina had survived again. The only challenge left to overcome was a cramp in Capel's left calf. In a scene that proved the depth of team togetherness, Curry, Forte, and several other players ran the length of the floor to help rub out the cramp.

The 86–83 win demoralized Maryland and enthused both the Tar Heel players and their fans.

After the game, Forte gave unusually quick answers during a postgame ESPN interview, jumped in the shower for a few minutes, and returned to the court, where his mother, brother, and assorted friends waited. Also waiting for him was Wootten, who immediately pulled him to a quiet spot to talk to his former player.

"I'm very proud of you, Joe," said Wootten in a grandfatherly tone. Forte, accustomed to praise and never lacking for confidence, was humbled. "It's obvious that you've really worked hard to improve, especially on defense. Your defense tonight was outstanding."

Wootten asked how Joe was enjoying the other parts of his college life in Chapel Hill, and the two talked about his roommates, classes, and his girlfriend. Forte, whose own father had not been a part of his life since the early years of elementary school, hung on every word of advice Wootten offered. The two embraced after a few minutes until Forte jogged to catch up with the bus.

Carolina had won nine straight games and was in first place in the ACC, and all was right with the world.

23

The Innocent Climb

T he bus ride to the airport following the win over Maryland was loose and giddy (but still without sight of any cell phones). Just as the bus pulled up to Reagan International Airport, Woody Durham, who had been listening to local AM radio on his headphones, announced that Carolina's next opponent, Marquette, had just defeated Cincinnati.

What looked like an easy, nonconference home game after two emotional ACC wins had just turned into (potentially) another tough battle.

Doherty raised his eyebrows at the news, but in truth Marquette's win would not change his (or his staff's) preparation at all. Doherty had already set a precedent of working hardest to prepare against teams they should defeat. Doherty's biggest fear wasn't losing to the good teams, it was being the victim of an upset.

Following the win at Maryland, everyone associated with Carolina basketball began to feel the momentum. The Tar Heels had moved back into the AP Top 10 (rising to No. 9) and had begun the ACC season 3–0, with wins over two of the top five teams in the league. More important, two of those wins had come on the road against teams that were expected to finish in the top division of the league.

No other ACC team could say that.

Duke had been Duke, crushing Florida State, Clemson, and Virginia by an average of 36 points per game. The Blue Devils' only test had been at NC State when the Wolfpack battled back from a 19-point deficit in the second half, only to lose by six. Tech's surprise win at Virginia the night before Carolina downed Maryland meant that only Duke, UNC, and Maryland owned winning records in ACC play, placing even more importance on the Tar Heels' win over the Terps in College Park.

The optimism among Carolina fans was palpable. When Doherty began doing his radio call-in show at Michael Jordan's 23 Restaurant in November, the crowds were sparse. The night after the Maryland game, it was a packed house, with fans surrounding Doherty at the broadcast position to ask an on-air question, congratulate their coach, or get an autograph.

But Doherty refused to get caught up in the excitement and good feelings surrounding his team and his first season as coach. He always felt as if it could all change for the worse in a heartbeat—or at least one game. Doherty knew that a loss at home in either of their next two games could turn all of those slaps on the back into stabs.

Which is why Doherty worked hardest and put the most pressure on himself and his team in preparing for games that looked like sure-fire wins. The next two on the schedule, Marquette—Carolina's lone non-conference opponent during its ACC season—and Clemson were just those types of games.

As it would turn out, Doherty's preparation and his team's belief in the new coaching staff (helped along, in large part, to their recent success) led to an easy 84–54 win over Marquette. Forte, suddenly the perimeter stopper on defense, drew Golden Eagles' star Brian Wardle, a burly two-guard with tremendous shooting range. Fresh from the pep talk from Wootten, Forte again responded, forcing Wardle to miss his first six shots as Carolina built an 18-point halftime lead. The Blue Team—Holmes, Brooker, Johnson, Melendez, and Bersticker—entered the game with about five minutes remaining to close out the impressive win on national television.

Still, Doherty was not outwardly pleased, nor did he allow himself to relax. While everyone in the media kept one eye on the schedule to more important games like Virginia, NC State, and (the granddaddy of important games) Duke, Doherty worked tirelessly to keep his team focused on only the next game: Clemson.

The Tigers had not won in Chapel Hill in 75 years (and 47 games), a fact Doherty had to comment on repeatedly in the days leading up to the game. He was able to joke when it was brought up, gently chastising reporters for "putting the jinx on," but it was exactly the kind of game—like the Winthrop and College of Charleston games earlier—that Doherty feared most. In other words, one Carolina could not afford to lose.

Doherty needed no help in finding ways to motivate his team in the two practices leading up to the Clemson game. While he avoided the "streak," he did post articles on Tigers' forward Chris Hobbs, a freshman from East Chapel Hill High School who made some relatively tame comments in the local papers about anxiously anticipating the return to his hometown. "It will be exciting. I can't wait," he said.

Doherty had the article's quotes highlighted and posted in the locker room. During practice, Michael Brooker, playing on the Blue Team, was given the role of playing Will Solomon, the Tigers' guard who was leading the ACC in scoring. Brooker took it to heart, lighting up the White Team while running Clemson's plays and giving Doherty all the fodder he needed to stop practice repeatedly and get on the White Team for not working hard enough (the two players Doherty had taken to riding the hardest were Haywood and Forte).

Again, despite (or because of) Doherty's constant worrying, Carolina came out and blew away the Tigers early en route to a 92–65 win. Capel hit two jumpers to put Carolina up 5–0 to start the game, but Solomon, Clemson's only serious offensive threat, answered with a three and a 15-footer of his own to tie the score. After his second bucket, Solomon began a running commentary on his own skills with Forte. Forte, never one to back down when someone else began the trash talk, colorfully reminded Solomon of the scoreboard as the first half progressed. Solomon kept shooting, scoring, and talking, but Carolina led at the half by 13 points.

Doherty, however, was not pleased. During a game, he will relay points of emphasis to MacKinnon, who will write them down for timeouts and halftime. During the first half against Clemson, everything MacKinnon wrote down concerned Carolina's lack of concentration. "We're shooting too many three-pointers," said Doherty. He went on to list the other instances of concentration lapses: "Kris, we've told you not to save the ball under the other team's basket how many times?" Doherty grabbed the legal pad out of MacKinnon's hands and read off the list. "Fumbled passes. Shooting too quickly. Missed free throws."

The message was received. Carolina came out in the second half and extended the 13-point lead to 22 in less than four minutes. Haywood was particularly inspired during the stretch, blocking three shots in four possessions. When he swatted an Ed Scott layup attempt, the normally reserved Haywood let a stare linger in Scott's face, which brought Clemson coach Larry Shyatt off the bench in protest. Tigers' assistant Bruce Martin joined in, yelling at official Ted Valentine: "That's taunting!" Valentine immediately turned and gave the Clemson bench a technical foul. Shyatt then went berserk and had to be restrained. Valentine—the same official who was part of one of college basketball's most infamous incidents when he tossed Indiana's Bobby Knight out of a game in Bloomington and was well known for his short fuse—walked away, visibly upset.

"It's kind of funny, really," Curry said with a grin after the game of Haywood's stare-down tactic. "I guess he's trying to be intimidating." Haywood, who spends the majority of his time playing PlayStation and watching cartoons, would be the least intimidating person on earth, if he wasn't seven feet tall.

The Blue Team got into the action in full swing with about five minutes remaining—and was promptly outscored by seven points. But they got their licks in, with Bersticker on the end of an alley-oop dunk and even Big-Jim-Sports-Camper Everett scoring his first basket of the season on a jump-hook in the lane with 56.5 seconds remaining.

The win was Carolina's fourth in a row in the ACC, a feat it had not accomplished in three seasons. Not that it would help Doherty sleep any easier; Carolina would enter its next—at Florida State—game as a heavy favorite.

Just what he hated.

24

Tallahassee

Team dynamics is a critical component to success. The players' egos, fragile from years of coddling in high school and AAU basketball, can be easily bruised in the harsher world of college basketball. At the same time, college basketball players are like any other 18- to 22-year-old college student in that they seek acceptance and friendship from their peers.

The young men who made up the Carolina basketball program represented a wide variety of backgrounds. Max Owens remembered his house being broken into as a child—a few weeks after a basketball hoop that was put up in his backyard in Macon, Georgia, as a Christmas present drew some of the neighborhood undesirables to his house. Brian Bersticker was born in Honolulu and had traveled the world with his father, who was in the Navy. Kris Lang got along with everyone, thanks in large part to a childhood spent in Gastonia, North Carolina, living amid highly diverse neighbors. Adam Boone had an academic background as strong as any player in the ACC, but he also possessed a sly sense of humor and cockiness that prompted his teammates to vote him the honor of being the freshman that carried the infamous green equipment bag on road trips.

It was a group that had grown very close in a short period of time.

That was not the case of the Tar Heels the year before, when many of Carolina's key players—Joseph Forte, Jason Capel, Brendan Haywood, Ed Cota—were not close friends. They did what they had to do on the court, but when practice ended, so did their time together, as all headed their separate ways to spend time with friends outside of the program. Often, the players would pass in the hallways of the Smith Center and barely acknowledge each other.

Enter Matt Doherty. His beliefs about building a team included getting along on and off the court. "You don't have to be best friends," he said, "but there has to be a trust and a bond that extends off the court." It also helped that Cota, a three-and-a-half year starter who had grown more and more critical of his teammates as his career had progressed, had graduated.

Immediately, Doherty's inclusive personality—and that of his staff—began to have an effect. Late summer cookouts outside of the coaches' offices at the Smith Center, tailgate parties before football games, and encouraging the players to go out to eat with each other (Outback Steakhouse was a team and staff favorite) forced the players to get to know one another. Slowly, friendships that had not been there the year before began to emerge. The team grew close.

Once the season started, the team dynamic was further strengthened by the physically challenging workouts—nothing bonds players more than collective pain—as well as the humor and sense of fun Doherty and the coaches brought to their informal interactions with the players. The result was that Capel and Forte and Haywood and the rest now joked around with each other more often and, in the words of one of the players, got along "like brothers." The rest of the team followed.

It was a tight-knit group—thanks in part to a fast start in the ACC regular season—that prepared to take on Florida State.

Six weeks before the Tar Heels visited, Tallahassee had been the center of the newsmaking universe, as boxes of uncounted ballots made their way to the capital of the state of Florida and the world wondered who would be the next president. Less than three weeks earlier, Florida State's football team had played for (and lost) the national championship.

At 4:00 on Saturday, January 20, 2001, the town was not nearly as energized. Typically, when North Carolina entered any college town to play a basketball game against the home team, it created a buzz. Carolina was the team everyone loved to hate (ABC—Anyone But Carolina—fans are in every ACC town), and it brought out the best in teams. Earlier in the season, the Tar Heels were the biggest story to hit Boone, North Carolina, in the last 10 years. In Tallahassee, no college basketball game—whether the opponent was North Carolina or North Texas State—ever created much of a ripple.

Steve Robinson, Florida State's coach, was in trouble. Athletic Director Dave Hart publicly denied any rumors regarding Robinson's job, but the few alumni who cared about basketball were beginning to grumble. The Seminoles were not very good in 2000–2001, having lost all four ACC games by an average of 21.5 points. In its nonconference games, FSU had been defeated by the likes of Furman and Cleveland State.

The most important by-product—given the modern-day fiscal realities of college basketball—was apathetic attendance. Leon County Civic Center had undergone extensive renovations two years earlier (upgrading the facility from the worst in the league to just *among* the worst in the league), but the poor record and lack of enthusiasm had resulted in an average attendance of just below 5,000 per game.

Even North Carolina coming to town couldn't change that number, as just 7,452 paid to see the Seminoles take on the Tar Heels on a sunny January afternoon.

Robinson's fate was hard for Doherty to ignore. The two are good friends, having served together on Williams' staff at Kansas for three years. Before Matt and Kelly had their own children, they used to play with Robinson's when the families met for dinner at each other's houses.

That's not to say the competitive juices didn't flow, even when they were on the same coaching staff. Like many athletic departments around the country, staff members played basketball at lunch time. At Kansas, the NBL (Noon Basketball League) met every Monday, Wednesday, and Friday and would include everyone from custodians to former college All-Americans. During the off-season, the games also included Doherty and Robinson. As two former players roughly equal in ability, they often had to guard each other. The results were often incendiary.

"They didn't like to do it, but it was the only way to keep it fair," recalled Dean Buchan, then the men's basketball sports information director at Kansas. "Matt would set up on the three-point line and shoot his set shot, while Steve liked to set up on the post and shoot jump-hooks. It would get into a physical battle down low. Someone would call a foul, and the other guy would say it was an offensive foul. Then the first guy would say that you can't call an offensive foul in a pick-up basketball game."

In one particularly hard-fought game, the argument over a foul call resulted in a stand-off, with Robinson taking his team to one end of the floor and Doherty's team remaining on the other. "They stayed there, neither one willing to budge, for 15 minutes, until lunch was over," said Buchan.

Carolina's practices between the Clemson and Florida State games were largely uneventful. Until late in the workout on Friday, that is. With practice set to conclude within minutes, Morrison rose to shoot over Forte during an intrasquad scrimmage. When he came down, his foot rolled over when it landed on Forte's foot, and the freshman fell to the floor and screamed in pain. "When he went down, I thought it was broken," said Adam Boone. "He was in serious pain."

Marc Davis quickly rushed to Morrison's side, as the team hustled to the other end of the floor to finish the late-game situations drill.

Doherty and the remainder of the team were concerned, but the coaches did not want an injury to be the last thing the players remembered as they left that night to fly to Tallahassee.

The ankle was badly sprained, Davis thought, but not broken. When Morrison's pain subsided somewhat after he was assisted to the training room, Davis's diagnosis strengthened. An X ray was taken as the other players boarded the bus for the airport. By the time they landed in Florida, Doherty had already received word that Morrison's ankle was just a sprain.

Heading into the game, Doherty felt as positive about the team as he had all season. Haywood had 16 blocks in the past two games and was zeroing in on the all-time blocks record at the school, held by Sam Perkins. As maligned as Haywood had been during his four seasons in Chapel Hill, he would likely conclude his career as the career leader in blocks and field goal percentage.

On defense, Curry and Peppers had brought the needed toughness, making Carolina's man-to-man as stingy as any in the league. Perhaps most amazing, the Tar Heels—the poster boys (or at least the video subjects) for the new initiative to clean up post play—were leading the country in fewest fouls per game.

On offense, Haywood and Lang were much-improved passers, particularly when getting double-teamed inside. Curry's ballhandling improved every day he spent on the court, and as he had proven against Maryland, he could hit an outside shot when he had to. Owens' confidence, although up and down, was holding steady at the moment, as he was providing important scoring punch off the bench. And if all else broke down, Forte had proven that he had a rare knack to know when a game's crucial moments occurred and when he needed to score. More important, he *could* score, virtually whenever he wanted.

The most obvious improvement from the previous season had been in sheer effort. Opposing league coaches were always careful not to diminish the accomplishments of previous Carolina teams or Bill Guthridge, but many commented privately that Carolina was now tougher to play against because they simply played harder.

 Doherty's last statement to his team as they prepared to take the floor against Florida State was simple: "Let's create our own energy out there."

"Out there" was definitely a place that needed some energy. When the Tar Heels took the court for pregame warm-ups the Leon County Civic Center was a morgue, with every word spoken on the bench and sneaker squeak on the court clearly audible. The year before, the arena's temperature (due to the renovations that left gaps in the walls and ceiling) had hovered around 55 degrees, which only proved that the situation could be worse. Some FSU students eventually made it to the arena about 10 minutes prior to game time, but every time a fan yelled from the stands it was possible to individually identify that person.

Of course, the person doing the majority of noisemaking was Matt Doherty. His defensive calls of "slide" and "get through" reverberated throughout the arena, and were adhered to well by his players. Florida State was able to score only four points in the game's first five and a half minutes.

After a mini-run by the Seminoles closed the gap to 14–11 with 12:43 on the clock, Owens took a pass from Lang and hit a three over the FSU zone. Over the next six minutes Carolina went on a 16–0 spurt. Defensively, Carolina was active in the passing lanes and in containing drivers. Without a post-up game, Florida State was relegated to drives and wild shots. The result was a 49–30 halftime lead for UNC.

Matt Doherty was pleased with his team's effort and execution in the first half, but, as had become the custom, he refused to allow his players to relax. "Whatever you do, don't let up. They can hit some shots, and if we let them think they can stay in it, they will."

The Tar Heels' play in the second half during many recent games had been extremely unpredictable. Against Georgia Tech, they had come back from 12 points down to win. Against UCLA, they had given back a 20-point lead, gotten behind, and then won. Against Maryland they had taken and *then* nearly given up a big lead. Against Kentucky, the Tar Heels had simply continued to play as poorly as they had in the first half.

There was no indicator or predictor as to which Carolina team would show up in the second half of any of those games, a fact that boggled the collective minds of the coaching staff. In this one, Doherty sensed that human nature would be to let up. He did everything he could think of—pleading, threatening, cajoling—to make sure it didn't happen.

It wouldn't work.

After flirting with 20-point leads twice in the first half before settling for a 17-point cushion at the half, Carolina let Florida State score the first five points of the second half. A 12-point deficit is viewed much differently than 20, and the Seminoles suddenly felt a rush. Doherty felt it, too. He immediately took Forte, Capel, and Lang out of the game and replaced them with fresh bodies. He also hoped to send a message to the starters.

Meanwhile, the few people in the arena sensed that maybe, just maybe, a game had broken out when Adrian Crawford hit a three-pointer off an out-of-bounds play. Doherty railed against his three starters on the bench. "We said that we needed to come out with energy! And we didn't!"

Florida State, however, did. For the next seven minutes it was an even game. Inside, Haywood and Lang, who had dominated inside in the first half, suddenly couldn't handle Nigel (Big Jelly) Dixon, the 6'7", 324-pound center for Florida State. Dixon did not score a point in the first half; in the second, he grabbed every stray rebound and loose ball and even scored six points.

Carolina did not score a field goal until Brian Bersticker took a pass from Owens and dunked at the 15:23 mark to boost Carolina back up to a 16-point lead. But a 10–2 FSU run—after the UNC starters were inserted back into the lineup—cut the lead to single digits. The wheels were wobbling, but they hadn't come off. Yet.

Florida State kept spreading the floor, and Carolina, so aggressive on defense in the first half, reverted back to early in the season when they played not to get beat. Which, of course, meant they most likely would. FSU point guard Delvon Arrington went around Boone and then Curry seemingly at will. Where the Seminoles couldn't buy a basket with their spread-the-floor-and-play-one-on-one offense in the first half, they couldn't miss in the second. With the crowd into the game for the first time all season, it became apparent that Carolina might lose this game, and thus, all of the positive feeling and momentum it had built up during its 11-game winning streak.

The tentative play culminated when, trying to make a simple pass from the point to the wing and hardly under intense pressure, Curry's pass to Capel was deflected by Arrington. Outracing Capel to the ball, Arrington then took it the length of the floor and scored to make the score 60–57 with 7:44 to play. Doherty, meanwhile, sat calmly on the bench, knowing that yelling and screaming would only tighten his team further. The game was slowly but surely getting away from North Carolina.

Enter Joe Forte.

It started with a basket that, while it wouldn't show up on any highlights show that night, was as impressive as any he had made all season. Unable to get the ball during most of the possession thanks to pressure from Crawford, Forte bided his time until Curry found him on the left wing. Haywood moved to set a screen, but instead backed into the post. Forte drove into the lane and rose off of two feet. In the air, he made contact with Monte Cummings, but Forte shielded the ball with his left shoulder, waited until Cummings came down, and then banked the ball off the glass on the right side. With his team struggling and all of his teammates looking to him, Forte delivered.

The Carolina bench breathed a huge sigh of relief. The defense reenergized and tightened. Haywood blocked a shot. Forte came down on the break and hit a 15-footer. After a Joiner hoop, Forte banged in a three from several feet behind the top of the key. Two possessions later, after a pass out of the post from Peppers, he hit another on the left wing. Then, on a beautiful backdoor cut and another pass from Peppers, he culminated the string with an uncontested dunk. Twelve straight points by Forte gave Carolina an 11-point lead.

And the game.

When it was over and the Tar Heels had escaped with a 10-point win, 80–70, Doherty was sufficiently upset. While careful to give Florida State—and his good buddy Robinson—plenty of credit for playing with more energy, he knew that his team had been out-hustled and out-played in the second half.

Doherty would grudgingly admit several days later that it was a blessing to have aspects of the game in which Carolina could improve—while still winning games. It allowed him to have his team's full attention in practice as they worked to "tighten the screws"—a favorite Doherty expression.

And the screws needed to be tight for the next stretch. Virginia, twice victors over Carolina the year before, was coming to town. After that, it was rivalry week: NC State and Duke.

25

"... A Good Problem to Have"

The game at Florida State had been, in Matt Doherty's mind, close to disastrous. Of course, a true disaster would have been a loss, but the Tar Heels' tentative play in the second half put their coach in a relatively foul mood during the next few days as he asked himself the same question he had after so many other games this season: Why does his team come out flat in the second half?

But Doherty's nature was to focus on the negatives. Without a doubt, there had been positives in Carolina's recent play and even during the win in Tallahassee. With 1:02 remaining in the game, Haywood had blocked a layup attempt by Nigel Dixon, giving him sole possession of the North Carolina career blocked-shots record. In four seasons, Haywood had blocked 246 shots, breaking the record previously held by Sam Perkins. Haywood's career may have been up and down in the eyes of many fans

247

and media, but he would be the only player in ACC history to leave his school as the career leader in blocks and field goal percentage.

Doherty, however, was quick to notice that on the very play Haywood recorded the record-breaking block, Dixon recovered the loose ball and scored two seconds later.

A similar good news–bad news situation was developing with Forte. The Carolina guard had scored 28 points at Florida State and had been arguably the best shooting guard in the country in the first half of the college basketball season. Inexplicably, Forte had been left off the list of 30 nominees for the Wooden National Player of the Year Award that was announced in late December. Although the Wooden Committee would not admit it, it was most obviously an error that could (and would) be corrected later in the season, but not one that went unnoticed by Forte. "I know I'm one of the 30 best players in the country," he said after a reporter informed him of the omission.

As the season progressed, Forte had displayed a knack for making big plays or scoring at crucial times. He had made the clutch plays in games against Charleston, Georgia Tech, Maryland, and Florida State. Even the winning play against Wake Forest went through Forte's hands, showing the maturity of having a year of college basketball under his belt.

When pressed, Doherty would grudgingly admit that Carolina had done well to avoid fouling, had improved its half-court defense (Carolina had held teams to just 35 percent from the field during its 12-game win streak), and when they were clicking, the team did a nice job of getting the ball inside and then back out for jump-shots. But the negatives—lack of concentration and turnovers in particular—weighed on his mind heavily, and he and his staff sought ways they could "tighten the screws" while keeping the team's confidence high.

Virginia came into the Smith Center after surviving a season's worth of peaks and valleys. Like Wake Forest, the Cavaliers had been a surprise in the preseason, winning 10 consecutive games to start the season, including a 19-point drubbing of then-No. 4 Tennessee on national television at the Jimmy V Classic in Madison Square Garden. Entering their first ACC game at Wake, the Cavs had risen all the way to No. 8 in the country.

But Pete Gillen's club was throttled by Wake Forest in Winston-Salem, losing by 23 points. The game was not that close, and the loss shook Virginia's confidence. A team made up of a tempestuous mix of talented young players (Travis Watson, Adam Hall, and Roger Mason Jr.) and holdovers from the Jeff Jones era (Chris Williams and Donald Hand), the Cavs were at their best when they played fast and loose. "We're not very good at half-court offense and half-court defense," admitted Gillen. "When one of our guys shot-fakes in practice, even the managers jump."

The Cavs wanted a full-court, frenetic game; exactly what Carolina wanted to avoid.

For the first 12 minutes, Carolina was effective at keeping the pace to their liking. A few communication errors in their half-court defense did not keep the Tar Heels from building a 29–20 lead with 8:24 remaining in the first half. Up to that point, UVa's pressure defense had been a nonfactor due to a simple equation: Virginia hadn't scored very much, therefore Carolina hadn't had to take the ball out against a set-up press. The lead continued to grow to as high as 16 points when Forte found Lang for a dunk at the 5:39 to make the score 39–23. At the half, Carolina held a 50–35 lead and appeared on its way to a blowout.

Doherty's halftime comments centered on the recurring problem of relaxing in the second half. "No letdowns. Come out as if the game is 0–0."

It didn't work. In less than five minutes, Virginia had the Carolina lead to three points. On the first possession of the second half, Curry threw it away trying to enter the ball to Haywood in the post. The Tar Heels' offense was stagnant; the movement was gone. Haywood was struggling to get free inside against Watson, a deceptively strong, if undersized, post player.

Again, it was Forte who came to the rescue. On 4-of-5 possessions (following a Williams three-pointer that cut the lead to 56–53), Forte scored, going on a personal 9–4 run. Doherty ran plays for Forte, free-ing him up at the top and setting screens for him on the left side (so he could penetrate into the lane). On all of them, Forte scored. With each basket, Doherty breathed a sigh of relief but was disturbed by the knowledge that the best teams weren't carried by one player. When he scored his 23rd point with a leaner in the lane that bounced high before dropping through, Forte did a very un-Forte-like thing; he gestured with a pumping fist to the students on the baseline. On the sideline, Doherty pumped his own fist, instructing Carolina to get back into a man-to-man defense. By the time Curry drove the baseline and scored two minutes later, Carolina was back up by 10 with 9:21 remaining.

But Virginia refused to quit. Watson continued to dominate inside, scoring twice on quick interior post moves. Hall dunked two minutes later, and again the lead was down to three points.

With just under 4:00 on the clock and Carolina ahead by five, 80–75, Forte made a rare mistake trying to break UVa's press and his pass to Lang was picked off. Watson rushed the ball into the frontcourt and hit Williams, who tried to get it back to Watson for what would be a bucket that would cut the lead to three points. But Peppers, who possesses remarkable hands for his size, stole the pass and threw a pass back up-court to Forte. With the numbers even, Forte slid to the baseline, and, to the disbelief of fans, his teammates, and, especially, his coach, threw up a fallaway jump-shot from 14 feet over two Virginia defenders. On the bench, the coaches looked stone-faced at the shot, knowing it was ill advised, but not wanting the ball in anyone else's hands. "I thought to myself, 'no, no, no,' " said Haywood later.

The ball seemed to hang in the air for several seconds before it came down clean through the net. The shot seemed to deflate the Cavaliers and Carolina went on to win 88–81, despite Curry missing four consecutive free throws in the game's last minute. Forte ended up with 33 points, none bigger than his fadeaway jumper with 3:41 left that sealed the win.

After the game, there was anything but euphoria on Doherty's face or in his words. "We didn't come out with the energy that I'd hoped in the second half, that's for sure," he told the players. "We've got practice tomorrow, and we're going to try to figure out what we need to do to play both halves of a game." Publicly, he praised Virginia for hanging tough; privately, he wondered what he was doing—or not doing—to make his team go into comas during key stretches.

Without Forte's constant heroics, Doherty knew, Carolina could easily be under .500 in the league.

That night, the frustration of letting leads slip away almost too much to bear, Doherty called Dean Smith at home, seeking advice and/or a knowing shoulder to cry on. What he got was much more valuable: a sense of perspective.

After Doherty explained the second-half struggles and wondered what he was doing wrong, Smith—who was quiet on the other end as Doherty explained all of the things the team was doing wrong—finally spoke. "Matt," said Smith, "you just defeated the No. 13 team in the country. Virginia's athletic and talented. You've won 13 games in a row, and you still have a lot of things to work on to get better.

"Sounds to me like a pretty good problem to have."

Class War

26

A beautiful, sunny, 55-degree day greeted the Tar Heels as they made the short trip to Raleigh for a Super Bowl Sunday show-down with NC State, a team Doherty had declared "the most dangerous team in the conference" to his players in the three days of practice that had come after the win over Virginia and before the matchup with the Wolfpack. While many of the players had understood their coach's need to build up the Pack (who were struggling at 2–4 in the ACC and 10–7 overall), the truth was, they didn't need any extrinsic motivation for this in-state rivalry.

More so than any other game—except maybe Duke—the Carolina–State rivalry was based on the raw emotion of the teams' fans and, to a lesser extent, the players, particularly those who grew up in-state, such as Brendan Haywood, Jason Capel, and Will Johnson. For the fans of both teams, the matchup was, for lack of a better description, a class war.

252

UNC–Chapel Hill and the students and alumni who attended the school were stereotyped as the social and academic elite of the state. To be a Carolina student/alumnus was to be part of southern gentry, to be from the best families and to become leaders in the state's economic, political, and cultural circles. This sense of entitlement had grown out of the university's status as one of the oldest and finest state universities in the nation—and the students and alumni both lived up to and enjoyed the benefits from that distinction.

NC State, meanwhile, was labeled as "the other state school" that produced students interested in "less noble" pursuits, such as agriculture and engineering. It was perceived that NCSU people were not a part of the southern aristocracy, but more of the down-home, good-ole boys (and women) who were somehow less cultured than those who were associated with UNC. Of course, this was a crass and exceedingly untrue overgeneralization, but the stereotype nonetheless lived on—and rankled NCSU alumni, students, and fans to such an extent that it bordered on cultural warfare. UNC people took an untold amount of pleasure from NC State's unbridled anger over the perception and further fanned the flames by pretending not to care.

Needless to say, the two regularly scheduled meetings of the school's basketball programs—which were the most visible manifestations of the stereotypes attached to the schools and had enjoyed great success and two national championships each in the modern, post-1960s era—were eagerly anticipated.

The rivalry had taken a hit recently due to Herb Sendek's difficulties in producing winning teams in Raleigh as well as NC State's abandoning its on-campus facility, Reynolds Coliseum, for the new and well-appointed (but significantly less intimate) Entertainment and Sports Arena (ESA), which it shared with the NHL's Carolina Hurricanes and was located several miles from the main academic campus. "Reynolds was the loudest place I ever played," recalled Doherty. "During my time as a player, the NC State rivalry was as big as any."

This season, Sendek was again facing the scrutiny that surrounded unrealized expectations. He had yet to lead an NC State team to the

NCAA Tournament, despite several recruiting classes ranked in the Top 10 nationally. Even with its past success—NCAA titles in 1974 and 1983—and brand-new arena, NC State was not North Carolina or Duke and often had to work exceptionally hard to land talented players. Much like a professional team consistently picking in the middle of a draft, Sendek had had to settle for the best athletes he could get, instead of the polished players who were also great athletes that landed in Chapel Hill and Durham.

The result in 2000–2001 had been a team filled with strong, athletic players who were largely unskilled. Sendek, a professorial coach who had worked under Rick Pitino at Kentucky before moving on to Miami of Ohio and then to Raleigh, had a strong belief in himself and his system and had been successful in getting his players to play hard. But without enough skill and finesse, the Wolfpack could not develop consistency on offense. Thus, NC State entered the game against UNC as the second-worst shooting team in the ACC, making just over 40 percent of its shots from the field against conference foes.

Sendek's headaches increased when his leading scorer, guard Anthony Grundy, was arrested early Saturday morning—before the Sunday afternoon game against UNC—on a charge of assaulting a female. After being released to the custody of Assistant Coach Larry Harris, Grundy met with Sendek on Saturday. Sendek heard Grundy's side of the story and announced that his starting guard would play against Carolina the next day and after until the judicial process had run its course. (Grundy would eventually be found innocent of the charges.)

Despite the Pack's struggles on and off the court, Doherty knew this was a very losable game, for several reasons. First, NC State was a relentless offensive rebounding team. Early in the season, boxing out had been a Carolina weakness, but since losing the battle on the boards to Kentucky, the Tar Heels had been out-rebounded only twice, against UMass and at Maryland. Second, the next game after NC State was at Duke, and the buildup had already begun in the local and national media. ESPN was running a weeklong series of games it was billing as "Rivalry Week," with the crown jewel being the Thursday night

Duke–Carolina matchup in Cameron. Doherty had consistently refused to answer any questions about the next game on the schedule, but he understood human nature was to look ahead. Third, Doherty knew that a team with its back to the wall, and as athletically gifted as NC State, would do anything for a big home win against a marquee team. The fact that Carolina—NC State's biggest rival—was riding a 13-game winning streak only made Doherty more focused in his preparations.

Practices that week included emphasis on offensive execution in the half-court and transition defense, both of which had been lacking against Virginia the game before. "It seems that as soon as we plug one hole in the dike, another opens," said Doherty.

The ESA, complete with a state-of-the-art lighting and sound system, was rocking. As had been the case in Reynolds, NC State had made the commitment to keep a good portion of its students near courtside, and the typical signs and chants—one veteran observer commented that the NC State crowd was a less clever version of the Cameron Crazies—were everywhere as the Tar Heels took the court. When the teams returned to the locker room for last-minute instructions, the crowd stood for the national anthem, which was being sung by an NC State student. When the student reached the middle of the song, the audio suddenly cut out. In a frantic attempt to fix the problem, an ESA technician accidentally plugged the Tar Heel Radio Network's feed into the PA system. Thus, with the entire ESA crowd silent and standing, expecting the ". . . home of the brave," they instead heard Doherty's voice—answering a Woody Durham question during a prerecorded, pregame interview—fill the arena for a few seconds.

There was no such awkward moment for Carolina early in the game, as it took an early lead despite turnovers on three of its first four possessions. The lead swelled to 10 points when Haywood scored on a feed from Forte at the 11:05 mark, but NC State came roaring back to within two when the Heels' offense struggled. But Carolina's defense stiffened when Doherty went to a zone to protect Lang, Haywood, Curry, Capel, and Peppers, all of whom were in foul trouble. NC State struggled against the zone, missing eight straight shots to end the half.

Meanwhile, Carolina came back to life, scoring on two Haywood dunks and a 15-foot Forte floater to take a 10-point lead into halftime.

At halftime, Doherty and his staff knew they were fortunate to lead. "That stretch [at the end of the first half] was key," he said. "We might need that cushion." Doherty knew that many of State's shots in the first half had been makeable. The physical play was something they knew was coming when they had scouted State, but Doherty thought the strength of the Wolfpack players had surprised many of Carolina's players. He was happy that they had only six turnovers, but he made a point to tell Curry and Boone to keep attacking and not be tentative with the ball. "They aren't going to back down," he said to the team. "This is their house, and they see this as their breakout game. Don't you dare let up."

Second-half letdowns, of course, had plagued Carolina all season. But against NC State, Doherty would admit later, the tentativeness of his offense was caused more by State's defensive intensity than anything his Tar Heels would do.

Capel picked up his fourth foul before the first media time-out when he charged into Damon Thornton. When he went out, Carolina led by nine points, 37–28. Lang was already out, replaced by Brian Bersticker, the forgotten big man on Carolina's bench. Of all Carolina's players who had reacted so well to their new coach's intense style, Bersticker was one whom it had hurt. Always laid back and rarely one to be fiery or emotional, Bersticker had played himself out of the regular rotation. But with foul trouble and a sagging State defense, he came off the bench for Haywood and immediately hit a 15-foot jumper to give Carolina its largest lead of the game at 39–28 with 15:21 remaining. But a minute later he allowed Thornton to push him off the block, and Bersticker was forced to foul. Immediately, Doherty reinserted Haywood.

Just as Doherty had feared, Carolina grew tentative as the game progressed and NC State would not give up. With just under 10 minutes remaining, Haywood missed two free throws and Grundy made a twisting layup to cut the Tar Heel lead to four points, 46–42. Forte again came to the forefront when his team needed him most, draining a three from the corner to push the lead back to seven points, but momentum kept rolling for State. For three minutes Carolina's offense was stagnant and, in the face of rising pressure, looked scared.

Clifford Crawford stripped a backpedaling Curry and drove the length of the floor to score and cut the lead to three with 4:43 remaining. Thirty seconds later, Cornelius Williams made his first basket of the game on a jump-hook over Haywood to cut the lead to one. Carolina and State traded baskets until Forte missed a 15-footer in the lane. Grundy rebounded and immediately hit Damien Wilkins down the sideline. The nephew of Dominique and the son of Gerald crossed over on his way to a one-handed dunk to pull the Pack to within one point, 53–52, with less than two minutes to play. The thought went through more minds than one on the Carolina bench—maybe today was the day that Forte's luck, and Carolina's win streak, ended.

Doherty took a time-out when Carolina again was slow to set up on offense. "I was grasping at straws at that point," Doherty would say later. "I had to burn through all of our time-outs because we looked so tentative with the ball." In the huddle, Doherty tried to both calm down his team and set up a play to get Haywood the ball inside. Haywood had struggled against State's double-teams inside, but Doherty trusted his big man to make the right decision when it counted most. When play resumed, State allowed the ball to get inside to Haywood and immediately doubled off of Lang with Kenny Inge, forcing Haywood to dribble back out all the way to the corner and call time-out with just seven seconds on the shot clock.

During the time-out, Doherty calmly consulted his ever-present blue index card, calling a side out-of-bounds play that would get the ball to Curry and spread the floor, allowing Curry to (hopefully) get in the lane and make a play.

He did just that, getting by Crawford in two dribbles, drawing inside help, and feeding Haywood, who was fouled by Inge as he attempted to dunk. The game rested on Haywood's free throws—he had made just two of his last 15 attempts from the line and was 0-for-2 on the day— with 1:17 remaining in the game.

Doherty called Haywood over to the sideline and told him to think about being back at Dudley High School and block out everything else.

Haywood understood: he had been so concerned about free throws earlier in the season that on Christmas morning, after his family had opened presents early, he had gone to a gym at Greensboro Day School alone and had shot free throws for over an hour and a half. It was typical of Haywood, who was as hard a worker as anyone on the Carolina team but was rarely given credit for it by Tar Heel fans.

With the arena erupting all around him, Haywood—the exact player Sendek would want on the line in that situation—calmly hit both free throws. For good measure, Haywood blocked a three-point attempt by Scooter Sherrill on the next possession to secure the win. The Tar Heels would go on to survive, 60–52.

As the team jogged off the court after the win, Lang jumped on Haywood's back. As the two front-court mates chest-bumped and celebrated in the tunnel to the locker room, Lang bellowed at the top of his lungs. "Seven-and-oh, baby!! Duke and Carolina; let's get it on!!"

In four days, they would.

27

The World Is Watching

Matt Doherty began—officially and publicly—preparing for Duke on the walk back to the visitor's locker room at NC State following Carolina's win, but he had really begun the process six months earlier.

In the late summer, during his family's vacation at Roy Williams's beach house in Charleston, Doherty had brought two game tapes with him, both of the Duke losses from the year before. Since that week, he had often informally reminded certain players on the team—particularly Forte and Capel, his personal favorites when delivering humorous, stinging jabs—about improvements they would have to make to successfully do battle against Duke. The majority of comments focused on defense and toughness. "Of course, he was right," said Forte. "But he was tough on us."

Following the hard-fought win at NC State, Doherty told his players to relax and not come into the arena on Monday. Even though

Monday would serve as the NCAA-mandated day off, Doherty knew that many of the players tended to come in on their own to shoot, lift weights, or just hang around the basketball office or locker room. Instead, he said, he wanted them to work on their studies and stay at home and relax. "Don't think about basketball," he told the team four days before they would take the floor of Cameron Indoor Stadium for the biggest college basketball game of the year.

Forte spent his afternoon off playing video games with suite-mates Clay Phillips and Chase Briggs. Capel spent his day off working on a paper for class. Doherty and the coaches had no such opportunity—nor would they have wanted to be any place in the world other than working on a game plan for Duke.

Doherty spent Monday morning downstairs in the coaches' locker room with Dean Smith, watching film on Duke. Smith's manner of breaking down tape was similar to Doherty's (and most every other coach); he rewound the tape constantly and pointed out aspects of footwork and poor positioning that led to plays being made. Their level of comfort together in their current roles was continuing to grow as they exchanged ideas on how to beat arguably the best college basketball team in the country.

The game plan Doherty came up with for Duke was not groundbreaking. Carolina's advantage was inside, where Haywood and Lang held a size advantage over Duke's Carlos Boozer and Shane Battier. Doherty was concerned about Jason Williams, Duke's outstanding and lightning-quick point guard. Ronald Curry had been less than confident in the last few minutes at NC State, and the result had been several turnovers in which he was stripped of the ball while dribbling. If Williams sensed that he could take the ball from Curry, he would attack like a piranha smelling blood.

"Ronald needs to be aggressive, to take it by Williams if he lunges at the ball," said Doherty to his coaches later at an impromptu staff meeting. (Rarely did the coaches have a scheduled staff meeting—most of the time Doherty called his assistants together on the spur of the moment.) In practices and in the media, Doherty had been quick to state his confidence in Curry, and it was no different with his coaches. Doherty was a big believer in showing the utmost confidence in players, particularly when the issue was one of their perceived weaknesses. For that reason, he built up Curry when he talked about his point guard's ballhandling and shooting skills.

As for the Duke game, Doherty kept his usual enthusiasm and competitive fire under wraps. For Florida State and Clemson, the players might need exterior motivation. Doherty knew that for Duke, they'd be focused and ready to practice, let alone play. Adding to the historical aspect of the event was this: never, in the long course of their storied rivalry, had both teams entered the game a perfect 7–0 in ACC play.

It nearly wasn't so. The night before Carolina defeated NC State, Duke played at Maryland in what turned out to be one of college basketball's most remarkable games in recent years. The Terps, who had downed Duke in Cameron a year ago for the Blue Devils' only conference loss in two seasons, played a tremendous game—for 39 minutes.

But ahead by 10 points with one minute remaining, Maryland inexplicably lost the game when Williams, who had turned the ball over 10 times to that point, took advantage of Maryland's Steve Blake fouling out and scored eight points in less than 20 seconds. Maryland continued to miss free throws and execute poorly on both ends of the floor as Duke first tied the game to send it into overtime and then won the game by two points when Shane Battier blocked a shot by Juan Dixon. "One of the most amazing games I've ever been a part of," said Duke coach Mike Krzyzewski after the game.

Forte watched the game in his suite at Granville Towers, shaking his head as Maryland imploded under Duke's late-game pressure. "They're pretty good," he said quietly in a colossal understatement.

Doherty had the same thought as he made notes on Duke's individual players for the scouting report. Williams, he thought, was the key to the team. "The point guard is the most important player on the floor," said Doherty. "And he's the best in the country at that position. Everything Duke does on offense goes through Williams." It seemed Doherty made similar notes on all of Duke's starters: can shoot or drive, likes to go one-on-one, great passer, and so on.

Doherty was also concerned about Kris Lang matching up with Battier. Battier—a player every Carolina fan loved to hate—had seemingly played at Duke for a decade. Lang had fueled the fire after Battier had fouled out against Stanford, allowing the Cardinal to hand the Blue Devils their only loss of the season. "You mean they fouled out the Golden Boy?" Lang said to several reporters. "I can't believe they fouled out the Golden Boy." Golden or not, Battier had improved each of his four seasons. As a freshman, he had established his reputation as a gritty defensive player who could guard post players inside or perimeter players outside. He had also earned a national reputation for taking charges; Carolina fans (and those of other teams in the ACC) accused him of flopping. But that charge was largely a result of frustration, as Battier and Duke enjoyed unparalleled success against conference foes. On the Carolina roster, only Brendan Haywood, Max Owens, and Michael Brooker—all seniors— had been on a Carolina team that had defeated Duke.

Duke's offense was not one that required a great deal of film analysis or breakdown. Other than a few set plays, Duke simply spread the floor and let Williams, Battier, freshman Chris Duhon, Mike Dunleavy, and Nate James drive and/or spot up. Duke shot almost 26 three-pointers per game and made an average of 10; both totals were by far the most of any team in the country.

"I'm thinking we should play some zone," Doherty offered as more of a question to his staff. The response was generally favorable, so Doherty worked into the practice plan—which he wrote early in the afternoon after watching tape and getting input from the staff in the meeting—20 minutes of work on their 2-zone. He didn't necessarily want to play zone, but if containing Williams and the others became too difficult or if Carolina got into foul trouble, playing a zone—one that was aggressive on the perimeter to contest three-point shooters—might be a necessity.

The game regularly captured the national sports spotlight, and this year, with Duke and Carolina 1–2 in the conference (and No. 2 and No. 4 nationally), was no different. On Tuesday, Doherty met the media in the memorabilia room and appeared relaxed, joking about his own role as a player (Doherty often displayed self-deprecating humor during press conferences) and about his biggest surprise since becoming the Carolina coach. "This biggest surprise?" Doherty wondered, repeating the question and laughing. "The fact that my wife hasn't left me."

Tuesday's practice, as Doherty predicted, was focused and intense—thanks to a special prepractice film session. Typically, the coaches would prepare a scouting video on the opponent, whittling down the hours and hours of videotape into about 20 minutes (so as not to lose the players' attention) that best summarize the other team's tendencies and strengths. Since the ACC was predominately a veteran conference and many of the players and plays on the majority of the teams were the same as the year before, the tape would include several cuts from last year's games. Frequently during these cuts—taken from the ESPN, CBS, or Raycom broadcasts—the voices of the commentators could be heard. For the Duke scouting tape clip of last season's game at Cameron, Doherty made certain that one announcer was clearly audible.

Throughout the 20 minutes, Doherty had made comments on Duke's players and team tendencies as they were appearing on the screen, sometimes stopping the action and rewinding the tape to make a specific point. With about a minute remaining on the tape he let the VCR run without stopping or commenting. He increased the volume on the projection television unit and let Dick Vitale's voice—screaming short sentence fragments to be heard over the Cameron Crazies—reverberate through the room. On the screen, the camera showed a dejected and sullen Carolina team as it lined up for a Duke free throw: "This isn't Carolina basketball!!! . . . Put 'em on the bus!! . . . This is EMBARASS-ING!!"

The screen went dark and Doherty let Vitale's voice hang in the air for several seconds. Then, the lights snapped on and Doherty stood, looking each of the players in the eye before speaking.

"Let's go practice."

 After his African American Studies class let out on Wednesday, Forte wanted to get "tight" the day before the big game.

The uniqueness of the Duke–Carolina rivalry for the players lay only in part in the history that so captivated fans and media on both sides. Rarely did the Tar Heel players, except maybe Jason Capel (whose brother Jeff played at Duke and hit one of the most storied shots in the rivalry in 1995), have more than a general knowledge of the important events in the history of the rivalry.

All they knew was that most all of them got their haircut at the same place, the 40 Below Barber Shop, which stood almost exactly halfway between the two campuses on the south side of Durham. It wasn't unusual to have UNC's Brendan Haywood in one chair, Duke's Nate James in another, and several players from both teams on one of the couches waiting for their turn.

Getting criticized in the press or by their classmates was one thing, but getting razzed by barbers Teddy McKoy (a self-proclaimed huge Duke fan who had cut Jason and Jeff Capel's hair when all three lived in Fayetteville, NC) or Len Lilly (a UNC fan) was brutal. Earlier in the year, after Haywood had not scored against Georgia Tech, McKoy had labeled the Carolina center "Doughnut"—complete with Haywood's stats written on the mirror.

Forte slinked into the place the day before the Duke game wearing sunglasses, but the disguise was quickly undone by McKoy. "Don't come in here trying to hide!" McKoy went on to predict a 15-point Duke win, a boast to which Forte and Haywood, who flatly refused to get his hair cut by the Duke-partial barber, were unresponsive.

"It's best to just be quiet," said Forte, leaving 40 Below looking decidedly tight. "Those guys are brutal."

Walking into the Smith Center the day before the Duke game, several players ran into Bill Guthridge. It wasn't rare for the players and Guthridge to talk—many of the players would seek out their former coach for advice on any number of subjects—but Guthridge was cognizant of appearances and did not want to get in the way of the new staff. But when Coach "Gut" did run into any of the players, he often flashed his well-known sense of humor and dry wit.

Several years earlier, during Dean Smith's second-to-last year coaching, Michael Jordan arrived at the Smith Center at the beginning of the school year. With the secretaries and current players fawning all over him, Guthridge slowly sidled up to the world's most recognized athlete in the tunnel that led from the locker room to the court, shook his hand, and asked—with a straight face and in a sincere voice—"So, Michael, what have you been doing with yourself since leaving Carolina?"

His question to the players the day before the biggest game of the year was equally deadpan. When he bumped into Forte in the hallway outside the basketball office, he warmly shook the sophomore's hand.

"So, Joseph," said Guthridge, who always referred to Forte by his full first name, "Who do you guys play tomorrow, Georgia Tech?"

Forte laughed, but played along. "No, Coach. We've got Duke."

"Oh, Duke," said Guthridge. "I've heard they're pretty good. Better not look past them to Tech, I suppose."

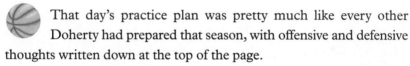

That day's practice plan was pretty much like every other Doherty had prepared that season, with offensive and defensive thoughts written down at the top of the page.

On offense, Doherty had written: "cut hard and 2nd TO." "Cut hard" referred to Doherty's observation that Duke overplayed on the perimeter and the way to defeat them was to cut hard to the wing and, if overplayed, to cut hard backdoor for a layup. The "2nd TO" was a reference to practice; if a player turned the ball over once, it went unpunished. A second turnover by the same player resulted in running. For the defensive emphasis, Doherty had a more simple, general message referring to disallowing Duke's penetration, open shots, and offensive rebounds: "contain, contest, and SCREEN OUT!"

The thought of the day was equally concise and to the point and referred to a vaunted Duke postvictory tradition: "Stop the Bonfire!" If the fire was to be extinguished in Cameron, Carolina would have to put together its best basketball game of the season.

And the world would be watching.

Duke at Duke

With a 9:00 P.M. start, the day of the Duke game was as long as any that the Carolina players or coaches could remember a game day being. No one wanted to wait all day to play the biggest game of the season.

Before heading off to pregame meal at 23, Doherty wanted to make a quick call and leave a message for Roy Williams on his voice mail. Doherty, who was always aware of the historic significance of every game and activity of his team, wanted to thank the man who, in more ways than one, had made this opportunity possible.

He dialed the number to Williams's office line and was surprised when, in the late afternoon, his old boss answered the phone. Doherty and Williams launched into a heartfelt and emotional conversation as the mentee thanked the mentor for all that he had done for him, personally and professionally.

"Matt," Williams said after Doherty had finished. "You're ready for this day. You've earned it. I know you'll do well tonight." The two men, both emotional and not scared to share their feelings, continued talking about the upcoming game. Williams reminded Doherty to be confident with the team, even if they got behind. Doherty thanked Williams one last time and hung up the phone, staring at the receiver.

He couldn't believe how lucky he was to be the coach at North Carolina, but more so, to have people in his life like Roy Williams.

When official Mike Wood tossed the ball up at exactly 9:08 P.M. to begin Duke at Duke 2001, Matt Doherty was seated calmly on the bench with his jacket on, his players to his right, his coaches to his left, and his dad, Walter—Doherty's parents were spending the month in Chapel Hill—and brother, John, directly behind him. His pregame speech had been quick and to the point, a repeat of the key points he and the coaches had focused on all week: contain Williams, take care of the ball, don't let a Duke run frustrate us.

Less than 30 seconds into the game, it appeared that all of Doherty's worst fears would come true. Duke won the tip and Williams, coming off an on-the-ball screen, hit a three-pointer from a step and a half behind the line. On its first possession, Carolina turned the ball over when Nate James stole Jason Capel's inbounds pass, starting a fast-break to the other end. Mike Dunleavy hit Carlos Boozer, who was fouled by Haywood.

Three possessions. Three of Doherty's worst fears realized.

The jacket came off immediately, and Doherty was up, already arguing the call by Wood. Doherty would not admit it publicly or privately, but he was determined not to be shown up by Krzyzewski, who had grown into a masterful manipulator of officials. When Krzyzewski was new to the league in the early 1980s, it was Smith who was perceived as the institution and successfully worked officials to his advantage. By 2000, it was Krzyzewski, the new legend, getting the calls. Although the two were cordial and respectful, both were hypercompetitive. No one would realize that quicker than the three officials who were working the game: Wood, John Clougherty, and Bob Donato.

Coming into the game, the Blue Devils had crushed ACC opponents at home by an *average* of 36 points—and two of the victims, Virginia and Wake Forest, were nationally ranked at the time. Many of those games were over before the first media time-out and were caused by the visiting team quickly getting intimidated. Doherty knew this, and continuously urged his team to attack and not be tentative with their drives or passes.

This strategy created an early tempo that appeared to favor Duke. After a brief Carolina lead at 5–4, Duke went on a 5–0 run, punctuated by a Williams-to-James alley-oop dunk. Capel quieted the Crazies momentarily with a spinning 15-foot jumper from the free throw line. On the bench, Doherty clapped twice—he knew Capel's scoring would be crucial if Carolina was to keep up.

But Williams answered with another three-pointer from the top of the key. The sequence was one that had demoralized other teams; a made two-pointer followed by a Duke three meant that even if a team played well and shot two-point field goals at an unheard-of rate of 61 percent from the field, it would still get beaten by the Blue Devils if they scored at their usual rate from behind the line (41 percent and almost 11 three-point field goals per game).

Just before the first media time-out, the pace looked to be getting to the Tar Heels, who were plodding through a set play, down 15–9. But Curry found Forte on a back-door cut (James was overplaying). Dunleavy and Lang swapped hoops and Carolina trailed by four, 17–13 with 14:39 on the clock. In the game's first five-plus minutes, Carolina had committed every mistake Doherty could imagine: stupid turnovers, silly fouls, bad three-point shots, and even a lane violation. Still, the Tar Heels had taken Duke's opening punch and were still standing.

Now, they would deliver one of their own.

Capel buried a three-pointer—after Adam Boone successfully negotiated Duke's press—and Carolina trailed by one, 17–16. As Capel backpedaled back down the court he glanced behind the Duke bench, where his brother Jeff sat. The elder Capel had been a three-year Duke starter in the mid-1990s, with varying success. It was the worst of times for the Duke program; Krzyzewski was sidelined with exhaustion and various physical ailments during the 1994–95 season, causing him to leave the team after 12 games. When Krzyzewski returned the next year, the program was not near what it was in the early 1990s, when the Blue Devils had won back-to-back NCAA titles. Capel was seen as a star player who could help Duke reclaim its rightful place among the elite teams. His career hit a peak when, on February 2, 1995, he hit a running jumper from 35 feet at the buzzer to tie Carolina and send the game to overtime. (Duke would go on to lose.) But when his play slumped as a junior and senior, he was periodically booed in several games at home. Jason, then in high school, never forgot hearing the Crazies boo his brother, and he wanted nothing more than to beat Jeff's former team.

Capel's three was followed by another from Max Owens, and Carolina had a two-point lead. As the lead grew, Doherty decided to implement his game plan and go into a 2-zone. It was a defense he had used extensively early in the season, but with the addition of Curry and Peppers and the development of Forte, Capel, and Haywood as solid-to-great man-to-man defenders, he had gone to it less. Doherty felt the zone would be effective, even though common thought might be that a zone was the worst defense to be in against a three-point shooting team like the Blue Devils. But Doherty and his staff had worked hard in the last few days of practice on a few important wrinkles to the zone: namely, to abandon the usual contain principles and instead fly out at shooters and make Duke pass the ball inside. It was a risky proposition: Duke was a great penetrating team, and Boozer and Battier had a quickness advantage inside against Haywood and Lang. But Doherty felt that relying on Haywood and Lang to be effective moving their feet (and not fouling) inside was a better option than letting Duke penetrate and pitch versus man-to-man all night.

The result was exactly what he had hoped. Upon seeing the zone set up, Williams and the other Duke perimeter players pulled up, looking to expose the zone's gaps with passes instead of dribble drives. They would still get shots from behind the arc, but almost always with a hand in their face—sometimes two. The result was a nearly four-minute drought by Duke, finally scoring again when Williams hit a three (after UNC went back to man-to-man) at the 10:42 mark.

Carolina, however, couldn't capitalize on the drought, as Curry missed a layup and was called for an offensive foul on successive possessions. With Carolina clinging to a 1-point lead, Chris Duhon stripped Boone and went the length of the floor for what would be the go-ahead basket—except the 6'1" guard couldn't decide whether to lay it in or dunk the wide-open attempt. The indecision caused him to miss the shot, and Carolina's good fortune was intact.

Duhon's miss seemed to energize Carolina, particularly Forte. With the overwhelming emotion of the game finally settling down, the Tar Heels made a realization: they could play with Duke. In the game's opening moments neither team had backed down. That was expected from Duke, but the toughness factor was still an unknown for Carolina. Doherty and his players had announced to the 9,314 in attendance and the millions nationwide (the game would earn the highest-ever rating among Carolina–Duke games on Raycom/Jefferson Pilot and would be the highest-rated regular-season game on ESPN2 for the year) that they were not the same as last year's team. They were not going away. Forte led a calm, collected offensive dissection of Duke that included a 15-foot floater and another back-door cut for a layup. Over the course of five minutes, Carolina increased its lead from 1 point to 13 with 4:46 remaining in the half. At one point, during a time-out, Doherty coached Boone: "Don't mess around with Williams and try to go side-to-side. Blow by him. If he cuts you off, pull it back out." Later, on defense, Boone even slapped the floor in a mock gesture at Duke's defensive trademark. On that same possession, Boone poked the ball away from Williams and Forte collected it and sped down-court for a breakaway dunk. When Krzyzewski was forced to call a time-out, the UNC bench celebrated like the game was over, causing Doherty to have to calm the team down in the huddle. Truth was, he was as excited as any of the players.

Duke recovered to hold Carolina to just three more points the rest of the half, cutting the UNC lead to seven points, 41–34, at the half.

It had been a remarkable 20 minutes of basketball. Forte had set a career high with 11 rebounds *in the first half*. Capel had scored 11 points. Haywood had held Boozer to one point; Lang allowed Battier to score just two. Most amazing (and most telling): Duke was just 4-of-12 from the free throw line.

The Carolina locker room was businesslike at the half as Doherty allowed the team time to rest before he went over some technical points of how he wanted to continue to guard Duke. Because of Duke's offense—which relied on quick ball movement and set its perimeter players up in a lot of one-on-one situations—Doherty knew that he needed to emphasize fundamentals more than he had to against other teams. "Play hard," he said as his last piece of instruction before bringing the players into a circle. "And don't back down from them."

Doherty decided to start the second half in the 2-zone—a move he would later regret. "It took some of our aggressiveness away." After two quick Carolina baskets, Battier responded with a three-pointer. Doherty responded by switching back to man-to-man, but Battier hit another one from 25 feet. Suddenly, the lead was down to five points, and the Crazies—whom Carolina had quieted as much as possible—came back to life.

Over the next two-minute stretch the "Duke Factor" took over. Carolina kept scoring two-pointers on a dunk by Capel and a short jumper by Curry, but Duke hit threes by Williams and James to cut the UNC lead to one point, 49–48. Following a media time-out, Williams went around Morrison easily and hit a 12-footer to give Duke its first lead, 50–49, since the 14:17 mark of the first half. But good fortune again smiled on Carolina, as Haywood hit a banked-in jump-hook from straight on in the lane. On the next Duke possession, Boozer attempted a 14-footer in the lane that missed—it was Boozer's first field goal attempt of the game.

Neither team would lead by more than two points over the next five minutes as each possession became a war.

Boozer finally scored from the field on a dunk at the 12:56 mark. Haywood answered with a dunk of his own. Battier followed with a three for a 55–53 Duke lead.

Neither team would lead by more than six points for the remainder of the game.

The score was tied at 57–57 when, after a time-out at the 9:54 mark, Krzyzewski gave Dunleavy a break and made a defensive switch, putting James (who was guarding Forte) on Capel, leaving Williams on Forte and Duhon on Curry. Not one to score in bunches, Curry nonetheless sensed an opportunity and scored three consecutive layups. With just under nine minutes remaining, Carolina suddenly appeared to be the fresher team.

But just when Carolina thought it had some breathing room, Haywood picked up his fourth foul at the 7:22 mark when he tried to block Boozer's layup attempt. Doherty quickly huddled with Bob MacKinnon. He had no choice; Haywood—who had been so instrumental down the stretch in earlier wins over NC State and Wake Forest—had to come out. He would stay out less than two minutes.

By the time he came back, UNC led by three points, 67–64. Duke immediately worked the ball inside to Boozer, who made a quick baseline move and appeared to have a step on Haywood. But Boozer's shot hit the underside of the backboard. Haywood collected the loose ball and, immediately trapped, called a time-out. A disaster—one that could have had game-altering conclusions—was averted.

A Forte three—on a play Doherty had called in the time-out—pushed the lead back to six at the 4:30 mark. "This is like Ali–Frazier," Tar Heel Radio Network analyst Mick Mixon yelled on air over the din. Every shot was contested; every loose ball caused a scrum; every whistle drew the ire of one coach or the other. Through it all, Duke continued to struggle from the free throw line.

Finally, with just over four minutes remaining, Battier hit two to cut the lead to two points, 70–68. A terrible pass by Curry led to a Williams three, and Duke had the lead back, 71–70. Another moment, another challenge. This time, it was Haywood battling on the offensive boards and getting fouled by Battier. Haywood went to the line—it was just Carolina's seventh and eighth free throw attempts of the night—and, despite shooting less then 50 percent from the line, buried both to give the Tar Heels a 72–71 lead with 3:34 on the clock.

During the media time-out, the crowd was as loud as it had been all night, and loud in Cameron can be disorienting and intimidating. Doherty—who had instructed the managers to set up collapsible stools away from the bench during time-outs, something UNC had never done—would have to yell to be heard by his players, who huddled in close.

Before he began his instructions, he made a little joke, one that he'd regret but was made only for his players' ears in an attempt to ease the tension. "Duke still has the ugliest cheerleaders in the ACC!" Doherty said. The players who could hear him smiled, but it was quickly back to business. Doherty reminded the players of the time-out situation, told them to play zone for the next possession, and ran down the offensive plays he wanted to run down the stretch.

The next minute and a half was all Carolina, as Haywood blocked a Boozer layup attempt, Peppers scored, and Dunleavy missed the front end of a one-and-one and a three-pointer. After Forte made two free throws with exactly 2:00 on the clock, Carolina was up 76–71. After another missed three by Dunleavy, Curry began walking the ball up the right sideline as the clock hit 1:30. Battier, knowing Curry was a poor foul shooter, rushed out to commit the foul. As he did, his left knee hit Curry high on his thigh. The rugged QB then limped in front of the Carolina bench and bent down for several seconds. Doherty, sensing an opportunity, turned and looked at his bench. The rule is clear: if the player fouled is injured and leaves the floor, the coach has discretion on a replacement. Just as Doherty called out for Max Owens (an 80 percent free throw shooter), Curry sat down on the court.

As Marc Davis kneeled over Curry, Krzyzewski was understandably angered. "That's bullshit!!" he yelled from his bench toward official John Clougherty. Assistant Coach Chris Collins took it a step further, becoming visibly irate to the point that Clougherty—who appeared unwilling to take profane criticism from another coach, particularly an assistant—

told Collins to keep quiet. Doherty put Owens in, and the senior calmly hit both free throws to put Carolina up 78–71 with 1:28 remaining.

Williams, who had single-handedly kept Duke close with 26 points to that point, then hit the most important Blue Devil basket of the game—a deep three-pointer. Forte took the inbounds pass and calmly dribbled the ball up-court as James, Duke's best perimeter defender, came out to matchup. It was exactly the situation Forte wanted: "I didn't want to have to score on a lesser player," he'd say later. Forte went right, into the lane, and hit a surprisingly open 12-footer to put Carolina up 80–74 with 1:00 remaining.

It was exactly this situation—down and seemingly out with less than one minute remaining—that Duke had faced against Maryland a week earlier. The Blue Devils had won that game, erasing a 10-point Terps' lead in the process. Many of Carolina's players had been watching that game and knew just how explosive Krzyzewski's team was. As if on cue, Dunleavy—recognizing that Capel was hobbling from a cramp—blew past Owens and dunked, drawing a foul on Capel. The ensuing free throw cut the UNC lead to three points—one possession—at 80–77. Fifty-one seconds remained.

Forte immediately grabbed the ball and, spying Lang long, fired a 75-foot pass that Battier got a hand on, batting it to Peppers at mid-court. Peppers began maniacally dribbling in toward the goal as Doherty and the coaching staff screamed to pull it out and work the clock. As he got closer, Lang attempted to clear Williams out of the lane to give Peppers room. Clougherty, one of the most experienced officials in the game, spotted it and whistled a foul. All Doherty could do was shake his head.

Making matters worse, the foul sent Williams to the free throw line. He could hit just 1-of-2, and Carolina led by two, 80–78. Forte caught the inbounds pass and brought the ball across half court. He was immediately double-teamed but found Peppers in the corner. Before Battier could get out to foul him, Peppers found Owens wide-open underneath and fired a high pass to him. Owens caught it and rose to lay the ball in, but Williams sprinted in, from out of nowhere, and blocked the shot.

Duke recovered the ball and came up-floor with a chance to take the lead. Williams came off an on-ball screen a few steps behind the top of the key and got a pretty good look. But the three-point attempt bounced off the front rim and skipped out. Dunleavy had to come over Capel's back to try to grab the rebound and was called for the foul.

No one wanted to see Jason Capel at the line any less than his brother, Jeff. Wearing an Old Dominion hat and T-shirt, Jeff held his head in his hands and tried to cover his face. He couldn't watch. He wanted Duke to win, but for his brother to do well. Both could not happen, as Jason held Carolina's fate largely in his hands. He made both ends of the one-and-one—giving Carolina an 82–78 lead with 0:25 on the clock—as Jeff, in a no-win situation, clapped twice and immediately yelled for Duke to push the ball up-court quickly.

The Blue Devils did just that, with Dunleavy finding Williams inside for a layup. Haywood goaltended the shot and Duke had scored in just five seconds. Taking the ball out, Capel wanted to find Forte, which he did, in the corner. Duke could not foul immediately, and Carolina effectively played keep-away until Capel was fouled with just 9.3 seconds remaining. Jeff had to endure once more, but this outcome was more what he might have scripted as his brother missed one and made one.

Carolina led by three, 83–80, with 9.3 on the clock. Duke needed a three to tie.

It took them just over six seconds to get it. With Carolina in a 2-zone, Williams let the ball roll in to almost half court. In one motion, he picked it up and threw a bullet into the opposite corner to James. Haywood, as he did late in the game against NC State, closed quickly as James rose to shoot, causing James to have to kick it to Dunleavy on the right wing. The sophomore rose up and, with Peppers hanging all over him, hit the biggest shot of his life to tie the score at 83–83.

3.9 seconds remained.

Doherty calmly called a 30-second time-out and set up a play that would get Forte the ball on the sideline, hopefully with a full head of steam heading down-court. But Forte caught the ball much closer to the end line than Doherty wanted—even with the free throw line—and alertly threw it deep to Haywood near the three-point line. "I figured he had a better shot at it from there than I did from 60 feet," he'd say later.

But Haywood never got the chance to take what would have been the first three-pointer of his career. Instead, Battier, going full-speed, dove for the ball and made significant contact with Haywood. The whistle blew. Mike Wood made the call: foul on Battier with 1.2 seconds remaining. It was Battier's fifth. The Carolina players on the bench jumped and cheered; the coaches remained stoic and calm; the Crazies began chanting, "Who's your daddy, Battier?!"

For the second consecutive game, Haywood would decide the outcome at the free throw line. "We only need one," Forte said in his ear as he stepped to the line. "I'm hitting both," Haywood answered. The roar was deafening as Haywood took a short stroll while the officials attempted to get players situated along the lane. Every player on the Carolina sideline held hands. Everyone else held their breath. Haywood received the ball from Mike Wood, bounced it once . . . twice . . . three times . . . rose up and without hesitation shot it.

Straight in.

The bench players celebrated wildly, grabbing each others' jerseys and raising their arms. The coaches did not move; Doherty remained crouched along the sideline, an expression completely void of emotion on his face. Before Haywood's next attempt, he slid over to the sideline. "Do you want me to miss the second?" Haywood asked as the crowd roared its disapproval. It would not be a bad strategy, but Doherty wanted none of it. "No, just make it!" answered Doherty.

He did. Carolina led 85–83 with 1.2 seconds remaining.

Duke called a time-out to set up a last-second play, but the miracles had run out. Duhon's half-court heave bounced high off the back rim ("To be honest, when it left his hand, I thought it was in. I thought we had won the game," said Krzyzewski later) and Carolina had won, 85–83. Considering the magnitude of the victory, the players were surprisingly subdued, raising their arms and embracing each other, but not dancing on the scorer's table or taunting the fans. The entire team, including Doherty and his coaches, moved quickly to shake hands before heading straight to the locker room. The players jogged, some pumping their fist, but none celebrating—publicly.

When the team was in the back hallway leading to the locker room, the jubilation broke out like water bursting through a dam. Everywhere, players began chest-bumping and jumping up and down. Forte hugged Boone, who hugged Haywood, and so on. The coaches did not have to show the players how to celebrate this time, as they had back in November following the win over Tulsa in the second game of the year. It was an instantaneous explosion of joy, culminating in a rousing, ear-splitting chant: "Who's House!? Heel's House!!!" Soon, a mosh pit ensued as players and coaches alike chest-bumped and shouted after achieving a win no one outside of themselves had believed possible. North Carolina had beaten Duke at Duke.

With Doherty's Midnight Rule in effect and a matchup with Georgia Tech less than 48 hours away, they would have exactly 47 minutes to enjoy it.

29

Almost Unfair

The North Carolina basketball program was different after it defeated Duke. The players were more confident, the fans more boastful, and the media more respectful. Outside of the players and coaches themselves, no one expected the Tar Heels to walk out of Cameron Indoor Stadium with a win.

Duke was not only the best team Carolina had played—and beaten—all season, it also launched a string of games Doherty would refer to as "almost unfair." After the emotionally draining win at Duke, Carolina had roughly 40 hours before it would take the Smith Center court against Georgia Tech, a team that had led the Tar Heels by 12 points at the half in the ACC opener. After that Saturday game, Carolina would play at Wake Forest on Tuesday and at home against Maryland on Saturday. Even the most optimistic Carolina fan had to be happy with two wins in those three games, given the impossible-to-avoid let-down that had to follow the Duke win.

Doherty's imposed Midnight Rule meant that the team would be told to forget the Duke game at the stroke of midnight—or approximately the same time as the bus hit the halfway point between the Duke and North Carolina campuses, eight miles apart. "We're going to call you around 1:30," Doherty told the players as the bus pulled into the back lot of the Smith Center. "Don't go out. We need our rest. Start thinking about Georgia Tech on Saturday."

During the short ride home, the players were euphoric, but not overly boisterous as they had been in the back hallway outside the visitor's locker room. With the cell phone rule momentarily ignored, the players called friends and girlfriends who were partying on Franklin Street. Most wanted to go out when they got home and enjoy the revelry downtown, where television news crews were gathering as UNC students took to the streets. Despite the temptations, all of the players were in their rooms when called at 1:30 by one of the four assistants.

All of the coaches left the Smith Center around 2:00 in the morning except Doherty, who remained in his office for another half-hour to familiarize himself with the Georgia Tech scouting report, which had been prepared by Bob MacKinnon. When he finally left his office, the building was deserted.

When Doherty reached the parking lot, he was surprised to find several dozen UNC students applauding him as he made his way to his car. Doherty politely signed autographs and posed for pictures and even sat on the curb to talk with the last group, inquiring about their majors and schoolwork. About 3:45 Doherty finally climbed into his car and made his way home.

He'd be back in the office less than five hours later.

Already scheduled for the next morning was a meeting between Doherty and the Executive Committee of the Educational Foundation, the athletic fund-raising club whose donations had built the

Smith Center and virtually every athletic building on campus. Doherty, UNC chancellor James Moeser, and Athletic Director Dick Baddour strode into the paneled conference room in the office suite of the Educational Foundation—located adjacent to the Smith Center—at 8:30 A.M. that morning.

Only one item was on the agenda: a new practice facility for men's basketball.

Doherty greeted everyone—"This is a great time to be able to ask for some things, huh?" he said with a smile—and stood at the front of the room, presenting the plans for the facility. The idea for it had begun with Dean Smith, and talks had continued while Bill Guthridge was in charge, but it was Doherty who had pushed the matter forward.

His reasoning to the committee was simple: practicing and working out in the Smith Center was not always private, nor was it always in the best interests of the university. Like Smith and Guthridge before him, Doherty had final say on all nonbasketball events that might be scheduled in the building. With a practice facility, he wouldn't have to say no to any revenue-producing concerts or other events. Another reason was the summertime; Carolina hosted basketball camps all during the month of June, and alumni (Hubert Davis and Eric Montross) also held camps in the Smith Center. With a private practice facility, the current players and the many alumni who come back to Chapel Hill to train would have a quiet, peaceful gym in which to work out.

Doherty also had a personal reason for wanting the new facility. "I like to have a walk-through just before the game," he explained. "[I like to have] the players meet an hour and a half before the game for about 20 minutes and have a walk-through. That way, we can have our dress rehearsal then. We did that at Notre Dame, and I thought that was helpful."

Another obvious, if unspoken, reason: the addition of a new practice facility and other improvements would also serve as an important step in Doherty truly taking the reigns of the program and making it his. A new space would be a physical and daily reminder to the players that the program was now being run by a different man, with different ideas and passions and practices, albeit with the same goals.

Doherty continued his presentation. The practice facility, if approved, would be located in what was now the Bowles Room—ironically, the same room that had been the site of Smith's retirement announcement and the press conferences announcing the hiring of both Guthridge and Doherty. In the late 1980s, the room was originally intended to be a practice basketball court until, as the legend goes, Smith walked in during construction and asked what the room was going to be. When he was told it was his new practice court, he reportedly said that no, his team would be practicing in the arena in which they played. Later, Skipper Bowles—a prominent alumnus—asked Smith if the room could become a large meeting room for the Educational Foundation.

The plans that would change the room back into its originally intended purpose also included renovating the basketball locker rooms and weight room. While nothing was in disrepair, the spaces could stand modernizing and, if done well, could be an important recruiting tool. It was noted more than once that Duke had recently completed a very attractive and impressive basketball tower, which contained brand-new offices, locker rooms, meeting rooms, and a stunning Hall of Fame adjacent to Cameron Indoor Stadium.

After Doherty's presentation Baddour discussed the cost of the new facility: $8 million. A little over $1 million would be provided by the state of North Carolina, while the remainder would be paid for by the Educational Foundation. Sitting at the head of the table, Maurice Koury—a Burlington, NC, businessman—paused and looked around the room. The most influential Ram's Club member, it was Koury's name that was on the building—a building that also housed the natatorium in addition to the Educational Foundation offices and the Bowles Room—that would be renovated. It went without saying that it would take a fair amount of donations from him and other foundation members to have the blueprints become a reality. Koury, like every other UNC alumnus and fan, was euphoric over the events of the last evening. Beating Duke at Duke could not have come at a better time, Doherty knew, even though the meeting had been scheduled for quite some time.

After a long pause, Koury spoke: "Give him what he wants."

And just like that, Doherty had his building.

The rest of the day quickly turned into a whirlwind as Doherty lived through exactly the kind of attention and constant distractions that had worn out Smith and Guthridge. Congratulatory calls came from all over the country—most important from Williams (who had watched the entire game with his wife, Wanda, and a Carolina friend) in Lawrence. "I've never been as nervous in my life watching any other game as I was watching the Duke game at Duke," said Williams later. Needless to say, Williams had reveled in watching his former assistant beat the hated Blue Devils.

Other calls came from friends and family in New York and from Smith in his downstairs office. As best he could, Doherty greeted each congratulations warmly, but in the back of his mind he knew all the good feelings and positive momentum would disappear in an instant with a loss to Tech the next day.

For the coaches, the quick turnaround only meant less time to do more work. The film breakdown took most of the morning, and planning practice took the bulk of the early afternoon. The players began to straggle in about an hour before practice, looking haggard and tired. "It's hard not to feel good today," said Boone. "But I admit I'm pretty tired."

Boone had played only 15 minutes.

The win put the Tar Heels in first place in the ACC with an undefeated 8–0 record, marking the first time in the conference's history that a first-year coach had guided his team to an undefeated record in his first go-round through the league. It was the first time the Tar Heels were undefeated in league play through the first swing since 1986–87, when UNC won all 14 regular-season ACC contests. The Heels' win streak had reached 15 games—trailing only No. 1 Stanford as the longest such streak in the nation in 2000–2001.

The rest of the ACC had fallen behind the Big Two of Carolina and Duke. The Blue Devils, at 7–1, were still very much in the hunt, but

Maryland's collapse since losing to Duke at home had stretched the league into two contenders, five spoilers, and two also-rans. The Terps, a consensus preseason Top 10 team, were a disappointing 5–3 but still led the "spoilers" category. Virginia, Wake Forest, and surprising Georgia Tech were all 4–4. The wolves were barking at the door for NC State's Herb Sendek, who, despite the backing of his AD Lee Fowler, was on the hot seat after guiding his team to a 2–6 ACC mark. Clemson and Florida State were both 1–7 and appeared incapable of beating anyone in the top tier.

Nationally, Carolina had put itself into position to move up from its current No. 4 ranking. Duke (previously at No. 2) and Michigan State (No. 3) had lost earlier in the week. No. 1 Stanford had a home game Saturday with UCLA, a contest it figured to win despite the Bruins' improvement in recent weeks. A win over Tech almost assured Carolina of a No. 2 ranking, and if UCLA pulled an upset in Palo Alto . . .

No. 1 was the last thing on the Tar Heels' minds as they walked through Georgia Tech's offenses and defenses and did some light shooting on Friday afternoon. Practice was upbeat, and Doherty kept it short. "Tech's a pressing team," he reminded the team just before they broke at the end of practice, "and we've done pretty well against pressing teams lately. But we can't come out flat. Championship teams win games like the one we're playing in tomorrow."

30

We're Number One

Matt Doherty's fear of a post-Duke letdown lasted four minutes. Looking to take advantage of the situation, Georgia Tech began the game with great energy and enthusiasm and extended to an 11–3 lead with 15:49 remaining in the first half. At the first media time-out, UNC trailed 11–7. In the huddle, Doherty stressed defense: "We need to pick up our energy down here [pointing to UNC's defensive end of the court]. They're setting hard screens, but we're letting them be effective. Fight harder to get around them. Pressure the ball more. And get in the passing lanes on the perimeter."

It looked like a long afternoon was in the making.

But Carolina responded to Doherty's plea for more intensity with its most impressive defensive performance of the season. With Doherty motioning to the student section for more noise (and getting it), the Tar Heels dug in. With 14:06 remaining in the first half, Tech point guard Tony Akins drove right around Adam Boone and missed a wide-open layup, but Alvin Jones was there for the follow-up dunk to push the Jackets' lead to 13–7.

It was the last basket Tech would get for over seven minutes.

North Carolina scored 23 consecutive points on dunks and tip-ins by Peppers, runners and free throws by Forte, several vehemently argued calls by Doherty, and about every other conceivable way Carolina could score. When the dust cleared and the crowd finally took another breath, the Tar Heels led by 17 points, 30–13. Except for some late-game three-pointers by Tech that cut the lead to nine points—and once to eight—the Tar Heels would keep the lead at double digits through-out and go on to win by 13 points.

In addition to getting the win, several other developments pleased Doherty, none more than the play of Boone. Pressed into service by the tired legs of several perimeter players, Boone played 28 minutes, the most since Ronald Curry had replaced him in the starting lineup. He had responded by handling the pressure well and even hitting a spinning 15-footer with 3:33 left and Tech mounting its last chal-lenge. He would go on to score a career-high 10 points and grab five rebounds.

During the first media time-out of the second half of the Georgia Tech game, an announcement was made over the Smith Center PA sys-tem: Stanford, the top-ranked team in the nation, had lost to UCLA. The Carolina student section recognized the significance immediately and began chanting, "We're Number One!" Several team managers at the end of the bench implored them to stop, but the players heard it and looked at the scoreboard, where the outcome was posted. "Don't look at the scoreboard!" Doherty yelled. "We can't worry about that now!" At most every break the rest of the game, the cheer would start again. As Capel dribbled out the clock for the 82–69 victory, the chant spread to the entire building.

Two days later, the coaches and the Associated Press confirmed what the Tar Heel faithful had predicted; North Carolina was the No. 1 team in the nation.

The graffiti first started after the win over Duke, but after Carolina beat Georgia Tech and reached No. 1, it began popping up everywhere around campus: on the sides of academic buildings and fraternity houses and cars. "Doherty is God," it read.

While Matt Doherty was most certainly not a deity, what he had accomplished in his first seven months as Carolina's head coach was astounding. It had begun slowly, as he and his brand-new staff tried to figure out what they had while they gained the trust of the players. It had taken time, and the growing pains had resulted in tough losses to Michigan State and Kentucky. The latter was much harder to take—due to it being a home game and given the poor play of the Tar Heels—but something important had begun: the players had begun to trust and follow their head coach.

Doherty didn't just want to win; he *needed* to win. And if the players didn't quickly develop their own competitive instincts, he would find a way to motivate them to. Doherty did (and does) raise his voice; he also used profanity or made a joke at the most tense time of a game. No matter what, he would not change his approach to coaching the team, using language as a tool, whether it was socially to loosen his guys up (such as telling a joke at the most stressful time of a big game) or to increase the volume and edginess to push them through a grueling preseason workout, a tough practice, or a crucial time in a close game. "These players needed a leader, and they've eagerly jumped into the foxhole with Matt," said Doug Wojcik.

The team did need a leader, but it couldn't be overlooked how much the players had been through the previous season and the willingness with which they accepted leadership as part of doing everything they could to avoid last year's near-disaster. "This year we're more together because of what we went through last year," said Will Johnson.

"It was tough, and we lost a lot of games. It forced us to come together during the off-season and into the year. We didn't want that year to happen again."

No one had been through more the previous year than Will Johnson. Exactly one week had gone by in his college life and he had already been called to Head Coach Bill Guthridge's office. What made it even odder was that his parents were there. They had something to tell him.

Will's brother, Daniel, a graduate of UNC and an ensign in the Navy, had been in an accident on board his ship, the *USS Blue Ridge*. Not much was known on that day, August 22, 1999, other than it was bad. Daniel was alive, but seriously injured.

The details would trickle in slowly, too slowly, as Will tried, over the course of the next few days, to concentrate on the normal adjustments to life in college. Daniel was indeed alive and would soon be transferred from Korea to Walter Reed Hospital in Washington, D.C. The accident had involved another sailor, named Steve, who was also injured.

The story, when all the specifics were known, would fill Will with both pride and terror.

Daniel was on the deck of the *USS Blue Ridge* during a routine towing procedure as the ship left Pusan harbor. The tugboat began pulling out too fast, and before anyone knew it, the leg of Seaman Steven Wright became tangled in a loop of what's called the messenger line. With great force, the line pulled Wright off his feet and across the deck, until his lower leg lodged in the "chock," an oval opening about a foot long and eight inches wide through which ropes pass. If left alone, Wright's body would rip apart in the chock.

Daniel, whose duty as safety observer at the aft mooring station put him in charge of Wright and seven other men overseeing the departure that morning, immediately ran to Wright and attempted to free him. The other seven men did not move. The rope would quickly sever Wright's foot from his leg, saving his life by freeing him from the chock.

But in trying to free Wright, Johnson's own legs were quickly wrapped by the violently jerking messenger line. Daniel Johnson would lose both of his legs below the knee as well as a finger.

But he was alive.

Will got to see him soon, in Washington, D.C., and was amazed at his brother's courage and outlook on the rest of his life. His own challenges of adjusting to college life and college basketball suddenly seemed small, in comparison.

The chances that Will would ever see significant playing time at North Carolina were slim—at least that's what most outside observers thought. He was a good player, many said, but not a UNC- or even ACC-caliber athlete. At 6'8" and 200 pounds, he lacked the size to play inside and the quickness to play on the perimeter. He hadn't even cost the basketball program a scholarship, they'd say, having come to UNC on a Morehead Scholarship, the most prestigious academic award given by the university.

Despite his low ranking in many national recruiting publications, Johnson was pursued by North Carolina, Indiana, Princeton, and Davidson during his junior and senior years in high school. Because he was an outstanding student (4.0 GPA at Hickory High School and president of the National Honor Society), he was seen as little risk and, maybe, some reward on the basketball floor. His recruitment by Guthridge was odd in that Guthridge was prohibited from talking to Will directly, as any contact would mean that Johnson would be counted against the basketball scholarship limit.

The recruitment process peaked for Will when, one morning during early August of his senior year in high school, he received a phone call from then–Indiana coach Bobby Knight. Knight chatted briefly with Johnson, telling him that, at that moment, he was sitting in the office of his good friend Tony LaRussa, manager of the St. Louis Cardinals. In an earlier conversation, Johnson had told Knight he was a Cardinals fan, and, even more, a fan of Mark McGwire, who was chasing (and would eventually surpass later that summer) Roger Maris's single-season home run record. LaRussa got on the phone to say hello to Johnson before passing the phone off to McGwire himself, who added some words of encouragement and wished the young basketball player well.

"I was stunned," said Johnson. "Later that day, he ended up getting thrown out of the game, so maybe it wasn't such a good omen."

Despite the McGwire phone call, Johnson chose UNC after he won the Morehead Scholarship—which he was awarded following a series of three grueling interviews over the course of three months. During his freshman season at Carolina, Will played only sparingly, but, due to injuries to Kris Lang, more than many would have predicted. More important, Johnson learned what he needed to do to compete at the highest level, which was get stronger and improve his perimeter skills.

The summer between his freshman and sophomore season Johnson made giant strides toward those two goals. He gained 15 pounds ("I still need about 15 more," he said) and became one of the best outside shooters on the team. "I just want to prove people wrong," said Johnson. "I know I can play at this level. But if it doesn't happen, that's OK. . . . I see my brother at many of our games, and it makes me put things in perspective."

Daniel Johnson was in the crowd in Winston-Salem, having made the short trip from Hickory to watch his younger brother's team play Wake Forest in what was the first game for the Tar Heels as the No. 1 team in the nation.

Matt Doherty took little solace in the top ranking and pushed his team as hard as he had all season in preparing for Wake Forest. The Deacons had not played well since Brendan Haywood beat them with a last-second layup in the Smith Center on January 6, losing 5-of-7 games and falling to No. 19 in the AP poll. But in Joel Coliseum—and with a brand-new target on their backs—any slight letdown would spell a quick loss for the Tar Heels. In the hopes of making his players understand this, Doherty had created a flyer with the NC logo in a bull's-eye. On the top of the page, he had written "Raise Your Level!"; on the bottom were the words "Raise Your Commitment!" The signs were plastered all over the locker room as a reminder of their new status.

In an attempt to further prepare the team, Doherty had made a cal-culated gamble in designing the travel schedule prior to the Wake game. With the game at 9:00 on Tuesday night—and Joel Coliseum an hour and a half from Chapel Hill—Doherty nonetheless decided to leave campus after practice Monday and stay the night a little over halfway in Greensboro. "We're tired," Doherty explained. "If we're away from cam-pus, maybe the guys can get some rest in the hotel the day of the game." In preparation for the game, he had talked little about the first meeting against Wake Forest, other than showing the players some film and dis-cussing offensive execution: Carolina had shot less than 40 percent from the field in the first Wake game.

In any road game, the start is much more important to the visitors than the home team—and the first few minutes against Wake went as well as Doherty could have hoped. Out of the gate, Forte scored an uncontested layup, and Capel hit a three off a set play. The Tar Heels wouldn't score over the next three minutes (committing three turnovers during the stretch), but active man-to-man defense did not allow Wake to jump out to more than an 8–5 lead. After Capel hit another three—on an assist from Curry—to tie the score at 8–8, neither team would lead by more than a basket until the 9:37 mark of the first half. That's when Curry—the player Odom had wanted left alone on the perimeter in the teams' first meeting—hit a three from the right wing when Broderick Hicks left him to put the Tar Heels up 23–18. Forte hit two free throws 35 seconds later to give UNC a seven-point lead.

It would be the largest advantage either team would hold until the final minute of the game.

Wake battled back to take a two-point lead on a jumper by Craig Dawson, but the seesaw half ended with Carolina in the lead, 38–37. In the locker room, Doherty was positive and energetic, pointing out that if Carolina had done a few things smarter—particularly taking care of the ball in the half-court—it would be in great shape. "Let's get a good shot every possession," he urged. "Don't rush things. When we've taken our time, we've scored." To his coaches, Doherty expressed concern that they'd taken too many three-pointers—almost half of their shot attempts were from behind the arc.

As close as the first half had been, it was even closer in the second. Wake began the half energized and attacking the offensive boards. Josh Shoemaker set the tone by outfighting both Capel and Lang and tipping in a Darius Songaila miss to give Wake a 39–38 lead. When Forte banged a three-point attempt off the back rim with 16:20 remaining, he had missed 10-of-15 shots on the night. Haywood finally got free—on a beautiful back-screen from Forte—and dunked with 16:50 remaining to cut the Wake lead to one, 46–45. On the sideline, Doherty pumped his fist and pumped up his players as they ran back on defense, trying to infuse his team with enough energy to overcome its fatigue. But Wake's defense again stiffened. When Forte banged another three-point attempt off the rim 30 seconds later it was his 10th miss in 15 shot attempts.

With Forte struggling in a close game, it appeared as if Carolina's luck might run out.

"We're fine," Doherty said in the huddle at the second half's first media time-out. "Don't rush it. We're going to win this game if we just make good decisions and play our game." The looks he got in return made him confident.

The lead changed four times over the course of the next nine minutes, and the Joel Coliseum crowd roared louder with each possession. Doherty continued to speak as calmly as he could and still be heard in the huddle. "Isn't this fun?" he asked during a time-out with 6:25 remaining and the Tar Heels down 65–62. "Won't it be more fun to quiet this crowd?"

Forty seconds later—and after a Lang layup—Capel hit two free throws, and Carolina had a 66–65 lead. "Get a stop!!" Doherty bellowed as he held his fist aloft, signaling Carolina's man-to-man. They did, as Haywood forced Howard to alter his short baseline jumper and Peppers rebounded the miss. Haywood then sprinted the length of the floor, took a Curry pass, and dunked to give Carolina a three-point lead. The Tar Heels extended the lead to seven on another bucket by Haywood and two free throws by Forte—all the while holding Wake without a point until Howard made two free throws with 2:49 remaining.

Two consecutive turnovers by Carolina allowed Dawson to pull the Deacs to within three with an 18-footer just right of the top of the key— ending a Wake Forest 0-for-10 drought from the field. Once more, UNC needed a late-game basket that would seal the win. Doherty called a 30-second time-out and called a play for Curry to fake coming off an on-ball screen and look for either Haywood posting up or Forte on the wing. But the timing was off, and Curry was able to get the ball to Forte with only four seconds remaining on the shot clock. He was 25 feet from the basket, with Howard—Wake's best perimeter defender—blanketed all over him.

Without hesitating, Forte dribbled hard to the right baseline. He was cut off by Vidauretta, and it looked like Wake would force a bad shot and get the ball back with a chance to cut the UNC lead to one or, per- haps, to tie. But just as soon as he was cut off, Forte rose up in the air. "His feet weren't even set," said Doherty later. The shot surprised Vidauretta and Howard so much that neither was able to get off the ground to try to block it. "I knew Howard had long arms, so I leaned back a little to get the shot off," explained Forte in a matter-of-fact tone after the game. The baseline fadeaway curled in the hoop with 1:13 remaining. Carolina led 74–69.

Dawson missed a rushed three on the other end, and free throws by Haywood, Forte, and Capel put the finishing touches on what Forte's jumper had already sealed: an 80–74 victory. The win streak, remark- ably, was at 17 games. "We feel that when the game gets into the last two minutes, we're going to win it," said Haywood.

Perhaps no other comment so crystallized the difference a year had made.

31

Getting to the Core

After elevating to the top spot in the polls, distractions had become the norm for Carolina, a fact Matt Doherty had grudgingly learned to accept. A welcome distraction came on the day after the Wake win: a recruiting trip to tiny Latta, South Carolina, to watch one of its top junior targets, Ray Felton, practice. Felton, a lightning-quick 6'1" guard, and his entire high school team had been in Chapel Hill for the Georgia Tech game, sitting behind the bench. After the game, the entire Latta team—"maybe the whole town," Doherty joked—had filed into Doherty's office for a light-hearted, 30-minute get-together. It had become a practice for Doherty to invite not only the recruit he was pursuing but that player's family and high school teammates to games; he had done it earlier in the season with a sought-after junior named Shavlik Randolph, an agile 6'10" forward from Raleigh whose college choices had already been whittled down to Duke and NC State (where Randolph's grandfather Ronnie Shavlik had been an All-American).

The slaps on the back and congratulations came fast and furious for every player, from Joe Forte to Jim Everett. Doherty, as would be expected, was being lauded state- and nationwide as a genius, a savior.

Nowhere was the adulation more apparent than at Doherty's live weekly radio show. When the show began in November, no more than a half-dozen fans comprised the show's live audience at Michael Jordan's 23 restaurant, watching Doherty and Woody Durham take calls. The week the Heels rose to No. 1, the place was packed with several hundred patrons, all clutching hats, T-shirts, and programs for Doherty to sign during breaks.

Doherty handled the attention extremely well. Callers to his show were treated with respect, and their questions were taken seriously— except when he was asked for tips on how the team might play an upcoming opponent. "If I tell you, I'd have to kill you," Doherty would joke. The crowd, adoring fans all, laughed heartily and often. It was a love-in—but Doherty knew it wasn't his jokes or personality that brought all the good feelings. It was the simple and incontrovertible fact that the team was winning games. "You can't let all this stuff get to your core," he said. Doherty was particularly good with children. One 11-year-old, Mike, called in and couldn't believe he was talking to the coach of North Carolina. "This is so cool," he said on the other end of the line. "It's really cool talking to you too, Mike," said Doherty, cementing another Carolina fan for life.

Later in the season, Doherty would notice that a group of student fans had attended every single show. "Do you have tickets to the game?" he asked at a commercial break. "No, we couldn't get any," replied one of the young women, wearing a "Doherty's Disciple" T-shirt. "Call my office tomorrow," said Doherty, scratching his number on a napkin. "There will be tickets waiting for you at will call."

Prior to practice that Thursday, the players had been asked to arrive early for one of the previously scheduled "signing days." Three of

Carolina's two dozen managers were designated "autograph managers" and worked with the staff in the basketball office to coordinate all autograph requests, of which there were several thousand each season. Spread out in the hallway outside the locker room were hundreds of basketballs, posters, T-shirts, and hats that had been sent in by fans. The players spread out and sat at one of the several tables and signed their names hundreds of times, until their hands literally cramped. When Doherty, who was signing the items right along with the players, noticed that some of the signatures were illegible, he admonished the players to take their time. "Guys, c'mon, I can't even tell what these names are," he said, a grin on his face. "Some kid out there will treasure what you sign forever. Let's sign them so they can read it."

Practices on Thursday and Friday before the rematch with Maryland were again very short. The Terps' game would be UNC's fourth in 10 days, and Doherty was extremely concerned about playing Maryland, even though the game was at home. He tried not to look ahead to the next week, when they wouldn't play again for eight days. To say he was looking forward to that break was an understatement. If they could get by the Terps, they'd have several days to rest and then several more to practice hard and get back to basics. Doherty had a list several pages long on a legal pad in his office with fundamental breakdowns he had observed over the course of the last two weeks. He was also looking forward to taking Sunday off—completely—his first such day off since Christmas day; a stretch of 47 days. His parents were still in town, and his sister Maureen had brought her kids down for the weekend. He didn't allow himself to think about how miserable he'd be if they lost Saturday, so he did what he always did: he threw himself into preparation, covering everything he could possibly think of, staying in the office past midnight on Thursday and Friday. His preparation was interrupted only on Friday, when he had to speak to print reporters, ESPN, and CBS (who would broadcast the game nationally the next day). Billy Packer was allowed to observe practice, a privilege almost no one, even Carolina's own radio announcers, was allowed.

To Packer, Doherty said the same things he had to anyone who would listen that week: "I'm very concerned about this game. Maryland may not be playing all that well, but they have as good a talent as anyone in the country. We can't afford to let up *at all*."

Maryland was a wounded team when it entered the Smith Center on February 10, 2001. It wasn't that they had suffered any physical injuries—in fact, none of the Terps had so much as a pulled muscle—but their psyche had yet to recover from the loss to Duke at home. Since that devastating defeat, Gary Williams' crew had lost at Georgia Tech and at Virginia and beaten only Clemson at home. Still, Maryland had won at Carolina in three of the last five meetings in the Smith Center. Terence Morris, Juan Dixon, and Lonny Baxter (all of whom had scored more than 20 points in the teams' previous matchup exactly one month earlier) were extremely talented and could break out of their slump at any time.

In addition to several newspaper articles that quoted Duke's Nate James as saying, "We still feel like the number one team in the country," tacked to the locker room bulletin board, Carolina received an extra boost of motivation just before game time. On his way into the arena several hours before the tip-off, CBS analyst Billy Packer passed one of the team managers, who casually asked Packer what he thought about the game. Packer, never one to withhold an opinion, spoke over his shoulder as he walked through the tunnel to the floor. "I'm taking Maryland by double digits." Within minutes, the comment had made its way back to the coaching staff. When Doherty heard it, he let out a sly smile.

When he repeated the comment moments before the Heels took the court, no one in the Carolina locker room was smiling.

Early on, Packer's prediction appeared on its way to becoming a reality. Doherty had decided not to start Kris Lang against Maryland, not because of anything strategic, but in the hopes of resting Lang's sore right ankle. Lang had first injured a tendon in the ankle against Duke 10 days earlier and with three games since, it had grown more tender. Last season, the injury would have been cause for great concern. But this season, the Tar Heels had Julius Peppers at the ready.

And ready he was. Peppers dominated inside, scoring six of Carolina's first 14 points, and adding an assist (he would go on to score a career-high 18). On television, Packer swooned; earlier in the season Packer had begun trumpeting the excellence of Peppers, both as an athlete and as an instinctive player. Peppers was both in the first few minutes against Maryland, but it wasn't enough to shake the Terps, who rode the strong play of Baxter and Drew Nicholas to take a 20–19 lead by the second media time-out.

Doherty sensed that an opportunity to put the game away early had slipped by, and he let the players know—in no uncertain terms—that they had come out flat and were not playing very hard. If Curry had not taken a charge from Steve Blake immediately prior to the time-out, the verbal undressing would likely have been worse. Doherty punctuated his displeasure by getting a technical foul from official Karl Hess—his second of the season—after Morrison was tied up by Dixon. Gary Williams had already received a technical foul earlier.

Doherty's technical did not fire up the Tar Heels, who quickly fell behind by eight points, 29–21, after Dixon hit a jump shot and a free throw to complete a three-point play. At the next time-out, Doherty was as calm and collected as he had been animated earlier. "We'll be all right, just take care of the ball and we'll get shots." Doherty subbed Curry, Capel, and Haywood back in toward the end of the half to get some more mature players on the court. The substitutions worked, as Carolina's defense stiffened. Maryland, which had been playing loose and free for the first fifteen minutes of the first half, suddenly tightened up. The Terps scored just two points over the last 3:56 before the break, while Jason Capel scored 11 straight points—nine on three consecutive threes—allowing Carolina to take a 43–42 halftime lead.

Earlier in the week, Barry Svrluga of the Raleigh *News and Observer* had written a very positive feature on Capel, with one disturbing (to Capel) phrase: role player. Capel had taken it as a slight to his abilities. (In fact, the term appeared nowhere in the article and only in the subheading.) "I'm not a role player," he said after the story came out. "I'm a player." It was exactly the type of piece that would have driven a wedge between players the year before; in fact, Capel and Forte had seemingly clashed at times the year before due to Forte's arrival as the team's designated star; a role Capel saw himself in. This year, however, the "slight" only caused the players to rally around one of their own.

At least for now.

Despite shooting nearly 60 percent from the field, Carolina led the Terps by only one point. "It's not hard to figure it out, guys," Doherty said to the team at halftime. "If we take care of the ball and box out, we'll win. Keep doing what we're doing, just pick up our intensity, and we'll get this one."

During warm-ups for the second half, Haywood, a player Doherty had encouraged to be more assertive as a leader in huddles and the locker room, walked over and sat down next to his coach. "Coach, we need to do something to get Joe off in the second half. Why don't we run '52' to get him a good look. Maybe it will get him going." Doherty, who encouraged and accepted input from the players during halftime and time-outs—sometimes beginning huddles by asking his players to "tell me what's going on out there"—had already had that exact plan in mind. Hearing Haywood suggest it struck him as a great sign.

"That's what this team is all about," he said later.

Doherty called the play Haywood had suggested, and Forte—who had made just 2-of-5 shots and scored only seven points in the first half—hit a double-pump runner in the lane. Then, as if Haywood was a prophet, Forte followed it up with a layup in traffic two possessions later, forcing Williams to call a time-out. From that point on, Carolina dominated Maryland on both ends of the court, putting together its best half of basketball all season. Capel, hoping to shed the "role player" label once and for all, scored 14 second-half points to go with the 13 he scored in the first half, giving him a career-high 27. Maryland, with shaky confidence coming in, imploded in the game's final 10 minutes.

Carolina went on to win by 14 points, 96–82, extending its win streak to 18 games and solidifying its spot atop the poles.

With the win and facing no games in eight days, Carolina was beginning to swagger. "We're number one in the country, man," said Capel after the game, sitting under the newspaper article in which Duke's Nate James begged to differ. "We're going to go out and prove to everyone we worked hard for the number one ranking, and you're going to have to take it."

Over the course of the next week, the swagger would turn into something much more deadly: complacency.

32

Bye, Bye Streak

Seven months into his tenure as head coach at North Carolina, Matt Doherty had learned a great deal about the job and how to handle being the most recognizable individual in the state as well as a nationally known figure. It had not been an innocent climb, but he had learned on the run how to manage the incredible workload generated by constant correspondence and demands on his time. The basketball requirements had been the easiest part of the job, and Doherty did not mind the public relations aspects as much as his two predecessors.

In his dealings with the media, Doherty had proven open and forthright, another change from Dean Smith and Bill Guthridge. Smith had a well-known reputation for dealing with the media as little as possible. Guthridge, while possessing a wonderful sense of humor and an active competitive streak, rarely displayed either in speaking with the press. Doherty's personality—emotional, honest, engaging, and trusting—had come through in personal conversations with writers and television commentators as well as during press conferences. "When I talk with the media, I like to have fun," said Doherty. "I like to get to know them, interact with them, be forthright. If I can't say something, I'll tell them. I think they respect that as opposed to dancing around the question. I think they appreciate it when I'm forthright."

It was those same personal qualities that also set Doherty up to grow angry and hurt when journalists, in his mind, took something he said out of context or treated him or his team unfairly. Given the fishbowl Carolina basketball constantly resides in, it was only a matter of time before such a disagreement occurred.

Doherty had been mildly irritated with a few of the stories through the year, the latest coming when Tim Crothers of *Sports Illustrated* wrote a largely glowing story following Carolina's win over Duke. For the most part, Doherty felt it was a positive article, but the last line, which repeated Doherty saying to his dad, "This doesn't suck, huh?" following the win over Duke, did disturb him somewhat. "It was a personal comment to my dad . . . I wish it hadn't been reported. I have a better vocabulary than that." But Doherty, understanding the media as well as anyone, knew it was still great publicity for his program. Carolina recruits would soon receive the article in mailings.

But the most publicized incident came following an Internet column by ESPN's Curry Kirkpatrick. Although he did not cite the source, Kirkpatrick had been forwarded an e-mail from a player's relative in which the relative—who had been sitting behind the Carolina bench during the Duke game—retold the story of Doherty commenting that "Duke still has the ugliest cheerleaders in the ACC." It was a comment intended for the players' ears only (many of them did not even hear it), and Doherty's hope was that it would loosen them up.

When the Kirkpatrick column went online, a local Raleigh television station did a live report from the Duke campus. When he heard about Kirkpatrick's story, Doherty was mildly irritated but hardly angry. But soon, the local writers, not wanting to get beat on a story, were forced to write about it. Doherty released a statement of apology and called the Duke cheerleader adviser, who was not in the least bothered by the private comment that Kirkpatrick (a Carolina graduate) had made public.

Heading into the second matchup with Clemson, Matt Doherty had exactly 11 ACC games under his belt as a head coach, but even he was experienced enough to know that every game was losable. He and his staff had prepared just as hard and worked just as tirelessly to get the players ready for the last-place Tigers as they had in preparation for Duke.

In fact, the week of practices had been as vigorous and competitive as any all season, except for the last two days, which had been marginal at best. He chalked that up to too many consecutive days without playing against someone other than teammates, but the lackadaisical play concerned him and gave him ammunition to use during one-on-one conversations with players as the Clemson game approached. By contrast, he had been very happy with the first two days of practice that week—Monday and Tuesday—when the team had been able to get back to some fundamental instruction. "Our sharpness was slipping," he said after Monday's workout. "It was a good, fun practice. We joked at times, but we worked hard, too. Sometimes, when players joke, it can get out of hand, and they get sloppy when it's time to work. That didn't happen today. I was pleased."

Tuesday wasn't quite as good a practice, but that was largely due to the schedule, which called for a lot of work on late-game situations, during which many of the players stood around. During the final stretch, Doherty called the situation out for the team and for Chad Webb, the head manager, who was working the clock. "Chad, put 30 seconds on the clock; White down two with the ball on the baseline." The players would sprint to either Doherty (the White—i.e., starters—coach) or MacKinnon (Blue Team) for instruction. Doherty would stop the action often, giving pointers on specific spacing and how to react in different situations—knowing that in a real game, he would not be heard over the crowd. "We have to get it right, or we'll lose in this situation." He was able to cover about two dozen different situations over the course of the last 30 minutes of practice; sometimes the White Team won, sometimes the Blue Team. Every time the Blues—made up of Jon Holmes, Will Johnson, Michael Brooker, Orlando Melendez, and Jim Everett—won, they celebrated for a few seconds before settling down and refocusing on improving their teammates.

The week's darkest moment didn't come on the court, but in the parking lot of a Harris-Teeter grocery store on a rainy Thursday night. Boone, who had played so well of late and become the most effective backup point guard in the ACC, was jogging through the downpour into the grocery store to pick up some bananas for breakfast the next morning. As he stepped onto the curb, he misjudged where the cart ramp was and rolled his ankle. He caught himself from falling, but pain immediately shot up his leg as he limped a few steps under the over-hang. He tried not to yell out, but the ankle was bad, he knew. He bent over and prayed that the pain would subside. It didn't. The ankle throbbed harder as he limped back to his car. He would be out at least a week.

On Friday morning, Doherty taped his television show segment with Woody Durham. After he had finished taping, Doherty remained in the studio to record a promo for an ESPN commercial that would run later that month. On the other end of the phone line, the commercial's producer gave Doherty the lines to read for the animated spot, which would run during Championship Week. "Try to do the first one sort of sugary," the producer explained. Doherty raised an eyebrow and smirked: "I'm not sure I have that in me, but I'll give it a shot."

Doherty got it on the first take.

As Matt Doherty drove into the Smith Center Saturday morning—the day before the Clemson game—he noticed the throng of students outside, lined up in front of the natatorium, which was adjacent to the arena. He remembered the reason as he pulled into the back lot: it was student ticket distribution day for the Duke game, two weeks and one day away. The students, wearing wristbands they had received in a lottery, were lined up according to their number. The number of students had swelled to several hundred, most of whom would purchase the maximum number of tickets they were allowed: four.

When he got into his office, Doherty called over to the ticket office and asked them to hold 30 or so student tickets for him. A half-hour later, he left his office, walked the short distance outside to the ticket office in the natatorium, chatted briefly with the student organizers, and grabbed his tickets. A buzz had already resounded through the line: Coach D was here! His appearance was nothing new—he had brought doughnuts and chatted with students before while they waited—but this time, he had something new in mind.

Doherty wandered out among the students and, as he truly enjoyed doing, began talking to them as if he were one of them, or, more accurately, as if he were a genial professor, asking them about their majors, classes, and campus life. At first the crowd around him was fairly small; no one wanted to lose their spot in line. Already knowing the answer, he turned to a short, blond, female student and asked her how big a fan she was of the Tar Heels. "Huge!!" she said with a huge smile. "Good answer," said Doherty, handing her four of the choicest student tickets in the arena.

Suddenly, no one cared about his or her spot in line. Coach D was handing out tickets! As the mob pushed in around him, Doherty (at 6'7", he stood out above the crowd and appeared like a shepherd spreading feed for the flock) knew he didn't have enough tickets to make everyone happy, so he changed his strategy.

"Who here can name the starting five on the 1982 championship team?" All at once, about a dozen of the students rattled off the names as if they were one: "Jordan-Worthy-Perkins-Doherty-Black." To about three students, Doherty handed tickets.

"Who here knows where Coach Guthridge is from?"

About half the students yelled back: "KANSAS!"

Doherty smirked. "No, I mean which *town* in Kansas?"

A short pause. "Parsons, Kansas," said a proud young man with an anti-Duke T-shirt on.

"Pretty good," said Doherty. He then proceeded to make the questions much more difficult, and focused on players from his era or on events or players who came before him. After a few stumpers, a student yelled out: "Coach, we were only two years old when you played!"

"No tickets for you," Doherty said, breaking the crowd up.

When the tickets were gone, Doherty shook everyone's hands and thanked them for their support. Even those who hadn't been lucky enough to snag a few ducats were all smiles, slapping their coach (key word: *their*) on the back and wishing him and the team good luck, among other things. "Tell Joe not to be shy! He has to shoot!" "Tell Jason he's not a role player to us!" "Wear a red tie tomorrow, Coach. Red looks good on you!"

Joe Forte awoke in the Greenville, South Carolina, Embassy Suites feeling very fresh and ready for the Clemson game that would be played that afternoon. A hard week of competitive practices was behind him, and he looked forward to playing in a real game again. His roommate for the trip, Will Johnson, was already up and waiting for him to get ready to head to the team breakfast in a meeting room downstairs. The sun shone bright outside; it was another beautiful mid-February day in the Carolinas. He was particularly looking forward to playing against Will Solomon, Clemson's score-first, talk-after guard.

Johnson, who had roomed with Forte on road trips all season, turned to Forte in the elevator. "The paper today said Solomon won't start against us." "Why?" Forte asked. "I don't know. Missed some classes or something," Johnson replied. "He'll play, though."

Forte, ever the competitor, was disappointed. He was looking forward to battling Solomon, the ACC's scoring leader (Forte was second), on both ends of the floor. He confirmed the information at breakfast and listened as the coaches went over the scouting report again. The rest of the day went by slowly, as the team shot and walked-through the

Tigers' sets at nearby Furman University around midday, ate pregame meal, and then relaxed for an hour in their rooms.

"I'm ready," Forte, a thin smile on his face, said as he boarded the bus for Clemson. "But I wish Solomon was going to start. I get fired up when he starts talking."

 Littlejohn Coliseum is a dank, charmless arena that looks—on the outside and inside—like a cow palace with a new coat of paint. When the Tigers aren't playing well (which they haven't for a good portion of their tenure in league play) and the opponent is not highly regarded, Littlejohn can be empty and cold, with all the energy of a rec league game at the YMCA. But given something to cheer about, the Clemson students and fans, and really the entire state of South Carolina (since there are no major professional sports teams, South Carolinians are rabid college sports fans), will rise to the occasion and create an atmosphere that is rowdy and intimidating. The students at Littlejohn may not be nearly as clever as those at Duke, but since they stand closer to the action—just a few feet off the baseline on both ends—they can and do present a distraction.

Many of the fans in the building during pregame warm-ups, however, were wearing Carolina blue. Haywood, almost always the first player on the floor to shoot prior to a game, was mobbed in one corner of the court by fans who, unable to obtain tickets to home games, made the two- to three-hour drive from western North Carolina to watch their beloved Heels on the road. When Joe Forte and Julius Peppers emerged from the tunnel a few minutes later, several hundred early arrivers cheered. The rock stars were in town.

As Forte had heard, freshman Tony Stockman replaced Will Solomon in the starting lineup. Without their leading scorer (Solomon scored approximately 28 percent of the Tigers' points), Clemson would have to search elsewhere for offense. Doherty was wary of the Tigers' finding balance—he knew that Solomon going for 25 or 30 points wouldn't hurt if the other Tigers didn't hurt them—as well as Clemson's penchant for playing junk defenses.

Both causes for concern would turn into realities—and lead to the most improbable upset of the season in college basketball.

With Solomon out, the other Tigers suddenly took it upon themselves to provide offense. Players who had not shown any inclination to shoot—let alone score—came alive. Forward Ray Henderson (averaging 5.4 points per game) hit a 15-footer to start the game. Stockman, Ed Scott, and Chris Hobbs got into the act. The result was a raucous arena and a 14–12 Clemson lead with 12:30 remaining.

On the other end of the floor, Carolina's offense was tentative to the point of comatose. The junk defenses—triangle-and-two and box-and-one—had effectively bottled up Forte and Jason Capel and dared Ronald Curry to shoot. With 2:25 remaining in the half, Doherty took his point guard out and urged him to take the shot if it was there. After hitting his first three-point attempt earlier in the half, Curry missed his next four shots in the first half and turned down countless others. He would play just 10 minutes in the second half.

Despite the anemic showing, Carolina led 35–30 at halftime. Doherty assured the players that the game was still in their control, if they could raise their level of intensity. On the way back out to the court, Doherty pulled his star, Forte, aside. "Are you OK?" he asked. Forte assured his coach that he was, despite not scoring a field goal in the first half. "I just haven't found my rhythm. I will."

To himself, Forte was surprised at how tired he and his teammates were. The game seemed to be moving quicker than any other he could remember. He felt so great coming in; rested and ready. Now, after 20 minutes, he felt sluggish, a step behind, like someone had put the game on fast forward and he was still on play. It was a feeling he couldn't ever remember having before on the court.

Try as he might, the rhythm never came to Forte. Not that he didn't try. He wouldn't score a field goal until 14:10 remained in the game, when he hit a contested 15-footer. But he followed it with a miss from behind the arc. Clemson's next possession was a microcosm of the game: Ahead 47–45, Solomon sprint-dribbled into the lane, where he was stripped by Owens. The ball bounded to the sideline, where

Stockman outraced Morrison and Forte to it. He then hit Jamar McKnight, who missed from the baseline, but Chris Hobbs outfought Haywood for the rebound. Solomon then backed it out, Clemson ran a play, and Stockman missed a jumper. Several Tigers got their hands on the ball, until Adam Allenspach knocked it out of bounds. North Carolina had not given up a basket, but they had been outhustled on at least six occasions.

Carolina looked tired and timid as Clemson's lead grew from two points to four to seven. Finally, with 10:00 to go, forward Tomas Nagys, 1-for-10 from behind the arc for his career, trailed a Tiger break, took a shovel pass from Scott and, without hesitation, rose up and swished a three from the top of the key. When Nagys hit an even more improbable shot over Peppers on the right side of the lane on the next possession, Clemson led 54–45 with 9:11 remaining.

Forte answered with six points over the next three and a half minutes, and Carolina climbed back into the game. With a little more than two minutes remaining and Carolina behind 64–62, Forte had the ball in his hands and the game on the line. Over and over, throughout the season, he had hit big shots (or a series of shots) during the guts of a game . . . at UCLA . . . College of Charleston . . . at Georgia Tech . . . Wake Forest . . . at Maryland . . . at Florida State . . . at NC State . . . at Duke . . . at Wake Forest. Each game needed a hero and he had risen to the challenge. Against Clemson, Carolina needed another miracle. With 2:14 on the clock and a chance to tie, Forte rose from just beyond the foul line with every intention of doing it one more time.

But he missed.

"He's allowed to miss one of those shots this year," Doherty said later, half joking. "Just one."

After the miss, Clemson regained its confidence. Chris Hobbs drove baseline and scored with one minute remaining. Forte missed a rushed three-pointer. Stockman, who would go on to earn freshman-of-the-year honors, rebounded, dribbled the length of the court, and instead of pulling it out as Shyatt yelled from the sideline, pulled up and calmly hit a three-pointer with 0:44 on the clock. The Littlejohn roof nearly came off as the crowd, which had entered the arena asking for Tar Heel autographs and cheering the opponent, erupted. The rest was missed UNC shots and Clemson free throws as the Tigers closed out the biggest win in its program's history, 75–65.

But not before one last bit of drama. With 5.5 seconds remaining and Will Solomon at the free throw line, Shyatt elected to call a time-out. The purpose? To celebrate the win over the No. 1 Tar Heels. It was a questionable decision that one of his assistant coaches tried to talk him out of, but his mind was made up. It was a time-out that would not be forgotten.

After the game, Doherty wasn't despondent. "You can look back and say, 'Why?' Was it just today? Was it the week off? Was it those kinds of things?" He was down and blamed himself for not preparing the team to face the junk defenses, but he was not at all like he had been earlier in the year following the loss to Kentucky. It had been 70 days and 18 games since that defeat. Over that period, Carolina had gone from a huge question mark, a team apparently still struggling against the indefinable sleeping sickness it had nearly succumbed to a season earlier, to the confident, swaggering North Carolina team that fans loved and opponents hated. Matt Doherty had made North Carolina cool again, creating a buzz of excitement that literally lifted the spirits of alumni, administrators, faculty, and students. He had lifted this weight with his own spirit and allowed his players to just play.

Now, the question was, could one loss undo everything they had accomplished?

Forty-five minutes after the game, Jason Capel fought through the several hundred fans who crowded around the bus, asking for autographs and pictures. His dad, Jeff, helped him push through the clamoring fans.

"I don't know what to say. I can't believe it," Capel said to his dad in a muted, defeatist voice. "I don't know what to do."

His dad, a lifelong coach, put his arm around his son until Jason lifted his head. "Just get on the bus and go home. It's all you can do."

33

Home

The plane carrying the Carolina basketball traveling party touched down on the runway at the Raleigh-Durham Airport and rolled to the terminal four and a half hours after losing to Clemson. As the plane began to taxi toward the gate, Doherty stood up and turned to face the players; an idea had been turning around inside his mind for several hours.

"Guys, I want to practice tomorrow," Doherty announced. Originally, Monday was supposed to be a day off, with practice resuming on Tuesday for Thursday's home game against Florida State. "I don't want us to have to sit around and stew on this loss for a full day. It's not a punishment; if it was, we'd be coming in at six (in the morning). I just want us to get back to ourselves. The game went to the team that played harder today. And it wasn't us."

310

He went on to explain, in very calm tones, the same thoughts he had expressed to his coaches during the trip home: We weren't ready to play. We didn't look aggressive on defense or offense. Maybe we worked too much on playing against the junk defenses instead of just *playing*. For that, he took the blame. He got done speaking just as the plane stopped at the gate. The players, who had been very quiet and hung their heads for the better part of the last five hours, rose to their feet and collected their personal bags.

They didn't feel any better after what Coach Doherty had said, but they were now anxious to do something about it.

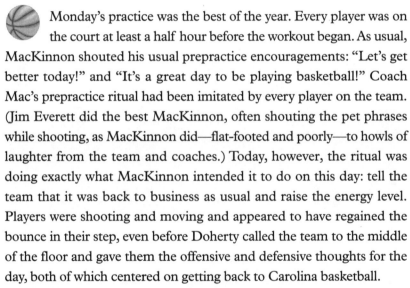 Monday's practice was the best of the year. Every player was on the court at least a half hour before the workout began. As usual, MacKinnon shouted his usual prepractice encouragements: "Let's get better today!" and "It's a great day to be playing basketball!" Coach Mac's prepractice ritual had been imitated by every player on the team. (Jim Everett did the best MacKinnon, often shouting the pet phrases while shooting, as MacKinnon did—flat-footed and poorly—to howls of laughter from the team and coaches.) Today, however, the ritual was doing exactly what MacKinnon intended it to do on this day: tell the team that it was back to business as usual and raise the energy level. Players were shooting and moving and appeared to have regained the bounce in their step, even before Doherty called the team to the middle of the floor and gave them the offensive and defensive thoughts for the day, both of which centered on getting back to Carolina basketball.

For the next hour and a half the players worked as hard as they had all year. During fundamental breakdown drills, the post players cut hard to the basket, received passes from the managers, drop-stepped, and dunked—all the while, Everett pounded them in the back and on the arms with the football blocking dummy. The perimeter players, meanwhile, sprinted between spots, shooting dozens of jumpers from all over the court. Teammates yelled encouragement at every opportunity.

During competitive drills and scrimmages, all 10 players on the floor battled and fought for position, for rebounds, for loose balls. Those on the sidelines shouted out when good plays were made. Only twice did Doherty raise his voice.

During a water break toward the end of the practice, Ronald Curry, who had played as poorly as any Tar Heel the day before but whose leadership on the team had risen steadily as the year progressed, walked over to Doherty.

"Coach," he said in his usual quiet voice, "this was the best coaching move you've made all season."

"What's that, Ronald?" Doherty asked.

"Having us practice today," Curry replied. "I think we're back now."

Doherty, who had slept barely two hours the night before, nodded and smiled.

"I hope so."

When he slipped into the building, he was barely noticed, except by several maintenance men. Immediately and as if they were old friends (which they were), he walked up to several of the building supers and electricians and shook hands and slapped backs all around, talking about the team, their new coach, and their prospects for the upcoming ACC and NCAA Tournaments. It was just four guys, old friends, talking basketball.

Perhaps the most striking aspect of Roy Williams's return to Chapel Hill (which served the dual purpose of allowing Williams to see his daughter, Kimberly, dance at halftime and see two of his old assistants, Doherty and Seminoles' coach Steve Robinson) was just how much the same it would have been if last summer had never happened. He greeted old friends and Tar Heel fans he had never met before with his characteristic smile, using their first names when making new acquaintances, answering questions, and asking questions back. He signed autographs and stood for pictures, and only once did a fan, from several rows over, yell anything derogatory.

"I'd be lying if I said I wasn't apprehensive about coming back," he said. "I've had a huge, huge, majority of people who have been very supportive. I've got some people again that I've disappointed. It's been harder for them to get over than maybe some other people. I don't know if they'll ever get over it, and I know I will never get over it."

At halftime, Williams—who was in town only for a couple of hours—ran out of the arena to call Dean Smith. Their relationship—thanks to Smith's inability to hold a grudge—was strong and getting stronger every day. Williams was back in his seat for the second half as North Carolina crushed Florida State, 95–67, putting together an overwhelming offensive and defensive effort.

When it was over, Williams spent time with both Robinson and Doherty before heading back out of town.

Back to Lawrence, his home.

34

Not-So-Happy Birthday

The decisive win over Florida State at home put a seed of hope in Matt Doherty's mind that the Clemson loss was an isolated incident. While he still held a great deal of optimism about the remainder of the season—it was, after all, just one loss—a nagging realization was just starting to take hold: his team had become complacent after reaching No. 1.

As it turned out, the eight-day stretch between the win at Wake and the loss at Clemson would be the most important period of the season. Nothing had occurred that week that would qualify as a turning point, other than the nagging thought in the coaches' minds that maybe, just maybe, their work ethic had slipped ever so slightly.

Florida State, Doherty hoped, had put them on the right track mentally; back in a hunter mode, instead of being the hunted. To test that optimistic theory, the Virginia game in Charlottesville would be key.

"Florida State was a good game to have," said Doherty. "Any time you lose—even though you've got a lot of confidence—any time you've been ranked high and won 18 games in a row, I think everyone begins to think 'what's wrong? Are we going to get it back?' And then when we got it back it brought our confidence back."

Chad Webb was used to running unusual errands. As the leader of the "Swat Team" (a name Doherty had given to the managers after watching them load and unload gear from airplanes and buses with well-oiled efficiency) he had attended to a wide variety of tasks, from as simple as running to a convenience store to get a coach a candy bar to, once, as a junior, riding in a cab on the mean streets of Manhattan, searching for an all-night laundry to wash the team's practice gear (he finally located one in the Bronx—the team was staying in midtown Manhattan). Now, as a senior, Webb was expected to see potential problems in traveling or moving gear for 15 players, five coaches, and numerous staff before they occurred. Every once in a while, he got to do something fun, like today.

It was a cold, gray, damp Sunday in Charlottesville, the clouds clinging to the tops of the rolling hills of central Virginia. It was the Tar Heels' third day in town, Doherty having decided to make the three-and-a-half-hour bus trip—instead of flying—on Friday after practice. Doherty figured that by the time they would get to the airport in Raleigh-Durham, wait for the charter, land in Charlottesville, and then drive over, flying would only save the team a half hour or so. "It's a little safer," said Doherty, the Oklahoma State tragedy from six weeks earlier (in which 10 members of the traveling party perished in a plane crash) perhaps fresh in his mind.

Sunday was also Doherty's 39th birthday. "I'm a little more concerned with Virginia than my birthday," said Doherty in his usual single-minded fashion. His family had made the trip, including his parents, Walter and Mary, who were nearing the end of their month-long stay in Chapel Hill. Even Doherty's kids, Tucker and Hattie, were there, although they stayed back in the hotel during the game. There would be no party or event to celebrate—until after the game (if it was a win). Webb, making a run to a local grocery store, picked up a cake that the team presented to their coach during pregame meal. All of the players sang "Happy Birthday" (poorly) and also gave Doherty a card.

"We'll give you a present later today," wrote Forte at the bottom.

Thirty minutes before the teams came out onto the University Hall floor for warm-ups, the arena doors were opened and the UVa students flooded in. Nine days earlier, the crowd had been instrumental in Virginia upsetting Duke, 91–89 (and keeping Carolina alone in first place in the ACC), and it hoped to have a similar effect on this day. Almost immediately, the students—who had been camped out for eight days prior to the game, prompting UVa coach Pete Gillen to send doughnuts and chicken wings during what was a cold, wet week—started in on Ronald Curry. Curry, who had spurned Virginia for North Carolina in what was a wild and highly controversial recruiting process, had become a symbol of loathing for Cavaliers fans.

Doherty was never one to back down from the catcalls of students. At Duke, he had disarmed a student heckler who got in his face as he walked onto the floor and yelled that he was the fourth choice to be the coach at UNC. "Actually," he said to the student upon walking closer, "I was the fifth choice." There was no comeback. At Virginia, Doherty walked over to the most raucous section of students at the end of the Carolina bench and began conversing with them, holding up his fists in a mock boxing stance, and generally enjoying the exchange. The day before, when Carolina had been walking past the camped-out students and into U-Hall for a practice, he had attempted to talk to some students in line. "I tried to talk to some of them, but they only growled at me," Doherty said.

There was plenty of talking early in the game, but not much scoring, at least in the first few minutes. Three consecutive turnovers (two by UVa and one by Carolina) seemed to signify an ugly game was coming. "We wanted to make it helter-skelter out there," said Gillen. "We figured, the uglier, the better [for us]." Entering the game, Virginia's Achilles heel had been half-court defense. The Cavs ranked last in the league in field goal percentage defense. In Chapel Hill, Carolina had scored easily—when they had broken Virginia's press. But it was obvious to Doherty on the bench that Virginia's defense was much more active. He was impressed with how well the athletic Cavs were getting around screens and closing out to the shooters.

Despite the improved Virginia defense, Carolina began to score. Or, more specifically, Forte began to score. His (and Carolina's) first bucket came on a 10-foot baseline jumper. After Chris Williams' two free throws and Travis Watson's layup, the Tar Heels ripped off eight straight points (five by Forte and three by Haywood) to take a 12–4 lead at the first media time-out.

But with 15:30 remaining and Carolina cruising, Roger Mason Jr. shot-faked Curry up into the air and smartly leaned into him, causing contact and the foul on Curry. It was his second, and the crowd erupted. To add insult, Mason had hit the shot and also connected on the free throw. The lead was now 12–7, UNC, but Curry had two fouls and had to sit. Boone was still nursing the ankle injury he sustained at the grocery store, so he was a step slower than usual. Carolina could not penetrate the Virginia defense, and it showed.

Forte, perhaps sensing his team needed him to score, kept Carolina in the game single-handedly. Throughout the season, Forte had developed an innate sense of knowing when to break out of the offense and score and when to play within the team framework. At this point in the game, with Curry out and no one else hitting consistently, Forte sensed he had to score. It was much earlier than usual—he almost always saved his scoring spurts for the second half—but he felt it was needed, if the Tar Heels were to keep up with Virginia, which had suddenly gotten very hot. Keith Friel came off the bench to hit two threes in transition, the second tying the game at 18–18. Forte then answered, drilling a three from the right wing for his 12th point, putting Carolina back ahead, 21–18, with 12:27 remaining.

Doherty then made a calculated gamble. Sensing his team's offense was not executing, he reinserted Curry. To try to protect his point guard, he assigned Curry to guard Mason instead of Donald Hand, who was the Cavs' point guard and had a knack for drawing fouls. Brian Morrison picked up Hand. But the two fouls weighed on Curry's mind and caused him to be less aggressive than he normally was. More than any other player, Carolina could not afford to lose Curry. Although he did not score much, his aggressiveness and leadership had largely been the reason for the team's turnaround after the Kentucky loss. Now, he couldn't play his normal game, and it hurt the Heels. Mason stepped behind a screen and hit a three, pulling the Cavs to within two, 25–23. A minute later, Hand lost Morrison and hit from the top of the key to put Virginia in the lead. Capel answered with a three from the corner on a pass from Forte. Carolina led 28–26. Both teams were on fire. The first one to blink would lose.

And then it happened: After Friel hit another three (the official play-by-play listed the play as: "Friel 3 PT jump; HEAD FAKE LOSES CURRY"), Curry, feeling the frustration of being unable to play his game in front of the most hostile of crowds, broke free from the Virginia press and blew past Hand. He sprint-dribbled to the lane and charged headlong into Friel, who was set up in the lane. The whistle blew: charging. It was Curry's third foul, and it came with 8:17 remaining in the first half. Without its defensive leader and with the U-Hall crowd screaming for blood, Carolina would get outscored, 29–14, the rest of the half. Even Forte, who scored 19 points in the first half, couldn't keep Carolina in the game as Virginia took a 56–42 lead at the half.

In the locker room, Doherty stared at the 56 points on the stat sheet. He was understandably upset and concerned with his team's defensive effort. He knew Virginia had shot extremely well, but he believed Carolina could do a better job of being active in getting around screens, containing dribblers, and getting a hand up on shots. Most of all, he was disgusted with the transition defense. "That's all effort, guys," he said. "It's nothing else but beating them down the floor and matching up. And we're not doing it." Offensively, Doherty was worried that too much had gone through Forte. At the same time, he did not want to stifle his best scorer. So he focused on executing, getting the ball to Lang and Haywood (who had scored 10 points in the first half on an assortment of post moves and put-backs), and working inside out. "Don't rely on one-on-one moves," he said as the team came together before heading out to the floor.

Carolina played a zone to start the second half, trying to cross up the offensive rhythm of Virginia. But the Cavs came out with as much, if not more, energy than they had in the first half, extending the 14-point lead to 17 . . . 19 . . . and then 20 points when Mason hit a three from a full step behind the line to give the Cavs a 74–54 lead with 10:24 remaining. Carolina's offensive execution continued to deteriorate—and Forte continued to break out of the offense and force the action.

Only in the second half, Forte wasn't hitting shots.

Just when everything looked its darkest, Carolina, through sheer force of will, began to battle back. It started on defense, as Carolina forced UVa into a 0-for-10 stretch from the field. On offense, Forte hit a three from the top of the key and then stole a pass intended for Friel and scored a layup on the other end—uncharacteristically arguing a no-call when Friel tagged him on the arm on his way up. A Capel three and another driving layup by Forte pulled the Tar Heels to within 76–66 with just under five minutes remaining. After another defensive stop, Carolina pushed the ball up the floor and caught Virginia in a scramble—and into a bad matchup: Watson on Forte. Reading the situation, Forte backed up and drove hard to the right baseline. But Watson, who, at 6'8", is incredibly agile, was able to cut him off, forcing Forte to stop and shoot a 15-foot fadeaway—very similar to the shot he had made to clinch the win at Wake; if it went in, Carolina would trail by eight with 4:30 remaining and still be very much in the game.

But the shot, online all the way, hit the back rim and bounced out.

Hand rebounded and pushed it ahead to Mason, who hit a reverse layup over Capel. The Virginia drought was over, and the Tar Heels were out of gas. Incredibly, Carolina would not score another point in the game as the Cavs matched UNC's 10–0 run with one of their own to close out the game. When the buzzer finally sounded, Carolina had lost, 86–66, and the Virginia crowd rushed the floor, pushing up against the scorer's table and forcing the Tar Heel players to escape through media row. Forte, as he left the floor, was as frustrated as he had ever been after a game, shouting at himself and punching the air in a rare show of emotion.

While Pete Gillen addressed the crowd over the U-Hall public address system—"You are the greatest fans in college basketball!!!"—the players in the Carolina locker room seethed. They had been outworked and outplayed. Their frustration was visible. No one said a word. Doherty addressed the players briefly, vowing to have more to say on the three-and-a-half-hour bus ride home. Not a single player looked up from the floor. When Doherty left for the coaches' postgame press conference, he called Forte out into the hallway and into a corner under the bleachers, where the two talked quietly. The other players slowly took showers and packed their bags. After talking to Doherty and taking a quick shower, Forte headed out the back door, refusing to speak with the media.

The ride home was as long as anyone could remember. As soon as the bus left the Charlottesville city limits, Doherty stood and asked for everyone to take their headphones off. "We're going to watch the film while we're riding home," he said solemnly. "We need to see what we didn't do."

As the film ran without interruption, the players watched intently—for about 20 minutes. Then some heads began to dip and eyes droop. "I watched it, but I knew we were going to see it again later," said Haywood later. The tape ended just as the bus crossed the North Carolina state line. The last vision on the screen was of the Virginia students storming the court. Only one player had watched every play without interruption, gluing his eyes to the screen without more than a blink for almost two hours.

Ronald Curry.

35

" . . . Worse than This Before"

Two losses in its last three games gave credence to a rising storm of controversy regarding Carolina basketball. Reporters began wondering what many fans were already saying: What's wrong with Carolina? Rumors swirled that Matt Doherty and Joe Forte engaged in a shouting match at halftime of the Virginia game (the truth was that the two had a quiet one-on-one conversation) and that Forte and Jason Capel were at odds, a clash of egos among Carolina's leaders.

The truth was, none of the players handled losing very well. Most of them would be terse or standoffish with media and others following a loss, knowing the incredible crush of naysayers that would begin jumping off the Carolina bandwagon. "We have some fans who stick with us no matter what," said Brendan Haywood on more than one occasion. "The others, I don't care what they do."

For many, the Capel-versus-Forte angle was one too easy to ignore. The story seemed simple: Capel was a star in high school, a McDonald's All-American with a pedigree as a coach's son, and now he was a secondary scorer, behind Forte, in Carolina's offensive attack. But the truth was that Capel had accepted Forte's role as a scorer and his own as a guy who could do other things to help the team win. "Everybody in the world knows that Joe is the best scorer in the country, so there is no reason for me to try to go out there and try to get 20 a game," said Capel.

But that didn't erase Capel's comments immediately following the Virginia loss, in which he appeared to target Forte's shot selection: "Whatever Coach says, that's what happened," said Capel. "You saw it just like I did. People took shots, some people didn't. That was it."

It was a comment made in the heat of the moment that was largely ignored by the two players but would, eventually, have to be addressed.

The most upset person about the Virginia loss was, not surprisingly, Matt Doherty. The Clemson loss had not been a one-time problem; a trend had developed. One reporter asked him if he was concerned about his team after the game, and he responded in frustration: "Heck yeah, I'm worried." He would end up regretting that comment (slightly) and blamed himself for adding to the public perception that the Tar Heels were a team in turmoil.

Doherty's initial analysis, without watching the tape, had been that the Virginia game was very much like the loss to Kentucky: too many open shots allowed, too many uncontested layups. All added up to a recipe for defeat. And all were unacceptable.

Doherty explained as much to the team during a meeting they had in the locker room when they returned to Chapel Hill on Sunday night. As he did in most team functions, Doherty sought feedback from the players after he gave them his impressions of what they had all just endured. He was careful not to sound too panicked: "We weren't very good," he told the team. "We didn't match their intensity, and that's the most disappointing thing. It's important we don't let this loss linger, but we have to realize that we can't let that happen again. Once we get into March, one game where we don't give everything we have can end our season."

The next day was a Monday, and Doherty asked all of the starters to come in for individual meetings. His main motivation for this was to make sure everyone was on the same page and there were no lingering effects from the loss—and he wanted to give any player an open and personal forum to express any doubts about the way things were being done. None of players expressed any doubt as to the roles on the team or the direction they were all heading in. At the end of his short meeting, Haywood, who had taken to speaking his mind more often as the year had progressed, summarized many of the players' feelings: "Coach," he said, "we've all been through worse than this before."

It was a comment that stuck with Doherty. He had to keep reminding himself that his was a mature team, one that had been to a Final Four and lost four consecutive games in ACC play in the same year. They were not going to be thrown by one loss on the road to a team that was hitting every shot it threw up, even if it was the worst loss UNC had suffered in its last 90 games. He was more angry now than worried—upset that his team had given up so many easy baskets in transition. He let them know during the usual prepractice huddle at center court. With his voice rising as he rattled off the things they didn't do against UVa, the players fidgeted, wanting to start working to atone for their lack of effort. When he was done, Doherty's voice echoed in the cavernous and quiet arena. "Bring it in," he said a little lower. The players' arms shot into the middle of the circle. Doherty looked each one in the eye, his head rotating around and bobbing up and down. "Let's go to work."

While NC State stood between Carolina and the regular-season finale against Duke (and the game that would likely decide the ACC regular-season champion and No. 1 ACC Tournament seed), the Blue Devils had to play Maryland in a rematch of the most remarkable college basketball game of the year. It had been exactly one month since Duke came back from 10 points down with a minute to go in College

Park and eventually defeated the Terrapins in overtime. Since that game, Gary Williams's shell-shocked team had been to the depths of college basketball, losing four out of five games, including an embarrassing defeat to then–last place Florida State *at home*. After that game, the Cole Field House crowd had booed the Terps in the waning moments, prompting Williams to admonish the fans during his postgame radio press conference, which takes place on the court and is broadcast over the PA system.

But a kinder, gentler (sort of) Williams had turned the team and the season around, starting with a win at Wake Forest. Further wins over NC State and Oklahoma had bolstered the Terps' confidence to the point that they truly believed they could go into Cameron and win. They were the only ones who believed it.

Doherty watched the game after having dinner at home with his parents, who were leaving the next day after spending a whirlwind month in Chapel Hill. Walter had seen his son lead UNC to a win over Duke in his first matchup with Mike Krzyzewski. About a week later, a cold that Walter was battling turned into pneumonia, and he spent several days at UNC hospital. He was feeling much better when he sat down with his firstborn son to watch the second half of Duke–Maryland, and when Matt turned the TV on just after the beginning of the second half, Duke held a one-point advantage.

"How about that?" said Walter.

"I'm not surprised," said Doherty. "I wouldn't want to play Maryland right now."

The second half continued on, and the two men talked about other things, family, kids, and so on. But when Duke center Carlos Boozer exited the game limping (it was later diagnosed as a broken third metatarsal in his foot) and Maryland went on a run to push their lead to nine points, all other talk stopped. "They might get 'em," said Walter.

"Still a lot of time left," responded his son.

When the game reached its final minute, the younger Doherty began to get into coaching mode. With exactly 1:00 remaining and Maryland clinging to a seven-point lead, Jason Williams sprint-dribbled down the lane and was fouled by Byron Mouton. "Don't foul 'em!" Doherty bellowed. "Putting them on the line is the worst thing you can do!" Williams missed both free throws, however, and Maryland pushed its lead back to nine points.

"It's not over yet," cautioned Doherty. Walter grinned, watching his son's casual off-court demeanor morph into his game face. Maryland continued to make errors—and Doherty continued to coach Williams' team through the screen—but Duke could not capitalize and the Terps got their revenge, 91–80. When it was over, Doherty turned to his father and smiled.

"Now, we have to take care of our own business."

With Duke's loss, the NC State game took on a new dimension. No longer was it just a game, but it was a chance to make history.

"We can hang a banner tonight," said Doherty in his pregame address to the players. "We have the chance to do something special. Something that hasn't been done here since 1998. We have to come out in a defensive frenzy. If not, we'll be making some substitutions." With a win, Carolina was assured of a share of the ACC regular-season title and, thanks to its earlier win over Duke and the Blue Devils' loss to Maryland (the ACC coaches had voted on the tiebreaker several years earlier and decided that, after head-to-head play, the next determining factor was losses from the top of the standings down), could earn a No. 1 ACC Tournament seed.

NC State rolled into the Smith Center with no such high aspirations. The Wolfpack was a team on the proverbial bubble—the NIT bubble. Herb Sendek's team had looked awful eight days earlier at Maryland, losing by 29 points, but had rebounded to crush Florida State at home five days later by 25. The Wolfpack was not much different a team than the one the Tar Heels had faced earlier in the season; State played extremely hard but rarely found any offensive rhythm.

What was expected was a bruising, ugly battle—and that's just what UNC got. Dean Smith, whose 70th birthday was on this day, had met with Doherty for 20 minutes the day before the game, sharing notes. Smith spoke little about the loss at Virginia as the conversation focused more on how to handle the team's emotions. When Doherty and Smith got together to talk about X's and O's, the meetings could last all morning; at other times, the two had shorter conversations that focused more on team dynamics and psychology. "As a coach, he's been in virtually every situation anyone can imagine with an incredibly wide variety of teams and personalities." On Tuesday, Smith reminded Doherty about the 1992–93 UNC team that lost by 26 points at Wake Forest and then won 17-of-19 games including the national championship, and the 1976–77 squad that was crushed at Clemson by 20 points, 93–73, and then ripped off 15 consecutive wins before losing to Marquette in the NCAA title game.

If Carolina was going to repeat that kind of history, it would have to win games like it had against the bruising Wolfpack. It was not a perfect performance, by any means. Offensively, the Heels still struggled to find consistency and balance; defensively, NC State got some open shots due to defensive miscommunications. Still, Carolina defeated a bully of a team 76–63 behind Joseph Forte's 27 points, Ronald Curry's career-high 14 points, Adam Boone's solid eight minutes, and Kris Lang's 10-point, seven-rebound outing. With the win, Matt Doherty became the first coach in the history of the ACC to win the regular season in his first go-round through the league. Carolina was the top seed in the ACC Tournament, with one game—Duke—remaining. No, not everything was perfect.

But it was pretty close.

36

Senior Day

Hype for the second installment of North Carolina versus Duke officially began on the first day of March when Joseph Forte made the six-mile trip into Durham to get his hair cut. Within 30 seconds of pulling his Ford Explorer Sport up to the 40 Below barber shop on Chapel Hill Road in Durham, he was being vigorously razzed (and defended) by the proprietors. It was just another day at ground central of one of sports' greatest rivalries.

Prior to the team's first matchup, Teddy McKoy (the barber with the bias for Duke) had been, for him, restrained. But with the ESPN cameras inside the shop filming a piece that would run the morning of the game, he was in full throat.

"I didn't like what Doherty said about the Duke cheerleaders!" bellowed Teddy before Forte could even sit down (even a star has to wait his turn at 40 Below). "You tell him he'd better look in the mirror!"

Forte just smiled and sunk into one of the torn faux-leather couches that lined the far wall of the shop. The long rectangular room was filled with regulars, some of whom would stay all afternoon. Lin Lilly, a barber and rabid UNC fan, immediately jumped to Forte's defense.

"What's Joe got to do with that!" yelled Lin as the other customers provided the laugh track. "How you doin' Joe Sprewell? I call him Joe Sprewell because, like [Latrell] Sprewell, he's two hard dribbles to the left, one dribble back to the right and *money*."

From there, it only got louder.

No one was immune from Teddy's barbs; it was as if the Carolina basketball players were all sitting in the front row of a Kings of Comedy concert, and Teddy, the insulting comic for the night, was letting them all have it as part of his act. It was Teddy who had bestowed the "doughnut" nickname on Haywood after the Georgia Tech game (in which Haywood hadn't scored). Now, Adam Boone, who had come in earlier, also had a nickname, courtesy of Teddy: "Yo, Apple Turnover, when you gonna learn how to dribble?!"

"Why you gotta be so hard on Boone, man?" asked Jason Capel, defending his teammate.

"Me? Ya'll are the ones who don't play him," answered Teddy to a chorus of laughter.

But it wasn't just the Carolina players who took abuse. Duke's Jason Williams and Dahntay Jones (who was red-shirting a year after transferring from Rutgers) took their share, as well, thanks to Lin. After a heated exchange between Lin and Jones, Lin shouted above the din: "You can't talk!! You ain't even *played* in the ACC yet!!" When asked if Shane Battier, as well known for his abilities in the classroom as he was for his exploits on the court, ever came in, Lin quickly responded: "Nope. We don't have a library in the back." Carlos Boozer and Chris Duhon would get their medicine later in the day, as well.

But it was Teddy, pictures of former and current Duke players behind him on his mirror, who roared loudest and cracked the most jokes for the ESPN cameras. And every Carolina player who walked in was his target. Teddy predicted how Sunday would go: "Forte, we're gonna give you 15 [points]. Haywood, you get five. We're gonna let Lang shoot, because he won't score. And Jason, I know we're family and all, but you're only getting seven." Then Teddy turned to Peppers—who, at 6'7", 270-pounds, was standing ominously nearby—and lowered his voice. "Peppers . . . we're gonna have to suspend you."

Throughout this wild scene, ESPN's Curry Kirkpatrick—the slim, slight, well-dressed broadcaster/writer for *ESPN* who had written about Doherty's comments on the Duke cheerleaders—meandered between the cameras, boom-mic operators, and his producer to try to lead the Carolina and Duke players into on-camera gibes at the other team's players. Most of the time, the players knew better. But not every time.

"I'd rather Boozer play against us," said Haywood in response to Kirkpatrick and Teddy. "I keep Boozer in my hip pocket. I let him out on weekends. . . . It wasn't like he scored 30 last game."

Even Kirkpatrick wasn't immune from Teddy, however, as the barber caught the famous sportswriter laughing at one of Lin's anti-Duke comments. "Yo, yo, what are you doing here? [ESPN sportscaster] Stuart Scott was busy? Why we got the 'B' team here?! We're not big-time enough?!"

Throughout the storm of comments and flurry of opinions, Forte remained his usual stoic self, only getting animated when he and Haywood reminded Teddy that he was crying after the last game between Carolina and Duke. "It was just one tear, but you were crying," said Forte.

About 45 minutes after he arrived, with his hair cut and his ego bloodied but intact, Forte climbed back in his car for the short trip back to Chapel Hill. "Man, I hope we win Sunday," he said. "If we don't, I'm not sure we can come back here."

More serious matters were taking place that same day in the Smith Center. Although the players had the day off, the coaches were holed up, watching film, and trying to figure out how Duke would change its lineup and game plan without Carlos Boozer. Shortly after Duke's loss to Maryland, it was determined that Boozer's broken foot would keep the 6'8" center out until at least after the ACC Tournament.

Immediately, speculation had begun on how Duke would attack Carolina—
and vice versa.

Boozer, as Haywood pointed out at the barber shop, had not been
a factor in the first game in Durham. Haywood had given his best defensive effort of the season in holding Boozer to just four points (on just five
shots) and five rebounds. But in the two most recent games before getting hurt he had scored 20 against Wake Forest and 16 versus Maryland.
In short, he had become the inside threat the Blue Devils needed to balance their outstanding perimeter game. Now, with Boozer out, Duke
would have to rely solely on outside shooting to score points.

But Boozer's injury caused more concern for Doherty and the staff
than if Duke was coming in at full strength. "They're used to being the
hunted," Doherty said more than once. "Now, they're the hunter." It
was true; the local and national media began counting Duke out, writing and commenting that without Boozer, Duke's chances for a No. 1
seed in the NCAA Tournament were slim, at best.

It was obvious to Doherty that Duke would make two strategic
moves to counter the loss of Boozer. First, Krzyzewski would use Casey
Sanders, a McDonald's high school All-American who, in his sophomore season at Duke, had yet to live up to his promise. Doherty had
recruited Sanders when he was an assistant at Kansas and knew
Sanders had rare speed and athleticism for a 6'10" player. He wasn't a
polished inside player, but he could run, and, more important, he gave
Duke a shot-blocking presence it normally did not have.

The other possibility open to Duke worried Doherty much more
than Sanders. With such a versatile defender as Shane Battier—perhaps
the best all-around defensive player ever to play college basketball—
Krzyzewski might play Chris Duhon at the 2-guard spot and shift Nate
James to the 3, Mike Dunleavy to the 4, and Battier to the 5. Battier had
the strength and, more important, the smarts, to play either Haywood
or Lang in the post, and the presence of five perimeter scorers in Duke's
offense could wreak havoc with Carolina's two-post-player lineup.

More important than the strategic moves Duke could make, however, was the one motivational advantage the Blue Devils had. "Coach

Krzyzewski has a lot of hot buttons to push," Doherty said. "He can use the 'underdog' angle, he can pull the team together and rally around Boozer. This is going to be a fired-up team that comes in here Sunday.

"I'll bet Duke shoots between 35 and 40 three-pointers," Doherty continued. "They can come in here and play loose. In Cameron, they didn't shoot well because they got a little tight, especially when we got ahead. The same thing can happen to us. We can't get behind double digits. If we do and they go small, it could be very difficult to catch up." On the other hand, Doherty knew, if Carolina could defend like it did in Cameron—when Duke rarely got a shot up without it being contested—then the Tar Heels could attack Duke offensively, getting the ball inside and forcing Duke to double-down with its perimeter players. In preparing for practice the next day, Doherty was stern and to the point. "We better not relax one bit," he said without a trace of doubt, "or Duke could come in here and run us out of our own place."

Michael Brooker and Jim Everett were almost always two of the first players to arrive at practice, and among the last to leave. No one was going to get more out of their last days in a Carolina uniform than the two players who were least likely to ever have been allowed to wear it. For Everett, the journey had been beyond a dream: from not starting as a high school senior to—just maybe—starting for North Carolina against Duke at home in his final college game. It was such a ridiculous notion that he tried not to think about it too much. But it was a feeble attempt; Everett's mind wandered to the point of daydreaming in class about hearing his name called over the PA system and coming out and hitting a three-pointer in the game's first minute. "I still can't believe I'm here," said Everett. "I'm going to make the most of it, to be sure."

Everett had begun counting down the days until the living dream would end (counting backwards from the national championship on April 2) about the time that Carolina made the turn and began its second go-around in ACC play. He X'd the days off of his calendar one by one: it was 32 days from now, 30 from the Duke game, which, as a senior, he was slated to start, if Coach Doherty held to tradition.

Every senior on the UNC roster had started his last home game since Dean Smith took over at Carolina in 1961–62. Bill Guthridge, as loyal a disciple as could be imagined, had continued the tradition without even giving a thought to it. It wasn't a tradition that hadn't backfired: in Smith's second-to-last season as coach, he had started the less-than-powerful lineup of Ed Geth, Dante Calabria, Clyde Lynn, David Neal (all seniors), and Serge Zwikker (the lone junior) in the last home game against Florida State. The Seminoles proceeded to storm out to a 10–0 lead before Smith could get the regular starters into the game and storm back for an improbable 84–80 comeback win. "It was the only game where I thought it [starting the seniors] ever hurt us," Smith told Doherty the week of the Duke game.

Doherty did not want that to happen against Duke on national television, but the decision to start the seniors was in line with everything he had been taught by Smith and Roy Williams. Not doing it entered his mind, but never seriously. Among the Tar Heel faithful, starting the seniors was one of those automatics that they never believed would be changed—it was one of those Carolina traditions that the true-blue fans believed made their program different from everyone else's (Duke nor NC State, for example, started their bench-warming seniors in their final home games). For Doherty, it wasn't nearly as automatic (he didn't announce he would start the seniors until talking to Woody Durham on the Tar Heel Sports Network broadcast a few minutes before the game), but it was close.

Brooker and Everett were the two seniors who would have been most affected if Doherty chose not to honor tradition. The other two seniors, Max Owens and Brendan Haywood, were going to see significant minutes. Without tradition, however, Brooker and Everett weren't going to sniff the court except during warm-ups.

It hadn't always been that way for Brooker, who had seemed on the cusp of receiving playing time on several occasions during his college career due to his shooting ability. At 6'4", he was tall enough to get his shot off against smaller guards, and it was a shot that, when he was feeling it, rarely hit anything but net. During Guthridge's coaching tenure, Brooker had been within an eyelash of being in the regular rotation, but his defensive liabilities (i.e., quickness) caused by repeated knee injuries always showed when the ACC schedule began. He first hurt the knee his senior year at Brentwood Academy in Sandersville, Georgia; not during a game but after the season was over and he was fooling around during a physical education class.

Brooker redshirted his first season at Carolina, thus becoming the only player to span the five years between playing for Dean Smith, Bill Guthridge, and Matt Doherty. When he was healthy, Brooker was a dangerous offensive player—in practice. "He's unstoppable when he gets going," said Forte. "There have been practices where he just lights up the White Team. He's caused us to run a lot of sprints." But the shooting sprees never led to serious minutes, even as a senior, when his best game came against Kentucky in a mop-up role when he scored five points in 12 minutes.

As much as Brooker was looking forward to starting against Duke, the last thing he wanted to do was hurt the team with his presence in the lineup. He had no idea what Coach Doherty was thinking when he approached his coach on Thursday. The two had a casual conversation when Brooker's tone changed. "Coach, I don't know what you're thinking about for Sunday, but you should do what's best for the team."

"What do you mean, Mike?" Doherty asked.

"I'm just saying that you shouldn't start the seniors if you think it's going to hurt our chances to win."

Doherty explained that he hadn't made up his mind yet, but he genuinely appreciated Brooker's unselfishness and it was likely he would start the seniors. The conversation reminded Doherty of the day before, after the NC State game, when he had made a point to explain to Max Owens why he hadn't played him more.

"Max, I really wanted to get you more minutes, but because State was using a bigger lineup with Inge, Thornton . . ."

Before he could finish, Owens, a soft-spoken player who had seen his career yo-yo up and down during his time at Carolina (and wasn't always happy about it), stopped Doherty in mid-explanation.

"Coach, don't worry about it. I want to do whatever is best for the team. All I care about is winning," said Owens as Doherty listened, a bit stunned by the truly selfless manner in which Owens spoke. "I appreciate you explaining it to me, though."

When Doherty relayed both the Owens and Brooker conversations to his assistants, they all remarked that it was a telling aspect to the team—and to the two players—that each would make such a selfless statement.

"I love this group of guys," Doherty said, never one to hide emotion.

The seniors expected word on Doherty's decision when he called a seniors-only prepractice meeting on Friday. But instead of addressing the issue of who would start, Doherty instead talked about managing their time—and helping their teammates to manage theirs—over the course of the next few days.

"Guys, this is a hectic time. We're all being pulled in different directions and dealing with family coming into town and our friends asking for tickets and everything that goes along with it. We can't let that distract us. We can't get too emotionally high. We have to take care of those things as quickly as possible and prepare to play this game. Make sure we're all doing that."

After the players' meeting in the back hallway by the locker room, Doherty ran into Chad Webb, the lone senior among the managerial crew, who was busy getting everything ready for practice.

"Chad, let me ask you a quick question," Doherty said. "Do we introduce senior managers before the last game?"

"No, Coach, not since I've been here," Webb replied.

Doherty paused. "Well, we did when I was at Kansas, and I also did it last year at Notre Dame, so tell your parents they should come down to the floor with the players' parents. I want them to be there when you get introduced."

Webb was floored, but managed a brief smile and a "Thanks" before heading off for more towels.

What Doherty didn't mention in the short five-minute players' meeting was the media swarm that had descended on Chapel Hill. Doherty had experienced the fan frenzy firsthand the night before at his coach's radio show. A crowd about one-third larger than any that had shown up during the season at Michael Jordan's 23 restaurant greeted Doherty and gave him the usual standing ovation. A steady stream of autograph seekers (one woman wanted Doherty to simply touch her collection of four-leaf clovers for luck) and well-wishers descended on Doherty, whose approachability was different than any of his predecessors. He greeted every fan with a smile and a handshake, even those who repeatedly interrupted his postshow dinner with Bob MacKinnon, his lawyer/friend Bill Bunch, and their wives.

But the media attention was even more intense. ESPN and ABC had begun hyping the game a week earlier. "It is sort of neat to be sitting in your living room the week before a game and see them hyping it on TV," Doherty said. "It's also kind of scary." Steve Kirschner had issued over 280 media credentials for the game, about 80 more than for any other game all year. Every media outlet from the Dunn (NC) *Daily Record* to *Gigante de Basket* (a Spanish basketball magazine) had sent a writer to cover the game. Dealing with this kind of scrutiny was nothing new for Carolina's coach and players, but the extra time spent answering questions could be draining.

As for practice, Doherty was pleased with the work that got done on both Friday and Saturday. "We practiced well, but Duke had an extra day [due to their previous game being on Tuesday]," Doherty said. "I hope we're ready."

 The seniors got the word at pregame meal: all four would be starting.

Doherty went on to thank each one for all they had done, on and off the court. Brooker, Owens, Haywood, and Everett took the news without any reaction, but their stomachs began churning as Doherty began his usual pregame quiz on the scouting report. Not surprisingly, no one missed any of the questions.

After he was done, Doherty paused a moment and looked at his notes, catching the name of Jim Everett, who would be matched up on Shane Battier in the game's first minute. The walk-on who had never even started for his high school team would be guarding not only an All-American but a player many had already tabbed as the best college player in the country. "Everett, if they back off of you and give you the shot, step up and bury the three."

The whole room laughed, but Doherty was only half kidding. He believed a strong start in the Duke game would be crucial; he knew getting behind—and thus allowing Duke to dictate tempo—would be very hard to overcome. If Everett (or Brooker, for that matter) was somehow able to get a hoop, Doherty knew the crowd would blow the Teflon lid off the arena. Last year at Notre Dame, Doherty remembered, one of the little-used seniors had hit a three and a walk-on had tipped in a miss; the crowd reaction had been enormous. But the chance of Everett rising up and hitting a three (he wasn't exactly Larry Bird) was pretty slim. That's why starting the seniors had been anything but a simple decision.

As one last insurance policy against a bad start—and to loosen himself up—Doherty grabbed Everett by the arm just as the team made its first entrance for warm-ups, 25 minutes before tip. "Jim," Doherty said with a slight grin as he crossed one forearm over the other, "if I give you the 'hack' sign, go over and foul Battier [so we can sub in the regular starters]."

As it would turn out, the short time the four seniors would be on the floor would be Carolina's best period of the game.

Senior day was emotional, as everyone had expected. Manager Chad Webb was the first one announced as the clock operator froze the clock with 3:12 showing prior to the game's start, followed by Everett, Brooker, Haywood (who received the loudest cheer), and finally, Owens. All hugged Doherty before moving down the line to embrace each parent. The ovation of 21,750 rained down on the four players, while the student section chanted, "Thank you."

The introduction of the seniors as starters brought even more cheers, but the crescendo was reached when Haywood timed the jump ball perfectly and tapped it to Everett. Thirteen seconds later, Haywood took a pass from Owens and dunked over Sanders.

With the crowd nearly jumping out of its seats, Haywood responded by blocking Jason Williams' shot in the lane. The sound drowned out Doherty's play call, but it hardly mattered, because Duke was trapping at midcourt almost immediately. "Write that down!" Doherty yelled to MacKinnon. "Battier's leaving his man and doubling the ball!"

Duke had shown its defensive strategy, and it was as simple as it was brilliant: Krzyzewski was using Battier as a rover, having him hawk the ball wherever it went. That left Sanders on the block and the other three Duke players guarding the perimeter. The middle was wide-open, where Carolina, in its secondary break, always placed either Lang or Haywood (or Peppers), whichever post player was the last one down the floor. Duke was conceding the 15-foot jumper to any of those players—if Carolina could break the half-court trap. Duke was going to force Carolina to play a scramble game. The Tar Heels would run very few offensive sets all afternoon.

Offensively, Duke had started Duhon and Sanders, sitting Nate James for the first few minutes of the game. The move allowed Duhon (who had scored over 12 points per game and shot nearly 50 percent from behind the three-point line over the last five games) to get more minutes and also put more speed on the floor.

Just as Doherty predicted (and Duke's defensive scheme solidified), Everett was left wide-open when Haywood reversed the ball to him to the left of the top of the key and behind the three-point line. Without hesitating, Everett launched the shot as the crowd grew suddenly silent . . . and missed off the left rim. Doherty subbed in his regulars 15 seconds later, and the battle was truly engaged. The first half would be all that the crowd in attendance, the thousands more watching along Franklin Street and on the Duke campus, and the millions watching on ABC could have hoped for.

The pace was furious, with Duke shooting 6 three-pointers (and making none) in the game's first four minutes. Carolina, however, could not take advantage due to turnovers and its own poor shooting, and the Blue Devils pushed out to an 8–4 lead after Dunleavy hit a short baseline jumper. Duke continued to trap out high, forcing Forte back to the midcourt line before he could get it off to Lang, open at the high post. He quickly fed Peppers, who rose up and dunked over Battier—and got the foul—to cut the Duke lead to 8–7 with 15:16 remaining.

But with all the openings on offense, Carolina could not take a lead until Capel hit a three-pointer from the top of the key with 13:37 remaining in the half to make the score 13–12. Duke, however, was beginning to reap the benefits of spreading Carolina's defense out. Playing with five perimeter players for a good portion of the first half, Duke spread the floor and isolated against Lang and Haywood, creating a scramble situation on almost every possession. Williams was the first beneficiary of such a scramble, when he collected a loose ball and drilled an open three-pointer at the 13:37 mark. It was Duke's first three-point goal in seven attempts. They would hit 13 of their next 31.

"We have to move our feet and contest every shot," Doherty yelled during the first media time-out. "Fly at the shooters!!" It was easier said than done. With Carolina scrambling to bother Duke's shooting, Williams was able to get into the lane almost at will. When Boone was in the game, Williams flew to the basket. Curry had better luck containing him, but Williams was definitely into the flow.

As was Battier. Five days earlier, Battier had his senior day ruined by Maryland. Now, he was determined to do the same to Carolina. Two consecutive Battier three-pointers erased Carolina's second lead, and Duke led by five points with just under five minutes remaining in the half. The last five minutes of the half were frantic, with Carolina climbing back into the lead when Forte hit a three from the top of the key coming out of a time-out. It was one of the few called plays Carolina was able to run successfully all afternoon. Carolina built its lead to three points as Haywood capped a 10–0 Carolina run when he put back a Curry miss for a 37–34 advantage with 1:28 remaining. But Battier answered with an offensive rebound put-back of his own on the next possession. Haywood then made one of two free throws, but Williams hit two threes around a Capel hoop to give Duke a two-point lead with under a minute before the half.

Carolina had a chance to tie or take the lead, but Forte missed the front end of a one-and-one. But the Heels forced a miss by Battier as the shot clock wound down for Duke and looked to have a semibreak when Forte collected the rebound with seven seconds on the clock and immediately sprint-dribbled up the floor. But Doherty just as quickly called a 30-second time-out (he would have lost the time-out if he had not used it) and set up a play in which Forte would get the pass in the middle of the court and read the defense. He did just that, finding Curry, who shot a short runner on the baseline that missed, sending Carolina into the locker room down by two points, 42–40.

Before he jogged into the tunnel, Doherty walked to midcourt to confront the three officials—Karl Hess, Frank Scagliotta, and Andre Pattillo—not about a specific call (although Doherty had been upset at several no-calls on Carolina's offensive end), but about their propensity for stopping and talking to Krzyzewski for long periods of time during the first half.

This practice had angered Doherty at Duke earlier in the season; it infuriated him in the Smith Center. "What's that!?" he yelled over and over at the officials when they stopped to talk to Krzyzewski for long periods of time. Late in the first half, Krzyzewski spent an entire time-out in conversation with Pattillo and Hess, never once bothering to address his team. After the break, Doherty walked down the line to express his displeasure with the officials' affording their time to Krzyzewski. As Pattillo, Hess, and Scagliotta walked briskly to the locker room, Doherty followed, again voicing his displeasure.

MacKinnon's notepad was filled with notes that Doherty had told him to write down during the first half, but when he addressed the team at halftime, Doherty boiled the game down to a few points. First, he diagrammed how he wanted to attack Duke's "soft trap," where Battier was floating around in the half-court. "Don't stop the offense when you catch it here," Doherty said, circling the high-post area. "We've got to attack the rim. Drive the ball in. Ronald, don't allow yourself to get trapped. When you see it coming, split it and drive the ball down the lane." Doherty also addressed the team's zone: "We can't be slow in our slides. We have to get out to the shooters and make them put it on the floor. In our man-to-man, big guys, you have to show yourself out more on the ball-screen. Don't let Williams get a free shot down the lane."

When the X's and O's were taken care of, Doherty talked about emotion. "We are right there, guys, RIGHT THERE! Do not give up any easy shots. Every possession is a war. Take it right at 'em on offense and don't let up if we get a lead or if we get down by a few buckets." As the team broke and headed out the tunnel, Capel pulled the team together. "Twenty more minutes!!" he shouted, the rest of the team echoing the chant.

In the other tunnel, Jason Williams was even more vociferous in getting his team fired up. The Blue Devils walked briskly to the opening of the arena, where Williams, soft-spoken off the court, pulled everyone in close. "NO F***ING LETDOWNS!!! NO F***ING WAY WE LOSE THIS GAME!!!" His voice was loud enough to be heard by a good portion of the Carolina fans near the tunnel, and Duke players were greeted even less warmly than they were typically. But the message got through: on Carolina's first possession of the second half, Curry split the trap—as he was told—only to see the ball stripped by Williams, who went the length of the floor and scored a layup.

Williams got a piece of the next pass as well, and a tone was set. Duke had raised the intensity. A few minutes later, Duke went on a 10–1 run, thanks to three-pointers from Williams and Duhon.

But it was a defensive play that led to Williams' three that turned the game in Duke's favor. With the score 50–47, Forte anticipated a move by Dunleavy at the top of the key and stripped him clean. With no one in front, Forte took off for what looked like an easy dunk. But Battier, starting in front of the Duke bench, sprinted toward the rim, hoping to get close. "I never saw him," said Forte afterward. "I didn't know he was with me." Forte closed in on the rim and rose to dunk with his right hand, but Battier timed his jump perfectly and just got a finger on the back of the ball. Forte lost control and pushed the ball against the rim, where it bounced off and was recovered by Dunleavy, who hit ahead to Williams, who hit a three.

After Lang missed a jump-hook, Dunleavy buried another three, and Duke suddenly led by nine, 56–47.

In the days leading up to the game, Doherty was most afraid of getting behind by more than double digits. If that happened, he knew, Duke could then go small and Carolina would have to matchup—thus losing its height advantage. A team behind by 10 points or more had to play a more frenzied game to try to make up the deficit. That style—quick up and down the floor, shooting threes, and trapping on defense—was the style Duke had played all season.

And that's exactly what happened. Once Duke's lead grew to double digits, Carolina was only able to get it under 10 points on three occasions, the last coming when Owens hit a three from the left corner with 13:36 remaining to cut the deficit to 64–57. The Blue Devils answered with an 8–0 run. The Smith Center got eerily quiet, with only the students on the floor making any noise at all. Doherty, who had been more than a little upset with the officials most of the afternoon, finally got a technical foul at the 9:31 mark, and Carolina was down by 13 points. Hess had avoided giving Doherty a technical foul on several occasions earlier only because Hess had successfully ignored him. But following a no-call in which Forte and Williams bumped as Forte took a 14-footer in the lane, Doherty slammed his feet and stormed onto the floor. "They've been fouling all damn game!!" Doherty screamed, punctuating his point with some more colorful language. "We are the home team!!" Hess had no choice but to give Doherty a "T."

The technical foul fired up Carolina, but only for two possessions. For the first time throughout the game, Duke was pressed to take a bad shot as the 0:35 clock ran down and Williams and Peppers collided on a layup attempt—with no call. On the other end, Owens shot-faked and hit a midrange jumper as the whistle sounded. Foul on Sanders (Hess made the call). Doherty jumped off both feet on the sideline, trying to will his team to victory. After Owens completed the three-point play, Carolina had the deficit to 10 points, 76–66, with 8:50 remaining.

But Carolina could not get the stops it needed. Even with Haywood and Lang on the bench from the 12:00 mark on, Carolina could not keep up with the quicker Blue Devils. Duhon and Dunleavy hit four straight free throws—and Duhon nailed a three from in front of the Duke bench—to push the lead back to 15. Layups and free throws kept Duke comfortably in front, and the first Smith Center fans headed for the exits with 3:30 remaining and Duke up by 17 points. The final margin was an afterthought: 95–81 Duke. The Blue Devils had put up a school-record 38 three-point shots (just as Doherty had predicted) and made 14.

As he ran off the court, Doherty waved at the students on the baseline and put his chin on his chest as he jogged through the tunnel to the locker room. The entire team jogged slowly and silently with him, wondering what would happen next. Would their coach, who hated losing more than anyone they had ever met, throw a tirade? Kick a chair? Slam his fist into the blackboard? Once inside the locker room, that question was answered.

"Congratulations, guys." Doherty said in a strangely upbeat voice and without a trace of sarcasm. "We have reached one of our goals. We've won the (ACC) regular season. That's a heck of an accomplishment. It would have been nice to win it outright, but we have no excuses. We got beat today. Think about why it happened until midnight, but rededicate yourself to what we're trying to do after that. All five of our goals—improve every day, win the next game, win the regular season, win the conference tournament, and win the national championship—are still there for us to achieve.

"Whether or not we achieve them will be based on how we react to this loss."

37

Tournament Time

All of Carolina's goals were indeed still achievable, but the team that won 18 straight games and climbed to the No. 1 ranking in mid-February was not the team Doherty saw before him now.

The thought had been nagging at him since the loss to Clemson two weeks earlier, but it now occupied every waking moment of his day: his team had not reacted well to becoming the No. 1 team in the country.

"We relaxed," said Doherty early in his preparations for the ACC Tournament. "We worked hard and made an amazing climb. Once we got there, we held on to the fire for a few games, but then, once we had the eight days off [with no games prior to Clemson], we stopped pushing ourselves." Doherty knew it was his job to snap his team out of its late-season funk, and he would try everything he knew in the week before the ACC Tournament to get his old Tar Heels back.

Doherty went over every team meeting, practice, and individual conversation in his head over the course of the last 15 days, searching for an answer. The problems were varied. Forte had struggled shooting the ball, and instead of letting the game come to him he had begun to force the action. The result had been an awful performance at Virginia. Capel, the most vocal team leader, had grown frustrated, and his teammates had followed suit.

The good news was that the ACC Tournament—and a chance to reclaim the good feelings and achieve more of the team's stated goals—was just a few days away, with the NCAA Tournament (and a likely 1 or 2 seed) around the corner.

"In a month from now they won't be talking much about today," said Doherty after the Duke loss.

Doherty was generally pleased with the week of practice prior to the ACC Tournament; he designed workouts heavy on shooting drills and scrimmaging. But that did not mean he relaxed or let the players forget the loss to Duke. "We have to regain that togetherness and toughness we had during February," Doherty said. Another concern he had—one that was relatively new to his thinking—was the team's confidence.

As a young coach—and one who makes a concerted effort to understand his players off the court as well as on—Doherty understands the power of popular media, music, friends, and other factors that add to or subtract from a young man's self-esteem. For that reason, Doherty and his staff were upbeat as well as tough during the week leading up to the ACC Tournament. In addition, Doherty asked Bob Ellis, the producer of Doherty's television show, to produce five- to six-minute highlight videos of each of the contributing players, set to music that the player chose. Doherty's plan was to show the videos to each player at some point prior to their first game on Friday as a way to bolster individual confidence.

On the court, Doherty did not change practice at all. The Tar Heels had now lost on three consecutive Sundays, however, and Doherty tirelessly searched for answers as to why. "We're a little banged up," he noted, "but so is every one else this time of year." As is the case whenever a team made up of over a dozen 18–22 year olds' struggles, there was more than one reason for the losses.

In his last three games, Forte had shot just 24-of-67 (36 percent). Defensively, Carolina was not as stingy as it had been. True, the Tar Heels still led the ACC in field goal percentage defense (the stat most coaches use in determining how good or bad a defense is), but in their last three losses to Clemson, Virginia, and Duke, the defense had allowed opponents to shoot 45 percent from the field (compared to a season average of 39 percent).

But the stats were just symptoms of the disease. The reasons for much of the struggles were that opponents were adjusting to what Carolina was able to do. With Curry's continued struggles from the field and Haywood's shaky passing out of the post, the Tar Heels had become very "guardable." Starting with Clemson's triangle-and-two defense and continuing with Virginia's pressure and Duke's use of Battier as a roving trapper, opponents had designed defenses that were structured to stop Forte, allow Haywood to catch the ball in the post (and then double-team him when he put the ball on the floor), and allow Curry to shoot virtually any time he wanted to.

The results, three losses in five games and a general degradation in the confidence of Curry, Haywood, and other players, did not bode well for the Tar Heels entering tournament season.

Predicting what the NCAA Men's Tournament Selection Committee does when it sequesters itself in a hotel conference room to select and seed the Field of 64 (actually 65 in 2001) is much like predicting the weather. The major storm fronts are easy to spot, but getting the specifics just right is next to impossible.

One of the specifics involved Carolina and Duke: the selection of the No. 1 seed in the East. It was highly likely that the Committee would put the East's No. 1 seed in Greensboro for rounds one and two. It was also highly likely that the No. 1 seed would go to either Duke or North Carolina if one of those teams was to win the ACC Tournament. If Carolina lost in the title game (or didn't make the final), it would likely be shipped to either Memphis or New Orleans as a No. 2 seed in the South. Duke, even if it lost, was likely to get a No. 1 seed, based on its win over Carolina and its strong showing without post man Carlos Boozer, who would not be back (after suffering a broken foot against Maryland) until the Sweet Sixteen, if at all.

Although the Carolina coaches kept an eye on the prevailing NCAA rumors regarding seeding and placement in the bracket, they did not talk about it with the players during the three days of practice leading up to the ACC Tournament in Atlanta. Carolina was the No. 1 seed due to a somewhat odd tiebreaker of looking at games against the third-place team (Maryland) and heading down the standings instead of starting from the bottom-up. It was a system ratified by the conference coaches several years earlier in the hopes of giving more emphasis to good wins than bad losses. Because Carolina defeated the Terrapins twice and Duke lost to the Terps on Senior Day in Cameron, UNC earned the top seed and Duke the second seed. It was a potentially important distinction, as Maryland was widely believed to be playing the best basketball of any team in the league, and as the No. 2 seed, Duke would have to face the Terps in the semifinals while Carolina played the winner of Georgia Tech and Virginia, should both teams advance that far.

The ACC Tournament bracket had also been changed. Since Florida State joined the league prior to the 1992 season and up through 1998, the nine-team tournament bracket was designed in such a way so that No. 8 and 9 seeds faced each other in a play-in game on Thursday. (This game was dubbed the "Les Robinson Game," after the former NC State coach and current Citadel athletic director who always seemed to guide the Wolfpack into the game.) But in 1999 and 2000, the ACC, in the hopes of making Thursday a more attractive day for fans, restructured the bracket so that the No. 9 and No. 1 seeds met on Thursday (with the winner getting a bye into the semifinals), as did the No. 7 and No. 8 seeds. The remainder of the teams played in the quarterfinal round, starting Friday. Complaints abounded about this setup, as coaches argued that the No. 1 seed no longer had to win three games in a row (Friday would be an off-day for the top seed) to win the event, while everyone else did (barring a No. 9 upset of No. 1). Likewise, fans did not like the two-games-on-Thursday, three-on-Friday schedule, preferring the four-games-on-Friday tradition that created one of the most anticipated days in college basketball. Thus, in 2001, the Les Robinson game returned.

Other traditions would be broken during the 2001 ACC Tournament, as the North Carolina basketball team participated in an open-to-the-public practice on Thursday. The seven top seeds traditionally practiced before the fans on the Thursday before they all played on Friday. Except North Carolina. Under Dean Smith and Bill Guthridge, Carolina did not take part in the one-hour practice sessions, preferring not to open practices. The only deviation had come in 1976 when the Tournament took place in Landover, Maryland, in an arena in which the Tar Heels had never before played.

Back in December, Assistant Commissioner Fred Barakat had called Doherty and personally asked him to conduct a practice on Thursday, as a show of goodwill to fans. Doherty, proving he was more open than his predecessors, had agreed without argument. "We want to be team players," Doherty said. "We want to participate. I think the players enjoy the excitement."

The fact that the tournament was moved to a domed stadium for the first time—and the media writing about and analyzing topics such as shooting backgrounds and the like—did not concern Doherty at all. "I don't make much of that," Doherty said. "The basket is still 10 feet and the court is 94. And if you want to advance [in the NCAAs] you'll play in a lot of domes."

With Carolina slated to practice before the public on Thursday at 1:00 in the afternoon, the team practiced on Wednesday in Chapel Hill before busing to their usual preflight dinner at the Angus Barn restaurant. And almost as routinely, their charter flight was delayed—it was the same plane that was taking Maryland from Washington, D.C., to Atlanta— causing the team to have to kill time after dinner. The mood was upbeat and light, with players playfully cracking on one another about recent haircuts or girls they were seen talking to lately. It was hardly the quarreling team filled with dissention that was being talked about on local sports radio stations and on Internet message boards.

"People will say whatever they want," said Forte, who was known to periodically jump on a message board under an alias and stoke the rumor fires, just for fun. "We're a close team. Anyone who spends time around us knows that. There's no problem at all between me and Cape. We're cool. Everyone on this team is cool. We just hate losing."

Thursday's fan-friendly practices began with hometown Georgia Tech taking the floor at 11:00 A.M.—to a "crowd" of exactly three Tech fans. Carolina took the floor two hours later to several hundred fans, but it was hardly the event it might have been. Except for the mass of media folks on the sidelines talking about Carolina's first open practice in recent memory at the ACC Tournament, there was little enthusiasm in the air. That is, until Duke's assistant coaches entered the arena about halfway through UNC's workout. With the Blue Devils next on the court, it wasn't odd for coaches and players to appear or remain in the arena before and after their practice, but the site of such bitter rivals watching each other practice struck more than one observer as bizarre.

After the players finished media interviews—conducted in the end-zone stands while Duke practiced—they made their way through the tunnel to the team bus. As he turned the corner, Lang was surprised by Doug Wojcik, who jokingly pushed the 6'11" center against a wall and held his forearm across the player's chest. Through a semigrin, Wojcik— nearly a foot shorter and 60-to-70 pounds lighter—mimicked a drill sergeant: "You got to promise me you're going to demand the ball tomorrow!" Lang sort of pushed back, and both play-wrestled until

Lang "gave up." "All right, all right," Lang said. Wojcik immediately relented. "OK, you can get on the bus then."

The bus was not, however, heading back to the Ritz Carlton (the team hotel in Atlanta). Instead, the team would make the 15-minute drive to Pace Academy (a private secondary school in Atlanta) where they would have their real (i.e., closed to the media) practice, in which they would go over the scouting reports for both Clemson and Florida State, who would play later that night in the play-in game for the right to face No. 1 seed Carolina.

Scouting opponents is tedious work that requires incredible attention to even the smallest detail, an experienced eye, and the kind of broad understanding of different basketball styles and strategies that can only come from years of experience around the game.

Prior to the beginning of the season, Wojcik was given the responsibility of devising the scouting schedule, splitting up the nonconference and conference opponents in such a way so that no assistant (Bob MacKinnon or Fred Quartlebaum were the other two scouting assistants) would be saddled with the job two games in a row. The job of scouting an opponent requires the breaking down of sometimes as many as a dozen tapes as well as making clandestine calls to colleagues in the coaching profession whose teams have played the opponent (and could thus give you their take on that team). After analyzing every piece of information possible on individual player tendencies, offensive sets, defensive strategies, under-out-of-bounds plays, and everything else imaginable (even down to when opposing coaches liked to call time-outs or come out of the locker room for warm-ups), the coach doing the scout would then whittle it all down to a one- or two-page scouting report to give to each Carolina player as well as a 10- to 15-minute videotape made up of clips of the opponent. After spending 20 to 40 hours on such tasks, the information had to be presented in such a way that 18–22-year-old players (with notoriously short attention spans) could learn the material and internalize it enough to understand what the player they would be guarding liked to do when he had the ball on the left wing or what play was coming when the opposing point guard signaled "thumbs down."

In addition to the assistants working on the scout, Doherty would watch every tape available (and with strength coach/video coordinator Ben Cook overseeing the recording of over 800 games per season, almost all tapes were available) and make his own notes, sometimes filling a legal pad with one team. The day of the game, the players would gather for a shootaround (or walk-through) practice in which the assistant who did the scout would instruct the Blue Team to walk-through the other team's sets while explaining to Forte or Capel or Lang what the man they would be guarding liked to do. (In practices leading up to the game, the Blue Team would run the opponents' sets and try to mimic individual tendencies, which brought about situations such as Jim Everett pretending to be Shane Battier. "I loved it," gushed Everett, "I could shoot at any time, take threes, drive, whatever.")

While the walk-through was occurring, Doherty would step in and explain to the players how he wanted them to defend each play or occurrence. For example, against a point guard who was not a great outside shooter, Doherty would want Curry to go "under" an on-the-ball screen at the top of the key, which allowed him to slide through the screen easier and stop penetration.

It was a fine line—and constituted the art of developing an effective scouting report—when a coach could analyze the voluminous amounts of information and condense it into a page of individual tendencies as well as several offensive and defensive keys.

Scouting was a particularly challenging task during the three-day ACC Tournament. With only 24 hours or less between games, much of the scouting work was done in the week leading up to the games. The ACC teams, of course, had already been played (and scouted) twice through the season. MacKinnon, for example (whose job it was to scout Duke), had every single Duke game from the entire season on tape; and he brought each and every one with him, should the Tar Heels face the Blue Devils in the final on Sunday.

And it was rare (though not unheard of) for a team to change what it did at that late point in the season. But the continued development of players and the short time frame did make scouting a difficult, ever-changing task and sleep a luxury. "You're lucky if you get four hours of sleep a night," said MacKinnon. "Let alone see the outside of your hotel room at any time other than going to and from games."

It is rare in this day and age of scouting (with every ACC regular-season game on television) to actually see and scout a team live, but MacKinnon (who was assigned Florida State) and Wojcik (Clemson) had the opportunity as the Tigers ended the Seminoles' season 66–64 in a relatively ugly Les Robinson game Thursday night. The Tigers led by as many as eight points in the second half, lost the lead late, but regained it when Will Solomon hit a three-pointer on the break with 1:45 remaining.

As they gathered up their notebooks and play charts at the conclusion of the game, Wojcik and MacKinnon suppressed a grin. When asked if Clemson was perhaps the team the Tar Heels wanted to see all along, Wojcik could hold back a devilish smile no longer. "Oh yeah," he said. "We can't wait."

As soon as the game ended, Wojcik drove back to the hotel to prepare his scouting report on Clemson (while at the same time the players were singing "Happy Birthday" to UNC alumnus Kenny Smith at halftime of TNT's NBA broadcast). Despite having already done 30 hours of preparation on the chance they'd face the Tigers, Wojcik would get only two hours of sleep that night as he worked on the scouting report and clips tape.

Down the hallway and in his room, Doherty would get even less sleep as he watched even more Clemson tapes. With their recent play and facing an opponent they had already lost to once that season, the Tar Heels could afford to leave nothing to chance.

38

Righting a Wrong

After the Clemson loss 19 days earlier, Matt Doherty had been careful not to comment publicly on Larry Shyatt calling for a late time-out for the specific purpose of celebrating his team's win over then-No. 1 Carolina. But privately, Doherty was angered; he thought the move was at best inconsiderate and, at worst, highly unsportsmanlike. The Tigers' coach defended the calling of the time-out by saying: "That would never be a slap in anybody's face. . . . You know what, our guys haven't had a lot of pleasurable moments. So why not enjoy it for 30 to 60 seconds?"

Doherty was so disgusted by Shyatt's move that he seriously considered reciprocating should Carolina hold a late lead in its ACC Tournament rematch. The night before the game, Doherty and Roy Williams discussed the possibility via telephone, but Williams talked Doherty out of such a plan.

That didn't mean he would drop it altogether.

Coaching in his first ACC Tournament, Doherty—as he did earlier in clips of television commentators making disparaging remarks about the Tar Heels—attached the Clemson time-out celebration to the end of the scouting video, again letting the scene play out without comment during the team's get-together early Friday morning in a hotel conference room.

The coaches had barely conducted their ritual pregame, all-staff "pound" before Carolina won the tip and Kris Lang—perhaps trying to avoid another hallway "confrontation" with Doug Wojcik—beat his man to the low post, received a pass from Jason Capel, and hit a short turn-around jumper. It was two more points than Lang had scored in the last game against Clemson.

Lang continued to work hard inside, and Carolina's offense looked more fluid than it had in recent weeks, but the Tigers shot freely and ran the floor. The result was a quick tempo and an even game throughout much of the first half. On the sideline, Doherty was actively encouraging his defense; at times jumping, spreading his arms, and moving his feet as if he was on the floor. But Carolina's defense did not respond. Will Solomon and Ed Scott got free in transition and hit open jumpers, igniting Clemson's confidence and tying the score 10–10 four minutes into the game.

With every basket by the Tigers, the Georgia Dome crowd roared. The "ABC" fans (for the tournament, that meant the fans of every other team in the league) wanted an upset and cheered loudly for every UNC turnover and Clemson hoop. On the Raycom television broadcast, analyst Billy Packer commented frequently on the lack of Carolina's intensity. In the huddles, Doherty vehemently pointed out the same thing.

In an attempt to infuse some energy, Doherty substituted liberally, bringing Julius Peppers and Adam Boone into the lineup earlier than usual. Even Brian Bersticker, who hadn't played meaningful minutes in a game since the early part of the ACC regular season, played three minutes. But the half belonged to Capel, who shredded the Clemson triangle-and-two defense (the same defense that had bottled up Carolina at

Clemson) for 3 three-pointers between the 5:12 and 3:38 marks of the first half. Doherty had made a strategic decision to play Capel at the 4-spot and not Lang or Peppers, meaning Capel was left alone at the top of the key. After each made shot, Capel's confidence grew. After his third three from the same spot on the floor, Capel backpedaled down the court and admonished his teammates to get him the ball.

Solomon hit a three with 1:07 remaining in the first half, cutting Carolina's lead to 44–42. But Capel, taking advantage of Clemson's stubbornness to change its defensive strategy, again answered with a three-pointer eight seconds later. Lang, who had continued to move his feet and demand the ball inside throughout the half, scored on a three-point play inside to push Carolina to a 50–45 lead at the half.

In the locker room, Doherty alternately praised his team's offense and lambasted its defense. "We're moving the ball very well," he said. "Keep looking inside and then out. But defensively we're not taking them out of anything. Our transition defense is poor; we have to find Solomon, Scott, and Stockman on the perimeter."

Doherty took a moment to collect his thoughts before pulling the team into the center of the room. "We just have to work harder, guys!"

The Tar Heels heeded their coach's advice. After shooting almost 53 percent in the first half, Clemson came out in the second and found Carolina defenders on them immediately upon catching the ball. The increased energy and aggressiveness—fueled by a hard foul and technical on Clemson's Ray Henderson—forced the Tigers into taking bad shots. Meanwhile, Carolina continued to pass the ball well and get good looks on virtually every possession. Clemson continued to lure Carolina into trying to take three-pointers. ("Our goal was to get them to shoot 25," said Shyatt.) Capel, however, picked up where he had left off, hitting his first three-point attempt—again from the top of the key. Lang and Haywood dominated the interior (they would finish with 33 points combined). Forte also played a solid floor game, totaling seven assists.

The Tigers continued to battle, hitting some improbable and well-guarded jumpers, but when Max Owens hit a 15-footer from the baseline for an 89–73 lead with 6:26 remaining, the game was all but over.

But not the drama.

As the clock wound down and the Carolina fans filled the cavernous dome with cheers, Doherty inserted the Blue Team (Everett, Holmes, Brooker, Melendez, and Johnson). When the final buzzer sounded on UNC's 99–81 victory, Doherty and Shyatt made their way to center court for the customary handshake between coaches.

Doherty had planned what he would say next. Despite Williams having talked him out of calling his own time-outs late—and many of the Carolina players joking on the bench as the clock wound down that he should call a time-out so they could celebrate—the anger over Shyatt's late-game action on February 18 lingered. Always possessing of pride and a strong sense of what is right and wrong, Doherty could not help but point out to Shyatt what he believed was an egregious error in sportsmanship his opponent had made three weeks earlier.

The two met at midcourt and shook hands—and to the world watching on television it looked amicable enough. But it was anything but friendly. "I'll tell you one thing," said Doherty, who, at 6'7", had to lean down so the 5'8" Shyatt could hear him, "my players wanted me to call time-out with five seconds to play, but I told them we weren't going to do that."

Shyatt understood the reference, but appeared to not want to get into it with Doherty. The two parted, and Shyatt moved on to shake hands with Quartlebaum. Once there, he tried to explain his earlier action late in the game in Littlejohn. "You talk to me!" said Doherty, turning back through the crowd of players and television cameras.

"You know why I called that time-out!?" Shyatt explained. "Because I wanted our players to have one good moment. I don't think there's anything wrong with that." The exchange got more heated as both coaches talked at once. Doherty had enough and began to turn away when Shyatt called out, "I'm rubbing your nose in it and you're the No. 1 team in the nation?!"

Doherty did not answer, having already started across the court to do a postgame television interview. While the exchange was not carried live on television (Raycom/Jefferson-Pilot, in fact, cut away from the exchange as it was happening and never mentioned it at all in its broadcast, even during the on-court, postgame interview with Doherty), it was caught by several television news cameras and was replayed extensively throughout the day and during the nightly highlights shows.

It was just one more example of the fight Doherty possessed—and the type of attitude he wanted to instill in his players. "Coach, he's that type of guy," said Forte. "He's not going to take crap from anybody. You embarrass him, he's going to try to embarrass you. That's his attitude."

With a potential third matchup with Duke—a team that had thoroughly embarrassed Carolina just five days earlier—looming, Doherty hoped it would be his team's attitude, as well.

39

First Team

The quick turnaround between games in a conference tournament is not so much a test of physical fitness as it is a test of mental stamina. From the time a team arrives in the host city, days turn into nothing but sleeping, eating, and playing basketball—with hours of boredom in between. Some players read or study for classes, but the majority of time is spent watching television and lying around a hotel. It is not the glamorous life many believe it to be.

North Carolina learned of its second-round opponent at dinner, three hours after defeating Clemson. Instead of Virginia—the team many wanted to play and, hopefully, gain some measure of revenge against—it would be Georgia Tech, who had upset the Cavaliers, 74–69. The loss completed a late-season slide for Pete Gillen's club, which was pummeled by 35 points at Maryland, two games after crushing Carolina at home.

Tech was a Fred Quartlebaum–assigned team, which meant the other three assistants would grade their own game with Clemson while Coach "Q" and Doherty focused on preparing for the Yellow Jackets. At the team meeting at 10:00 Friday night, the team watched some cuts from the last UNC–Tech game. "This team is much more confident than the team we played in early February. We can't take them lightly at all, or they'll blow us out." After the team meeting, the Tar Heel players had lights-out at 11:00 P.M., while the coaches stayed up most of the night to fine-tune the game plan.

One player that had trouble sleeping was Brendan Haywood. Haywood would be matched up with Tech center Alvin Jones in the semifinals. Jones (who had a strong game against UVa in the quarterfinals of the ACC Tournament with 20 points, 12 rebounds, 6 blocks) had come on strong late in the season and been voted to the First Team All-ACC ahead of Haywood. The announcement had come earlier in the week, and had not gone unnoticed by Haywood's teammates, who playfully teased the starting center. Haywood kept very quiet on the subject; the vote by the ACC's sportswriters was further proof to him that he was never given his due by the media.

In the past, Haywood may have sulked and gone into a shell. But this, his senior season, had been different. It had been a more mature Brendan Haywood; one who hit winning free throws and blocked shots to seal wins in several key games and gave an all-out effort every game.

Many believed that Haywood's improvement was a simple case of a maturing young man. But a lot of the credit went to Doherty, whose hands-on, personal style worked well with Haywood, who thrived when he was given attention—and sometimes disappeared when he didn't. Doherty rode Haywood harder than any coach (or person) he had ever been around, but Doherty also let Haywood know how important he was to the team in a positive, nondemeaning manner. It was obvious from the first few individual workouts that Haywood was going to give a sincere, constant effort. Which is all anyone—even the media—could ever ask.

On five occasions through the season, Georgia Tech had defeated top 15 teams. But none of those upsets had been at the expense of North Carolina. On the strength of those wins, Tech had been almost assured of gaining a bid to the NCAA Tournament, but a win over Carolina would send Tech into that even with a head of steam—and would be a serious blow to the confidence of the Tar Heels heading into the NCAAs.

Despite all that was on the line—and for the second consecutive game—Doherty felt like his team did not come out with any fire. Fortunately, Tech did not play much better early, which led to both teams missing their first nine combined shots (including two free throws) of the game. Alvin Jones finally broke the ineptitude with a dunk 2:28 into the game.

Down three at the first media time-out, Doherty blasted his team for getting out-hustled. "They're getting every loose ball!!" he yelled. The Tech lead got to 10–3 (thanks to two Curry turnovers and four missed shots by Forte), with just under 14 minutes remaining in the first half, and 15–7 by the second media time-out. This time, Doherty was calmer, imploring the perimeter players to push the ball down the floor on offense. "Brendan and Kris are beating their big men down the floor," Doherty noted. "Let's get it to 'em."

After scoring his team's first five points, Haywood picked up his second foul with 12:25 remaining trying to contain Jones. Earlier in the season, Doherty may very well have taken his big man out with nearly three-quarters of the game remaining. But he thought back to the advice of Dean Smith earlier in the season, following the Michigan State game, when his old coach advised him that the more veteran players—such as the senior Haywood—knew how to play with two and even three fouls. Instead of sitting his center until the half, Doherty decided to sit Haywood (and Owens, who also had two) for a few minutes, let him get a rest, and then put him back in.

It was a decision that turned the game.

When Haywood reentered the game (when Lang went out with a twisted ankle at the 9:16 mark), he played hard and smart, scoring two quick hoops and making a key steal that erased Tech's seven-point lead. When Brian Morrison found Capel in the corner for a three-pointer (Capel's seventh in a row, going back to the Clemson game), the game was tied at 23. On the sideline, Doherty pumped his fist and bade the UNC fans to make noise. Carolina's defense tightened, forcing Tech to miss 13 shots in a row and go 4:21 without scoring.

With just over one minute remaining in the first half, Forte was trapped hard by Tech's Jon Babul and Shaun Fein. Babul reached in and knocked the ball loose and while the two players battled for the ball, got tangled up, and fell. Official Larry Rose blew his whistle and ran in, pointing at Forte. It was his third. On the sideline, Doherty lost it. He stomped his foot several times and clapped in Rose's direction. Seeing that their coach was in danger of getting a technical (Rose, notorious for a quick trigger, had begun walking over to Doherty with his whistle in his mouth) at an inopportune time, Curry, Haywood, and Morrison surrounded Rose so he could not walk any closer to engage Doherty, who had thought better of it and moved to the end of the bench.

Another official's decision—this time a no-call—went in Carolina's favor as the halftime buzzer sounded. With Julius Peppers and Alvin Jones battling for the rebound, official Duke Edsall blew his whistle a split second before the horn sounded, ending the half. Instead of making the foul call on Peppers, Edsall made the call that the horn and whistle were simultaneous, and the foul was waved off. The no-call sent Hewitt into a rage; he ran the length of the floor—right past Doherty—and got in Edsall's face.

Neither would be the last controversial call of the game.

Carolina was ahead at the half, 29–25. When he entered the locker room, Doherty was immediately approached by Haywood, who had an idea. "Coach, I think I should guard Jones from behind." Doherty thought about it and agreed. Although Jones had scored only four points, Doherty knew that Haywood playing behind—and not fighting Jones for position and perhaps picking up cheap holding fouls—made a lot of sense. "OK, Brendan," Doherty said, "good idea. Let's start playing Jones from behind."

Doherty also spoke about taking care of the ball versus Tech's half-court press, which had caused many of Carolina's 12 first-half turnovers. Otherwise, the story was the same: "We have to play harder than they do," Doherty said. "They aren't going away."

It was Carolina that came out hungry to start the second half. Thanks to continued defensive intensity (the Yellow Jackets shot just 27 percent in the first half and scored just six points in the first six minutes of the second half) and better ball movement, UNC jumped out to a 13-point lead by the first media time-out of the second half. On the sideline, however, Doherty was worried. He had watched his defense hold an NCAA-bound team without a field goal for more than 14 minutes of play, but all the Heels had been able to build was a 43–30 lead.

The tide turned two minutes later when Forte picked up his fourth foul when he went over the back of LaBarrie trying to follow his own miss. On the sideline, Doherty kneeled in front of his assistants and discussed how long they could afford to leave their best offensive player on the bench in a tight tournament game.

Fein made Doherty's decision for him. After threes by Tony Akins and Marvin Lewis cut the Carolina lead to 45–40 with 12:00 remaining, Fein, a Division II transfer who had developed into a solid ACC guard, got hot. In the span of one minute and eight seconds Fein scored eight points (he had shot just 2-for-10 from the field, and 0-for-6 from behind the arc, up to that point). After Fein hit a three to cut the lead to 50–47 at the 9:07 mark, Doherty came back with Forte. "Just go out and play hard," he said to Forte as he put him into the game. "Don't worry about fouling."

The lead was completely gone 37 seconds later when T. J. Vines hit a free throw and Curry responded by throwing a pass 10 feet over Owens's head. Robert Brooks followed with a layup—giving Tech its first lead since the 6:22 mark in the first half. The crowd, 44,000 strong, suddenly came alive—with 8/9ths of it cheering wildly for Georgia Tech.

Carolina looked to be in serious trouble.

Capel broke the UNC scoring drought, and tied the game, with a twisting layup inside. The Tar Heels took back the lead for good when Owens hit a 12-footer on the next possession. But Owens, who had provided a key spark off the bench, fouled Darryl LaBarrie on a drive with 5:30 remaining. It was Owens's fifth foul.

UNC's lead rose as high as five points to 64–59 after an acrobatic layup by Capel with just over one minute remaining, but Fein followed a free throw with a three-pointer from the left corner with 0:48 on the clock. Doherty called a timeout with Carolina ahead by one, 64–63.

After successfully breaking Tech's press, Morrison crossed halfcourt and found Forte on the wing, in front of the Carolina bench. Without hesitating, Forte drove left, but Vines, a strong and quick defender, stayed close. As he neared the baseline, Forte and Vines made contact, causing Forte to stumble and fall. Official Larry Rose did not hesitate in calling a foul on Vines. "It was a good, savvy play on my part," Forte said later in a comment that would get printed in every newspaper account of the game. "I couldn't quite get my shot up like I wanted to, so I just fell because he was so close to me. I figured I'd get the foul." (The next day, Doherty would call Rose and apologize for Forte's comments.)

Forte hit both free throws to push the lead to 66–63. Doherty called a time-out to reinforce how he wanted the Yellow Jackets who were on the floor—specifically Fein—to be guarded. When play resumed, Akins came off an on-the-ball screen and hit Vines with a perfect pass: the only problem was, Vines had just been pulled out of the game and was standing out-of-bounds. After the time-out and with Tech in a scramble situation, Peppers was able to get free for a dunk (and get away with a travel) with 0:14 on the clock, Forte added a late layup, and the game was over: 70–63 UNC.

When the wave of media bolted into the locker room 10 minutes later, Haywood fielded a flurry of questions about his outplaying of Jones, whom he had outscored by six points and held to 3-of-16 from the field. "I wanted to prove my dominance," Haywood said. "He's an all-ACC-caliber player, and, in my mind, that meant a lot of people thought he was better than me. I think I'm the best in the ACC, so I took it as a personal challenge."

Half an hour after the win (with Wojcik and MacKinnon already sitting courtside, scouting the Duke–Maryland semifinal) the players were milling around in a back hallway, watching the game on one of the jumbo screens—and rooting for the Terps. Whenever a reporter would scurry by, the players would be careful not to make any comment or give away their preferred opponent, but when the coast was clear, the preference would come out. "We know we can beat them," said Forte of Maryland. After thinking a moment, he nodded. "Of course, we know we can beat Duke, too." Just then, Maryland's Lonny Baxter hit a jumper to push the Terps' lead to 10–0—and the Tar Heels did everything they could to contain their glee.

 It hadn't been easy, but after two ragged ACC Tournament games, the prize was in front of him.

Matt Doherty had already become the first coach in league history to win a share of the ACC regular-season crown in his first season; now he had a chance to become just the second first-year coach to win an ACC Tournament title. Still, due to the 18-game win streak, the No. 1 ranking, and the unusually high expectations of Carolina fans everywhere, the season was still being touted with a "wait and see" attitude. A loss in the final to Duke (the Blue Devils would overcome its early deficit to Maryland in the semifinal and win on a tip-in by Nate James) would, without a doubt, sour the already incredible accomplishments.

The team that had been through a coaching change, had been picked third in the ACC in the preseason poll, was thought to have no point guard, team speed, or reliable outside shooter, and was beaten badly in two of its first four games was a win away from completing a sweep of the conference regular-season and tournament titles.

40

Falling Apart

Entering the most important game of his coaching career, Matt Doherty felt confident, if uneasy. Over the course of the past two games, his Tar Heels had proven resilient, winning games without playing their best basketball. But the lack of offensive flow and the sporadic defensive intensity was as perplexing to him as it would be to any coach in his situation. Both previous North Carolina coaches had gone through similar periods in their careers; Dean Smith fairly regularly in his first three seasons in Chapel Hill, Bill Guthridge as recently as last season.

Like Guthridge, Doherty was receiving no leeway from fans and media regarding the recent struggles. Both wanted to see Carolina win, particularly against Duke.

Doherty's main concerns entering the ACC Tournament final against the Blue Devils were matchups. His best defensive team often included Capel at the 4-spot, as the majority of opponents (Duke included) possessed a 4-man who was more of a small forward than a back-to-the-basket post player. But Carolina's advantage lay in its size, so the coach was faced with a conundrum: play his big lineup and risk being unable to chase Duke's three-point shooters (particularly Battier), or go small and negate his size advantage. "There are mismatches on both sides," Doherty said prior to the game. "We just have to put ourselves in position to take advantage of them."

With Duke's Carlos Boozer still in street clothes on the sideline, Doherty and Bob MacKinnon (after consulting the more than 30 Duke tapes he had brought with him) devised a game plan to attack Duke inside early. Carolina did exactly that, as Lang took Carolina's first four shots, making two. Both teams appeared to be suffering from big-game jitters, as the play was ragged and disjointed in front of the 44,000 fans, many of whom (at least two-thirds were from other schools) would have been happy to see *both* teams lose.

After missing two free throws, Haywood scored twice inside to give the Heels an early 8–7 lead. The bigger, stronger Haywood was also playing harder than Casey Sanders—which Doherty took as a very good sign. "Keep getting the ball inside!" he bellowed after the team retreated down-court after Haywood's second hoop.

When Doherty went to his bench, the tempo changed slightly. Mike Dunleavy, Duke's 6'9" guard, scored seven consecutive points against Brian Morrison, who gave up seven inches to the man he was guarding. Doherty quickly reinserted Haywood for Lang and went small, putting Capel at the 4-spot. The move stemmed the tide for a period and allowed Capel to get free for an offensive rebound dunk that cut the Duke lead to two points.

Carolina entered the second media time-out down by five, 19–14, but energized by the fact that Duke had missed six of its first nine free throw attempts. Poor free throw shooting by Duke had been a major factor in UNC's win in Cameron on February 1. A quick Forte three-pointer out of the time-out cut the lead to two and seemed to set the tone for what would be a hard-fought, back-and-forth final game between two great teams.

It never materialized.

Forte's three, which came very quickly in the possession, was a turning point, but not for the right reason. The shot added to a false belief in the Tar Heel players that they could play Duke basketball; quick shots, scrambling defense, outside-in offense. Over the next two minutes, Forte would miss a quick three, Haywood would miss an offensive put-back, and not once would a Carolina player make a post entry to Lang or Haywood.

Meanwhile, Duke—playing like Duke—started to make a run. Shane Battier and Nate James made back-to-back threes from the same spot in the right corner; forcing Doherty to call a 30-second time-out. Krzyzewski came out of the break in a half-court trap that immediately forced a bad pass from Curry that Williams turned into a dunk. Suddenly, the Duke lead was 31–20 with eight minutes remaining.

But it didn't end there. Forte forced up another quick three on a four-on-three break—with Capel open on the left wing. With the floor spread, Duke pushed it ahead to Chris Duhon for a wide-open layup. Forte missed from behind the arc again on UNC's next possession, got an offensive rebound, and missed an open 15-footer. Williams collected the rebound, pushed the ball down the floor, and found the trailing Sanders, who was fouled as he scored a layup. Two more turnovers by Lang and Boone led to a Battier three and a Williams layup.

When the dust cleared, Duke had outscored Carolina 23-to-4 over a six-and-a-half-minute span and led 42–21.

Just like that, the game was over.

The remaining 25 minutes of the game were a period of great frustration for Doherty, the players, and everyone associated with the program. For the fans, it was almost unbearable. Because its best style was a controlled, inside-out attack and a consistent defense, Carolina—like a ground-attack team in football—had no chance to come back. In the days following, many in the media would question Carolina's heart, but it was not a lack of heart that was at fault. Like a miler who had gone out and run too fast too early, Carolina simply did not have the ability to play the way the faster Blue Devils could play, no matter how much the will was pushed.

When the final horn mercifully sounded, Duke had won 79–53. Carolina had been beaten every way a team could be beaten; on the boards (Duke 54, Carolina 47), at the free throw line (18-of-32 to 10-of-14), and from the field (38 percent to 29 percent). All that was left to do was forget about it.

"We've got to get ready for the NCAA Tournament," Doherty said to the players in the locker room. It was a short address. The room was deathly silent; heads were down. "We have to put this behind us immediately. We can't afford to let this linger."

Doherty brought the team into the center of the room and ordered them to meet his eyes. "We have a goal left," he said. "We can still win the NCAA Tournament. But to do it, we have to move on right now."

41

"... Never Saw the Sun"

The mood was predictably somber at the Ritz Carlton in Atlanta, several hours after Carolina had been embarrassed by Duke in the ACC Tournament Final. The presence of the families of the coaches lightened the atmosphere somewhat—something about the laughter of three-year-old Tucker Doherty, and the sounds of infants Hattie Doherty, Paxson Wojcik, and Trey Quartlebaum, took the edge off the loss.

But just a little.

Just after 6:00 P.M. the players, team personnel, and the coaches' families (Bob MacKinnon, the only coach with school-age children, had left earlier to make the six-hour drive home with his family) were just finishing dinner and getting ready to see what fate—and the NCAA Tournament Selection Committee—would bring them.

"I have no idea what they'll do," said Doherty, who last year at the same time was agonizing with a Notre Dame team that was hoping against hope to be included among the 64 teams heading to the NCAA Tournament. That team had not made it, but Doherty and his staff were able to turn that negative into a positive as the Fighting Irish made it to the NIT Championship game. "Maybe we can still get a No. 1 seed," Forte said, trying to disappear in a corner of the couch.

At 6:30 the selection show started on a television brought into the dining room, but it would be an agonizing 15 minutes until North Carolina would appear on the screen. Greg Gumbel and Clark Kellogg of CBS ran through the East (Duke had indeed clinched the No. 1 seed in the East and would play in Greensboro) and West, with little or no reaction from any of the players. After a commercial break, the bracket-watching resumed. The Midwest was unveiled, and still no Carolina. Then the South—and Michigan State was revealed as the No. 1 seed. "We're No. 2 and in New Orleans," Doherty said in a low voice. All that was left was seeing who else would be in their draw. With the Tar Heels in News Orleans would be ... Texas ... Temple ... Florida ... Western Kentucky ... Providence ... Penn State ... and Carolina's first-round opponent would be ...

... Princeton.

When the opponent's name went on the board, the players' heads turned, trying to gauge a reaction from their teammates. For several seconds, no one said a word. Then, knowing the Tigers always seemed to either pull an upset or come close almost every year, many of the players grinned with eyes wide. Others muttered under their breath. Some were louder and more boastful, saying they were looking for-ward to it.

Drawing Princeton got the players' attention.

Doherty quickly sensed his team's trepidation and spoke about how it would be a great challenge. His thoughts turned immediately to how they needed to prepare for a Tigers team short on size, very well schooled in a difficult-to-defend style, and, coming out of the

Ivy League, relishing yet another opportunity to sling a stone at a giant.

And there was no bigger Goliath than North Carolina.

Within seconds after the bracket was unveiled on television, Bob MacKinnon's cell phone was ringing. He was just crossing the Georgia–South Carolina state line in his car, his kids in the backseat closing in on sleep and his wife reading in the passenger seat.

"Hello," he said, answering the phone.

"It's Princeton," said Fred Quartlebaum in lieu of a greeting. The players' yelps could be heard in the background.

"Where?" MacKinnon asked, already making travel plans in his head.

"New Orleans."

"Who else is there?"

"Providence and Penn State are in our side of the draw; Temple, Florida, Texas, and Western Kentucky are also there."

MacKinnon was beginning to formulate a list of people to call for scouting reports and tapes. They had prepared for Providence before while at Notre Dame (both are in the Big East). "I'll start making calls."

"So will I," said Quartlebaum. "I'll see you in the office in a little while."

The plane touched down at Raleigh-Durham Airport that night around 10:00. The "Swat Team" moved all the gear from the plane to the bus, and they were rolling within 20 minutes for the 30-minute drive to the Smith Center. When the coaches walked into the office, MacKinnon was already there, his head cradling the phone. When he hung up, he got together with the other coaches in the video room. David Cason began going through the over 800 game tapes Ben Cook had recorded off the satellite during the season.

"We've got two tapes for Princeton and about a half dozen each for Providence and Penn State, including the conference tournament games for each," announced Cason. "We'll work on getting more tomorrow."

"Good," said Doherty, snatching up one of the Princeton tapes to watch that night at home. "Let's get to work."

The coaches then split the scouting duties among the teams in their bracket and for anyone else they might see down the road in the tournament. The players, who had been buoyed by their draw, were growing increasingly positive about playing in the NCAAs—and in New Orleans.

Twice North Carolina had won national championships under Dean Smith, and twice (1982 and 1993) it had done so in New Orleans. None of the players mentioned this bit of history as few of them were aware of it. The real interest in their host city was much more what you'd expect from a group of 18–22-year-old men.

"At least we're not going to Boise, Idaho," said Haywood with a wry grin.

After leaving the office just after two o'clock in the morning, MacKinnon was up by 6:00 A.M. and in the office for a travel meeting at 7:00. Monday was an NCAA-prescribed off-day, and the Tar Heels didn't play until Friday, so the entire coaching staff concentrated on grading film (Doherty, as he always did, had watched the Duke game on a personal digital video player on the flight back) and preparing scouting reports for all the teams in their region. All day long, FedEx packages arrived with game tapes, and the coaches worked the phones, watched the game films, and made clip tapes. The players, meanwhile, straggled in to work out on their own or lift weights.

It was a hectic day that flew by. But it was not a new experience for anyone on the staff.

"The NIT came at you faster than this tournament," said Doherty. "Last year, we lost to Miami on a Friday and we had to turn around and play on a Wednesday. In the NIT you have to fly by the seat of your pants. They'll call you up and say, 'You're playing tomorrow at home against Xavier.' A lot was thrown at us last year. It was good preparation for this year."

When the long day was over, the enthusiasm was still high.

"I never saw the sun," said MacKinnon, who occupied the only office (other than Cason's) that did not have windows. "But, of course, I wouldn't have it any other way."

It might be expected that, during arguably the most frenetic time of the season, little to no time would be spent on recruiting. Nothing could be further from the truth.

In an effort to strike while the iron was hot, Doug Wojcik, Fred Quartlebaum, and Matt Doherty sent personal notes and made their one allowed call per week to the several seniors still in the mix and many juniors whom the coaching staff had targeted.

Carolina's search for a center was still project 1A for the staff. Over the course of the late season, it had become more and more obvious to the UNC coaches that DeSagana Diop, the 7'0" Senegalese center who was playing this season at Oak Hill Academy, would bypass high school and declare himself eligible for the NBA Draft. He continued to profess that his choice was not yet made, but the enthusiasm he showed during his visit to Chapel Hill (when he was cheered and chanted to during the Blue–White game) had decreased. Diop had been hurt the last few weeks of the season and would not play in any all-star games following the season, but some NBA scouts had projected him as a lottery pick, which made a serious impression on the young man from Africa, who had not grown up dreaming of one day playing college basketball. But the allure of becoming instantly rich was universal.

UNC and Virginia were still in the mix, Diop told the coaches and media who covered recruiting, but all signals were he was a lost cause.

The other player the coaches had focused on was David Harrison of Brentwood Academy in Tennessee. Not as physically developed as Diop, Harrison was still a very talented 6'11" center who fit the Doherty mold as an athlete: long, lean, and quick. Harrison's interest in North Carolina had increased as the year progressed. It was largely a contest between hometown Vanderbilt, where Harrison's father was a defensive line coach for the Commodores; and Colorado, where Harrison's brother D.J., was the leading scorer for the Buffaloes. On his visit to Chapel Hill for the Maryland game, Harrison—a quiet, introspective, and intelligent young man—had been impressed with the coaches and players. "It's going to be hard to get him away from Vanderbilt," thought Jon Holmes, who had been one of Harrison's hosts. "But I think he liked us."

Doherty had picked up his wooing of Harrison, and it seemed to be working. A boost to the effort came accidentally when North Carolina hired John Bunting as its new football coach. Bunting, it turned out, had played in the NFL with Harrison's father. The square-built coach even sat next to Harrison's mother during the Maryland game.

The fact that Harrison's other two choices—Colorado and Vanderbilt—were not in the NCAA Tournament was not lost on the Carolina coaches in their call to Harrison that week.

As for juniors, Carolina had singled out several high-profile players and was aggressively recruiting them. Atop the list was Latta's own Ray Felton (whose entire school had been in Doherty's office after the Georgia Tech game). Felton would commit to North Carolina a few weeks later.

Other current high school juniors on Carolina's list included top-recruit Shavlik Randolph of Raleigh's Broughton High School. Proving his recruiting creativity had not lessened, Doherty would convince Michael Jordan to don a "Shav's Country" T-shirt (worn by Randolph's high school classmates during games) for a photo that Doherty would send to Randolph.

Felton, Randolph, and the other junior recruits further reflected Doherty's philosophy to recruit the best athletes he could find. The more, the better.

It was a bruised and battered Carolina team that prepared for the NCAA Tournament and their first-round opponent, Princeton. Lang, who spent more time with trainer Marc Davis than he did with his teammates, was still suffering the lingering effects of the

ankle he sprained against Tech in the ACC semifinals. It was also discovered that Capel had chipped a bone in his left wrist against Duke.
Many other players were nursing minor injuries.

After watching the Duke film several times, Doherty, like many fans
and media, had been disappointed in the team's effort. "We're in the
process of licking our wounds," Doherty said. "We have a quiet group.
You look [and ask] who's the best leader on the team? To have good
leaders, you have to have followers. Sometimes, we haven't had that one
guy that can snap everybody in line. A lot of times, that falls to me. It
should start with me, but you need somebody in the locker room that
supports that and has some charisma that people will listen to.
Sometimes it's there and sometimes it might not be there. It's something
you try to massage every day.

"We've got good players; we just need to click again. And that can happen again in the matter of a game or a half. . . . We are confident we can fix
it. There hasn't been a fight or anything like that [among the players]. There
is a respect among everyone on the team. We're all in this together."

While there may not have been any fights among the members of
the team, there was one issue that needed resolving. Prior to practice on
Tuesday, Doherty called Forte and Capel into his office for a frank discussion on the dynamics of the team as a whole—and the relationship
between the two of them, in particular. Forte admitted being stung by
Capel's public comments after the Virginia game, when Capel said that
"some people took shots and some didn't," believing that Capel was
referring to him specifically. Capel assured Forte that he meant nothing
by the comment and apologized, saying that he was just frustrated.

The issue was further resolved by the two players immediately after
they left Doherty's office. "Joe and I talked and everything was cool,"
said Capel. "We talked again on the phone that night to make sure. We
were just frustrated, that's all. None of us liked losing. There was nothing wrong between Joe and me."

After their conversation, the relationship between Capel and Forte
was patched up. Much had been made about a perceived problem

between the two, but, in truth, they were fairly close friends. They may not have spent every moment together, but they were most definitely friends and could count on one another at any time.

Hard practices were one of the remedies Doherty and his staff utilized to try to cure the recent disease of losing—as was bringing the team together for dinner on Tuesday night. During practice, Jim Everett once again took on the role of playing the opponent's key player—this time it was Nate Walton, son of Bill Walton, legendary UCLA and NBA player. This time Everett did not need to add any temporary tattoos (as he had earlier when he was getting into the character of Maryland's Lonny Baxter); Walton was a fundamentally sound if undersized center who often stepped out to the three-point line to shoot or, more often, to find cutting teammates.

Brendan Haywood would draw the challenging assignment of guarding Walton, meaning he would have to step out, move his feet, and contest outside shots. It was a task to which he was unaccustomed, requiring a good deal of prodding and motivation from Doherty during practices held on Tuesday and Wednesday afternoons.

As he walked out of the basketball office and made his way to the bus that would take the team to the airport following practice on Wednesday, Doherty, his briefcase slung over his shoulder, gazed up at the large 6-by-5-foot photo he had had installed on the wall earlier in the year. It was a shot of the famous game winner that Michael Jordan hit from out on the left wing during the 1982 NCAA title game versus Georgetown, with Doherty in the background, standing in the lane, his hands up at his shoulders on the off-chance Jordan passed instead of shot.

"People ask me where I was when Michael Jordan hit that shot," joked Doherty. "I was wide-open at the foul line, but he didn't pass me the ball. Michael wanted tickets [to the NCAA Tournament game with Princeton] and I told him no because I'm still mad at him."

Three hours later the team plane touched down in the same city that produced the most memorable game in the program's storied history—and this time the ball would be in Doherty's hands.

Knockout

In the midst of preparing for the NCAA Tournament, it was not hard for Carolina to forget the struggles of the past few weeks. The excitement of a brand-new opportunity to prove themselves put a bounce in the step of the players. "We did it last year when no one thought we could," said Haywood. "We can definitely do it again."

For the coaches, the burden of fixing the problems that led to those struggles, however, was causing more than a few headaches. "I think they really rallied around Coach Guthridge last year," said Doherty. "I hope we can rally again. I don't know what the rallying cry should be this year. We shouldn't have to search for a rallying cry. It should be a matter of pride. It should be an opportunity to win. It should be the feeling they got last year from going to the Final Four and wanting that feeling again."

The Tar Heels' stay in New Orleans had begun with some free time on Bourbon Street, the players breaking into small groups and heading off on their own. As it so happened, Carolina's team hotel, Le Meridien, was just steps from the French Quarter. The proximity did not concern Doherty. "We wanted to give them some free time, but we had our normal pregame curfew. It's important guys get a feel for the excitement of a Final Four. It will be good for us."

As the players headed out for a few hours away from basketball, the staff spent a few hours with their families, most of whom had made the trip down with the team. Doherty and his wife, Kelly, had dinner alone in a romantic bistro a few blocks down from the hotel.

By midnight, all the players were in their rooms (all made the mandatory curfew) while the coaches settled into Doherty's hotel room for a late-night film session. "You have to understand that Princeton's pretty good," Doherty said, getting back to business. "They've played some pretty good folks. I'd love to win by one point. We understand that the game could be in the 40s or the low 50s, and we have to be ready for that."

As they had prior to the ACC Tournament in Atlanta a week earlier, the Tar Heels held an open practice on Thursday in which they did little more than some full-court drills to get the legs moving, shooting drills, and free throws. Later, they would walk through Princeton's methodical, back-door offense at a closed practice at Tulane.

While the team stretched on the Superdome floor, Doherty (after his usual stroll around the wide circle of players, giving each a "pound") casually grabbed a ball off the rack and dribbled to a spot on the left wing, in front of the bench that would be used by the home team. His toes on the three-point line, Doherty began launching set shots from the exact same spot on the floor as Michael Jordan's game-and-championship winning shot almost 19 years earlier.

"I missed the 1985 Final Four, but from '86 on I've been to every Final Four since," Doherty said. "That includes when I wasn't coaching. A lot has happened in a short period of time. I went to Davidson in '89 and one thing led to another and here I am, the head coach at North Carolina, coaching in New Orleans in the NCAA Tournament. It's exciting. . . . I hope my team comes out and performs well, plays hard and advances."

After stretching, the players broke out their best dunks during two-line layups. Julius Peppers and Orlando Melendez wowed those in attendance—and even their own teammates—with several impressive efforts. But the highlight of the warm-ups came when 7'6" Neil Fingleton, coming in from the left side, jumped as high as he could (several inches, at least), cupped the ball in his left hand, and, after actually *landing on both feet*, threw down a windmill dunk. While his teammates erupted in laughter and bent over at the waist, Fingleton, in on the joke, went around and chest-bumped his teammates.

Even the coaching staff broke up.

The end of practice was equally as entertaining, with the entire team (coaches included) lining up at the top of the key for a game of knock-out. The game's rules are simple: everyone forms a single-file line, with the first two players having basketballs. The first player in line shoots, and, if he misses and the second shooter hits, the first shooter is "knocked out." "The key is to get in front of a bad shooter," said MacKinnon.

After a protracted battle, Jon Holmes bested Joe Forte. More important, the team was as loose and together as it had been all season.

North Carolina began its 27th consecutive NCAA Tournament (by far the longest such streak in the nation) with a flurry. Princeton, a team coached by the son—John Thompson III—of the man Dean Smith's 1982 NCAA champs defeated, did not start a player over 6'7". As a team, the Tigers had not dunked once *during the entire season*. Jason Capel, the Tar Heels' 3-man, was about an inch taller than the Tigers' tallest player.

"We just hope they have an off-night while at the same time we can't do anything wrong," said Thompson prior to the game.

Thompson, certainly, had a reason to worry. He had ascended to the head coach's job after Bill Carmody had bolted for Northwestern in September. In addition to losing their coach, the Tigers also suffered when center Chris Young opted to forego his remaining college basketball career and instead threw his name into the baseball draft. (The Ivy League prohibits a pro in one sport to compete as an amateur in another.) In addition, Princeton's best outside scoring threat transferred to UCLA.

While it was not one of the more talented Princeton teams that would take the floor against Carolina, it was still dangerous due, of course, to its renowned patient style of play that balanced adept outside shooting with quick passing and back-door cuts.

It was a style that obviously concerned the coaching staff.

"I've seen some quality teams try to speed them up," Doherty said. "Xavier is a very good pressure defensive team with great quickness and forces 20-something turnovers a game. Princeton only had about 11 against them. They handle pressure very well. They invite pressure. You have to understand that they are going to take the whole shot clock to get the shot they want. You have to be mentally tough to hang in there for 35 seconds per possession on defense. People talk a lot about being patient on offense, but you have to be patient on defense, too, because a lot of times you get anxious and go for a steal that's not there and you're giving up a back-door layup."

Doherty had decided by the team's pregame meal that he would start Peppers instead of Lang, who was still hobbling from the leg injury he suffered in the ACC Tournament. "He probably should have played more in Atlanta, but I also don't think he was as sharp in Atlanta," said Doherty of Peppers. "I think he'd be the first to admit that. Kris hadn't practiced all week because of his leg, so I thought it would be good to start Pep because they were a little quicker, [they have] more perimeter players, and Pep does a good job of chasing guys around. Then, when Brendan gets tired, put in Kris as opposed to Kris and Brendan getting tired at the same time. Then, give Brendan a break and slide Cape to the four."

But substitution rotation wasn't the only thought in Doherty's mind. He knew his team needed to regain a spark. He thought back to when the Heels were playing well and wondered how he could recapture that swagger. "The best game we played all year was against Maryland, and Pep started," Doherty explained. "Maybe this would wake Pep up, too. And then it might just wake our team up."

Whether it was Peppers starting, the looseness that came from giving the players some free time, or the Louisiana air ("I did spit in the Mississippi for good luck," admitted Doherty), the Tar Heels started the game looking sharp and playing hard.

After winning the tip, Carolina executed a picture-perfect offensive possession, swinging the ball around the perimeter twice before finding Haywood inside. The seven-footer was quickly swarmed and kicked it out to Curry, who found Forte, who found the bottom of the net with a three-pointer. With Haywood heeding his coach's not-so-gentle prodding in chasing Nate Walton all over the floor, Princeton found the going tough on its offensive end. A Haywood block and three consecutive missed three-pointers by Princeton—followed by a Curry layup in transition and a Capel three-pointer on the other end—put the Tar Heels in front early, 8–0.

The first 10 minutes were close to perfect for Carolina, despite giving up some signature back-door cuts to the Tigers. But it was obvious early that this was not a great Princeton team. With a record of 16–10 in a weaker-than-usual Ivy League, Thompson's squad, despite fighting hard, was woefully overmatched from the beginning. It didn't help that Carolina was playing at midseason form, moving the ball inside-out and being patient on defense. A switch to a zone by Doherty midway through the first half caused Princeton to score only once in 12 possessions and effectively ended any chance of an upset.

Up 23–8 with eight minutes remaining, Doherty was able to go deep into his bench, using Will Johnson, Adam Boone, and Brian Morrison extensively. When the starters did return, all semblance of the last month's struggles appeared to have disappeared. So did any appearance of animosity between Forte and Capel. Following yet another missed three by the Tigers (this time it was freshman Andre Logan from the top of the key), Curry pushed the ball ahead, finding Capel at the top of the key for a quick three-pointer. The shot missed, but Haywood, hustling the length of the floor, gathered in the offensive rebound and kicked it out to Forte, who was wide-open on the opposite wing.

But instead of shooting what would have been a perfectly legitimate shot in anyone's mind, Forte one-touched a pass to Capel, who had moved into the lane, just under the free throw line. Capel's 12-footer found nothing but net, and, as Princeton called a time-out, Capel and Forte chest-bumped one another as the Heels sprinted for the huddle.

So much for team dissension.

A 36–16 halftime lead (the lowest point total by an opponent all season) forced Doherty to dust off his let's-win-the-second-half speech. "You knew they were going to make a little bit of a run and they did and I thought we answered it," said Doherty after the game. "No sense in panicking, because if you panic guys will sense that. I thought we did a good job of answering their runs. We took some bad shots, we turned the ball over a little bit, but in the end we came through."

The final was a workmanlike 70–48 first-round win—despite a 13-point explosion by Princeton's Ed Persia in the second half—that produced a relieved coach and players. Even the Blue Team—Brooker, Everett, Holmes, Bersticker, and Melendez—got into the game with 1:13 remaining. Just enough time for Everett to dive into media row for a loose ball and have his name uttered by Billy Packer.

As he always did, however, Doherty took no time to enjoy his first-ever NCAA Tournament win. Instead, he began thinking about the second-round opponent—Penn State had surprised many by beating Providence earlier in the afternoon—as he was walking off the floor after the Princeton win.

For the players, as it was for the coach, the win was a relief. "This is definitely a good game to get us back on track. A lot of teams were going down in the first round," said Haywood, memories of Weber State undoubtedly in his mind. "We didn't want to be one of those teams."

Doherty was more reserved in his judgment.

"We were better today, but we have to sustain it and get our rhythm back for a full game," said Doherty later that night. "We have some big goals."

43

"... I Gave It My Best Effort"

The first weekend of the NCAA Tournament is a showcase for the midmajor schools and a potential nightmare for programs from the major conferences. The equation is simple: the smaller the school, the less pressure to advance; the larger the school (and the stronger the tradition), the more pressure to avoid the upset. Consequently, the midmajor schools—some of which are very good basketball teams—play looser and more open, creating a flurry of "upsets" over big schools that are expected to win, and thus play much tighter.

No team in America has played better—when the pressure is at its height in March—than North Carolina.

Seventeen times in the past 19 years the Tar Heels had reached the Sweet Sixteen. The predictable results of such a run are incredibly high—and often unfair—expectations. Anything short of a Final Four is considered a failure—and sometimes, even that isn't good enough.

Bill Guthridge had led the program to two such finishes in his three seasons at the helm and was rewarded by ever-increasing pressure to retire.

The pressure of outside expectations was nothing new to Matt Doherty as a player, but as a head coach, it was a situation for which he could never have prepared. In truth, no person could prepare himself to be in the North Carolina fishbowl, leading America's most-watched and analyzed college basketball program, no matter what that coach's background. Of course, the outside pressure didn't measure up to the internal drive Doherty possessed; a truth that was easily discernible by the dark circles under the head coach's eyes and the increasing volume of gray hair that appeared as the season progressed.

"We're under a lot of stress," Doherty admitted during the day in between the first- and second-round NCAA Tournament games. "You put a lot of energy into trying to coach a basketball team. I hope we play for a few more weeks, and then after that I think I deserve to go play any golf course in North Carolina I want to play."

Carolina's second-round opponent would be Penn State, a school much better known for its powerhouse football program under legendary coach Joe Paterno than for its basketball program. The reverse similarities between the two schools were not lost on the players. "Penn State basketball is a lot like North Carolina football. Neither gets a whole lot of attention because of Penn State football and North Carolina basketball," observed Joe Crispin, the Nittany Lions' starting point guard and team leader.

Doherty, one year removed from a similar position at Notre Dame, concurred. "It's a tough situation. It's kind of on the outskirts of the Big Ten. It's somewhere where football is very important, and I dealt with that at Notre Dame."

In its less-than-glorious basketball history, Penn State had reached the NCAA Tournament on eight occasions and had only once advanced to the Final Four: in 1954. Not one Nittany Lion had played in an NCAA Tournament game. Penn State was hardly a basketball factory; the basketball media guide devoted an entire page to Calvin Booth,

Penn State's "first-ever NBA second-round draft pick." By comparison, North Carolina had produced 29 *first-round* selections.

But the Nittany Lions were hardly a pushover. As the 11th member of the Big Ten, Coach Jerry Dunn's squad had, in past years, taken its lumps in the rugged conference. But in 2000–2001, Penn State had slugged back, starting with a five-point win at Kentucky in late November—one week before the Wildcats came into the Smith Center and spanked the Tar Heels. The Nittany Lions went on to beat Temple (a team that would go on to the Elite Eight) out of conference and Illinois and Michigan State in conference. The latter victory occurred in the Big Ten Tournament semifinals just eight days before Penn State would take the floor against North Carolina.

By that time, Doherty had watched the tape of that game (along with games against Iowa, Wisconsin, and the first-round win over Providence) almost around the clock following the Princeton game. "They're a different team because they're experienced," said Doherty prior to his team's practice on Saturday. "[Gyasi] Cline-Heard is a different player this year. He's really improved. The confidence they have. They beat Kentucky; we lost to Kentucky. They beat Michigan State; we lost to Michigan State. They're a darn good basketball team."

During his preparations with his staff (Doug Wojcik had the scout for Penn State), Doherty confided that he was very worried about the Nittany Lions, not because of the way they were playing or their confidence in coming from the Big Ten, but because his Tar Heels were far from playing their best. "We came out well against Princeton, but we regressed some in the second half," Doherty said. "We're still not clicking completely." Doherty's biggest concern was the effort. At times, he believed that the effort was there, but the execution was poor. At other times, he felt the effort lacked—a reality he couldn't accept. He knew he had pushed hard over the course of the last month.

But the NCAA Tournament was no place to back off. The players seemed relaxed and loose through the closed practice on Saturday and into Sunday. "I like the look in our kids' eyes," said Doherty. "I think they're focused. I think they're attentive. I didn't feel like we were for maybe that month's stretch, but I think we're back on the same page."

It would be the fifth consecutive Sunday on which Carolina had played—with the previous four ending in losses. Try as he might not to succumb to superstition, Doherty nonetheless wore St. Patrick's Day beads over the weekend in an attempt to bring the luck of the Irish to the Heels. (Earlier in the season, during the 18-game winning streak, Doherty had taken to entering and exiting rooms in his house using the same route each time so as not to tempt fate.)

It was the first weekend of the NCAA Tournament, and Carolina, like the other remaining 31 teams, needed all the luck it could get.

The mood of the starters from both teams as they took to the floor for the final NCAA Tournament game of the weekend in the Superdome was one of contrasts. In an atmosphere largely devoid of energy—any noise made by the 12,684 in attendance dissipated in the cavernous dome-like dandelion spores in the wind—the Penn State players appeared almost giddy, smiling and chest-bumping each other as they came out of the huddle. Out of the other huddle came the Tar Heels, serious-minded with the facial expressions to match. The pressure was most definitely on Carolina, as a win over UNC would constitute the greatest victory in Penn State athletics that did not involve an oblong ball—a prospect that many in Penn State blue and white still considered more a dream than a potential reality.

The first few minutes of the game did nothing to portend that history would not hold up. As it had against Princeton, Carolina was determined to get the ball inside to start the game. "We wanted to make sure we shared the ball and got it inside, and I thought we did a good job of that," said Doherty after the Princeton win. In preparation for the second round, Doherty had obviously noted the size and strength disparity and designed a similar game plan.

And Brendan Haywood responded. In addition to scoring six of Carolina's first nine points, he also intimidated Penn State's front line with two blocked shots in the game's first three and a half minutes. After Haywood's second block, Joe Forte was able to get free in transition, make a pretty behind-the-back dribble move, and hit a 15-footer to push the early lead to 11–4 and force Jerry Dunn to call a 30-second time-out.

On the bench, Doherty had the fleeting thought that maybe, just maybe, his team was back in the groove.

Doherty gave Haywood a needed break, and Penn State, finding the middle suddenly open, took advantage. Two dunks and a 15-footer by Gyasi Cline-Heard—the player Doherty feared even more than Joe Crispin, the Lions' all–Big Ten point guard—and a layup by 6'8" Tyler Smith brought Penn State back to within three at 19–16. In their first-round win the Tar Heels had dominated an all-important segment of the game—the four minutes between the first and second media time-outs. But Penn State—accustomed to hard-fought, physical games—did not panic.

Thanks to Cline-Heard's play, the Lions' confidence grew. Titus Ivory, a guard who had grown up in Charlotte and dreamed of being a Tar Heel, hit his first jumper to pull Penn State to within three, 27–24. The momentum was beginning to swing. Penn State, mixing up its zone and man-to-man, began to make it tougher for UNC to get the ball to its front-court players, who had scored all but 5 of the team's first 19 points. When senior Max Owens took an ill-advised jumper after no passes in the offense, Doherty chided his senior guard for taking bad shots. On the other end, Penn State's perimeter players had been missing shots early, but Joe Crispin had surprised Curry with his quickness. It appeared that it was only a matter of time before Jon Crispin, bigger but not nearly as dangerous as his older brother, and Ivory began to find the range.

After Ivory's three-pointer at the 7:30 mark, the game became a struggle to gain a stronghold. Carolina dominated on the boards, grabbing 20 rebounds to Penn State's four, but sloppy turnovers—the Tar Heels would give up the ball 12 times in the first half against little to no pressure from Penn State—by Curry and Peppers meant Carolina could not sustain any offensive consistency.

Cline-Heard, his confidence growing by the minute, scored inside on a twisting reverse layup to give Penn State its first lead, 30–29, at the 5:35

mark. Ivory hit another three from the right wing 30 seconds later to push the lead to four points. Its inside game getting shut down, Carolina began to rely on Forte and Capel (and Curry, who banked in a three-pointer), who answered jumpers by Joe Crispin and Ivory with shots of their own. When Curry found Haywood for a dunk 10 seconds before the half, Carolina had regained the lead, 40–39. It would stay that way into the halftime, as Joe Crispin's 27-footer bounced off the front rim.

The two teams left the floor as they had come onto it: Carolina dour and concerned; Penn State elated and energized.

At the half, Doherty talked about little other than turnovers. "We shot 56 percent in the first half," he said to his staff, "but we should be getting more shots." The turnovers, Doherty noted to the team, were the result of sloppy play against a physical and athletic team. "We knew coming in they'd be a physical team. We've got to match their physical play and be strong when the ball gets into the post," Doherty said. He called the players into the middle of the locker room, where they all put their hands together up high and waited for one last point of emphasis.

"Take care of the ball and we'll win this game."

In the other locker room, the Penn State players felt it was their game to win. Joe Crispin, the Nittany Lions' leading scorer, had shot just 3-for-10 from the field. They could run their offense largely unimpeded (Penn State only turned the ball over three times in the first half), and it was only a matter of time until their shots began falling. "You get a feel for the game after a while," said Joe Crispin. "In the first five minutes [of the game] I knew we could beat them."

The game continued to be a grind-it-out affair through the first three minutes of the second half. But then Joe Crispin hit a three on a nifty step-back on the right wing to push the Nittany Lions out to a 49–44 advantage with just over 17 minutes remaining. And then the Tar Heels' offense crossed the thin line from grinding to a full-blown breakdown, scoring just once—on a layup by Lang—over the next five minutes of play. Thanks to solid defense—Penn State could only manage six points over that same span—Carolina was able to stay within striking distance, down just nine points before Peppers' two free throws broke the drought and pulled the Heels to within seven with 12:53 remaining.

The rather small Carolina contingent—many fans had elected to hold off on traveling to New Orleans and instead had decided to catch up with the Heels in Atlanta for the South Regional—held its breath. Reserves Brian Morrison and Max Owens did little to raise the level of Carolina's play. On the sideline, Doherty continued to inspire intensity on defense, but how does a coach will a team to make better decisions, to play with more flow? It's like a dance instructor admonishing a pupil to have more rhythm. On the CBS broadcast, Billy Packer began to, once again, question Carolina's heart. But it wasn't heart that was lacking; it was confidence and trust in each other.

Over and over, Carolina's offensive possessions ended with dropped passes, missed short jumpers followed by missed tip-ins, air ball layups, or offensive goaltending calls. Forte, who had so often bailed out the offense during similar situations, was just as out-of-sync, forcing jump-shots and missing runners. With 13:00 remaining, Forte had made just 2-of-9 shots.

But the Tar Heels did not quit. In fact, it was the determination of the coach and the players that pushed them through the frustration to play the kind of defense that kept them in the game. A Peppers layup with 10:09 remaining cut the deficit to 57–53. Following a Cline-Heard bucket inside, Ivory picked up his fourth foul trying to defend Morrison on a drive. Another Peppers hoop inside seemed to give UNC's offense some juice. After a rain-making three by Jon Crispin gave Penn State a 60–53 lead, Forte scored on a signature twisting shot inside. Suddenly, the Tar Heels appeared to be poised to recapture their confidence on offense with Forte leading the way.

But Forte, a consensus first-team All-American and Carolina's designated go-to guy, would not score another point.

North Carolina's run continued, cutting into Penn State's lead slowly and steadily, until Haywood broke through the invisible ceiling on a drop-step layup while being fouled by Joe Crispin. It was Haywood's first basket since the first-half-ending dunk. The ensuing free throw tied the game at 62–62 with 7:25 remaining.

UNC's lead swelled to four points on layups by Lang and Curry. Another defensive stop gave Carolina the ball with under five minutes remaining and a chance to take control of the game. Running its secondary break, Carolina got the ball exactly where it wanted it; on the right block to Lang, who quickly attempted a jump-hook.

No good.

Lang immediately put his head down and sprinted back on defense where Cline-Heard, obviously tired, used his right arm to push Lang to try to gain position. Official Reggie Greenwood, however, called the foul on Lang. Even Packer wondered how the call could go against Lang: "That's a foul on Lang?!" he barked on TV.

It was Lang's fourth foul. On the next two Penn State possessions, Ivory, also playing with four fouls, answered with two free throws and a three to give Penn State back a one-point lead. After two more free throws by Cline-Heard (following Haywood's fourth foul), Capel scored in the lane to make the score 71–70, Penn State, with 3:29 remaining in the game.

Then came the possession that ended Carolina's season.

It began innocently enough. Joe Crispin walked the ball up, content to use as much of the shot clock as Penn State could against Carolina's man-to-man defense. The clock crossed the 3:00 mark as Brandon Watkins, a little-used backup guard, missed a three-pointer from the left wing. But the rebound bounced to Cline-Heard, who handed it off to Joe Crispin. As he penetrated, looking for an open teammate on the perimeter, Dunn screamed for patience from the sideline. Crispin got it back and called a play; a high on-ball screen for himself. But Haywood blocked Crispin's layup attempt out of bounds with 0:08 on the shot clock and 2:30 on the game clock. An out-of-bounds underneath play resulted in a deep three attempt, again by Joe Crispin, that bounced off the front rim.

But again the rebound went to a Nittany Lion, this time to the 6'1" Watkins, who got around a block-out attempt by Curry. Dunn called for his team to spread the floor before, with 0:13 on the shot clock, Watkins got around Forte and found Smith for a short baseline jumper that went through the net with 2:02 remaining in the game. Penn State had run a full minute and a half off the clock and now led 73–70. "That possession characterized what our team is about," said Dunn later. "We wanted it more."

A tired and erratic Carolina team answered with two critical mistakes.

First, Haywood took the ball out. In Carolina's system, it is the 4-man who takes the ball out, but with Haywood panicking and grabbing the ball on the baseline, it forced Peppers to move to the free throw line. Penn State was pressing, and Cline-Heard was blanketing Curry, so Haywood hit the only open man, Peppers. Already with six turnovers, Peppers tried to force it to Curry, but it was swatted away and stolen by Watkins. Following a 30-second time-out by Dunn, Joe Crispin split a Carolina double-team and found Ivory, who buried an 18-footer for a 75–70 lead with 1:29 remaining. In over two minutes of game time, Carolina had handled the basketball for approximately three seconds.

The game was over. Carolina tried to force turnovers in the last minute with a half-court trap, but Penn State was too smart and too good. When the buzzer sounded, Carolina had been beaten, 82–74. There would be no storybook ending.

The season was over.

The locker room assigned to North Carolina at the Superdome could have been located in any high school in the country. In front of the iron mesh lockers, on wooden benches, sat all of the players, silent, with heads bowed. No one looked up or spoke, because there was nothing to say or do. Sixty-four of the 65 teams in the NCAA Tournament ended their seasons this way; with a loss as jarring as an automobile crashing into a brick wall. No matter how successful a season or a tournament run was, the finality of it being over produces a unique and heart-wrenching scene; young men realizing that, for many, their lives will never be the same.

As miserable as all of the players felt about losing, all but Haywood, Owens, Michael Brooker, and Jim Everett knew that, if they chose to, they'd have this experience again. But it wouldn't be together, with the same bunch of guys. It was not the pain of a loss that they all felt (although they themselves believed it was) but the sudden realization that the people with whom you had shared so much in your life would no longer be there at the same level.

Several players cried, as did their coach, Matt Doherty. Not much was said; words are rarely heard through the veil of emotions following the last game. After just 10 minutes, the door at the end of the locker room burst open, and the media rushed in like the bulls at Pamplona to record the moment. The more than two dozen television videographers were the most aggressive, pushing and elbowing each other in front of the most distraught and/or star players.

Suffering sells.

"When we took care of the ball, we got the ball inside," Capel said into the bank of cameras and bright lights, his voice barely audible. "We just gave up the ball too much."

"It's bigger than losing a game," said Peppers. "We had a close team. That's the sad part. We didn't want to lose, but never being together as a team . . . that's hard."

Fifty yards down the hall, Forte and Haywood sat on a podium and gamely addressed even more media during the postgame press conference. Both spoke to the high number of Carolina turnovers (21) and gave credit to the opponent. Haywood, distrustful of the press on his best days, gave a glimpse into his thoughts regarding his mercurial career at Carolina. "I've had a lot of good times and a lot of bad times at this university. Obviously, this is one of those bad times. I've had a lot of good moments here, and I was happy with my career here, and I made a lot of good friends."

Haywood looked over at Forte for a moment and grinned. "I've met a lot of different coaches. I'll always have a lot of context, I guess."

Off in the wings, Doherty, his tie tight around the neck of his sweat-stained white shirt, studied a stat sheet. On it, he saw Carolina advantages in all but two areas of the game: turnovers and three-point shooting. His thoughts were still on the immediate past, about what he could have done to stem the tide during his team's offensive struggles during the middle 10 minutes of the second half. As for the larger questions, there would be time to analyze what happened to the team that was No. 1 in the nation just five Sundays ago.

When the players were done, Doherty straightened his back and braced himself to face the music. Sitting in the crowd, out of Doherty's sight, were a number of Carolina athletic administrators, including Athletic Director Dick Baddour, the man who had taken the reigns of the hiring process from Dean Smith following Roy Williams' decision to remain at Kansas more than eight months earlier. It was Baddour, as much as anyone, who had put Doherty in this position.

Doherty walked to the dais, patted both Haywood and Forte on the back, and sat down. After crediting Penn State and speaking to the turnovers, the inevitable questions came about where the season went wrong. It wasn't long before the always-emotional coach was fighting through tears.

"My expectations are higher than anybody's in this room . . . so . . . you judge . . . you judge effort. I thought our effort was very good. One thing I congratulated our team on today, there were a couple times this year where we gave in. As hard as it is for me to admit that, we did. But we didn't give in today. There's one lesson we learned from athletics this year is—not to steal a Jimmy Valvano line—but not to give up. I don't think we did today. We had some great moments. We were ranked No. 1 in the country. We had an 18-game winning streak, which was the second highest winning streak in the country, the fourth or fifth highest winning streak in Carolina history. We beat Duke at Duke, Maryland twice, Wake Forest at home, which was an exciting win. UCLA at UCLA. We had some great moments."

He spoke to the disappointment he felt that the team did not react well after reaching No. 1. And he spoke about expectations.

"I know at North Carolina you're not really content unless you win a national championship. But I can't fault the guys' effort. You try to play up to your potential and look yourself in the mirror and say, 'We gave a good effort. We put in a good day's work and a good year's work.' I think for the most part we did a pretty good job. We just didn't play well at the right time, and that's at the end of the season."

The moderator called for one last question, which came from a veteran beat writer often critical of the program. How would Doherty grade the team's performance on the season? And how would Doherty grade his own performance?

About the team, Doherty said: "Well . . . we want to win the whole thing. It's hard for me to sit here and feel satisfied right now. As you put distance between the loss you do get to see a bigger picture."

And about his own performance, Doherty struggled to fight back emotion and find the words: "The only thing I'll tell you . . . is I gave it my best effort."

The Superdome crowd was long gone when Joseph Forte stood from his stool in the locker room, slung his duffel bag over his shoulder, and headed for the door. His Tar Heel teammates were already on the bus that would take them to the airport and, eventually, home. It was a trip none of them thought would occur so early in March.

With a customary grin and in a lower-than-normal voice, Forte had answered all of the reporters' questions about the team's late-season slide and his own future. He did not seem haunted by the loss, as other players had, many of whom had stared blankly at the floor or the walls in stunned silence. Like every development that had occurred throughout the season, Forte seemed to take it in stride, holding his head up high as he walked outside the locker room and toward the deserted court.

"The past six games have been tough," Forte said. "I felt as if all the teams we've played have focused on me. It's been very frustrating."

He went on to talk about the decision that faced him; the one so many reporters had already asked him about: Would he leave North Carolina for the NBA? Throughout the year, he would tell anyone who listened that he dreamed about playing in the league constantly; "every morning when I wake up," he'd said. He wanted to discuss his options with his mother (who had left her job at Hewlett-Packard and taken one with Octagon Sports Marketing—an agency that represented professional athletes) and his brother, who would be heading to Brown the next year. He would also listen to Matt Doherty and to Dean Smith, who would utilize his extensive network to gain information for Forte on his draft prospects.

Forte thought back to the first time he met Doherty when his new coach stopped by his house in Rockville, Maryland, to speak with his mother and him just a few days after taking the job. Doherty had greeted him with a "pound" and asked him, "What's up, dog?" Forte smiled at the memory. "I knew then it was going to be different."

As the year progressed, Doherty rode Forte as hard as anyone (except for maybe Brendan Haywood). Forte, self-described as "not a rah-rah guy," reacted well to the more aggressive extrinsic motivation when the team won and he was scoring, but when his shot began misfiring and the team struggled, he found the criticism tougher to take.

As did his teammates, all of whom had signed up to play in a program led by a reserved, somewhat hands-off coach in Bill Guthridge. Doherty's style was much more assertive and took some getting used to. Once the players did, they banded together and played beyond their capabilities, eventually reaching No. 1 and winning the ACC regular season. Then came the five consecutive Sunday losses, and frustrations grew.

"What would I do differently?" Doherty said. "Maybe cut back on practice time. A lot of the losing was out of our control. A lot of it is knowing players and their personalities and histories. Knowing what affects them, positively and negatively."

If nothing else, Doherty definitely knew his players better by the end of the season. He knew what to expect from those who would return. He just wasn't sure who would be returning.

"Coach and I are fine," said Forte, standing at midcourt in the darkened Superdome. "My teammates and I are fine. I have two great options to choose from: I can either go to the NBA or I can come back to North Carolina. I can't go wrong either way."

Asked what he was going to do between the Penn State loss and the time he would make his decision on whether to stay in Chapel Hill or declare himself eligible for the NBA draft, Forte regained the twinkle in his eye: "I'm going to be young and have fun."

He then turned and walked out of the empty arena. He never looked back.

Epilogue

The record will show that the 2000–2001 North Carolina basketball team—the first under Matt Doherty—won 26 games and lost 7, finished in a tie for first place during the regular season of the ACC, finished as the runner-up in the ACC Tournament, and reached the second round of the NCAA Tournament. Most important, it was a team that added one more number to each of The Streaks:

31 consecutive seasons of 20 or more wins
27 straight NCAA Tournament appearances
37 years in a row of finishing no worse than third in the ACC
    regular-season race

It was a season of incredible highs and equally miserable lows. It was a team that struggled to find itself as a new coaching staff attempted to make a connection to a group of young men understandably chafing under the change in leadership. One of the reasons many had chosen North Carolina in the first place was because it was a place where being a part of a family—and the stability that came with it—was what they sought. Dealing with the changes that occurred over the course of the past three years—from Dean Smith to Bill Guthridge to Matt Doherty—was difficult.

Beyond the numbers, the coaches, players, and fans will remember the public triumphs and disappointments: the pain following the second-worst home loss ever in the Smith Center to Kentucky . . . the release of emotion after beating Wake Forest on Brendan Haywood's last-second layup . . . the unbridled joy of beating archrival Duke at Duke . . . the sense of pride of attaining the top ranking in college basketball . . . the shock of the upset loss to Clemson . . . the bitter disappointment of losing to Duke on Senior Day . . . the questioning of heart and desire after a blowout loss in the ACC Tournament final . . . the sudden halt to the ride in the second round of the NCAA Tournament.

But it was the moments in between that meant the most to the 16 players and five coaches thrown together and forced to learn about each other under the most pressure-filled of circumstances.

Each one has his own personal memory: Haywood getting his water break back after the win at Appalachian State and winning the endearing respect of Carolina fans for game-winning plays against Wake Forest, NC State, and Duke . . . Jim Everett walking into the coaches' locker room in early January and learning he had been put on scholarship for the second semester . . . Joseph Forte playing well in front of—and earning praise for his defense from—his high school coach, Morgan Wootten . . . Jon Holmes dealing with his disappointment as others played in front of him, but never losing his will to compete and help the team when he was called on . . . seniors Max Owens and Michael Brooker putting individual accolades aside and making selfless sacrifices for the good of the team late in the season—and earning the undying respect and gratitude of their coaches and teammates . . . Forte calling Coach "D" from several yards away in the Atlanta airport to remind his coach about the team rule banning cell phones.

Most of all, the individuals who made up the 2000–2001 North Carolina basketball team will remember their time spent with one another in constant pursuit of a common goal. It wasn't always easy, and they weren't always good times, but like a family the Tar Heels came together, for better and worse. During a season jam-packed with what seemed like 10 years of wins and losses, joy and emotion, it was the ties to each other that will stand the test of time.

"The moment I remember the most was during the final seconds of our game at Maryland," said Jason Capel. "Everyone was on the other end of the court, and I had a cramp and was lying down, trying to rub it out. When I looked up, I saw all my teammates running down-court toward me to check to see if I was OK and to help me massage out my cramp. We were such a close team—people didn't understand that. I hadn't been on a team as close as that since high school. That moment was something I'll never forget."

The Matt Doherty era will not be judged on this one season, following which he was named the Associated Press National Coach of the Year. His first-year record was markedly better than those of the two local legends against which he will always be measured: Dean Smith and Mike Krzyzewski, both of whom struggled mightily until their fourth season at the helm of their respective programs.

Nor will it be judged by the next two or three seasons, during which it is quite possible Carolina will struggle.

Forte, after weighing his options, chose to chase his NBA dream and leave Chapel Hill behind. Ronald Curry and Julius Peppers are unlikely to continue playing basketball, sacrificing the game for their futures as professional football players. Michael Brooker will try to keep playing—maybe in Europe—as will Max Owens. All of the seniors, including NBA first-round draft pick Brendan Haywood and Wall Street's own Jim Everett, earned their degrees.

Three talented players (Jawad Williams, Jackie Manuel, and Melvin Scott) enter a Carolina program that will be led by seniors Jason Capel and Kris Lang (if he can stay out of the training room) and will try desperately to continue a legacy of success.

It won't be easy. Duke won the NCAA Championship two weeks after Carolina lost in New Orleans to Penn State, only increasing the expectations on Doherty's shoulders to close the gap quickly. Doug Wojcik briefly considered leaving North Carolina for the head coach's job at Ohio University, but he pulled his name out of consideration, wanting instead to chase after a national championship in Chapel Hill. As expected, center recruit DeSagana Diop opted to enter the NBA, while David Harrison chose Colorado. The lack of depth inside (caused, in large part, by the Jason Parker saga) would most definitely be felt.

"It will be a challenging season for the program," Doherty said. "But you have to take inventory of our players' hearts and see how they react."

No franchise in any sport—amateur or professional—has set as high a standard of uninterrupted excellence as has North Carolina basketball over as long a period of time. On the court, it has been since 1962 that Carolina has had a season in which it lost more games than it won. Off the court, the program continues to stand for the best in the achievements of student-athletes. It is a fact punctuated in the off-season by Vince Carter's dedication to his former coach and the legacy of UNC players graduating when—under intense media scrutiny—he insisted on appearing at the UNC graduation and receiving his college degree on the same day his Toronto Raptors played in a deciding playoff game.

It is the enormous responsibility of guiding this franchise and all for which it stands that faces Matt Doherty every day. It is one he, as a former player and member of the Carolina Family, works to come to grips with and live up to. With each passing day, the shadow of Dean Smith may fade, but the sheer scope of what it means to lead the program comes into focus for Doherty. He is more than just a coach, he is the CEO of an entity that, for better or worse, is a daily source of pride and hope for its legion of fans. As such, he must be everything to everybody: a moral compass, a stirring orator, an effective fund-raiser, a grand motivator, a winner. And he must be these things every day.

In addition, his perch atop the program comes at a time when loyalties are strained. Larry Brown, despite leading the Philadelphia 76ers to the NBA Finals, is still hurt by the way he was treated during the hiring process. George Karl had his contract with the Milwaukee Bucks rewritten to include a clause stating he could entertain the option of leaving for North Carolina, if the job should ever reopen. The loyalty of many former

Tar Heels remains torn as Dean Smith continues to ease out of the picture and a new, different program emerges.

Leading that program is a position of immense influence and responsibility with which few can empathize and for which no one can prepare. To that, add the youth and inevitable missteps of a coach in his first few years of leading any program, and the pressure multiplies. Of course, no outside force can put as much pressure on Doherty as he himself does. His intense desire to win comes from a lifetime of success in the sport, but also from personal failure. Just as he will never forget the joy and sense of accomplishment of being on a team that won the 1982 NCAA Championship, he is also tortured by the loss to Indiana that ended his college career and his inability to reach the goal of playing in the NBA.

He is driven as much, if not more, by his personal flight from failure as he is by his chase for the dream.

The long-term effects of the constant pressure from internal and external sources will undoubtedly change Doherty as his tenure at Carolina progresses. Following a first year of such pressure he has already shown some reluctance to be as open and honest with reporters as he was when he arrived. While far from jaded, it would only be natural for Doherty—after several more years of living in the fishbowl of Carolina basketball—to become as guarded in his comments as Dean Smith or Mike Krzyzewski eventually did.

How will he do? What will be Matt Doherty's coaching legacy? It will take many years—and the understanding that can only be gained with experience—for that answer to come. Along the way, he will be himself: emotional, highly organized (even anal), demanding, intelligent, driven, funny, and honest. To many of his players and those who know him well, he sometimes seems like two people; a hard-driving, demanding disciplinarian who pushes his players and staff beyond their comfort zones while at the same time a good friend who enjoys the personal interaction with young people and colleagues alike. But his devotion to attaining the goals he sets for the team and himself will be absolute and unwavering.

Using the words with which he ended his first season as the head coach at North Carolina: He will give it his best effort.